Making Medical History

TIME

THE WEEKLY NEWSMAGAZINE

Holmes I. Mettee

JOHNS HOPKINS' SIGERIST
His philosophy: History spirals toward Socialization.
(Medicine)

Edited by Elizabeth Fee
and Theodore M. Brown

Making Medical History

THE LIFE AND TIMES OF

HENRY E. SIGERIST

The Johns Hopkins University Press

Baltimore & London

06 05 04 03 02 01 00 99 98 97   5 4 3 2 1

Frontispiece: The *Time* magazine cover featuring "Johns Hopkins'
Sigerist," January 30, 1939. Copyright 1939 Time Inc. Reprinted
by permission.

The Johns Hopkins University Press
2715 North Charles Street, Baltimore, Maryland 21218-4319
The Johns Hopkins Press Ltd., London

Library of Congress Cataloging-in-Publication Data and illustration credits
will be found at the end of this book.
A catalog record for this book is available from the British Library.

ISBN 0-8018-5355-9

To the memory of our fathers,

John A. T. Fee and Philip Brown

CONTENTS

ILLUSTRATIONS

ACKNOWLEDGMENTS

We would like to thank the members of the Sigerist Circle, founded in Baltimore in 1990, for providing the initial enthusiasm that culminated in this project. One of the first activities of the group was to organize a luncheon session, marking the centenary of Sigerist's birth, at the 1991 meeting of the American Association for the History of Medicine. Several of the papers in this volume were developed from presentations at that luncheon; Pauline Mazumdar, editor of the Sigerist Circle *Newsletter,* was helpful in publishing abstracts of these talks. We also appreciate the contributions of Charles E. Rosenberg and John Eyler to the success of this event.

For the development of this volume, we are grateful to the National Library of Medicine Publication Grants Program for financial support. These funds were invaluable in allowing us time to work intensively together in writing our own chapters and working with the contributors to this volume. We would also like to thank Charles E. Phelps, former chair of the Department of Community and Preventive Medicine and now provost of the University of Rochester, Stephen J. Kunitz, current acting chair of the department, and Gert H. Brieger, chair of the Department of the History of Science, Medicine, and Technology of the Johns Hopkins University, for their assistance in the publication of this volume. Thanks also to the Dean's Office of the College of Arts and Science at the University of Rochester for providing Theodore Brown with travel funds.

We are especially indebted to Nora Sigerist Beeson for her continuing interest in and assistance with this volume. She gave generous and expert editorial advice, helped with photographs and other sources, and provided warm hospitality. We are also grateful to those who shared their memories of Sigerist, especially Owsei and the late Lilian Temkin, George and Mitzi Silver, and Leslie A. Falk, and to Jacalyn Duffin and John Farley, who shared their knowledge of Sigerist's visits to Canada and South Africa.

As we were working on this book, we benefited from several opportunities to clarify our ideas by presenting papers on aspects of Sigerist's career. Dorothy Porter and Roy Porter organized a conference at the Wellcome Institute for the History of Medicine, "Doctors, Politics and Society." Elizabeth Fee is grateful to the participants in this meeting for their stimulating comments and to Edward T. Morman for his collaboration on a joint paper, "Doing History, Making Revolution: The Aspirations of Henry E. Sigerist and George Rosen." Lewis Pyenson organized a plenary session, "A la Recherche du Temps Perdu," at the annual meeting of the History of Science Society in Santa Fe, New Mexico. We are grateful for the opportunity to present a joint paper "Henry Sigerist's Progress toward a Social History of Medicine," which served as the first draft of our chapter, "Intellectual Legacy and Political Quest: The Shaping of a Historical Ambition." Elizabeth Fee would like to thank the members of the History of Medicine Division and the audience at the National Library of Medicine where she discussed "Henry E. Sigerist and the Social History of Medicine." She is also grateful to Stanley Jackson, William Summers, and the members of the Beaumont Medical Club of Connecticut for inviting her to give the annual Beaumont lecture "The Pleasures and Perils of Prophetic Advocacy: Henry E. Sigerist and the Politics of Medical Care," which served as the basis for her essay in this volume. Mervyn Susser, Carole Leach-Lemons, and Mina Chung were most helpful in arranging for the publication of a revised, and much shorter, version of this paper in the *American Journal of Public Health*.

In all stages of our research, the staffs of the Yale University Archives, the Alan Mason Chesney Archives of the Johns Hopkins Medical Institutions, the Hamburger Archives of the Johns Hopkins University, and the Rockefeller Archive Center were gracious and helpful. Gerard Shorb of the Alan Mason Chesney Archives and Tom Rosenbaum of the Rockefeller Archive Center were especially generous in sharing their knowledge of the collections. Nora Sigerist Beeson, Marcel Bickel, Ingrid Kästner, Genevieve Miller, and Walter Lear provided photographs for this volume as did the Alan Mason Chesney Archives, the Rockefeller Archive Center, and Time-Warner Publications. Saul Benison and the anonymous reviewers for the Johns Hopkins University Press gave us helpful advice and suggestions.

Our work was made easier and more efficient by the invaluable assistance of Ann Smith at the Johns Hopkins University School of Hygiene and Public Health. We are also grateful to Helen Weeks and Constance French of the Department of Community and Preventive Medicine at the University of Rochester for their secretarial help. Wilhelm Braun of the University of Rochester helped us translate some of the more difficult German passages. Chris Bigenwald at the University of Rochester and Joanne Riley at the Johns Hopkins University introduced us to the information superhighway.

We thank Jacqueline Wehmueller, our wise and patient editor at the Johns Hopkins University Press, for her warm encouragement and astute advice. We also appreciate our colleagues, students, friends, and families, who have accepted and sympathized in our preoccupation with this project. Finally, we owe Corinne Sutter-Brown special gratitude for her unfailing good humor and her intellectual and emotional support.

Making Medical History

The Renaissance of a Reputation

Elizabeth Fee and Theodore M. Brown

For close to three decades in the first half of this century, Henry Ernest Sigerist was widely admired as the world's leading historian of medicine. In 1925, at the precocious age of thirty-four, he succeeded Karl Sudhoff as director of the University of Leipzig's Institute of the History of Medicine. The institute had been a pioneering center for medicohistorical research, and its founding director, Sudhoff, was a scholar of towering international reputation. Yet Sigerist, a youthful Swiss national with cosmopolitan tastes, quickly impressed his personal stamp on Weimar Leipzig. He reorganized and refocused the work of the institute and created a vibrant sense of shared intellectual community in which unprecedented numbers of students and young scholars participated.

In 1932, Sigerist succeeded William Henry Welch as director of the Johns Hopkins University Institute of the History of Medicine, recently created on the Leipzig model. Sigerist was expected to bring with him a high level of German scholarship and to employ his influence and diplomatic skill to transform the widespread but largely amateur American interest into serious professional work in the history of medicine.

With consistent financial support from Rockefeller philanthropy, Sigerist turned the Institute into a national center for the history of medicine in the United States. He transferred his own research to Baltimore and arranged for several exceptional junior colleagues to join him. He nurtured American efforts already under way and elevated scholarly standards, most notably by publishing the *Bulletin of the History of Medicine* and by raising the professional tone of the American Association for the History of Medicine.[1]

During his American years, Sigerist also played an important public role. Welcomed as an urbane and eloquent lecturer, he enjoyed celebrity status at medical society meetings, before civic organizations and women's clubs, in colleges and universities, and at intellectual fora and student conventions. He was regularly called upon by philanthropic foundations, public agencies, labor unions, and the media. His 1937 book *Socialized Medicine in the Soviet Union* created a sensation.[2] Sigerist portrayed the radically transformed health care system of the Soviet Union as a model for public health and medical care worldwide, the final stage in a long historical evolution of health services. Widely read and both criticized and admired, this book brought him to the attention of the cultural and scientific left and made him the hero of many progressive young medical students and interns.

Sigerist now emerged as a major spokesman for compulsory health insurance, being much sought after as a lecturer, popular author, and radio commentator. He published articles in mass circulation magazines and left-wing reviews such as *Atlantic Monthly, PM, Science and Society,* and the *New Masses.*[3] On January 30, 1939, *Time* magazine published his portrait on its cover and described him in the accompanying article as both the world's greatest medical historian and the nation's most widely respected authority on compulsory health insurance and health policy.[4] Because of his dual reputation in historical scholarship and medical politics, Sigerist was invited to visit South Africa, and later Canada and India, as a distinguished lecturer and consultant.

In June 1947, when Sigerist left the United States to take up residence in the Ticino region of Switzerland, his circumstances were dramatically different. He had now been attacked by the American Medical Association, criticized by Hopkins medical alumni, and declared unfit for government service by the Civil Service Commission. Tired and physically debilitated, he suffered from a variety of health problems including chronic sinusitis and hypertension. Under severe strain, he felt the need to defend himself against assault and struggled to continue writing his long-promised and recently begun multivolume *History of Medicine.*[5] Although Sigerist felt that he had worn out his welcome in the United States, he was still cherished by many of his colleagues and students as was evident in the outpouring of heartfelt testimonials offered during the period of his departure.[6] Among the many statements of appreciation and expressions of grief and loss, Alan Gregg of the Rockefeller Foundation perhaps best captured the essence of Sigerist's contribution: "Beyond and above anyone else Henry Sigerist made us aware of the fact that medicine is the study and application of biology in a matrix that is at once historical, social, political, economic, and cultural. . . . Sir Oliver Lodge once remarked that the last thing in the world that a deep sea fish could discover would be salt water. Henry Sigerist removed us, with a historian's landing net, from a circumambient present into the atmosphere of the past and thus discovered to us the nature of the milieu in which we were swimming, floating, and betimes stagnating."[7]

When volume I of Sigerist's *History* appeared in 1951, complete with a lucid introduction to the socioeconomic analysis of health and disease, it had a relatively limited impact on the history of medicine. The book was very positively reviewed in the leading English-language journals in the history of science and medicine, and elsewhere, but the reviewers, while congratulatory, were less than consistently rhapsodic about its historiographic innovations.[8] The American Association for the History of Medicine awarded Sigerist its first William Henry Welch Medal for outstanding scholarly achievement, but its members, by and large, followed other models of scholarship.[9] In the America of the fifties, given the atmosphere of cold war foreign policy and domestic witch hunting, most historians tended toward forms of analysis safer than the implicit Marxist materialism of Sigerist's volume I.

When Sigerist died in 1957, scholars around the world stopped to honor his memory. Historical journals mourned his loss and acknowledged his stature and influence.[10] Medical journals from the *Lancet* to the *New England Journal of Medicine* noted his passing.[11] The obituary in the *Journal of the American Medical Association* was, however, decidedly revisionist and chose to ignore both Sigerist's defense of Soviet medicine and his role in the campaigns for compulsory national health insurance.[12] The obituary in the *New York Times* was also strangely truncated; Sigerist's 1937 book *Socialized Medicine in the Soviet Union* received no mention, and the only reference to his involvement in campaigns for health reform was brief and apologetic.[13] *Time* magazine, which had earlier published glowing accounts of his work, failed even to note his death.[14] America was in the second term of the Eisenhower presidency, still caught in the aftermath of the McCarthy era, and living under the shadow of the House Un-American Activities Committee. In the context of this political chill, when the Soviet Union was being denounced as the "enemy" and compulsory health insurance was dismissed as tantamount to communism, historians who were writing the social history of medicine proceeded in a less confrontational manner. Thus began the eclipse of Sigerist's American reputation.

In the next decade and a half, a steady stream of scholarly publications kept the memory of Sigerist alive but failed to resurrect either his full reputation or the power of his personal influence. In 1960, two of Sigerist's friends and admirers published volumes of his collected papers. Felix Marti-Ibañez edited *On the History of Medicine,* and Milton I. Roemer edited a companion volume, *On the Sociology of Medicine.*[15] In 1966, another close friend, Genevieve Miller, published the comprehensive *Bibliography of the Writings of Henry E. Sigerist* and his daughter, Nora Sigerist Beeson, published an engaging volume of his selected *Autobiographical Writings.*[16] Over the next few years, several short essays celebrated specific aspects of Sigerist's work and influence.[17]

Despite the appearance in the 1960s of these significant publications on Sigerist's life and work, most American historians of science and medicine seemed to pay little attention to his contributions. Especially in the history of science but to some extent also in the history of medicine, professionalization and specialization were redefining disciplinary boundaries and content. Both fields were heavily influenced, though to different degrees, by the conceptual orientation known as the "internalist" approach to the history of science.[18] The history of medicine was also influenced by new trends in American social history of a largely apolitical character.[19] In health policy, the broader goal of universal health insurance had narrowed to the more limited if successful campaign for Medicare and Medicaid. Even in this policy domain, discussion and debate were quickly dominated by concerns about costs in the context of close attention to technical and administrative details. There seemed to be little room for the kind of vision, moral urgency, and projected sense of historical inevitability that Sigerist had once provided.

In Europe, however, a continuing lively interest in Sigerist's work was reflected in substantial scholarly contributions, most notably Elisabeth Berg-Schorn's doctoral dissertation of 1978 and Achim Thom and Karl-Heinz Karbe's long interpretative essay published with selections from Sigerist's works in 1981.[20] Several American authors wrote shorter essays, the majority of them in European publications.[21] In the United States, Sigerist's role in medical politics was made visible again by a series of essays addressed primarily to students of health policy: Arthur Viseltear's historical study of the formation of the Medical Care Section of the American Public Health Association, Milton Terris's essay on Sigerist's contributions to health service organization, and George Silver's article on social medicine and social policy.[22] In 1978, Lloyd Stevenson, then the editor of the *Bulletin of the History of Medicine*, decided to launch a new supplement series, named the Henry E. Sigerist supplements, and chose as the first volume Ronald L. Numbers, *Almost Persuaded: The First American Debate over Compulsory Health Insurance, 1912–1920*, noting that this subject was a particularly appropriate one, given Sigerist's own interests.[23]

A year later, two young social historians of medicine, representing a new generation, distinguished Sigerist's work, with its sharp, often quite contemporary political edge, from the more apolitical work of the dominant school of social history. Susan Reverby and David Rosner began their collection of essays with a manifesto, "Beyond 'The Great Doctors,'" calling for social history in a political and intellectual spirit that Sigerist would have warmly applauded.[24] Their title, however, added some confusion, as it seemed to associate Sigerist—author of *The Great Doctors*—with an intellectualist and iatrocentric tradition that he had in fact struggled hard to overcome.[25]

In the last decade, the pace of rediscovery has accelerated. Scholarship relating to Sigerist's work has broadened and deepened.[26] By the time of the one-hundredth anniversary of Sigerist's birth, sufficient interest had developed to support celebrations in Leipzig and at the annual meeting of the American Association for the History of Medicine.[27] A new organization of medical historians, the Sigerist Circle, adopted his name and with it his dual legacy of scholarship and activism.

This book is intended to continue this process of reacquaintance and rediscovery by offering a collective assessment of Sigerist's work by an international, intergenerational, and multidisciplinary group of scholars. The contributors include several of his former colleagues and students, and members of his family; some are physicians and physician-activists, and others are historians of different areas of expertise. A number of the authors knew Henry Sigerist personally; most have come to know him through his work, his published writings, and the immense archival records of his correspondence, diaries, and collected papers at the universities of Leipzig, Johns Hopkins, and Yale. Together these authors' papers provide insight into Sigerist's personality, a close scrutiny of his major scholarly endeavors, and an analysis of his political efforts, engagements, and influence.

The essays in this volume are organized into three main sections: biographical, historiographical, and political, with two concluding essays about Sigerist's influence on medical sociology and health policy, and on the history of medicine. The first, biographical section consists of essays written, for the most part, by scholars who knew Sigerist intimately. Marcel Bickel, Henry Sigerist's nephew, writes about Sigerist's background and his early years in Paris and Zurich and supplements the more readily available printed and archival materials with personal family documents. Ingrid Kästner, professor of medical history at the Karl-Sudhoff-Institute of the University of Leipzig, then takes up the development of Sigerist's career from his assumption of the directorship of the Institute of the History of Medicine at Leipzig in 1925. Genevieve Miller, Sigerist's graduate student and research secretary during his Baltimore years, reviews Sigerist's fifteen-year tenure as director of the Johns Hopkins Institute of the History of Medicine. Ilza Veith, Sigerist's only doctoral student in the United States, then discusses Sigerist's lifelong interest in oriental languages, history, and culture. Concluding this section, Nora Sigerist Beeson, Sigerist's daughter, offers an intimate and personal account of her father and their family life.

The essays in the second, historiographic section are less personal and more analytical. Owsei Temkin, Sigerist's colleague in Germany and the United States, writes of the originality and power of Sigerist's work and of his interests and assumptions, achievements, and limitations as a historian. Originally published in 1958, shortly after Sigerist's death, this essay remains fresh and insightful more than thirty-five years later. Heinrich von Staden, a professor of classics and comparative literature, locates Sigerist's complex attitudes toward ancient Greece within a context of European historical scholarship and culture. Michael R. McVaugh, an authority on medieval medicine, evaluates the recurrent attraction that medieval studies held for Sigerist and scrutinizes his contributions to that field over the course of his career. The final essay in this section, by the editors, confronts Sigerist's failure to complete his projected multivolume *History of Medicine,* examining the conflicts he experienced between his intellectual inheritance and his political commitments, yet celebrating the synthesis ultimately achieved in volume 1.

The third section addresses Sigerist's involvement with American politics—broadly construed to include his advocacy of national health insurance, his ideas about the social determinants of health and medicine, his political interest in the Soviet Union, and his surprising relationship with the Rockefeller Foundation. In the first essay, Elizabeth Fee explores Sigerist's interest in innovative approaches to health care organization, his active role in contemporary campaigns for national health insurance, and his dedication to the ideals he believed embodied in the Soviet system of health care. Next, John Hutchinson, an authority on the history of public health in revolutionary Russia, analyzes Sigerist's romantic idealization of the Soviet Union and demonstrates his highly selective perception of Soviet realities. Walter J. Lear then explains how Sigerist helped found the American-Soviet Medical Society and how its fate was determined by political shifts in American-Soviet relations during World War II and the cold war period. In the concluding essay of this section, Theodore M. Brown explores the development of an intriguing and somewhat paradoxical friendship between the socialist scholar, Sigerist, and Alan Gregg, the powerful director of medical sciences at the Rockefeller Foundation.

The first of the two concluding essays is written by Milton I. Roemer, Sigerist's long-time friend and an authority on international health care, Leslie A. Falk, Sigerist's student and a committed activist in social medicine, and Theodore M. Brown. They show that although Sigerist's program for medical sociology had little influence on the subsequent development of the professional discipline, it had a major and continuing impact on a generation of students turned medical and public health reformers. In the final essay, Theodore M. Brown and Elizabeth Fee examine Sigerist's impact on the development of the history of medicine in the United States. They find that his legacy was complex: although Sigerist did much to upgrade the scholarly standards of the field, nurturing a successor generation and building an organizational infrastructure, his influence was mediated by the uncertain process of professionalization with which the field is still engaged.

By bringing their different perspectives to bear on selected aspects of Sigerist's life and work, the authors of these essays show us the contradictions and complexities of the man as well as the challenges of his times. Other scholars would perhaps have undertaken different explorations. But we have selected these essays to highlight Sigerist's persistent struggle to bring together his intellectual and political interests. This fundamental tension of his career has a significance that transcends his particular historical context and reminds us that although both theory and practice have value, the synergy of the two can be especially powerful. Many of our generation have wanted our intellectual work to be consistent with our political commitments. No one desired this convergence more than Henry Sigerist, and he pursued that quest with passion, intelligence, and courage. We hope that the essays presented here will contribute toward the renaissance of his reputation and the fuller recovery of his legacy.

Notes

1. Genevieve Miller, "The Missing Seal, or Highlights of the First Half Century of the American Association for the History of Medicine," *Bulletin of the History of Medicine* 50 (1976): 93–115, and E. B. Krumbhaar, "Notes on the Early Days of the American Association of the History of Medicine," *Bulletin of the History of Medicine* 23 (1949): 577–82.

2. Henry E. Sigerist, *Socialized Medicine in the Soviet Union* (New York: W. W. Norton, 1937).

3. Henry E. Sigerist, "The Realities of Socialized Medicine," *Atlantic Monthly* 163 (1939): 794–804; Henry E. Sigerist, "Science and Democracy," *Science and Society* 2 (1938): 291–99; Henry E. Sigerist, "What Happened to the Health Program?" *New Masses*, June 18, 1940, 14–16; for Sigerist's series of articles in the progressive newspaper *PM*, dealing with innovative medical care programs, see Elizabeth Fee's chapter in this volume.

4. "History in a Tea Wagon," *Time*, 33 (January 30, 1939): 51–53.

5. Ultimately published, unfinished, in two volumes: Henry E. Sigerist, *A History of Medicine,* vol. I, *Primitive and Archaic Medicine* and vol. II, *Early Greek, Hindu, and Persian Medicine* (New York: Oxford University Press, 1961).

6. See, for example, the statements by Genevieve Miller, John Fulton, Leslie A. Falk, Stuart Mudd, Richard H. Shryock, Arturo Castiglioni, George Sarton, and Alan Gregg in the *Bulletin of the History of Medicine* 22 (1948): 3–34. These were read at Sigerist's farewell dinner, described in the essay by Genevieve Miller in this volume. Other tributes appeared in *Journal of the History of Medicine, PM, Soviet Russia Today,* and *Time* magazine.

7. Alan Gregg, "Henry E. Sigerist: His Impact on American Medicine," *Bulletin of the History of Medicine* 22 (1948): 32.

8. Charles Singer's review in the *Bulletin of the History of Medicine* 25 (1951): 91–93, was enthusiastic but seemed to miss the point of Sigerist's historiographic innovations; J. B. DeC. M. Saunders's review in *Isis* 42 (1951): 278–81 was, at best, tepid.

9. The award of the Welch Medal to Sigerist is noted in the *Bulletin of the History of Medicine* 25 (1951): 100.

10. See the essays "In Memory of Henry E. Sigerist" by Owsei Temkin, Ludwig Edelstein, Sanford V. Larkey, Victor A. McKusick, and Richard H. Shryock in *Bulletin of the History of Medicine* 31 (1957): 295–308; Walter Pagel, "Obituary," *Medical History* 1 (1957): 285–89; H. Fischer, "Obituary," *Gesnerus* 14 (1957): 173–74; P. Huard, "Henry Sigerist (1891–1957)," *Revue d'Histoire des Sciences et de leurs Applications* 10 (1957): 261–63; Erna Lesky, "Henry Ernest Sigerist," *Gnomon* 29 (1957): 638–40; Richard H. Shryock, "Henry E. Sigerist," *Archives Internationales d'Histoire des Sciences* 10 (1957): 299–301; Leo Norpoth, "Henry E. Sigerist zum Gedächtnis," *Nachrichtenblatt der Deutschen Vereinigung für Geschichte der Medizin, Naturwissenschaft und Technik* 9 (1957): 4; George Rosen, "Toward a Historical Sociology of Medicine: The Endeavor of Henry E. Sigerist," *Bulletin of the History of Medicine* 32 (1958): 500–516; the essays by John F. Fulton, George Rosen, Erwin H. Ackerknecht, Henry B. Makover, Leslie A. Falk, Milton I. Roemer, Gregory Zilboorg, Ilza Veith, Lloyd

G. Stevenson, Walter Pagel, Genevieve Miller, and Felix Marti-Ibañez in *Journal of the History of Medicine and Allied Sciences* 13 (1958): 125–250.

11. See the obituaries in *Lancet* 1 (1957): 692–93; *Canadian Medical Association Journal* 76 (1957): 794; Henry Viets, "Henry E. Sigerist (1891–1957)," *New England Journal of Medicine* 256 (1957): 831; A. E. Underwood and D. G. Underwood, "Obituary," *British Medical Journal* 157 (1957): 767–68. See also George Rosen, "Henry E. Sigerist, Social Historian of Medicine," *Science* 126 (1957): 551–52; Milton I. Roemer, "Medical Care Programs in Other Countries. Henry Sigerist and International Medicine," *American Journal of Public Health* 48 (1958): 425–27.

12. "Obituary," *Journal of the American Medical Association* 164 (1957): 476.

13. "Dr. Sigerist Dies; Historian was 65," *New York Times,* March 18, 1957.

14. "History in a Tea Wagon," *Time,* 33 (January 30, 1939): 51–53; "Doctor's Project," *Time,* 49 (March 10, 1947): 50–52.

15. Felix Marti-Ibañez, ed., *Henry E. Sigerist on the History of Medicine* (New York: MD Publications, 1960); Milton I. Roemer, *Henry E. Sigerist on the Sociology of Medicine* (New York: MD Publications, 1960).

16. Genevieve Miller, *A Bibliography of the Writings of Henry E. Sigerist* (Montreal: McGill University Press, 1966); Nora Sigerist Beeson, ed., *Henry E. Sigerist: Autobiographical Writings* (Montreal: McGill University Press, 1966).

17. Nikolaus Mani, "Some Aspects of Medical Historiography," in A. Berman, *Pharmaceutical Historiography: Proceedings of a Colloquium* (Madison, Wis.: American Institute of the History of Pharmacy, 1967), 109–15; H. Wissel, "Der Medizinhistoriker Henry E. Sigerist 'Über die Zukunft der Medizin,'" *Wissenschaftliche Zeitschrift der Humboldt-Universität zu Berlin: Mathematisch-naturwissenschaftliche Reihe* 17 (1968): 813–16; B. Gebhard, "Henry E. Sigerist—ein enttäuschter Amerikaner?" *Medizinhistorisches Journal* 4 (1969): 89–98; D. V. Subba Reddy, "What a Modern Seer Said Twenty-five Years Ago. The Need for an Institute of the History of Medicine in India," *Bulletin of the Institute of the History of Medicine (Hyderabad)* 1 (1971): 49–58.

18. Arnold Thackray, "Science: Has Its Present Past a Future?" *Minnesota Studies in the Philosophy of Science* 5 (1970): 116–19, 121.

19. For an analysis of American social history critical of its apolitical character, see Elizabeth Fox-Genovese and Eugene D. Genovese, "The Political Crisis of Social History: A Marxian Perspective," *Journal of Social History* 10 (1976): 205–20.

20. Elisabeth Berg-Schorn, *Henry E. Sigerist (1891–1957): Medizinhistoriker in Leipzig und Baltimore. Standpunkt und Wirkung* (Cologne: Kölner Medizinhistorische Beiträge, Band 9, Med. diss. 1978). Berg-Schorn's work is a comprehensive and ambitious monograph, meticulous in its research and rich in insight. Also of great interest is Achim Thom and Karl-Heinz Karbe, *Henry Ernest Sigerist (1891–1957): Ausgewählte Texte* (Leipzig: Johann Ambrosius Barth, 1981). See also Heinrich Buess, "Henry E. Sigerist und die erste Medizinhistorische Konferenz in Pura," *Gesnerus* 37 (1980): 104–12.

21. Glenn Sonnedecker, "The American Correspondence between George Urdang and Henry E. Sigerist, 1941–1948," in *Perspektiven der Pharmaziegeschichte. Festschrift für Rudolf Schmitz zum 65. Geburtstag* (Graz, 1983), 343–63; F. G. Vescia, "Henry E. Sigerist: The Years in America," *Medizinhistorisches Jour-*

nal 14 (1979): 218-32; Genevieve Miller, "Henry E. Sigerist," *Dictionary of American Biography,* suppl. 6 (New York: Scribner's, 1980), 580-81.

22. Arthur J. Viseltear, *Emergence of the Medical Care Section of the American Public Health Association, 1926-1948* (Washington, D.C.: American Public Health Association, 1972); Milton I. Terris, "The Contributions of Henry E. Sigerist to Health Service Organization," *Milbank Memorial Fund Quarterly* 53 (1975): 489-530; George Silver, "Social Medicine and Social Policy," *Yale Journal of Biology and Medicine* 57 (1984): 851-64.

23. Lloyd G. Stevenson, "The Henry E. Sigerist Supplements," *Bulletin of the History of Medicine* 52 (1978): 1-4; Ronald L. Numbers, *Almost Persuaded: The First American Debate over Compulsory Health Insurance, 1912-1920* (Baltimore: Johns Hopkins University Press, 1978).

24. Susan Reverby and David Rosner, "Beyond 'The Great Doctors,'" in *Health Care in America: Essays in Social History,* eds. Susan Reverby and David Rosner (Philadelphia: Temple University Press, 1979), 3-16.

25. Henry E. Sigerist, *The Great Doctors: A Biographical History of Medicine* (New York: W. W. Norton, 1933). A number of politically minded scholars in this period were trying to come to terms with Sigerist's apparent contradictions. For one sharply critical discussion, see Ronald Frankenberg, "Functionalism and After? Theory and Developments in Social Science Applied to the Health Field," *International Journal of Health Services* 4 (1974): 411-27.

26. Charles E. Rosenberg, "Disease and Social Order in America: Perceptions and Expectations," *Milbank Quarterly* 64, suppl. 1 (1986): 34-55; Elizabeth Fee, "Henry E. Sigerist: From the Social Production of Disease to Medical Management and Scientific Socialism," *Milbank Quarterly* 67, suppl. 1 (1989): 127-50; Dorothy Porter and Roy Porter, "What Was Social Medicine? An Historiographical Essay," *Journal of Historical Sociology* 1 (1989): 90-106; Elizabeth Fee and Edward T. Morman, "Doing History, Making Revolution: The Aspirations of Henry E. Sigerist and George Rosen," in *Doctors, Politics and Society: Historical Essays,* eds. Dorothy Porter and Roy Porter (Amsterdam: Rodopi, 1993), 275-311; P. Schneck, "Henry Ernest Sigerist—Begründer der Soziologisch Orientierten Medizingeschichte. Eine Einführung zu seinem Aufsatz 'Das Leben unter dem Schatten,'" *Zeitschrift für die Gesamte Hygiene und Ihre Grenzgebiete* 35 (1989): 750-56; C. Mörgeli and A. Blaser, "Henry E. Sigerist: Die Gestaltung des medizinhistorischen Unterrichts. Ein unpubliziertes Manuskript im Zürcher Medizinhistorischen Institut," *Gesnerus* 46 (1989): 45-53; M. C. Wäspi, *Die Anfänge des Medizinhistorikers Henry E. Sigerist in Zürich* (Zurich: Zürcher Medizingeschichtliche Abhandlungen, Nr. 206, Juris Druck und Verlag, 1989); G. Schmidt, "Henry E. Sigerists Auffassung vom Sinn medizinhistorischer Arbeit und seine Beziehung zu Wien," *Wiener Klinische Wochenschrift* 103 (1991): 487-92; Everardo Duarte Nunes, "Henry Ernest Sigerist—Pioneiro da História Social da Medicina e da Sociologia Médica," *Educatión Médica y Salud* 26 (1992): 70-81.

27. Susanne Hahn and Achim Thom, eds., *Ergebnisse und Perspektiven sozialhistorischer Forschung in der Medizingeschichte. Kolloquium zum 100. Geburtstag Sigerists, 12-14 Juni 1991* (Leipzig: Karl-Sudhoff-Institut, 1991); Elizabeth Fee, "Sigerist and Scientific Optimism," *Sigerist Circle Newsletter* 2 (winter 1991): 1-3;

Genevieve Miller, "Sigerist at Hopkins," *Sigerist Circle Newsletter* 2 (winter 1991): 1, 4–5; Leslie A. Falk, "Henry Sigerist as a Life Model," *Sigerist Circle Newsletter* 3 (spring 1992): 3–4; Theodore M. Brown, "Henry Sigerist and the Rockefeller Foundation," *Sigerist Circle Newsletter* 3 (spring 1992): 4–6; Gert H. Brieger and Owsei Temkin, "Editorial," *Bulletin of the History of Medicine* 65 (1991): 1–3; Owsei Temkin and Gert H. Brieger, "Two Institutions and Two Eras: Reflections on the Field of Medical History" (Baltimore: Institute of the History of Medicine, Johns Hopkins University School of Medicine, 1991, videocassette [69 min.]).

PART 1

The Life of Henry Sigerist

CHAPTER 1

Family Background and Early Years
in Paris and Zurich, 1891–1925

Marcel H. Bickel

Henry E. Sigerist's fame is based on his activities and success in Leipzig (1925–32) and Baltimore (1932–47). Much less well known are his origins, his youth in Paris and Zurich, his early development as a medical historian, and his first contributions to the history of medicine. Although Sigerist's life and career have been widely discussed in an extensive secondary literature, these sources usually treat his early years only briefly.[1] The following draws on family documents as well as published sources to sketch Sigerist's formative years and discuss his earliest contributions to the history of medicine.

Family Background

Sigerist's mother, Emma Wiskemann (1865–1954), was born and raised in Zurich. Her grandfather was a goldsmith from Kassel, Germany, who in his wanderings came to Zurich, fell in love with a local girl, and settled in her town. His son was also a goldsmith and so were most of Emma Wiskemann's brothers and their sons. A lively city girl, Emma in her twenties married Ernst Heinrich Sigerist, with whom she moved to Paris. This unique city and its social life strongly appealed to her taste. On April 7, 1891, she gave birth to Henry Ernest Sigerist, her first child,

in her apartment on 42 Rue d'Hauteville. Her second son, Edmond, died of typhoid fever as an infant, and her daughter, Marguerite, was born in 1894. Widowed in 1901 at only thirty-five years of age, this previously enterprising woman became fearful and overprotective toward her children, to whom she devoted her life, never considering another marriage. Well read, music loving, and an enthusiastic traveler, she did all she could to give her children, Henry in particular, the best education possible. She provided strong support for his studies and interests, and when he became too much of a bookworm, she encouraged him to play the piano and cello and exercise his body with tennis, fencing, and horseback riding. She also took her children to the Swiss mountains and repeatedly traveled with them abroad. In later years, when her successful son had become famous in foreign lands, he was his mother's pride. Her grandchildren used to tease her by declaiming, "Mein Sohn, der Herr Professor." Pride and love between mother and son were mutual. Sigerist had a strong attachment to and affection for his mother, and while living in Germany and the

United States, he visited her regularly. When she died at age eighty-eight, he experienced an emotional crisis.

Sigerist's paternal ancestors had been citizens of Schaffhausen, in northern Switzerland. For generations since the sixteenth century they had been tanners, and in the nineteenth century they became wine merchants. Sigerist's father, Ernst Heinrich Sigerist (1859–1901), might have taken over the family business but instead became one of the many hardworking and enterprising Swiss who left their small country with its lack of opportunities and went abroad for a career in foreign lands. In Paris he worked first in a bank, then as a representative of a chemical enterprise, and eventually he founded a shoe company of which he was the first director. He managed an empire with over a hundred outlets in France and abroad. A most successful businessman, he was also a loving husband and father. His intense feelings are evident in an emotional letter to his son, Henry, who was then only three months old:

2. Sigerist's mother, Emma Wiskemann Sigerist, photographed in Zurich.

Back in Paris for just a week, it seems like an eternity since I last held you in my arms and to my heart, my little darling . . . you did not refuse a last smile for your daddy; but now I'm gone and far from you, yet out of sight means close to the heart because I keep thinking of you, my dear, and all day long I look at the picture of my dear baby with his serious face, worthy of a man of your importance in front of the photographic lens.[2]

Sigerist's father later had troubles with his company, possibly resulting from his being too susceptible to flattery and trusting people more than some of them deserved. He became entangled in a law suit, which he won, but at the price of his health. In 1900 he became fatally ill with stomach cancer, from which he died in the summer of 1901, when he was only forty-two years old. About two months before his death (and his family's move from Paris to Zurich), he wrote from a sanitarium in Switzerland to his ten-year-old son:

My dear son Henry

Tomorrow is your tenth birthday, and with all my heart I wish you many happy returns of the day.

So here you are ten years old, which means no longer quite a child but rather a little man! That's why you have to act your age, that is to work diligently, to become serious, not to tease your little sister. Turn your thoughts from play to work in order to become a man. Mom has certainly told you the good news of our moving to Switzerland; thus, a new life will begin for you, and I hope that once in Switzerland our relatives and friends will be able to compliment us about you.

Be always polite to everybody, obedient and frank; you have reached the age of reason, so never tell a lie. Love your parents and prove it to them by your good behavior.

I love you and I hug you once more and I bless you,
    your Dad[3]

Sigerist remembered his father as a righteous and kind man, hard working, generous, and good to his employees.[4] He was attached to his family and to his hometown, Schaffhausen. His highly successful business left the family well provided for, so that his widow was able to enjoy a high standard of living for the rest of her long life.

Many features of Sigerist's personality are recognizable in his parents. With his mother he shared the love of music, art, and literature; the desire to see foreign countries; the ability to enjoy the pleasant facets of life; and also a sense of humor. But unlike his mother, who had an aristo-

3. Sigerist in Paris at age two.

cratic penchant, Sigerist was interested in society as a whole and liked to communicate with people in all walks of life, including the most humble. Sigerist was like his father in being gentle, sensitive and generous, hard working, enterprising, and a good organizer. With both his parents he shared a strong sense of family.

Sigerist's world was one of books and learning, and this orientation started early in adolescence while he shared the quiet life with his widowed mother and sister in Zurich. This is surprising if one considers a family background without any academic tradition. Sigerist's male ancestors and relatives were in business and crafts. None of his eight uncles and many cousins was a professional, let alone a scholar, or had a university education. Sigerist's own outstanding academic career would not have been possible without the wealth provided by his father. Schooling

4. Sigerist and his sister Marguerite, about 1898.

and even university in Switzerland were free of charge but still a burden for families without financial resources. Much more pronounced were the problems for those heading toward academic careers. They would work for years as assistants to a professor for a token salary or none at all. If successful in research, they would become *Privatdozent,* which made them eligible for a professorship. To reach this goal and thus a decent salary required several more years. Sigerist was thus in a very comfortable position, able to study what he wanted and for as long as he wanted, without the necessity of looking for a job.

Childhood in Paris; Education in Zurich, London, Munich

When Sigerist was born in Paris, the Belle Époque was in full swing. But the Sigerists' apartment, as was standard at that time, had no electricity, no bathroom, no hot water, no central heating, and only a primitive kitchen. Seven years later, the family moved into an apartment at 16 Rue d'Abbeville that had all the comforts of modern living, including an elevator. Sigerist went to a small private elementary school, where he quickly learned to read and write and where he was happy. One of his earliest written documents is the following note:

Dear Santa

    I have received your letter with great pleasure I promise to be a good boy to correct my faults and I will be good to the poor

    Henry [5]

The summer months were spent in Montmorency outside the city. The small country house with its garden and adjacent orchard became a source of much happiness, beginning his love for the countryside. At the height of the summer the family would travel to Switzerland to spend some time in the mountains and to see their relatives and friends in Schaffhausen and Zurich. It was with them that Sigerist learned some Swiss German, the language spoken at home being strictly French. But much as his parents loved Paris, they felt attached to their homeland.

Sigerist considered having spent the first ten years of his life in Paris a blessing, for it broadened his horizons and kept him from becoming provincially narrow at an early age. He dearly loved French, his first language, and later in life considered it his real mother tongue, even though the languages of his professional life were German and English. He associated Paris and France with a happy childhood, and they remained close to his heart all his life. He returned to the city every year, except during the world wars, sometimes for months of work. No wonder the very first sentence of his unfinished autobiography reads, "To me Paris is the most wonderful city on earth." [6]

Life for Sigerist took a sudden turn in 1901, when the family moved to Zurich as a result of his father's terminal illness. The family had a comfortable flat on the Eastern shore of the lake in central Zurich, where Sigerist lived with his mother and sister. However, painful humiliations awaited him at the beginning of this new life. In Paris at that time, a wealthy boy of ten would not, as nowadays, run around in blue jeans, but would rather behave and be treated like a little gentleman; he would be called "monsieur," wear a bowler hat and gloves, and carry a cane in his hand. To the more provincial boys of Zurich this seemed ridiculous, and sure enough, the young Parisian gentleman was teased and ridiculed. Equally distressing was the fact that although he was able to communicate with people in Swiss German, he had no knowledge of High German, which was used at school. However, Sigerist learned to adapt to his new environment, first in dress and later in language.

Sigerist described his education in the Zurich schools and university in his autobiographical writings and in his essay "University Education." [7] At the time of his first unsettling experiences in Zurich, his mother

5. Sigerist with his mother and sister at their home in Zurich, about 1912.

wisely selected an excellent private school for her children. The school practiced progressive educational methods that contrasted with the traditional, formalistic teaching common at the time. Learning came not only from books but equally from observation and manual work. The children made herbariums, relief maps, and sundials and learned botany on excursions into the countryside. The headmaster, Fritz von Beust, was the first of Sigerist's gifted teachers, an enthusiastic scientist able to instill in his pupils a love of nature and a deep interest in science. Thus, after the somber beginnings, Sigerist spent three happy years at this school, where he experienced the joy of learning.

Secondary school education in Switzerland was offered on several levels, the highest of which prepared students for university and was called gymnasium in accordance with its German model.[8] Sigerist entered the humanistic division of the Zurich Gymnasium in 1904 at age 13. Even though the classical languages were at the center of the curriculum, science and mathematics were not neglected. Soon another fine teacher deeply influenced Sigerist, the historian Otto Markwart, who had himself been a student of Jacob Burckhardt. A passionate teacher, Markwart's broad approach to history demonstrated to his students that history was not a dead subject but a living force. His enthusiasm for Italy and Italian culture meant that this country became the major destination of the Sigerist family's summer travels and a source of inspiration for the boy. Latin, and even more so Greek, excited the young student, so much so that in addition to the six to eight hours per week devoted to each of these languages throughout the six years of school, Sigerist decided to add an extra hour every day in the early morning to improve his knowledge of Greek grammar. Books became his passion. He felt joy and inspiration reading the ancient poets, historians, and philosophers, including the church fathers. Then his interests shifted to the East, and the Orient became his fascination. The early morning hour was now devoted to the study of Arabic, and Hebrew and religion were substituted for Italian and English as electives.

Even in his early adolescence, Sigerist seemed likely to become a scholar, even a passionate one. Yet he was by no means a model pupil. Not all his grades were the highest, but there was no subject in which he did poorly. His learning grew out of his own interests and was not pursued for the purpose of pleasing his teachers. Clearly, he owed a great deal to the gymnasium, which aroused his intellectual curiosity and prepared him for the university. In 1910, at age nineteen, he passed his final examinations, considered a license for university studies.

Sigerist had not the slightest doubt that the subject of his university studies would be oriental philology. In 1910, Sigerist went to the University of Zurich, which had been founded in 1833 and had a good reputation for its high academic standards. But because it was rather weak in oriental languages, Sigerist decided to continue his oriental studies in London at University College and Kings College. Under pressure from his teachers to choose between the Near East, India, or the Far East, Sigerist rejected the idea of specialization. He wanted to pursue the study of comparative literature and religion, but under an ever-increasing work load, he was eventually forced to comply with his teachers' advice and define an area of concentration.

Surprisingly, he decided to abandon oriental studies altogether and to go into science. It seems difficult to understand that after all he had invested, he took such a radical turn. Yet with his background of extremely broad interests, his horror of specialization is understandable. Another reason for the change may have been his overprotective mother, who even settled with him in London. She could never have tolerated, without suffering, her son's required travels and studies in oriental countries.[9] Thus, Sigerist's first and promising career came to a sudden end. Yet his interest in the Orient never waned, and the the many years he had invested in studying classical and oriental languages deepened the cultural background he brought to his future work as a medical historian.[10]

Sigerist went back to the University of Zurich and took the introductory science courses offered to students of both science and medicine. Ever since his school days with von Beust he had felt a certain attachment to science. However, at the end of a year of science, the phantom of specialization arose once more. Rather than decide for one of the many sciences, he chose medicine, which he considered the broadest of all fields.

Sigerist enrolled in the School of Medicine in 1912 and became an enthusiastic medical student. For his clinical studies, he moved to Munich in 1914; this time he was not accompanied by his mother but by his lifelong friend, the future radiologist Hans Schinz. He learned how to evaluate and manage patients from Friedrich von Müller, the professor of internal medicine. But Munich was also the art capital of Germany. Sigerist spent his days in museums and art galleries and his evenings in concert halls and theaters, rather than in the hospital. Occasionally, he dreamed of a theater career.[11] He developed doubts about medicine and in a crisis fled to Italy, plunging once more into a world of art and history. In Venice, as he recalls, he was struck by the thought that the history of medicine might be the field in which he could best combine his interests in medicine, history, languages, and the humanities.[12] If this was indeed a sudden intuition, that day in Venice must be called a crucial one in Sigerist's life. He hurried back to Munich, where he rediscovered his enthusiasm for medicine and started to collect materials on the history of medicine. He soon came across names like Karl Sudhoff's, and medical history remained on his mind for the rest of his medical studies. His stay in Munich ended abruptly when World War I broke out in the summer of that year.

Back in Zurich, he was called to active duty in the Swiss army, which was then guarding the country's borders. The years to come had to be split between periods spent in the army and at the university medical school. During these clinical years in Zurich, Ferdinand Sauerbruch, a famous surgeon, became another of Sigerist's outstanding teachers. Sauerbruch, like von Müller, was interested in the history of medicine, a fact clearly shown in his lectures. Sigerist got to know Sauerbruch personally and joined him on a tour of German military hospitals in 1915. Sigerist found World War I a shattering experience even though Switzerland, at least militarily, was not drawn into the conflict. In his own retrospective words, "The young generation will never understand what a shock this war was to us. . . . That Europeans, Christians, humans of one culture would suddenly assault and kill each other had been simply unthinkable." [13]

At the end of his clinical years Sigerist did research in the Department of Pharmacology with Max Cloetta. The results became the basis of his medical thesis, entitled "Experimental Studies on the Effect of the Chronic Administration of Camphor on the Normal and Pathologic Heart." [14] With this thesis and the state board examination, Sigerist obtained his M.D. and his license to practice in 1917.

His doctoral thesis was not Sigerist's first publication. Several times in his student years he had contributed essays to the "Feuilleton" column of the *Neue Zürcher Zeitung,* a daily newspaper of considerable reputation even outside Switzerland. The very first of these articles, written in 1910 at age nineteen, was on a visit to San Lazzaro, an island near Venice with an Armenian monastery.[15] As a medical student he wrote a review of Sauerbruch's book on a new hand prosthesis[16] and a brief article about his impressions of the tour of German military hospitals in 1915.[17] In the latter he praised the public assistance granted to amputated and other disabled soldiers and the impressive efforts at their social rehabilitation.

In addition to the university, the Swiss army was a school that taught Sigerist a great deal. After his military training in 1912, he was called for active duty during World War I for periods of several months. He spent a total of two years in the army, during which he gradually advanced to

6. Henry E. Sigerist, first lieutenant of the Swiss Army Medical Corps, during World War I.

7. Sigerist with his fiancée, Emmy Escher, in Zurich, 1915.

first lieutenant. As a member of the medical corps, he had the only opportunity of his life to treat patients, usually troops, but also civilians in the
remote mountain valleys. Sigerist likewise became acquainted with practical public health work during the 1918 influenza epidemic, which took
a heavy toll in Switzerland. He was assigned to the Surgeon General's Influenza Bureau and from there was sent on epidemiological surveys all
over the country. The army taught him additional lessons that had lasting consequences throughout his life. Previously he had been embedded
in the upper middle class and in academic life. In the army, he came into
close contact with the working class for the first time. The soldiers' views
on the war, on society and, of course, on the Russian Revolution seemed
more convincing to Sigerist than the conservative views circulating in the
officers' mess.

Building a Career in Medical History

After graduating from medical school in 1917, Sigerist wrote to the German scholar, Karl Sudhoff, the world's undisputed leader in the field of
medical history. First describing his studies and interests, Sigerist continued:

Last June I passed my State Board Examination, and shortly after that obtained my MD degree with a thesis in pharmacology which I had started two years ago. Now I have to make up my mind whether I should devote my career to medical practice or to the history of medicine. Since I feel rather helpless, I would like to ask for your opinion. Little is left of my former philologic knowledge, but Greek and Latin are still present, and I am fluent in French, English, and Italian. In our Swiss universities history of medicine is much neglected, but there seems to be no lack of interest. If we were at peace I would like to go to Leipzig and become your student. As long as there is war I am quite absorbed by military duty, and I would not be eligible for a permit to go abroad. For your information I may add that I am married and that financially I am in a position to embark on a career which is not exactly profitable. May I now ask you, dear Professor Sudhoff, to advise me how best to organize my future studies. In doing so, you would earn my deep gratitude.[18]

Sudhoff's encouraging answer tipped the balance, for from then on, Sigerist had no doubt that his career and his future would be in the history of medicine. His sudden intuition in Venice in 1914 and considerable enthusiasm and study since then were not in themselves sufficient. It was Sudhoff's endorsement in 1917 that helped Sigerist clearly see his future. His medical teachers in Zurich, however, were dismayed about his prospects; to them, medical history was a delightful hobby for retired physicians but not a career, let alone a financially secure one. They were certainly right about the immediate career prospects; none of the Swiss universities had a professorship or a department in the history of medicine.

Sigerist immediately began reading Greek and Latin medical texts with the classical philologist Ernst Howald.[19] He wrote to Sudhoff thanking him for his advice and expressing a hope that the spring of 1918 would bring peace so that he could visit him in Leipzig. In March 1918, with Europe still at war, Sigerist informed Sudhoff enthusiastically and in detail about his studies with Howald. In November of that year the war was finally over and with it also Sigerist's active duty in the army. He now was free to start his career as an independent scholar. But he had to wait a whole year until the dismal conditions in postwar Germany permitted him to visit Sudhoff.

December 1919 finally saw Sigerist in Leipzig. Many years later he wrote about the crucially important weeks he spent there.[20] Sudhoff introduced Sigerist to the rich library and to his manuscript collection, and they later discussed Sigerist's future projects. Sigerist had thought of working on Albrecht von Haller and the eighteenth century, to which he had a sentimental attachment, but Sudhoff convinced him to take up the early Middle Ages. This would require painstaking philological analysis of a great many manuscripts, exactly the way Sudhoff had built his own reputation. Sigerist returned to Switzerland with much material and immediately began the study of early medieval manuscripts. The result of this direct encounter with Sudhoff was a student-teacher relationship and the creation of an outpost of the Leipzig Institute in Zurich. Sigerist's gratitude and attachment to Sudhoff, to whom he owed so much, lasted most of his life.[21]

The delay of Sigerist's first visit to Leipzig, caused by the war, had allowed for preparatory studies during 1918 and 1919. He studied the history of medicine in antiquity and later periods and also took courses in Arabic, Syrian, and Persian. This was not a nostalgic repeat of his orientalist period but a recognition of the fact that Greco-Roman medicine had been transmitted to the Orient before being rediscovered in Europe. During these two years, Sigerist's first medicohistorical publications appeared. Two of them, published in German and Swiss medical journals, dealt with military medicine at the time of civil war in early eighteenth-century Switzerland.[22] In another article, published in the *Neue Zürcher Zeitung,* he presented a timely account of the history of influenza, comparing the anxieties and rumors circulating during former epidemics with those current in 1918.[23]

Back from Leipzig and inspired by Sudhoff, Sigerist's studies and literary production became more professional, better organized, and clearly directed toward a career in the history of medicine. His amateur period was over. Sigerist was still an independent scholar working in libraries and in the house at Ebelstrasse 7 in Zurich where he lived with his young wife, Emmy Escher, and in later years with their daughters, Erica and Nora.

In 1920 and 1921 more of his publications appeared in medical and medicohistorical journals.[24] The most important of these studies focused on Sigerist's main concern in this period, early medieval medicine. In the "Cirurgia Eliodori" he offered a philological commentary on the originality of this medieval text as well as an inventory of the operations performed by the Greek surgeon Heliodoros.[25] Erwin Ackerknecht called this Sigerist's "first serious medico-historical publication."[26] Another philological study analyzed the origins of Master Blumentrost's book on the art of healing.[27] In "Tradition and Nature Observation in Medieval Medicine," he traced the transmission of Greco-Roman medicine into the Arabic and German Middle Ages.[28]

Sigerist's most important work of these years was an in-depth study of early medieval drug formularies. The resulting *Studien und Texte zur frühmittelalterlichen Rezeptliteratur* (Studies and Texts on Early Medieval Drug Formularies) was an edited collection of seven manuscripts with an index of the materia medica of the period; it demonstrated a clear continuity from antiquity to the early Middle Ages but revealed some complexities in the transmission of early medieval material to the School of Salerno.[29] The manuscript was completed in 1921 and appeared in 1923 as Sigerist's first book.

One of Sigerist's goals on the way to his academic career was to achieve *Habilitation* in order to become *Privatdozent,* the first academic teaching rank in the German university system.[30] He applied for *Habilitation* by presenting his opus on early medieval formularies and received a highly favorable report from the committee responsible for commenting on his qualifications. On June 22, 1921, he had to present himself to the faculty of the medical school; his lecture was titled "Paracelsus and the Reaction against Galenism." Then, at the age of thirty, he was nominated *Privatdozent.* On November 26, 1921, he delivered his public inaugural lecture, "Tasks and Aims of the History of Medicine."[31] Sigerist was only the fourth *Privatdozent* of medical history since the foundation of the University of Zurich.[32]

Sigerist's inaugural lecture deserves particular attention as the first of his programmatic statements on the subject of medical history.[33] The text starts with an overview of the field as it had developed by 1920. Until the early nineteenth century, the history of medicine was not taught separately but was integrated into the teaching of individual medical subjects and considered part of practical medicine. Hippocratic classical medicine was still alive; its influence gradually waned with the advent of modern scientific medicine in the middle of the nineteenth century. The breathtaking developments in the second half of the century generated excitement and optimism among physicians and laymen alike. Leading physicians were conscious of the history of medicine; not so the rank and file who, out of ignorance, tended to despise the modest past of medicine in contrast to its glorious present and future. The few good historians of medicine had little following in the medical community. In the early twentieth century the pace of scientific advance had slowed, and medicine entered a stage of self-reflection. Interest in the past again increased, and this was favorable to the development of the history of medicine, which indeed witnessed a remarkable growth after about 1900. Libraries and societies dedicated to medical history were founded in many countries, international congresses were held, and a dozen journals as well as classic texts in new editions began to appear. In most German universities, the history of medicine became a teaching subject, and full professorships were created in Leipzig and Vienna. The history of medicine became an organized and acknowledged subject, having entered the stage of independence and institutionalization.

In his inaugural lecture, Sigerist also discussed the tasks of medical history, tasks that varied with respect to each historical period. Greek medicine was marked by a lack of knowledge, an abundance of hypotheses, and a great need for definitive editions of texts that might be discovered in Arabic medical literature. By contrast, modern medicine was characterized by an abundance of sources, and its major task was to isolate the leading ideas from a thicket of speculations, to reveal the roots of modern thinking.

Sigerist then turned to the aims of medical history and the demands made on medical historians. He pleaded for a high standard of professionalism and asked that the history of medicine not be considered merely a collection of curiosities and anecdotes. The history of medicine was not only "part of the general history of civilization, it should also be in close contact with modern medicine, giving and taking. . . . History will make the modern physician aware that his medicine is not the product of recent decades but rather the result of a long and troubled development, and that our grains of truth emerged from a sea of errors, a sea we are still wading in."[34] Apodictic statements in medicine should be met with skepticism, and hubris, a companion of rapid progress, should be countered with the modesty engendered by historical knowledge. Sigerist also suggested that medical history could be of immediate practical importance; for example, it could provide accumulated epidemiological experience. The recent influenza epidemic occurred when the younger generation of physicians had no experience at all of similar outbreaks. In such instances, the literature of past epidemics could prove invaluable.

Finally, Sigerist emphasized the value of medical history as a bridge between science and humanities, as a means of avoiding the dangers of narrowness in the study of medicine and of overestimating science. Science had become so important that it could no longer be ignored by historians and philologists. For them, the history of medicine and science could also fill the gap between science and the humanities. Physicians might then cease to think of philologists as useless dreamers, and philologists in turn might come to understand the eternal beauty of science. The historian of medicine or science, who had to keep up with the results of both history and medicine, would be a facilitator, moving toward the goal of a new humanism. Sigerist concluded: "The optional subject of the history of medicine is also meant to instill an idealism into the young students of medicine, an idealism more desirable than ever and without which life would not be worth living." [35]

The Range of Sigerist's Medicohistorical Interests

Although Sudhoff had suggested medieval studies, Sigerist did not concentrate on the Middle Ages alone. During the years 1921–24, he gave the following lecture courses and seminars, on a wide range of topics:

History of medicine
Reading of *De Medicina* by Celsus
Reading a text by Aristotle and discussing its medieval repercussions
The role of diseases and of the fight against them in world history
History of medicine and science in antiquity
History of anatomy
Reading of selected texts of the Corpus Hippocraticum
    Paracelsus and the spiritual trends of the Renaissance
The development of medicine in the nineteenth century
Reading of texts by Galen

The audience for these courses varied in number from one to twenty-nine. In addition, Sigerist had six medical students who carried out historical theses under his guidance. He was also one of the founders of the Swiss Society of the History of Medicine and Sciences, and he served as secretary to the young organization during its first four years, from 1920 to 1924.[36]

The same broad range of interests was evident in Sigerist's publications. In 1923, in addition to his monograph on medieval formularia, he published three edited books. One was *The Book of Cirurgia* by Hieronymus Brunschwig, a facsimile of Brunschwig's *Cirurgia* of 1497, to which Sigerist added an essay on this author's life and work.[37] In the context of then backward German surgery, Brunschwig had been important as the first German surgeon to write a practical manual based on Italian and French sources. In this manual, he described the typical problems of general surgery, such as wounds, dislocations, fractures, and amputations. At that time, wounds caused by firearms were an important problem; they were considered to be poisoned by gunpowder, which complicated their treatment. Brunschwig wrote about such technical matters as antidotary, soporific sponges containing scopolamine, and he also wrote about social problems. According to Sigerist, however, Brunschwig was still a man of the Middle Ages and his book, although a useful compilation, had few original contributions.

Ambroise Paré, by contrast, was a surgeon who crossed the threshold of Renaissance medicine in his willingness to adopt true innovations. His masterpiece of 1545, "The Treatment of Gunshot Wounds," was usually available only in debased modern editions. Thus, when Sigerist succeeded in finding the original text in Paris, he prepared a book, published in Sudhoff's series, *Klassiker der Medizin,* containing a German translation of Paré's French text and an essay on the author's life and work.[38] Paré, whose parents were poor, started out as a barber's apprentice and then became a field surgeon. He first treated gunshot wounds according to Vigo's accepted dogma that these poisoned wounds had to be cauterized with a red-hot iron or boiling oil, but on a military campaign in 1537, when he ran out of boiling oil, he had instead used a mixture of egg yolk, rose oil, and turpentine. The treatment was successful, proving that these wounds were not poisoned by gunpowder and sparing the wounded the additional torture of cauterization. Sigerist argued that Paré, in contrast to Brunschwig, was a Renaissance man, who emphasized observation and experience over the authority of the ancients.

Had Sudhoff not intervened, Sigerist's love of the eighteenth century and his interest in Albrecht von Haller (1708–77) would have dominated his early career. Sigerist's admiration for Haller was rekindled when he found Haller's original Latin letters to the physician and botanist Johannes Gesner in a Zurich library. This sparked Sigerist's fourth book of 1923, *Albrecht von Haller's Letters to Johannes Gesner.*[39] This collection of 549 letters reflected the full span of Haller's life and showed his development as a physician and poet, as a protagonist of modern experimental science, and as a universal scholar embracing all the knowledge of his time. Sigerist insisted on printing the letters in their original language; a German translation is preserved in typescript. The published volume contains Sigerist's sympathetically written biography of Haller up to the beginning of his correspondence with Gesner. Every letter—the originals in Haller's almost indecipherable handwriting—was commented on in footnotes that identified the countless scholars, books, and places mentioned. Reading the book and its introduction, one recognizes that Haller and Sigerist were truly congenial and that the young scholar felt a strong emotional and intellectual attachment to his predecessor.

Sigerist's enthusiasm for the eighteenth century made Sudhoff suspect that his disciple might be deserting the Middle Ages. Thus Sudhoff persuaded Sigerist to edit the *Herbal of Pseudo-Apuleius* for the *Corpus Medicorum Latinorum* to get his disciple back on track. This task took Sigerist and Ernst Howald many years of hard philological work and required the study of manuscripts at the British Museum and the monastery of Monte Cassino. A critical, illustrated edition was eventually produced and printed in 1927.[40]

In addition to these major works, Sigerist's last years in Zurich (1922–25) saw publications on a variety of medicohistorical subjects as well as his launching of the *Monumenta Medica,* a series of facsimiles of medical books. Among his important lesser works was an essay on the course and nature of Greek medicine.[41] He presented Greek medicine as subdivided into a prelude of protomedicine, a period of assimilation of foreign medicine, a struggle for new ideas, a climax (Hippocratic medicine), a period of extension (Hellenism), and finally, a long-lasting decline.

In another essay, Sigerist presented the birth of occidental medicine in a dramatic way: he argued that unlike Greece or other great civilizations, which created their medicine out of their own culture, the West had to live with a grafted foreign medicine, transmitted in a corrupted form, for a thousand years of its history. Only the Renaissance brought about a truly occidental medicine, not by rediscovering antiquity, but by making anatomical thinking the centerpiece of a new medicine.[42] Sigerist dealt elaborately with the medieval prehistory of occidental medicine and lets the reader feel his joy of years of medieval study:

> The investigation of medieval medicine is fascinating. Just fifty years ago it was hidden in a mist which has been dissolved by Sudhoff. The whole era has come alive. . . . The monks talk to us through thousands of manuscripts. In excitement we experience the idyllic episode of Salerno. We belong to the guilds of surgeons and take part in their struggles. With the lepers we flee into the wilderness, exiled, dead to society. We experience panic when the black death strikes, the whipped-up passions of the people, and we feel relief when the epidemic fades away. . . . The solemn mood of the cathedrals and the fervor of medieval madonnas move and enthrall us.[43]

Writing about the history of medicine in Switzerland, Sigerist presented his country as remarkable not so much for its original contributions, as for its role as a mediator of medical knowledge among the larger countries of Europe.[44] He published the letters of Swiss scholars to Johannes Gesner, thus providing further examples of eighteenth century correspondence among the learned.[45]

Altogether, Sigerist published fifty-six titles during his Zurich period; of these, about half could be considered serious scholarly works.[46] Eager to address a larger public, Sigerist also published a total of twenty-two articles in the *Neue Zürcher Zeitung* on such topics as Semmelweis, Pasteur, English surgery, and smallpox vaccination.[47]

In 1924 Sudhoff's successor was being discussed in Leipzig. Sigerist knew he was a candidate and so did the faculty of medicine in Zurich. The faculty discussed ways to keep Sigerist in Zurich, but dismissed the idea of creating a chair in the history of medicine, on the grounds that it was a minor subject and that the faculty was already too large and the students overburdened with the existing subjects. However, by a unanimous vote of the faculty, Sigerist was made *Titularprofessor,* i.e., he was given the title of a professor, but without rights and duties. Sigerist's time as a formally designated professor in Zurich lasted less than a year. On April 24, 1925, he wrote to the chancellor of education that he had accepted the call from Leipzig as of October 1 and that he would terminate his teaching at the University of Zurich by the end of the summer semester.

Conclusion

There can be no doubt that Sigerist's relatively little known years in Zurich were of decisive importance for his education and for his professional career as a leading historian of medicine. Medical historians usually have basic training in either medicine or history. In contrast, Sigerist combined training in medicine with pre- and postdoctoral studies in philology, based on a rare knowledge of several modern and ancient languages. The importance of Sudhoff is obvious; it was he who directed Sigerist toward medieval medicine, a field that allowed him to make full use of his philological abilities. But in addition to meeting Sudhoff's expectations, Sigerist was interested very early in the Renaissance, in the eighteenth century, and in a variety of other periods. Thus, even in Zurich, Sigerist was far from being a narrow specialist or a timid disciple.

Being guided by Sudhoff yet living geographically distant from his authoritarian teacher was another decisive circumstance. It allowed Sigerist to build an independent career. During the years from 1920 to 1925, he grew from student to scholar and developed his own distinctive style.[48] Clearly, these were years of a gradual emancipation from Sudhoff, visible in his choice of topics and in his increasingly synthetic approach. In his development as a scholar, Sigerist was also influenced by Max Neuburger (1868–1955), professor of medical history in Vienna, a fact Sigerist himself emphasized.[49] As early as 1904, Neuburger had pointed out the importance of the history of medicine as a bridge between science and the humanities and the practical consequences of its close contacts with modern medicine.[50] In a letter to Neuburger in the early 1920s Sigerist wrote, "Only he who is actively involved in research in the history of medicine knows how much this field owes to you. I for one have been stimulated and enriched by your works, and your great textbook is my steady companion." [51]

Sigerist's open letter to Neuburger in 1943 was more explicit:

> Great monographs came from your pen. They revealed profound historical understanding and a broad philosophical outlook. Most medical historians at that time were philologists, interested in texts and engaged in analytical work. Your mind was bent on synthesis. You did not edit texts but you wrote history, and you did it in a brilliant style which makes the reading of your books so captivating. . . . [Your two volumes of "History of Medicine"] gave inspiration and guidance to a whole generation of students of medical history, and I for one can testify how much they meant to us. They gave us not only facts but a philosophy of medicine. In your hands medical history evolved from being an antiquarian subject to be a vital matter full of significance for our day. . . . It was not easy to hold a leading position in medical history in a German-speaking university at the time of Karl Sudhoff. His domineering and aggressive personality tolerated disciples but not competitors, and he was often unfair to you. But to the students of my generation it meant a great deal to have two men like you, leaders both and yet as different as they could be: Sudhoff, the philologist engaged in analytic work; you, the philosopher bent on synthesis. You supplemented each other in an ideal way and it is a great pity that Sudhoff's attitude made it impossible for you to work together. As a close student of Sudhoff I wish to testify how much I owe to you, to your writings that I studied and digested, and to the warm interest that you always showed for my work from the first days of my career.[52]

Neuburger stood in Sudhoff's shadow not only in life but also with regard to his influence on Sigerist, which has been grossly underestimated. Sigerist certainly admired Sudhoff for his knowledge and abilities and for having guided his early work in the history of medicine. However, much that Sigerist became known for later in his career is really more reminiscent of Neuburger: his synthetic approach to medical history, his philosophical outlook, and his persuasive yet unauthoritarian personality.

Many topics that Sigerist dealt with repeatedly during his professional life thus had their origins in the early years in Zurich: the medicine of the Middle Ages and of the eighteenth century; the history of surgery, gynecology, and pharmacology, of epidemics, and of syphilis; and the history of medicine as a discipline, its institutionalization, methodology, and teaching. The one theme missing from Sigerist's Zurich works is an explicit interest in the social aspects of medicine, so characteristic of his work in America. These social and political issues were not even touched on in Sigerist's inaugural lecture, in which he defined the tasks and aims of medical history.[53] When returning to Switzerland at the end of his academic career, Sigerist gave a lecture in 1948 at the University of Berne entitled "Tasks and Aims of the History of Medicine"—the same title he had used for his inaugural lecture of 1921. This second lecture, by contrast, emphasized the issues not touched upon during his early Zurich years: "[Medical history] studies the ways a society and its individuals tried to improve health, to prevent disease, to restore health, and socially to rehabilitate the former patient. . . . Whether we will succeed in using the results of medical science for the benefit of all the people will depend on many non-medical, social, economic, religious, philosophic, and political factors."[54]

His Zurich years gave Sigerist the foundation for his life's work. They provided favorable conditions for the development of his personality and his ideas. When he left Zurich in 1925 to assume the Leipzig chair, Sigerist was no longer Sudhoff's humble student, but a mature, enthusiastic, and original scholar and visionary, ready to give medical history new directions and new dimensions.

Notes

1. See, for example, C. Becker, "Schriften über Henry E. Sigerist (1891–1957) —eine Bibliographie," in *Ergebnisse und Perspektiven sozialhistorischer Forschung in der Medizingeschichte. Kolloquium zum 100. Geburtstag von H. E. Sigerist,* eds. S. Hahn and A. Thom (Leipzig: Karl-Sudhoff-Institut, 1991), 37–45; M. C. Wäspi, *Die Anfänge des Medizinhistorikers Henry E. Sigerist in Zürich* (Zurich: Zürcher Medizingeschichtliche Abhandlungen, Nr. 206, Juris Druck und Verlag, 1989); E. Berg-Schorn, *Henry E. Sigerist (1891–1957). Medizinhistoriker in Leipzig und Baltimore. Standpunkt und Wirkung* (Cologne: Arbeiten der Forschungsstelle des Instituts für Geschichte der Medizin der Universität Köln, vol. 9, 1978).

2. Ernst H. Sigerist to Henry E. Sigerist, August 4, 1891. Private collection of M. H. Bickel, Bern, Switzerland (translated from French by the author).

3. Ernst H. Sigerist to Henry E. Sigerist, April 6, 1901. Private collection of M. H. Bickel (translated from French by the author).

4. N. Sigerist Beeson, ed., *Henry E. Sigerist: Autobiographical Writings* (Montreal: McGill University Press, 1966).

5. Henry E. Sigerist to Santa Claus, about 1897. Private collection of M. H. Bickel (translated from French by the author).

6. N. Sigerist Beeson, ed., *Henry E. Sigerist: Autobiographical Writings* (Montreal: McGill University Press, 1966), 8.

7. H. E. Sigerist, "University Education," *Bulletin of the History of Medicine* 8 (1940): 3–21.

8. The scholastic system in Zurich in the early twentieth century was the following. Elementary school *(Primarschule)* was for all children ages six to twelve. Secondary education for most was another three years of *Sekundarschule* or *Realschule* to complete the legal minimum of nine years. In many cases this was followed by an apprenticeship or a vocational school. A minority heading toward academic studies took their secondary education at the gymnasium. This was terminated at age eighteen or nineteen with the *Maturität,* i.e., the certificate that was a prerequisite for entry to a university.

9. H. E. Sigerist, personal communication.

10. For Sigerist's lifelong interests in oriental studies, see Ilza Veith's essay in this volume.

11. H. E. Sigerist, personal communication.

12. H. E. Sigerist, "University Education," *Bulletin of the History of Medicine* 8 (1940): 3–21.

13. H. E. Sigerist, "Prof. Dr. Hans R. Schinz zum 60. Geburtstag am 13 Dezember 1951," *Schweizerische Medizinische Wochenschrift* 81 (1951): 1189–90.

14. H. E. Sigerist, *Experimentelle Untersuchungen über die Einwirkung chronischer Kampherzufuhr auf das normale und pathologische Herz* (Zurich: thesis, Lehmann, 1917). See also H. E. Sigerist, "Ueber die Einwirkung chronischer Kampherzufuhr auf das Herz," *Korrespondenzblatt für Schweizer Aerzte* 47 (1917): 1748–52.

15. H. E. Sigerist, "Ein Besuch auf San Lazzaro," *Neue Zürcher Zeitung,* August 30, 1910.

16. H. E. Sigerist, "Die künstliche Hand," *Neue Zürcher Zeitung,* May 25, 1916.

17. H. E. Sigerist, "Deutsche Invalidenfürsorge," *Neue Zürcher Zeitung,* August 15, 1915.

18. Henry E. Sigerist to Karl Sudhoff, August 25, 1917. Karl-Sudhoff-Institut Medizinhistorische Sammlung D807, University of Leipzig (translated from German by the author).

19. Howald (1887–1967) was professor of Greek and Latin literature at the University of Zurich from 1918 to 1952. He was Sigerist's authority and collaborator in matters of classical philology and one of the first to practice interdisciplinary collaboration.

20. H. E. Sigerist, "The Medical Literature of the Early Middle Ages. A Program and a Report of a Summer of Research in Italy," *Bulletin of the Institute of the History of Medicine* 2 (1934): 26–50. See also H. E. Sigerist, "Erinnerungen an Karl Sudhoff," *Sudhoffs Archiv für Geschichte der Medizin* 37 (1953): 97–103.

21. Sigerist was later clearly dismayed by Sudhoff's association with the Nazi

Party; he tended, however, to explain it as a consequence of senility or opportunism rather than conviction.

22. H. E. Sigerist, "Läuse und Entlausung im 2. Villmergerkrieg," *Deutsche Medizinische Wochenschrift* 44 (1918): 189; H. E. Sigerist, "Aus einem Lazarett im zweiten Villmergerkrieg 1712. Die Schrift des Johann Kupfferschmid 'De morbis praeliantum' Basel 1715," *Korrespondenzblatt für Schweizer Aerzte* 48 (1918): 1000-1007.

23. H. E. Sigerist, "Zur Geschichte der epidemischen Grippe," *Neue Zürcher Zeitung,* October 29, 1918.

24. H. E. Sigerist, "Zur Frühgeschichte der Syphilis," *Münchener Medizinische Wochenschrift* 68 (1921): 1257-58; H. E. Sigerist, "Zur Geschichte der Geschlechtsprognostik," *Fortschritte der Medizin* 39 (1921): 965-66; H. E. Sigerist, "Die Verdienste zweier Schaffhauser Aerzte (Joh. Conr. Peyer und Joh. Conr. Brunner) um die Erforschung der Darmdrüsen," *Verhandlungen der Schweizerischen Naturforschenden Gesellschaft* (1921): 153-54.

25. H. E. Sigerist, "Die 'Cirurgia Eliodori,'" *Archiv für Geschichte der Medizin* 12 (1920): 1-9.

26. E. Ackerknecht, introduction to *A Bibliography of the Writings of Henry E. Sigerist,* edited by Genevieve Miller (Montreal: McGill University Press, 1966), 1.

27. H. E. Sigerist, "Meister Blumentrosts Arzneibuch," *Archiv für Geschichte der Medizin* 12 (1920): 70-73.

28. H. E. Sigerist, "Tradition und Naturbeobachtung in der mittelalterlichen Medizin," *Schweizerische Medizinische Wochenschrift* 2 (1921): 745-48.

29. H. E. Sigerist, *Studien und Texte zur frühmittelalterlichen Rezeptliteratur* (Leipzig: Studien zur Geschichte der Medizin herausgegeben von der Puschmann-Stiftung an der Universität Leipzig, Heft 13, Verlag Johann Ambrosius Barth, 1923). For more detailed analysis, see Michael McVaugh's chapter in this volume.

30. The process of *Habilitation* required a doctoral degree, years of research, and the presentation of an elaborate scholarly *Habilitationsschrift*. A committee of the faculty judged this work and the candidate's achievements, whereupon the candidate had to deliver a *Probevortrag* (trial lecture) to prove his talent for teaching. If accepted by the faculty, the government would bestow the title of *Privatdozent* on the candidate, who was then licensed to give courses at the university, usually outside the regular curriculum.

31. H. E. Sigerist, "Aufgaben und Ziele der Medizingeschichte," *Schweizerische Medizinische Wochenschrift* 3 (1922): 318-22 (quotations translated from German by the author).

32. The third was G. A. Wehrli, a practicing physician who published on the history of popular and local medicine. Wehrli's large collection of medical paraphernalia became the nucleus for the foundation of the Department of the History of Medicine in 1951. See U. Boschung, "Gustav Adolf Wehrli (1888-1949), Gründer der Medizinhistorischen Sammlung der Universität Zürich," *Gesnerus* 37 (1980): 91-102.

33. For further discussion of the central themes of this lecture, see also Temkin's essay in this volume.

34. H. E. Sigerist, "Aufgaben und Ziele der Medizingeschichte."

35. Ibid.

36. In the first annual report, Sigerist claimed the society had 120 members; its honorary members included Karl Sudhoff and Max Neuburger.

37. H. E. Sigerist, *The Book of Cirurgia by Hieronymus Brunschwig. Strassburg, Johann Grüninger, 1497. With a Study on Hieronymus Brunschwig and his Work* (Milan: R. Lier & Co., 1923).

38. H. E. Sigerist, *Ambroise Paré. Die Behandlung der Schusswunden (1545). Eingeleitet, übersetzt und herausgegeben* (Leipzig: Verlag Ambrosius Barth, 1923).

39. H. E. Sigerist, *Albrecht von Hallers Briefe an Johannes Gesner (1728-1777). Herausgegeben, eingeleitet und mit Anmerkungen versehen* (Berlin: Weidmannsche Buchhandlung, 1923).

40. E. Howald and H. E. Sigerist, eds., *Antonii Musae de herba vettonica liber. Pseudoapulei herbarius. Anonymi de taxone liber. Sexti Placiti liber medicinae ex animalibus etc.* (Leipzig and Berlin: Teubner, 1927). For further discussion, see McVaugh's essay in this volume.

41. H. E. Sigerist, "Beiträge zur Geschichte der griechischen Medizin," *Schweizerische Medizinische Wochenschrift* 6 (1925): 188-92. See also Heinrich von Staden's important discussion of Sigerist's ideas on ancient medicine in his essay in this volume.

42. In his essay in this volume, Owsei Temkin comments on Sigerist's overstatement of the novelty of anatomical thinking in Renaissance medicine.

43. H. E. Sigerist, "Die Geburt der abendländischen Medizin," in *Essays on the History of Medicine Presented to Karl Sudhoff on the Occasion of his Seventieth Birthday, November 26th 1923*, eds. C. Singer and H. E. Sigerist (London and Zurich: Oxford University Press and Verlag Seldwyla, 1924), 185-205 (quotation from p. 190, translated from German by the author).

44. H. E. Sigerist, "Die Rolle der Schweiz in der Entwicklung der Medizin," *Schweizerische Medizinische Wochenschrift* 6 (1925): 929-32.

45. H. E. Sigerist, "Beiträge zur Geschichte der Naturwissenschaft und Medizin in der Schweiz: 1. Zwei Briefe von Micheli du Crest an Johannes Gesner; 2. Ein Brief von Johann Melchior Eppli an Johannes Gesner," *Vierteljahrsschrift der naturforschenden Gesellschaft Zürich* 68 (1923): 554-69; H. E. Sigerist, "Beiträge zur Geschichte der Naturwissenschaft und Medizin in der Schweiz: 3. Die Briefe von Johann (II.) Bernoulli an Johannes Gesner," *Vierteljahrsschrift der naturforschenden Gesellschaft Zürich* 69 (1924): 326-41.

46. Among his many publications were a translation of Ketham's gynecology, a manuscript from the monastery of Einsiedeln, a review of literature on the history of dentistry, and a bibliography of Sudhoff's medicohistorical works: H. E. Sigerist, "Eine deutsche Uebersetzung der Kethamschen Gynäkologie," *Archiv für Geschichte der Medizin* 14 (1923): 169-78; H. E. Sigerist, "Deutsche medizinische Handschriften aus Schweizer Bibliotheken. I. Die Handschrift 297 der Einsiedler Stiftsbibliothek," *Archiv der Geschichte der Medizin* 17 (1925): 205-40; H. E. Sigerist, "Neue Literatur zur Geschichte der Zahnheilkunde," *Schweizerische Monatsschrift für Zahnheilkunde* 32 (1922): 157-64; H. E. Sigerist, "Bibliographie der medizingeschichtlichen Arbeiten von Karl Sudhoff, nach Materien geordnet," in *Essays on the History of Medicine Presented to Karl Sudhoff on the Occasion of his Seventieth Birthday, November 26th 1923*, eds. C. Singer and H. E. Sigerist (London and Zurich: Oxford University Press and Verlag Seldwyla, 1924), 389-418.

47. H. E. Sigerist, "Ignaz Philipp Semmelweis," *Neue Zürcher Zeitung,* August 13, 1918; H. E. Sigerist, "Louis Pasteur (Zu seinem 100. Geburtstag, 27. Dezember)," *Neue Zürcher Zeitung,* December 27, 1922; H. E. Sigerist, "Englische Chirurgie," *Neue Zürcher Zeitung,* September 15, 1924; H. E. Sigerist, "Zur Geschichte der Pockenschutzimpfung," *Neue Zürcher Zeitung,* May 28, 1921.

48. For the best expression of his independent views in this period, see especially H. E. Sigerist, "Aufgaben und Ziele der Medizingeschichte," *Schweizerische Medizinische Wochenschrift* 3 (1922): 318-22.

49. H. E. Sigerist, "A Tribute to Max Neuburger on the Occasion of his 75th Birthday, December 8, 1943," *Bulletin of the History of Medicine* 14 (1943): 417-21; see also G. Schmidt, "H. E. Sigerists Auffassung vom Sinn medizinhistorischer Arbeit," *Wiener klinische Wochenschrift* 103 (1991): 487-92.

50. M. Neuburger, "Die Geschichte der Medizin als akademischer Lehrgegenstand," *Wiener klinische Wochenschrift* 17 (1904): 1214-19.

51. G. Schmidt, "H. E. Sigerists Auffassung vom Sinn medizinhistorischer Arbeit," *Wiener klinische Wochenschrift* 103 (1991): 487-92 (the quoted letter is translated from German by the author).

52. H. E. Sigerist, "A Tribute to Max Neuburger on the Occasion of his 75th Birthday, December 8, 1943," *Bulletin of the History of Medicine* 14 (1943): 417-21.

53. H. E. Sigerist, "Aufgaben und Ziele der Medizingeschichte," *Schweizerische Medizinische Wochenschrift* 3 (1922): 318-22.

54. H. E. Sigerist, "Aufgaben und Ziele der Medizingeschichte," *Mitteilungen der naturforschenden Gesellschaft Bern, Neue Folge* 6 (1948): xxii-xxiii.

CHAPTER 2

The Leipzig Period, 1925–1932

Ingrid Kästner

Henry Sigerist's seven years in Leipzig were a particularly fruitful period.[1] Despite increasing material difficulties in the university, he built a research and teaching program in the history of medicine, organized a productive institute, and had his work recognized far beyond Leipzig. Always full of plans and ideas, Sigerist enjoyed interested and talented colleagues, enthusiastic students, and acceptance by both the faculty of medicine and Leipzig intellectuals. As medical historians from many countries came to work in his institute and to receive his guidance, Sigerist maintained close contacts in many countries, including those of Eastern Europe.

Call to Leipzig and Organization of Research and Teaching

Just how much the young *Titularprofessor* of medical history at the University of Zurich craved a new field of action we learn from a letter of October 9, 1924, to his teacher Karl Sudhoff: "We often think back to the Innsbruck meeting, to the beautiful days we spent with you in the Inn Valley, to the Congress' stimulation. By contrast, the Lucerne meeting was quite pallid and I returned rather depressed. Switzerland is really awfully small for a field like ours, and it is crippling to lecture to people who are not able to judge what is said."[2]

Sigerist had already had similar feelings in January 1924 when, at the urging of Sudhoff, he was invited to give guest lectures at Munich and was very cordially received there by Ferdinand Sauerbruch, among others.

As I recall it, that week seemed to me like a whole semester [he wrote to Sud-
hoff]. In the very first hour I declared myself to be your disciple, and when
the experience was good it was thanks to you. And now I am in Zurich again,
where life continues in ordinary fashion, and all seems small and narrow to
me. I wish that a call to an appointment would come! Then, immersed in the
intellectual life, able really to teach, everything would be marvelous. My wife
and I both agree that we will accept any call to Germany, even if we were
promised wonders in Zurich.[3]

On July 15, 1924, then nearly seventy-one years old, Karl Sudhoff recommended to the search commission for his successor, "in the first category and in alphabetical order," Paul Diepgen (*Honorar-Ordinarius* in
Freiburg im Breisgau), Theodor Meyer-Steineg (*Titularprofessor* in Jena),
Max Neuburger (*Ordinarius* in Vienna), Henry E. Sigerist (*Titularprofessor* in Zurich), and Georg Sticker (*Ordinarius* in Würzburg).[4] Sudhoff justified his recommendation of Sigerist as follows: "Henry E. Sigerist . . .
is an exceedingly competent man, I daresay the 'best horse in the stable'
of lecturers in the history of medicine. . . . Sigerist has a splendid way
of lecturing, animated and interesting; he is an amiable person, experienced in worldly affairs, a man with a great future."[5] The Dresden Ministry decided in favor of Sigerist, despite his youth, as both Sudhoff and
the faculty of medicine had warmly supported him. For Sigerist, the call
to Leipzig came as a great surprise. At the age of thirty-four he was the
youngest of all the candidates and not a *Reichsdeutscher* (German from
the Reich).[6]

What sort of situation did Sigerist find in Leipzig? Despite extremely
difficult postwar material conditions and the restrictions of the Versailles
Treaty, the faculty of medicine—supported by the Dresden ministry and
financed by state and private resources—had been successful in regaining
international acclaim. Acknowledging modern trends in the development
of science, professorships *(Ordinarius)* were established in 1919 in the
history of medicine, otorhinolaryngology, dermatology and venereology,
pediatrics, and physiological chemistry.[7] Great university teachers and
physicians, such as the internist Paul Morawitz, the surgeon Erwin Payr,
the gynecologist Hugo Sellheim, and the anatomist Werner Spalteholz,
emulated the great traditions of the faculty of medicine in the last third
of the nineteenth century, when men like Carl Ludwig, Wilhelm His, and
Paul Flechsig made Leipzig a mecca for physicians and scientists from
all over the world. In this city with nearly 680,000 inhabitants (then the
fifth largest city in Germany), a free and open intellectual climate flourished. As seat of the *Deutscher Bürsenverein der Buchhändler zu Leipzig*

(German Booksellers' Association), Leipzig was the center of the German book trade as well as an important center for publishing, the visual arts, and music.

In 1906, one year after Sudhoff's appointment to a professorship *(Extraordinarius)* of the history of medicine, the Institute of the History of Medicine opened with resources from the Puschmann Foundation.[8] After several moves, in 1916 it came to occupy the ground floor of the Institute of Mineralogy in Talstrasse. Until Sigerist's appointment, the institute had been Sudhoff's personal realm. Without assistants and with the help of only one attendant, he achieved immense organizational and scientific success. During his twenty-year tenure, the library grew to twenty thousand volumes and included manuscript archives and collections of medicohistorical objects. Aside from his own voluminous scholarly work, Sudhoff supervised numerous dissertations. With the "Mitteilungen zur Geschichte der Medizin und der Naturwissenschaften" (Contributions to the History of Medicine and the Natural Sciences), the "Archiv für Geschichte der Medizin" (Archive of the History of Medicine), and the "Studien zur Geschichte der Medizin" (Studies on the History of Medicine) as well as "Klassiker der Medizin" (Classics of Medicine), Sudhoff initiated his own publication series. When he retired in 1925, "an exemplary institute had been established and history of medicine had its definite place in the realm of scholarship."[9]

When Sigerist took over the institute in 1925, it consisted of a seminar room used as a workroom by the members of the institute, two other workrooms with three and six workplaces, respectively, and another work space in a small room that contained the collections. In addition to the director's office and a room for his assistant, Sudhoff used the room set aside for the archives of the "Gesellschaft Deutscher Naturforscher und Ärzte" (Society of German Naturalists and Physicians) as a study. The institute also had a library, a room for a secretary, a photo and darkroom, and a small auditorium.

On January 13, 1926, Sigerist gave his Leipzig inaugural lecture, "The Historical Aspects of Medicine."[10] Whereas in his Zurich inaugural lecture of 1921, "Tasks and Aims of the History of Medicine,"[11] he had insisted that the history of medicine could be useful as a mediator between ancient humanism and modern natural science, in his Leipzig lecture he placed the development of medicine in a larger scientific and cultural context. Sigerist's very broadly conceived research program, which took into consideration the philosophical and ethical problems of medicine, regarded the history of medicine as the "most general subject of medicine . . . whose task it is to examine the universal questions of medicine

8. Sigerist in his study at the Leipzig Institute.

and also the experiences of the specialty disciplines and the experiences of the past."[12] This cultural-historical and philosophical orientation to medical history was partially based on Sigerist's own broad education; placing medical history within the intellectual and cultural currents of the time gave it new relevance to the contemporary practice of medicine.[13]

Scientific medicine, which was supposed to have irresistibly revealed all the secrets of health and illness, entered a severe crisis after World War I. Just as the historical sciences had already gone beyond the mere gathering of facts and the discovery of sources, medicine now realized that the exclusively "objective" natural-scientific consideration of man was inadequate and needed supplementation. The rediscovery of the connection between mind and body, the increasing interest in Freudian theories, and the unquestionable success of medical psychotherapy stimulated new thinking. Disciplinary fragmentation in medicine had also generated uncertainty about the place of medical care and physicians within the system of the sciences and in society. This loss of certainty in medicine's conception of itself was experienced as a state of crisis leading to a yearning for a universe of perfect harmony; the revival of the ideas of Hippocrates and Paracelsus may best be understood in this context. The history of medicine was now expected to answer many questions; it was being called upon by clinicians such as August Bier, Ferdinand Sauerbruch, and Ludolf von Krehl to help create a philosophy of medicine.

> We approached history from a point of view that had shifted 180 degrees. The fundamental questions did not arise from the past or from individual cultural epochs but from living medicine. The point at issue was to form from a specialized research institute a general medical institute which dealt with the history of medicine not as an end in itself but as a method of inquiry.[14]

Full of energy, Sigerist set about realizing his plans, organizing the work of the institute and medicohistorical teaching and research. He intended to use the history of medicine to explain the relationship of medicine as a whole to the natural sciences and to society. He opened the Leipzig Institute to interdisciplinary debate on the burning issues in medical science, turning it into an open forum for discussion. For Sudhoff, who still worked at the institute, these many changes were somewhat surprising, but "without much ado he put up with the new situation, for he was basically a kind-hearted man."[15] Sometimes he "thundered" through the institute—he fancied himself a "Jupiter Tonans"—and he may have been surprised at the large number of young colleagues and students, for his dry delivery and awe-inspiring manner had never attracted so many. Sigerist was glad that he could turn to Sudhoff when arranging the extensive stock of materials in the institute, and there was never any discord between these two very different personalities. After the first weeks together in the institute, Sigerist wrote to Sudhoff: "I cannot tell you enough how grateful I am that I can now work in such close proximity to you. In Zurich I was quite isolated professionally and never had a person with whom I could talk about the things in which I was most interested. Thus, all the more do I enjoy our daily conversations and the harmonious cooperation with you."[16]

Sigerist considerably enlarged the subjects of instruction and, in addition to his lectures, began a regular seminar series on a wide variety of topics. The "Einführung in die Medizin" (Introduction to Medicine) lectures—which were published as a book by Georg Thieme in 1931[17] and translated into six languages—along with special lectures and a course, "Medical Ethics," drew an increasing number of listeners. Sigerist's lectures were crowded although attendance was optional. When he first started his "Introduction to Medicine" lecture series in 1927, twenty-one students attended, but soon the number grew to about one hundred, among them first- and second-year students, advanced students, young physicians in practice, and even undergraduates and specialists from other subject areas. The extensive range of subject matter can be seen in the titles of the special lectures: "Medicine and Religion," "The Logic of Medicine," "Introduction to Philosophy," "Philosophic Anthropology," "History of Anatomy and Anatomical Illustration," "Leonardo da Vinci and the Natural Science of the Renaissance," "Primitive Therapeutics," "Hippocratic Therapeutics," and "Therapeutics of the Ancient Orient."

Sigerist was a brilliant teacher who called his own teaching method "most primitive." "It consists merely in thinking aloud," he wrote, "and working in public so that students have a chance to watch me as I think and to help me in my work. In this fashion I hope to inspire the students and challenge them. I try never to give students facts that they can read in a book. What they must be taught is where you can find facts and how they must be approached and interpreted. In other words, I try to show them methods of working." [18] He urged his students to strive for the truth. In his lecture "Problems of Medical Historiography" at the Eighth International Congress of the History of Medicine in Rome in 1930 he said: "The historical methods create an iron discipline which we must heed. Anyone who in writing the history of trends misuses history to prove a thesis is no different from an experimenter who falsifies laboratory protocols. As historians who serve the truth we are working to advance medicine itself." [19]

The *Kyklos* Period

The idea of a "bridge function" for the history of medicine and the interdisciplinary consideration of fundamental problems in the history of science in connection with contemporary science stimulated the interest of students, assistants, and junior faculty. It also stimulated colleagues in other faculties and Leipzig physicians, so that participation in the institute's activities steadily increased. The themes Sigerist chose for the medicohistorical colloquia demonstrate that topics came from "living medicine": "Foundations and Aims of Contemporary Medicine," "The Physician and the State," "Philosophical Borderline Questions of Medicine," and "The Problem of Culture in Medical Psychology." Colloquium papers were published in four volumes of "Lectures of the Institute of the History of Medicine at the University of Leipzig." Among the colloquium speakers were Alfred Grotjahn, Erwin Liek, and Hans Driesch. Sigerist made the institute known as an intellectual center far beyond the University of Leipzig. His coworkers admired him as an excellent organizer and a very liberal director who never forced his opinions on others and whose optimism, joy of living, and enthusiasm for his field were contagious. [20]

According to the December 1926 statutes of the institute, any interested person, after having introduced himself personally to the director and paid a small sum, could become a member of the institute for one term. If that individual was engaged in scholarly research, he received a fixed workplace in the room set aside for doctoral candidates. The institute was open daily from 8 A.M. to 10 P.M., and on Sundays and holidays from 9 A.M. to 1 P.M. Because the central heating was turned off in the evening during the winter months, Sigerist asked the treasurer's office for the installation of stoves, for—so he wrote—"The opinion is incorrect that an eight-hour day is relevant in a research institute and that no work is done on Sundays and holidays. Indeed, the institute is most frequented in the evening hours and on holidays." [21]

There were nineteen registered institute members in the 1926–27 winter term, and the numbers steadily increased; the sixty-five members enrolled in the 1929 summer term corresponded to more than 10 percent of the total Leipzig medical student body. For space reasons alone, certain limits on the enrollment of interested persons became necessary. With the growing number of institute members, research productivity also increased. Although the "Archiv für Geschichte der Medizin" as well as "Studien zur Geschichte der Medizin" were published in Leipzig by the Johann Ambrosius Barth Publishing House, Sigerist looked for other possible publishing outlets for the institute's work. Thanks to his friendship with Bruno Hauff, the liberal publisher and owner of the Georg Thieme Publishing House, it was possible, despite difficult economic times, to publish ten volumes from 1928 to 1932: four volumes of the institute's yearbook, four volumes of lectures, and two volumes of research papers.

The yearbooks of the institute (vol. 1 [1928], vol. 2 [1929], vol. 3 [1930], and vol. 4 [1932]) were published under the *Kyklos* symbol, which represented the working program of the institute.[22] As Sigerist explained the meaning of the symbol:

The triangle symbolized the working program of the institute, the connection between medicine, history, and philosophy. Above it was an elongated Omega, leading to a circle. This was to express the thought that when medicine, conscious of its historical position and permeated by philosophy, is guided by the intellect, then the pathway to a better and more perfect medicine results, expressed by the circle. Wicked tongues, however, said that the circle stood for the soap bubbles ascending from the institute.[23]

9. The *Kyklos* logo.

The first *Kyklos* volume was dedicated to Karl Sudhoff, with an explicit acknowledgment that his work was prerequisite to, and the foundation of, the institute's work. In the preface, Sigerist referred to the gratifying growth of the institute, the extra subsidies from the ministry, the valuable donation of books by the *Vereinigung der Föderer und Freunde der Universität Leipzig* (Association of Sponsors and Friends of the University of Leipzig), and the establishment of a department for the history of pharmacology, made possible by the Sandoz Company of Basel and Nuremberg. In one year alone, 590 books and reprints, as well as numerous objects for the collection, had been given to the institute. All this shows how greatly Sigerist had been able to stimulate public interest in the work of his institute. The *Kyklos* volumes give detailed information about the institute's activities, lectures, seminars, and colloquia, the increasing numbers of affiliated scholars and registered members, and the enlargement of the library, collections, and manuscript archives. They also contain information about the international development of the field and list the numerous visitors who came to Leipzig from all over the world.

Because Sigerist made gentle suggestions for research without forcing specific topics on anyone, members of the institute worked on a wide variety of problems. Consisting of individualists like Sigerist himself, the *Kyklos* group formed an "organic team without teamwork." [24] Sigerist described his institute as the "Institute of the Kyklos-group" — in contrast to Sudhoff's institute, which was a one-man establishment.

The institute was subdivided into four departments. The Department of General Medicine dealt with the history of medical thinking, the development and problems of hospitals and nursing care, the conceptions of inflammation and constitution, and the history of physiology. Research on Hippocrates and Paracelsus was also conducted in the Department of General Medicine. Sudhoff continued working on his Paracelsus edition, and in 1931, Owsei Temkin habilitated as *Privatdozent* with a thesis on the history of Hippocratism at the end of antiquity. A group of institute members was engaged in translating Hippocratic works and in compiling a dictionary of Greek medical concepts. Their scholarly approach was represented with particular clarity in Owsei Temkin's study "The Systematic Coherence of the Corpus Hippocraticum." [25]

The Department of Pathology studied the relationship between disease and culture, for example in the case of syphilis, chlorosis, or cardiac diseases. In his programmatic outline "Culture and Disease," [26] Sigerist explained the thrust of this research, which aimed to show the cultural affiliations and "style" of certain diseases. Thus, he characterized the plague as an epidemic of great societal upheavals during the Middle Ages, syphilis as typical of the individualistic attitude of the Renaissance, and chlorosis as connected to the type of young women of the Biedermeier period (early nineteenth century). These reflections, deepened in seminars, were developed much later in the book *Civilization and Disease*.[27]

The work of the Department of Pharmacology, which had its own room with reference library, drug collection, and herbaria, was directed to the history of certain drugs—such as scilla, crocus, and varieties of allium—showing how their application changed in relation to the theoretical conceptions of the time. Pharmacology was regarded as a purely medical science, but research into related areas was encouraged. Thus Heyser, in his research on varieties of allium,[28] made use of philosophical ideas and knowledge about drugs, botanical literature, general pharmacognostic descriptions, and collections of prescriptions and was able to conclude his work with an actual bedside demonstration. Such pharmacological-historical investigations showed in general how the pharmacological knowledge of former times might be made useful for the present.

The Department of Cultural History dealt with the evaluation of well-established sources relevant to the history of ideas and the generation of new, philologically refined editions of hitherto unknown texts. An example is Wlaschky's publication and evaluation of an early medieval compendium of medicine.[29] This department also included investigations of early medieval and baroque medicine. Convinced that medical ideas were bound to the contemporary world view and that the "style" of an epoch influences its medicine, Sigerist concluded that William Harvey's physiology was "born from the spirit of the Baroque," and that "Harvey thus comes close to men like Michelangelo and Galilei, in whom quite a similar shift from static to dynamic thinking took place in the field of physics."[30] Bilikiewicz's essay on embryology, published as volume 2 of the proceedings of the institute, may also be understood as an example of "cultural history."[31]

Sigerist paid particular attention to medicine of the romantic period, aware that it had been unappreciated and unjustly treated in the second half of the nineteenth century, but also that it shared a certain intellectual affinity with the present: "We too approach [Romantic medicine] critically and do not overlook the numerous errors in which it frequently lost itself. But we are free of the resentment that former historians held against it. As a result of the entire situation in which we find ourselves, we feel related to it in many ways and it is therefore easier for us to recognize its many fruitful ideas."[32]

Ernst Hirschfeld especially applied himself to the romantic period of medicine[33] and compiled a specialized library and a bibliography of appropriate periodicals.

Two paid assistants and one unsalaried assistant worked at the institute. After Johann Daniel Achelis (1927), who soon returned to the Leipzig Institute of Physiology, came Hermann Scheer (1927–28), who had been Sigerist's unsalaried assistant since 1926. Ernst Hirschfeld, an unsalaried assistant in 1927, remained at the institute from 1928 to 1930 and then went to Berlin. Owsei Temkin, after working for two months as unsalaried assistant, became Sigerist's paid assistant and in 1932 followed him to Baltimore. Walter Pagel was at the Leipzig Institute from April to August 1930, and Ingo Krumbiegel, who began as an assistant to Sigerist in 1929, left the institute in 1934.[34] Among Sigerist's colleagues in Leipzig were Stephen d'Irsay, who especially in 1927–28 dealt with the history of physiology; Erwin H. Ackerknecht, a member of the institute from 1929 to 1931; and Leo Norpoth, from 1927 to 1930.

The wide range of subjects at the institute, the good working conditions, and, above all, the personality of the director made the Leipzig Institute of the History of Medicine an important center of the faculty of medicine as well as a place furthering interdisciplinary exchange. The institute not only maintained scholarly cooperation with other university institutions like the Institute of Social and Universal History and the Egyptological Institute but also kept in close contact with the physicians of the Leipzig Medical Society and the Leipzig *Bibliophilen-Abend* (the legendary "Leipzig 99," a local book club founded in 1904 with a strict quota system limiting membership to ninety-nine at any one time). The "Leipzig 99" dissolved itself in 1933 in response to attempts at *Gleichschaltung* (political purge) by the Nazi *Reichspropagandaministerium*.

The institute's central core was the library with a collection of sixty current periodicals. Besides the specialty journals there were also newspapers and journals of various schools, for example of the homeopaths and the anthroposophers, because Sigerist believed it important to study these movements. Thus the institute received the *Allgemeine Homöopathische Zeitung* (the General Homeopathic Newspaper) from the Leipzig firm Homöopathische Central-Officin Dr. Willmar Schwabe. In 1927, Dr. Gerhard Madaus, who in 1924 had founded his Dresden company for the production of naturopathic preparations, asked Sigerist if he was willing to become editor of the journal *Biologische Heilkunst* (the Biological Art of Healing). Madaus explained his request, "You are one of the few leading professors who has recognized the deficiencies of traditional medicine. Nevertheless, you will still have to contend with scant understanding from the traditional medical press, because this press in its advertising pages is dependent upon an industry which wants to and will advance in Germany by every means possible."[35]

On January 1, 1929, Sigerist joined the scientific advisory council of the Hippocrates Publishing House in Stuttgart.[36] At his first meeting, the editorial staff of the journal *Hippocrates* discussed the key ideas of "unity" and "constitution" and agreed:

> Apart from homeopathy, psychotherapy occupies a privileged position in our work done thus far; here Freud had as strong an impact as Hahnemann had in former times. Thus the catalysts to our work are the following: in pharmacotherapy homeopathy, in psychotherapy psychoanalysis, in constitutional therapy the humoral-pathological perspective. And so we feel that we are continuing along the road marked by the likes of Hippocrates, Paracelsus, and Hahnemann.[37]

Besides his many-sided tasks of teaching, scholarship, public relations, editorial work, and lecturing, Sigerist belonged to many different scholarly societies, including the Paracelsus Society founded in 1929 and the Pan European Union of Germany. The executive committee of the Society for the History of Pharmacy considered him "the current leader in all fields of the history of the natural sciences and the professions practicing them."[38]

Despite many obligations and the enormous amount of work of the *Kyklos* period, which Temkin called the "romantic period,"[39] this was a happy time for the teacher as well as for his students. Sigerist lived in close contact with the members of his institute, and after the joint work of the semester drew to a close, costume balls and bathing trips were organized. The members of the institute thoroughly enjoyed Sigerist's memorable parties. Many undergraduates had girlfriends among the students of the Leipzig Academy of Bookmaking and Graphic Arts, and these young women designed fancy costumes and decorations for the parties. On one occasion they turned the basement of the institute into a jungle, on another the theme was "Tramps and Gentlemen." Dancing lasted into the early morning hours, and the institute was repeatedly criticized for disturbing the peace with music and laughter.

Sigerist maintained an extensive correspondence with colleagues and former members of the institute in all parts of the world. The numerous visitors to the Leipzig Institute included, among many others, William Henry Welch (Baltimore), Arturo Castiglioni (Padua), Georges Duhamel

(Paris), Fielding H. Garrison (Washington), Arnold C. Klebs (Nyon), and I. D. Strashun (Moscow). In 1929 Sigerist took twelve members of the institute with him to Budapest, to the annual meeting of the German Society for the History of Medicine and Natural Sciences, after which the group also visited the institute of Max Neuburger in Vienna and then went on to Prague.

Sigerist remained particularly close to Neuburger throughout his Leipzig years. They exchanged publications, scholarly news, and personal opinions as they replaced their original, mutually respectful teacher-pupil relationship with a more equal exchange of views. Neuburger wrote to Sigerist on September 4, 1928:

> Dear Colleague,
>
> Please let me express my admiration for your activity as researcher, writer, lecturer and teacher. I particularly appreciate that you do not continue treading well-worn paths as others do but have taken new directions and that you understand how to impress physicians with the value of historical research. I regard it as particularly fortunate for the academic future of the subject that you hold the Leipzig chair, thus guarding against any threat of sterility. Don't take these words as presumptuousness on my part, for they are the judgment of an old medical historian who belongs to an era that has already passed away.[40]

The Social-Historical Period and Sigerist's Departure from Leipzig

Berg-Schorn[41] correctly points out that Sigerist's turn to social problems did not represent a renunciation of his former point of view and that he never gave up his philosophical-idealistic foundational principles for materialistic ones. Yet it must also be noted that the issue was not a new orientation but a certain displacement of emphasis, for according to his own statement, when he took over the Leipzig Institute, Sigerist had already developed a plan to treat the history of medicine from a sociological standpoint.[42] He intended to investigate the development of medical science and its applications with reference to determining "factors of an ideological, philosophical, religious, economic, or generally sociological sort."[43]

Various reasons account for Sigerist's increasing interest in these problems by 1930. Apart from the recognition that the problems in question are important in medicohistorical research, the political and economic situation of the Weimar Republic drew attention to these issues. In Germany during the years from 1926 to 1929 temporary prosperity was followed by a deep economic depression. Many of the expenditures for social welfare measures introduced by the Social Democratic government could no longer be sustained, health insurance was more and more criticized, and many younger physicians had to struggle for economic survival. The health care program of the Social Democratic Party contained such goals as community health care, uniform social insurance, planned distribution of medical institutions in both town and country, and the creation of a central board of health. In Sigerist's colloquia at the institute these problems and proposals were discussed together by sociologists and practicing physicians. Thus Erwin Liek, one of the severest critics of the health insurance system, in his lecture "Medical Practice" had turned against a social-medical service conducted by the state.[44] Sigerist, however, saw important new tasks for the physician in just this field. In "Changes in the Model of the Physician," he wrote, "Never in history has the state given the physician such great possibilities for influence on such a broad field of action as today. Instead of standing back and keeping aloof, we should willingly seize these opportunities and be equal to the manifold tasks set for us by society."[45]

Social hygiene and social medicine had become academically established disciplines in Germany by the twenties. Considering social conditions the main cause of disease, these disciplines regarded social legislation and communal policy as appropriate methods for improving public health. Along these same lines, contact with Russian scholars led Sigerist to become interested in state-run public health in the Soviet Union. In June 1930 Sigerist invited I. D. Strashun, who was the deputy of the Russian federal commissioner for the hygiene exhibition in Dresden, to lecture at the Leipzig Institute. While Strashun's account "The Development of Soviet Medicine" was received with great interest by the students, the faculty reacted very negatively and informed Sigerist that they regarded it as politically dangerous and unwise for a Russian to speak at the institute.[46]

During the economic depression, Sigerist found it increasingly difficult to maintain the activities of the institute. For a long time he paid the staff from his own pocket while he attempted to interest private sponsors in the institute. He was also very disappointed not to be called to the vacant Berlin chair in the history of medicine, which went to Paul Diepgen. Sudhoff, when asked by the Berlin medical faculty to evaluate Sigerist, had given him an excellent testimonial. After praising his major scholarly achievements and commenting on the other candidates in the field, Sudhoff emphasized the vitality Sigerist had brought to the institute: "And how is Sigerist as a teacher? Perfectly excellent. The students are fond of him and follow him enthusiastically owing to his vital, perfectly splendid lecture style; and from the large flock of those attending the institute mainly for the purpose of absorbing information, he knows how to captivate the most talented and to interest them in later doing independent research, for which purpose he cleverly preconditions them in his seminars. His lecture courses are always full." [47]

The Leipzig faculty, which in 1925 had already regarded Sigerist as the only candidate worthy to succeed Sudhoff, warmly recommended him for Berlin. [48] The greater was Sigerist's disappointment when he failed to obtain the position. Stephen d'Irsay, who at this time was working in Baltimore, wrote him a letter of consolation and also mentioned possible causes for his being bypassed:

> You can imagine that I was amazed and that I sympathize with you entirely in this matter. You were certainly disappointed. But is it so great a catastrophe? It is indisputable that one would not be able to work as well in Berlin as in Leipzig for years to come. And would a Göttingen mathematician trade places with one in Berlin? I don't think so. The whole world knows that Leipzig is the central location for medico-historical studies and activities. . . . I really think that they have used your relationship with homeopaths, with Aschner, Honigmann, etc. against you. Couldn't you distance yourself from these inferior people? [49]

Considering the institute's productivity and its influence beyond Germany, it must have been galling to Sigerist when, without his knowledge, the rooms of the medicohistorical institute were promised to the newly appointed director of the mineralogical institute. [50] With the library increasing annually by about one thousand volumes, the proposed new space for the institute was unrealistic. [51] Moreover, because of cost considerations, the plans for a new building were constantly changed. Finally, Sigerist was pressured to consent to a relatively small building without an auditorium, which he regarded as an indication of complete disregard for his personal standing and official position. When, after all this, *Geheimrat* von Seydewitz reproached him in the Dresden ministry for ill will and even shouted at him, Sigerist lost his patience. Embittered as well as depressed by constant financial difficulties and the general political situation, on December 22, 1930, Sigerist sent his request for dismissal to the Dresden ministry. His letter read, in part, as follows:

> I depart without bitterness. During these five years I have learnt much, in both the human and the scholarly sense. . . . I hope that my endeavors will bear fruit in a better time. It is completely clear to me what I give up. Although I can im-

prove my material position, I nevertheless give up an undertaking to which I have given all my energy for five years, and I will sorely miss my Leipzig students, to whom I feel so closely tied.[52]

After a discussion in the ministry, Sigerist was persuaded to withdraw his resignation and was granted a leave of absence for the 1931–32 winter term, which he used for a seven-month lecture and study tour in the United States. During that tour he was offered the directorship of the Institute of the History of Medicine at the Johns Hopkins University in Baltimore, to succeed William H. Welch. On his return to Germany, Sigerist saw the strengthening of National Socialism and understood that as a Social Democrat and advocate of the Weimar Republic his future would not have been promising. He had participated in the publication of the journal *Neue Blätter für den Sozialismus* (New Journal for Socialism), which appeared in Potsdam between 1930 and 1933, edited by Edward Heimann, Fritz Klatt, and Paul Tillich; Sigerist was a member of the editorial board in 1930–31. Among the authors of the journal's articles on political, social, and cultural problems were notable left-wing intellectuals, and in 1930 Sigerist himself published an article on the image of man in modern medicine.[53] He had also participated in several political activities. In 1926 he had been among the university professors who had declared their support for the Weimar Republic, and he had thrown two students wearing Nazi uniforms out of his lecture room. Sigerist thus had clear reason to accept the Hopkins appointment.

The Leipzig medical faculty very much regretted his departure. On March 1, 1932, the dean, the physiologist Gildemeister, wrote to Sigerist:

We receive with mixed feelings the news of the honorable call you have received. It is very flattering to us that you represent our faculty in such a splendid way; but the prospect that we shall lose you for this reason is very distressing. Above all, cordial congratulations on your great success and especially the offer! Would we be able to keep you as we should like to do? Is competition with Baltimore even possible to imagine? Can our poor country outbid the rich foundation? Hopefully, some means can still be found to keep you. Our faculty will find it very difficult to bear yet more blood-lettings, as seems to be in store for it nonetheless.[54]

Gildemeister had foreseen how devastating the National Socialist seizure of power would be for German scholarship.[55] Among the measures the Nazis enacted was the *Gesetz zur Wiederherstellung des Berufsbeamtentums* (Law of the Reinstitution of the Permanent Civil Service) passed

10. Sigerist leaving the Leipzig train station on his way to the United States, August 2, 1932.

on April 7, 1933. This provided a pseudolegal basis for removing democratically minded civil servants and those of "non-Aryan" descent. University teachers affected by this law were deprived of their *venia legendi* (official qualification to teach at a German university). Among those affected was Owsei Temkin, Sigerist's assistant and former student. News of the suspension of his *venia legendi* reached him in Baltimore, where he was already securely employed in a position that Sigerist had arranged.[56]

In August 1935 Sigerist's successor, Walter von Brunn (who had taken over the institute in November 1934), answered a letter from the Organization of National Socialist Assistant Professors: "Whether Professor Henry E. Sigerist was a non-Aryan in the sense of your inquiry (he left for Baltimore three years ago) I do not know exactly. From the list of Institute members during Sigerist's period of appointment one can see that of the seventy members, according to their names, a good many were non-Aryans."[57]

Scholarly publications and news continued to be exchanged between the Leipzig Institute and the Institute in Baltimore, until Walter von Brunn, according to the advice of the rector and dean, broke off relations. The immediate cause was Sigerist's signature on a petition of the Anti-Nazi League.[58]

Sigerist continued to feel closely connected to the Leipzig Institute and particularly to his teacher Sudhoff. When he heard about Sudhoff's death in 1938, he was very deeply moved. "I loved him like a father. . . . I do not know what my career would have been without him." That Sudhoff, "an old liberal, a democrat at the time of the Kaiser, a follower of the Volkspartei during the days of the Republic, who before 1933 loathed the Nazis," had become a member of the Nazi Party distressed Sigerist. "What were his motives? Vanity, the desire to be one of them at the top, patriotism, or just senility?" he wrote in his diary.[59]

On the instigation of certain German colleagues, Sigerist was ultimately expelled from the *Deutsche Gesellschaft für Geschichte der Medizin, Naturwissenschaft und Technik* (German Society for the History of Medicine, Science, and Technology) with insinuations of spreading Communist and anti-German attitudes and propaganda.[60] In spite of these bitter experiences and the intensifying political situation in Europe, Sigerist always felt himself a European and maintained confidence in the future of the continent. "Since 1911 Europe has been going through a very serious crisis, but it will be reborn, regenerated, and rejuvenated," he wrote in his diary in 1940.[61]

When Sigerist retired in 1947, he returned to Switzerland. On June 15, 1950, by order of the Leipzig Faculty of Medicine, Walter von Brunn wrote to him to ask whether he would be inclined to take over the Leipzig chair and the directorship of the institute.[62] On July 1, 1950, Sigerist answered:

> I thank you very much for your kind letter of June 15, and I deeply regret that your state of health makes your retirement necessary. That the Leipzig Faculty thought of me gives me great pleasure and satisfaction. If I were younger and in better health, I would accept my former chair with enthusiasm. . . . I am glad that I succeeded in carrying on the best traditions of German medical history in America, at a time when Geheimrat Sudhoff and other colleagues acceded to the National Socialist Party. And I am glad that I succeeded in saving Mr. Ackerknecht, Mr. Edelstein, and Mr. Temkin from Germany and in providing work opportunities for them in America. Today, all three have distinguished chairs and without doubt they are among the leading historians of medicine. I wish to express to the faculty my wholehearted thanks for the confidence placed in me and to say how much I regret that a return to Leipzig is not possible for me.[63]

For Henry E. Sigerist, the years in the United States were especially productive, as measured both by his publications and by his public impact.[64] Yet the roots for this success lay in his Leipzig activities. Here his attention was increasingly drawn to philosophical problems and to the social history of medicine. For the Leipzig Institute, the years under Sigerist's direction were the most brilliant ones in its history. Because of the intellectual atmosphere of the Weimar Republic and Sigerist's own verve and talent, German medical history, as Ackerknecht has stated, also had its "Weimar" period.[65]

Notes

1. For this description of Sigerist's work in Leipzig, in addition to autobiographical sources and institute publications, I have used materials from the Archives of the University of Leipzig and from the collection of documents in the Karl Sudhoff Institute of the History of Medicine and the Natural Sciences.

2. Henry E. Sigerist to Karl Sudhoff, October 9, 1924 (Universität Leipzig, Karl-Sudhoff-Institut, Collection of Documents, 1924), fol. 466.

3. Henry E. Sigerist to Karl Sudhoff, January 26, 1924 (Universität Leipzig, Karl-Sudhoff-Institut, Collection of Documents, 1924), fols. 499–500.

4. Sudhoff's notes concerning his potential successors (Universitätsarchiv Leipzig, Medical Faculty Archives, B III, no. 31), fols. 3–4.

5. Ibid., fol. 5.

6. Henry E. Sigerist, "Erinnerungen an meine Leipziger Tätigkeit," *Wissenschaftliche Zeitschrift der Karl-Marx-Universität Leipzig,* Mathematisch-Naturwissenschaftliche Reihe 5 (1955/56): 17–21.

7. Susanne Hahn, "Von 1918 bis 1933," in *575 Jahre Medizinische Fakultät der Universität Leipzig,* eds. Ingrid Kästner and Achim Thom (Leipzig: Johann Ambrosius Barth, 1990), 118–61.

8. Wilhelm Katner, "Die Puschmann-Stiftung," *Wissenschaftliche Zeitschrift der Karl-Marx-Universität Leipzig,* Mathematisch-Naturwissenschaftliche Reihe 5 (1955/56): 9–15.

9. Henry E. Sigerist, "Forschungsinstitute für Geschichte der Medizin und der Naturwissenschaften," in *Forschungsinstitute, ihre Geschichte, Organisation und Ziele,* eds. Ludolph Brauer, Albrecht Mendelssohn Bartholdy, and Adolf Meyer (Hamburg: Paul Hartung, 1930), vol. 1, 391–405.

10. The lecture is published in *Archiv für Geschichte der Medizin* 18 (1926): 1–19.

11. Henry E. Sigerist, "Aufgaben und Ziele der Medizingeschichte," *Schweizerische Medizinische Wochenschrift* 3 (1922): 318–22. See also the discussion in Marcel Bickel's essay in this volume.

12. Henry E. Sigerist, "Die Geschichte der Medizin in ihrer Bedeutung für die Gegenwart," *Lijecnički Vjesnik* (Zagreb) 53 (1931): 315–18.

13. Elisabeth Berg-Schorn, *Henry E. Sigerist (1891–1957). Medizinhistoriker in Leipzig und Baltimore. Standpunkt und Wirkung* (Cologne: Kölner Medizinhistorische Beiträge, vol. 9, 1978).

14. Henry E. Sigerist, "Forschungsinstitute," 397.

15. Henry E. Sigerist, "Erinnerungen an Karl Sudhoff," *Sudhoffs Archiv für Geschichte der Medizin* 37 (1953): 97–193.

16. Henry E. Sigerist to Karl Sudhoff, December 26, 1925 (Universität Leipzig, Karl-Sudhoff-Institut, Collection of Documents, 1925), fols. 40–42.

17. Henry E. Sigerist, *Einführung in die Medizin* (Leipzig: Georg Thieme, 1931).

18. Nora Sigerist Beeson, ed., *Henry E. Sigerist: Autobiographical Writings* (Montreal: McGill University Press, 1966), Diary, January 9, 1939, 143.

19. Henry E. Sigerist, "Probleme der Medizinischen Historiographie," *Sudhoffs Archiv für Geschichte der Medizin* 24 (1931): 1–18.

20. Erwin H. Ackerknecht, "Recollections of a Former Leipzig Student," *Journal of the History of Medicine and Allied Sciences* 13 (1958): 147–50.

21. Henry E. Sigerist to the Revenue Office, January 19, 1928 (Universitätsarchiv Leipzig, RA 1384 II), fol. 78.

22. Sigerist considered the *Kyklos* symbol so critical an expression of the institute's spirit that he had it imprinted on the institute's official stationery and cigarettes. See Erwin H. Ackerknecht, "Recollections of a Former Leipzig Student," *Journal of the History of Medicine and Allied Sciences* 13 (1958): 149.

23. Henry E. Sigerist, "Erinnerungen an meine Leipziger Tätigkeit."

24. Owsei Temkin and Gert H. Brieger, "Two Institutions and Two Eras: Reflections on the Field of Medical History" (Baltimore: Institute of the History of Medicine, Johns Hopkins University School of Medicine, 1991, videocassette [69 min.]).

25. Owsei Temkin, "Der Systematische Zusammenhang im Corpus Hippocraticum," *Kyklos* 1 (1928): 9–43.

26. Henry E. Sigerist, "Kultur und Krankheit," *Kyklos* 1 (1928): 60–63.

27. Henry E. Sigerist, *Civilization and Disease* (Ithaca: Cornell University Press, 1943).

28. Kurt Heyser, "Die Alliumarten als Arzneimittel im Gebrauch der Abendländischen Medizin," *Kyklos* 1 (1928): 64–102.

29. Momtschil Wlaschky, "Sapientia Artis Medicinae. Ein Frühmittelalterliches Kompendium der Medizin," *Kyklos* 1 (1928): 103–13.

30. Henry E. Sigerist, "William Harvey's Stellung in der Europäischen Geistesgeschichte," *Archiv für Kulturgeschichte* 19 (1928): 158–68.

31. Taduesz Bilikiewicz, *Die Embryologie im Zeitalter des Barock und des Rokoko* (Leipzig: Arbeiten des Instituts für Geschichte der Medizin an der Universität Leipzig, vol. 2, 1932).

32. Henry E. Sigerist, "Forschungsinstitute," 401.

33. Ernst Hirschfeld, "Romantische Medizin. Zu einer Künftigen Geschichte der Naturphilosophischen ära," *Kyklos* 3 (1930): 1–89.

34. Liselotte Buchheim, "Direktoren und Assistenten des Karl-Sudhoff-Instituts seit seiner Gründung," *Wissenschaftliche Zeitschrift der Karl-Marx-Universität Leipzig,* Mathematisch-Naturwissenschaftliche Reihe 5 (1955/1956): 16.

35. Gerhard Madaus to Henry E. Sigerist, June 22, 1927 (Universität Leipzig, Karl-Sudhoff-Institut, Collection of Documents, 1927), fol. 818.

36. Contract between Hippokrates Verlag G.m.b.H. Stuttgart and Henry E. Sigerist, January 1, 1929 (Universität Leipzig, Karl-Sudhoff-Institut, Collection of Documents, 1928), fol. 565.

37. Minutes of the first editorial staff meeting of the journal "Hippokrates," September 16, 1928 (Universität Leipzig, Karl-Sudhoff-Institut, Collection of Documents, 1928), fol. 574.

38. Georg Urdang to Henry E. Sigerist, April 21, 1929 (Universität Leipzig, Karl-Sudhoff-Institut, Collection of Documents, 1929), fol. 1556.

39. Owsei Temkin and Gert H. Brieger, "Two Institutions."

40. Max Neuburger to Henry E. Sigerist, September 4, 1928 (Universität Leipzig, Karl-Sudhoff-Institut, Collection of Documents, 1928), fol. 968.

41. Berg-Schorn, *Henry E. Sigerist*, 25.

42. Henry E. Sigerist, "Erinnerungen an meine Leipziger Tätigkeit."

43. Henry E. Sigerist, "Soziologische Faktoren in der Medizin," in *Zangger-Festschrift* (Zurich: Rascher & Cie., 1934), 749–58.

44. Erwin Liek, "Die Ärztliche Praxis," in *Grundlagen und Ziele der Medizin* (Leipzig: Vorträge des Instituts für Geschichte der Medizin an der Universität Leipzig, vol. 1, 1928), 72–115.

45. Henry E. Sigerist, "Wandlungen des Ärztideals," *Soziale Medizin* 3 (1930): 665–70.

46. Henry E. Sigerist to Fjodor A. Stepun, July 17, 1930 (Universität Leipzig, Karl-Sudhoff-Institut, Collection of Documents, 1930), fol. 462.

47. Testimonial for Sigerist by Sudhoff, February 17, 1929 (Universität Leipzig, Karl-Sudhoff-Institut, Collection of Documents, 1929), fol. 36–39.

48. Erwin Payr to Otto Lubarsch, February 23, 1929 (Universitätsarchiv der Humboldt-Universität zu Berlin, Med. Fak., Dekanat, no. 1388), fol. 158.

49. Stephen d'Irsay to Henry E. Sigerist, November 16, 1929 (Universität Leipzig, Karl-Sudhoff-Institut, Collection of Documents, 1929), fol. 596.

50. Landbauamt Leipzig to Ministerium für Volksbildung Dresden, June 3, 1929 (Universitätsarchiv Leipzig, RA 1599 I), fol. 125.

51. Henry E. Sigerist to Revenue Office, "Concerning the Proposed Move of the Institute to Carolinenstrasse," undated [August 1928] (Universitätsarchiv Leipzig, RA 858 VIII), fol. 209–16.

52. Sigerist's letter of resignation to the Ministerium für Volksbildung, December 22, 1930 (Universitätsarchiv Leipzig, PA 1579), fol. 8–23.

53. Henry E. Sigerist, "Das Bild des Menschen in der Modernen Medizin," *Neue Blätter für den Sozialismus* 1 (1930): 97–106.

54. Martin Gildemeister to Henry E. Sigerist, March 1, 1932 (Universitätsarchiv Leipzig, PA 1579), fol. 55.

55. A number of Sigerist's students were directly affected. Bernhard Katz, who as a student had been a member of the Leipzig Institute and whom Gildemeister could still advance to the doctorate in 1934, went to England and later was awarded the Nobel Prize for his investigations of the nervous system. The physician Margarethe Blank, who received her doctor's degree under Sigerist, was executed in 1945 because of antifascist activities, especially her aid to Russian forced laborers.

56. Ministerium für Volksbildung to Owsei Temkin, September 6, 1933 (Universität Leipzig, Karl-Sudhoff-Institut, Collection of Documents, 1933), fol. 28.

57. Walter von Brunn to Dozentenschaft, Universität Leipzig, August 10, 1935 (Universität Leipzig, Karl-Sudhoff-Institut, Collection of Documents, 1935), fol. unnumbered.

58. Walter von Brunn to Dean of the Medical Faculty Robert Schröder, July 1937 (Universitätsarchiv Leipzig, PA 1579), fol. 59.

59. Henry E. Sigerist, Diary, October 20, 1938; *Autobiographical Writings*, 138.

60. Thomas Jaehn, *Der Medizinhistoriker Paul Diepgen 1878–1966* (Berlin: Humboldt-Universität zu Berlin Medical Dissertation, Med. Fak. [Charité], 1990), 126.

61. Henry E. Sigerist, Diary, January 29, 1940; *Autobiographical Writings*, 163.

62. In 1938, on the suggestion of Walter von Brunn, the Leipzig Institute had been named the "Karl-Sudhoff-Institut für Geschichte der Medizin und der Naturwissenschaften." Letter from Walter von Brunn, November 15, 1938 (Universität Leipzig, Karl-Sudhoff-Institut, Collection of Documents, Acta Karl Sudhoff, 1938), fol. unnumbered.

63. Henry E. Sigerist to Walter von Brunn, July 1, 1950 (Universität Leipzig, Karl-Sudhoff-Institut, Collection of Documents, 1950), fol. 110a.

64. Fernando G. Vescia, "Henry E. Sigerist: The Years in America," *Medizinhistorisches Journal* 14 (1979): 218–32.

65. Erwin H. Ackerknecht, "Recollections."

CHAPTER 3

A European Outpost in America:
The Hopkins Institute, 1932–1947

Genevieve Miller

The first time I heard Henry Sigerist lecture was in 1934 when I was a student at Goucher College taking Dorothy Stimson's pioneering course in the history of science. She invited him to speak to our class, and for an hour we were fascinated by the polish and elegance with which he spoke about basic principles of historiography: what source materials are, how one approaches them, what questions one asks, etc. He could make any subject interesting because of his charming enthusiasm and devotion to scholarship. He always lectured with graceful gestures and, when asked about it later, explained that the European universities had a great tradition of academic oratory, an art that was not taught in courses but passed on from master to student through example and by the mere force of personality. Later our class visited the Hopkins Institute, where we again heard Dr. Sigerist and also met Dr. Fielding Garrison and were shown the first edition of Vesalius—my first encounter with a rare book!

A bored chemistry major who had become fascinated with the history of science through Dr. Stimson's course, I graduated from Goucher College in June 1935 and applied to Johns Hopkins to become a graduate student in the field, naively unaware that in 1935 no American university had such a graduate department. I was finally accepted by the history department with members of the Institute of the History of Medicine as

63

11. The staff of the Institute of the History of Medicine, with Arturo Castiglioni. Standing, *left to right:* Wilhelmina Broemer (Welch's secretary), Helen Brooke (Sigerist's secretary), John Rathbone Oliver, Owsei Temkin, and two Institute secretaries. Seated, *left to right:* Sigerist, Castiglioni, and Fielding H. Garrison.

12. Genevieve Miller and Henry Sigerist during the writing of *Civilization and Disease,* Bolton Landing, New York, August 1942.

my course advisors. Thus began a twelve-year collaboration with Henry Sigerist, first as student, then as research secretary, and finally as a junior member of the faculty, teaching the history of American medicine and serving as associate editor of the *Bulletin of the History of Medicine*.

The tremendous energy and drive of the "Boss," as we called him, were overwhelming. He worked himself even harder than he worked us, staying up late at night to prepare papers or books, which he wrote in longhand in special notebooks that he bought in Switzerland, but sometimes when a deadline was imminent, he dictated papers directly to his research secretary's typewriter. He made very few changes in his manuscripts, for he had the ability to formulate in advance exactly what he wanted to say. He was constantly receiving visitors from all over the world. One day it would be his lifelong friend, Professor Hans Schinz, who was a radiologist in Zurich; the next day it might be Andrija Štampar, the public health leader from Yugoslavia; Arturo Castiglioni, the Italian medical historian; Gregory Zilboorg, a New York psychiatrist whom he had known from Leipzig days; or George Urdang, who came to solicit Sigerist's advice when he was in the process of creating the Institute of the History of Pharmacy at the University of Wisconsin. Urdang neatly summarized the eagerness with which visitors approached their meetings: "I am anticipating the pleasure to breathe once again the atmosphere of intensity, inspiration and personal charm so characteristically distinguishing you."[1]

Sigerist's Recruitment to Hopkins

SIGERIST HAS CAPTIVATED EVERYONE HERE BY HIS MODESTY, LEARNING, LIVELY INTEREST IN EVERYTHING, AND PERSONAL CHARM. I CANNOT IMAGINE A MORE SUITABLE PERSON FOR THE POST OR ONE MORE CERTAIN TO DEVELOP IT IN THE WAY YOU WOULD DESIRE. HE IS CERTAIN TO HAVE A GREAT FOLLOWING. AMERICA FASCINATES HIM AND I BELIEVE HE WOULD FIND AN OFFER DIFFICULT TO REFUSE.[2]

At the end of November 1931, this telegram had been sent to William H. Welch, professor of the history of medicine at the Johns Hopkins School of Medicine, by Harvey Cushing, the famous Harvard neurosurgeon and bibliophile, whom Welch had been trying to persuade to become his successor in the Hopkins Institute of the History of Medicine. Sigerist had been visiting lecturer at the Institute in October and November 1931, was now touring the country in great demand among medicohistorical afficionados, and had just given a lecture in Boston.

Welch, the former dean of the Johns Hopkins School of Medicine and the retired director of the School of Hygiene and Public Health, at the age of seventy-seven had been persuaded by Abraham Flexner, the director of the General Education Board of the Rockefeller Foundation, to create an American center for medicohistorical studies. The Johns Hopkins School of Medicine had a long tradition of interest in medical history, with John Shaw Billings, William Osler, Howard A. Kelly, Harvey Cushing, and Henry Barton Jacobs among the early participants. All were also bibliophiles, a component of the Victorian ideal of a gentleman physician who must be a scholar and a lover of books as well as a scientist. The Johns Hopkins Hospital Medical History Club had been founded in 1890 under the leadership of Osler and Kelly.

It was not until the 1920s, however, that medical history took on a wider importance as a humanistic and integrative discipline at Hopkins. This occurred in conjunction with the creation of a new centralized medical library to bring together those of the hospital, medical school, and School of Hygiene. The "Plan for a Central Library," which was submitted in 1923 to the Rockefeller General Education Board for funding, included an area for the planned "department of the history of medicine."[3] The new library, which was formally opened on October 17, 1929, was named for Welch, and on the following day the Department of the History of Medicine was inaugurated, with Karl Sudhoff from Leipzig, Germany, as the principal speaker. Welch introduced him as the "foremost medical historian living in the world today" whose Leipzig Institute was a model of what an institute should be.[4]

The new department occupied (and still does) the entire third floor of the William H. Welch Medical Library and included a lecture room on the northeast corner, with a raised podium accessible with a handrail built especially for Dr. Welch, and a smaller seminar room on the northwest corner, surrounded by bookcases containing reference works. In between was the eighth floor of the library's book stacks, with cubicles along the north wall for students (who were greatly entertained by the monkeys in cages on the balcony of the medical research building facing the court behind the library). A large exhibition hall, with movable exhibition cases and upright supports for pictures and legends, occupied the center of the floor, the first space one entered when leaving the elevator. The director's office and study, both fitted with ceiling-high shelves, occupied the southeast corner of the floor, with his secretary's office adjoining to the west and his research secretary across the hall. The rooms on the west side of the floor, across from the seminar room, were designed for the rest of the staff, and two huge walk-in safes for rare books were nearby.

It is not surprising that when Welch had gone to Europe in May 1927 to buy books for his new department and to consult with European medico-historical colleagues, he went after several weeks in England to Leipzig, which was then led by a young Swiss medical historian, Henry E. Sigerist. Although Sudhoff had officially retired in 1925, Welch conferred daily with him and with Sigerist during the week of his visit to Leipzig. One day, while he and Sigerist were having lunch at Auerbach's Keller, a famous old Leipzig inn, Welch realized that they were seated at the same table where he had drunk beer with John Shaw Billings the day he first met him, in 1877. While Sigerist listened to Welch reminisce, he could not foresee that he would succeed Welch in America within five years.[5]

When Welch became the first professor of medical history, in 1927, as part of his program to stimulate interest in this new academic field, he began inviting professional historians from abroad to stay for a month or two and to lead seminars and give lectures. These included Sir D'Arcy Power, a British surgeon and medical historian, and Charles and Dorothea Waley Singer. Henry Sigerist was thus one of a series of distinguished visiting lecturers. Even before Sigerist's arrival in America in the fall of 1931, Welch predicted accurately in his diary that the visit "will be the greatest stimulus ever given to appreciation of the importance of medical history in America."[6] When Sigerist came to Hopkins, he became acquainted with Fielding H. Garrison, who had been appointed the first librarian of the new Welch Medical Library and with whom he discussed the current state of medical history in the United States. Sigerist wrote in his diary:

My opinion: the interest is enormous, much greater than in any European country. A great deal is published, but most of it is very amateurish. The task of the Institute in Baltimore is to break the way for really professional work. It will have to be done very slowly and nicely, without hurting feelings, more by example than by criticism.[7]

After sending his telegram to Welch, Harvey Cushing had withdrawn as a candidate for Welch's chair. At the end of December 1931 Welch appeared in Sigerist's hotel room in Minneapolis, bringing an invitation to come to Hopkins, "a unanimous decision by the faculty."[8] The invitation came as a great surprise to Sigerist, and he waited until he had returned to Leipzig to make his final decision. During his seven months' absence, the political situation in Germany had worsened considerably, and the more he traveled and saw in America, the more America fascinated him. He was collecting materials for his book *American Medicine,* which he had decided to write because he felt that America was now the center of the most advanced developments in medicine.

In April 1932 Sigerist accepted the Hopkins offer. His decision was based on two factors—the rapidly deteriorating situation in Germany and the hope that he could make a positive contribution to American medicine. As he wrote in the introduction to *American Medicine:*

> I saw great possibilities for the development of my subject in America. Wherever I had been I had found a keen interest in the History of Medicine. . . . Medical history in most countries is a purely antiquarian subject. My approach was somewhat different. Although I went through a strict philological school, and although I am still doing a good deal of philological work, I was always primarily interested in all the general problems of modern medicine; investigating the past in order to get to a clearer understanding of our own time, and to help in preparing the future. . . . I felt that an institute founded by Dr. Welch, backed by his authority, could not but be a vital Institute, an ideal place for such studies.[9]

Sigerist as Director of the Institute

Sigerist and his family moved to Baltimore in the fall of 1932. He arranged for his former student and assistant in the Leipzig Institute, Owsei Temkin, to be appointed to his staff, and he set himself the task of creating "a nucleus of German learning in foreign lands."[10] Fielding H. Garrison and John Rathbone Oliver, a Baltimore psychiatrist who had been lecturing on medical history at the University of Maryland since 1927, had already been appointed by Welch. In 1933 a teaching position was made for Ludwig Edelstein, an outstanding classicist from Berlin who had fled Nazi persecution. After Garrison's death in 1935, a Renaissance scholar and physician from California, Sanford V. Larkey, became the director of the Welch Medical Library and joined the Institute faculty. After World War II broke out, another of Sigerist's former German students, Erwin Ackerknecht, who had been living in France, also joined the Institute staff. They were all *sehr gründlich* (very thorough) scholars, especially for us American students who had not grown up speaking at least three languages and had not learned both Latin and Greek by the age of twelve.

In his first academic year (1932–33) Sigerist developed a program of lectures and seminars similar to those he had given at Leipzig. During the first quarter Sigerist gave a course on problems and methods of medical history, to introduce medical students to the field, and in the fourth quarter he gave illustrated lectures on the relations between civilization and disease.[11] He also gave a one-year course on the history of science to undergraduates of the Johns Hopkins University at the Homewood campus. He and his associate, Owsei Temkin, collaborated in a two-quarter seminar course on the evolution of anatomy and anatomical illustrations and on the history of the principal physiological problems. Courses were given by the other members of the Institute faculty: Garrison gave courses on how to use the medical library and medical writing and lectures on miscellaneous topics; Temkin gave a course on early scholastic medicine; and Oliver gave a general course in the history of medicine and a course introducing undergraduates at Homewood to medicine from the standpoint of history and of ethics.[12]

During his first Hopkins year Sigerist created the *Bulletin of the Institute of the History of Medicine* (first published in 1933 and 1934 as a supplement to the *Johns Hopkins Hospital Bulletin*). Eight months after coming to Baltimore he wrote to Arnold Klebs, a Swiss medicohistorical bibliophile:

> The Institute is developing very nicely. I am sending you under separate cover the first issues of our new bulletin, in which you will find reports on the activities of the Institute. I had an excellent group of students working with me, and I am very satisfied with the result of our courses. The students have less book-knowledge than the German students, but they are much brighter, much more open-minded, and the way they attack a problem is just splendid.[13]

Each year Sigerist described the various Institute activities in detail in the *Bulletin*. In addition to listing the courses given, he described special events, such as the celebration of the four hundredth anniversary of the publication of François Rabelais' *Gargantua* or the three hundredth anniversary of Anton van Leeuwenhoek's birth, when Dr. Welch was the principal speaker and a film demonstrating Leeuwenhoek's achievements was shown for the first time in the United States. Distinguished European scholars, such as Erwin Panofsky, an art historian, and Hermann Ranke, an Egyptologist, were invited to give lectures that illustrated the close collaboration Sigerist insisted must exist between historians of different nations and disciplines.

Sigerist taught mainly by example, and he tried to interest students in history by exposing them to many sorts of stimuli: brilliantly executed lectures; visual presentations of books, slides, or movies; projects such as a history of anatomy course that involved the students in preparing an

13. Erwin Acker-
knecht singing at a
New Year's Eve party
at the Sigerist home,
December 31, 1942.

exhibit and a subsequent publication; and exposure to outstanding scholars from all fields. He was very sociable, filled with energy, and liked by
almost everyone. When he came to his office, there was always someone
waiting in his secretary's office to see him.

During the early years in Baltimore, Sigerist tried to continue his philological study of the early Middle Ages with which he had begun his career.
His Institute study was lined with boxes containing photostats of medieval manuscripts obtained on summer visits to European libraries. But his
basic interest had shifted to current history. After finishing the book on
American medicine, which his initial trip to the United States had generated,[14] he resolved to study medicine in the Soviet Union, a nation he
thought embodied the socialist economy that he had come to regard as a
rational solution to social and economic inequalities.[15] At the same time
Sigerist was busy promoting history of medicine and the Institute in every

14. Owsei Temkin singing at a New Year's Eve party at the Sigerist home, December 31, 1942.

possible way. As early as February 1934, only sixteen months after arriving in Baltimore, he wrote to a friend, "I had to give so many lectures this winter that I am worn out." [16] He gave forty outside lectures in the academic year 1936–37; in May 1937 he wrote of having completed two chapters of his Soviet book, three papers, and four book reviews in four weeks' time, and by 1939 he was also serving on twenty-two committees and boards.[17]

Each summer before World War II the Sigerist family went back to Switzerland where they had a summer house at Kastanienbaum near Lucerne. A note, which I wrote in September 1936 while still a student, describes the anticipation of the Boss's return by the Institute staff:

> Everyone's hearts are beating excitedly—the Boss is returning tomorrow! After the last frantic week of preparation everything at last seems in readiness. The windows have been cleaned, the walls of the exhibit hall painted, all the pic-

tures are rehung, floors waxed, and the rug relaid in the Boss' office. Everything seems ready, down to his supply of paper clips and a fresh inkwell. Hope [Hope Trebing, his personal secretary] has brought in a lovely bouquet of dahlias to place on his desk. . . . We look forward eagerly to the beginning of a new academic year.

This is going to be a record year too. Dr. Sigerist does not plan to go away often on lecture trips, but to devote all of his time to the Institute and to the Medical History Club meetings. These latter have fallen off considerably without the full impetus of his genius and personal appeal to guide them. He will be more careful in selecting interesting speakers . . . I hope the Boss will give more lectures himself because he is the best speaker of them all. After all, everyone does not have his stimulating manner and extraordinary personality, which make him a born leader. He is fortunate indeed, in a sense, to be so gifted, but his life is probably no more happy than another's because by his very talent he must accept innumerable responsibilities and is keenly aware of the numerous ailments of society. The thought of war distresses him so. . . . He is alarmed by the menace of Fascism and would fight at any time for Democracy. He keeps his fingers on the pulse of all of society and recognizes its alternating tempos. A man of vision—an extraordinary individual. But with all his grandeur of personal appeal and his international reputation, a very simple human being lies underneath it all. He is very kind and considerate always. He doesn't hesitate to vent his feelings or express his opinions with some profanity, and he loves his food and drink. He bought a white suit this summer and told Hope and Polly [Pauline Brown, his research secretary] that he felt like a "new June bride" strutting around in it.—We all get a big kick out of him.[18]

For the secretarial staff, which was totally ignorant about Germanic manners and customs, it was also a great relief to have the Boss back again. The brilliant young Owsei Temkin, who became the acting head of the Institute during the summers when Sigerist was away, seemed very difficult to work with then, because of his highly analytical perception that extended to everyday events and his overly meticulous attention to details. The classicist Ludwig Edelstein, whose English was still quite difficult to understand, was more relaxed, except when he tried to make himself understood by telephone operators in those pre–automatic telephone days. Sanford Larkey was very friendly, outgoing, and a lot of fun to talk with when he came up to the Institute from his librarian's office on the first floor. We saw relatively little of John Rathbone Oliver, who only came in once or twice a week and whose health had begun to decline. For us students, the contact with these men steeped in scholarship was an overwhelming experience.

Sigerist felt that it was his obligation not only to promote medical history, but also to raise its standards in America. Previously it had been cultivated mostly by devoted amateurs, whose standards of scholarship in the eyes of philologically trained European scholars sometimes left much to be desired. Writing about a paper on Arnold Klebs that had been sent for publication in the *Bulletin*, Sigerist said:

> He was a follower of Osler and I think I found a name for their historical approach: *historia amabilis*. They "had a good time" studying history. Their subjects were limited and never offensive.

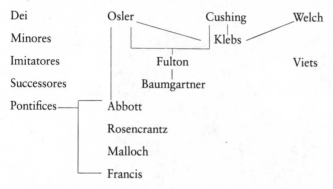

> Here you have the whole school! My history—I'm sorry to say—is anything but *amabilis* but is meant to be stirring, moving people into action.[19]

Yet, as seen in the scholarly articles published in the *Bulletin of the History of Medicine*, Sigerist tried to teach without offending people. He treated his students in the same respectful manner. In 1938–39, the graduate students at the Institute were Helen Paulson, Morris Leikind, Nell Snow Talbot, Elizabeth Longley, and Genevieve Miller; of this group, I was the only one to get a degree. (Ilza Veith came later and received her Ph.D. in 1947.) We students were never cruelly criticized for our sophomoric efforts, but we were shown a more sophisticated approach. In our seminars Sigerist discussed his own work in progress, his latest findings, and how he came to his conclusions. He urged us to read original sources, in foreign languages or Latin if necessary, and not to rely on secondary works in our research. He taught us to be critical. At first some of us spoon-fed American students tried to figure out what it was that the professor wanted of us, what we were supposed to learn. We were never told *what* to learn; this was frustrating until we finally realized that we were being taught *how* to be historians.

An example of his scholarly enthusiasm is the following note sent to me when I was his research secretary:

15. Ilza Veith, first recipient of a doctoral degree in the history of medicine from the Johns Hopkins University, May 29, 1947.

It is not yet 1 A.M. and I have written 10 pages, and good ones. No martyrdom but the joy of creative work. Gosh, I feel good. . . . I think you will be able to type it Saturday morning in no time. So long.

In addition to his scholarly activities, Sigerist was an avid photographer who took his Leica camera everywhere with him, and he even developed and printed his photos in a darkroom that he had set up on the first floor of the library. He frequently spent his lunch hours there. He also loved to cook and often, for special occasions such as birthdays and promotions, spent entire days creating elegant dinners, usually with French cuisine, and sometimes assisted by his female staff as scullery maids. An elaborate handwritten menu bearing a portrait of the cook wearing a chef's hat would always accompany the dinner. As with his daily activities schedule, he always created work plans, written in French, for these dinners, giving the times when various items should be prepared, cooked, and served. Every afternoon that he spent at his Hopkins office, he made tea in his study, which he frequently shared with staff or friends.

In addition to courses in the history of various periods or specialties of medicine, in his second academic year Sigerist began giving courses in medical economics and sociology. Such courses were especially popular with students from the Hopkins School of Hygiene and Public Health, and some were attended by more than one hundred students, of whom a number went on to careers relating to health service organization.[20]

To reach people outside the university, Sigerist and his Institute staff gave three Graduate Weeks in Medical History, in 1938, 1939, and 1942.[21] These were high-level postgraduate courses (open to anyone for a small fee) that consisted of lectures, seminars, and demonstrations by example that showed how medical history could be used to interpret events or discoveries, not simply to chronicle them. The topics included interpretation of an ancient medical text, how to organize a course in medical history, the selection of a subject of research in medical history, the history of disease, and contributions of Greece and Rome to medicine. Some of the forty or fifty participants per postgraduate course were Victor Robinson, Richard H. Shryock, Maude E. Abbott, George Rosen, Logan Clendening, and W. B. McDaniel II. The participants "looked over the shoulders" of the scholars as they analyzed and interpreted data. Elaborate exhibits were prepared as well as special events. One highlight was a concert given in the Great Hall of the Welch Medical Library at which a string quartet played music relating to medicine: a sixteenth-century frottola about the syphilis of a Mantuan marchese, a seventeenth-century tarentella written originally to cure the bite of a tarantula and recorded in a treatise by Athanasius Kircher, and a baroque song about St. Sebastian and the plague, sung by the director's wife, Mrs. Emmy Sigerist.

In a further attempt to raise the standards of American medical historiography, Sigerist reorganized the American Association for the History of Medicine, which had held its first meeting in 1925 as the American Section of the International Society of the History of Medicine through the efforts of Edward H. Krumbhaar of Philadelphia. Immediately after coming to Hopkins, Sigerist was invited to give papers at the annual meetings, and in 1936 he was elected president. Since he found the meetings rather amateurish and without real guidance (at one annual meeting an after-dinner speaker went on for over two hours!), Sigerist gradually transformed the association into a truly professional organization. He suggested establishing constituent societies, publication of the transactions of the annual meeting, creation of an annual honorary lecture, and establishing two medals to be awarded to outstanding medical historians. In 1938 the *Bulletin of the Institute of the History of Medicine* was renamed the *Bulletin of the History of Medicine* and became the official organ of the association. Sigerist and Sanford Larkey were elected secretary and treasurer, and for five years the association's headquarters were in the Hopkins Institute.[22]

The Impact of World War II

Unable to spend their summers in Switzerland during World War II, the Sigerist family found a new summer place in New York State. During the summers of 1941–43 they went to Bolton Landing on Lake George, where Sigerist hoped to escape the flood of people, mail, and other obstacles, to concentrate on the various books and papers he wished to write. A letter of July 14, 1941, describes his plight:

> I don't think I have left my study twice except for meals. I have not had a swim yet. I just managed to see the Lake. Somehow, everybody seems to have my address. . . . every few hours I get a telegram, long distance call or special delivery letter. People call and want me to go immediately to New York for a meeting and when I refuse they are offended. . . . I'll do the Paracelsus at night, but it's just as bad as in Baltimore.[23]

After the United States entered the war, the Institute became busier than ever, as members of the staff began a variety of wartime activities as well as their medicohistorical research and teaching. Because Sigerist was still a Swiss citizen,[24] he was first appointed a member of a mixed medical commission whose function was to examine prisoners of war in Canada to determine their eligibility for repatriation or internment in a neutral country. As the war progressed he was appointed consultant to the Board of Economic Warfare, a position that took him to Washington one day a week.

During the war Sigerist also was closely involved with activities relating to his interest in Soviet medicine. Early in 1943 he helped organize the American-Soviet Medical Society, created to acquaint American physicians with the "results and achievements of Soviet Medicine."[25] He also participated in a summer course, an intensive study of contemporary Russian civilization, at Cornell University where he led a workshop on Soviet medicine and health for a week in July 1943.

The following spring the stress of Sigerist's many jobs began to overwhelm him. He had been appointed acting librarian of the Welch Medical Library in October 1942 after Sanford Larkey had been called to the Army medical corps. These added burdens, together with a growing feeling of alienation and lack of support and understanding from Alan Chesney, dean of the Medical School, and Isaiah Bowman, president of the Johns Hopkins University, led him to think seriously about looking for another position.[26] Meanwhile his health was declining. In November 1943 he had written in his diary:

> A miserable week and I am in miserable health. The last two nights I slept only three hours and I am under constant terrific pressure. Everybody wants something, everybody hammers at me and there is no escape.
>
> The most depressing thought is to know that my research career is ended. Even if the war should end soon and if I got rid of the library, I would be used up, unable to give a synthesis, good only for little odds and ends.[27]

Except for the great stress that all his jobs put upon him, which was obvious to all of us, we staff members were not made aware of Sigerist's inner feelings about the opposition that he felt from Hopkins colleagues or of his growing desire to find a job elsewhere. In April 1945 his physician, Warfield T. Longcope, hospitalized him for a week's rest and declared that he should be relieved of the library directorship. In June Sigerist went to Saratoga Springs for three weeks of restorative treatment for his hypertension, followed by two quiet months with his family in Ithaca, N.Y., where he had ready access to the Cornell Library. On July 15 he wrote in his diary:

> A great day. Today, the fifteenth of July, I began my History of Medicine. I have prepared for and spoken of this book for more than twenty years. And finally the day has come. From today on this book will be at the center of all my thoughts and all my actions. I will not think whether my health will permit me to finish the book, but I will act as if I had eight more years to live.[28]

When the war ended, the Institute returned more or less to normal, as staff members resumed full-time service. In the academic year 1945–46, Sigerist gave seminars on the historical approach to medicine and problems of the sociology and economics of medicine. The American Association for the History of Medicine, which had suspended its annual meetings in 1942, met in Atlantic City in May 1946, and the complete proceedings were published as a 290-page issue of the *Bulletin*.[29]

Leaving the Institute

During the summer of 1946 when the Sigerist family resumed its annual Swiss summer sojourn, the professor was urged by his friends in Zurich to return permanently, and they tempted him with the possibility that a chair in medical history might be created for him at the university. After returning to Baltimore in September, Sigerist wrote in his diary: "I begin to feel a stranger here," since he felt that Hopkins was changing, "rapidly becoming some kind of technological institute." [30] By the middle of November he had decided to leave Hopkins at the end of the 1946–47 academic year. He wished to devote full time to writing his magnum opus and vowed to decline the Zurich professorship should it be offered to him. In January 1947 he sent his official letter of resignation from Hopkins to President Isaiah Bowman, and it was accepted. "On the way home I bought flowers and a bottle of champagne to celebrate," he wrote in his diary on January 23, 1947. [31]

To lose the Boss was disastrous news for us staff members, although we could certainly understand why he was leaving. The Institute had been a paradise for some of us, a place where we met so many interesting people who came to see Sigerist, were constantly stimulated to be curious and to learn more, witnessed such vitality and knowledge, and had such fun. When news of Sigerist's resignation became known, his friends and admirers from all over the country showed their appreciation for what he had achieved. A committee led by John Fulton of Yale organized a farewell dinner at the Plaza Hotel in New York on May 9, 1947. It was attended by over three hundred friends, colleagues, and former students. [32]

When Sigerist departed from the United States for the last time, on June 27, 1947, he left behind a huge legacy. A total of 472 books and articles were produced by the Johns Hopkins Institute of the History of Medicine during his tenure, of which Sigerist alone had produced 23 books in various editions and translations and 195 articles. [33]

In one of his farewell addresses Sigerist reviewed the achievements of the Hopkins Institute, which had been accomplished even though "the entire history of the Institute so far has fallen into the years of depression, war, and post-war confusion. . . . We had extraordinarily difficult years when we did not know how to carry on, and some very promising and timely projects could not even be considered for lack of funds. During those years, no other university could possibly have created a new department of the history of medicine." [34]

Notes

1. George Urdang to Henry E. Sigerist, May 12, 1941 (Johns Hopkins Medical Institutions, Alan Mason Chesney Archives, Institute of the History of Medicine Papers; hereafter referred to as Institute Papers).

2. John F. Fulton, *Harvey Cushing, a Biography* (Springfield, Ill.: Charles C. Thomas, 1946), 613.

3. "A plea for a central medical library (Johns Hopkins Medical School) Col. Fielding H. Garrison to be its librarian," 1923 (Johns Hopkins Medical Institutions, Alan Mason Chesney Archives, William Henry Welch Papers; hereafter referred to as Welch Papers).

4. "The William H. Welch Medical Library of the Johns Hopkins University," *Bulletin of the Johns Hopkins Hospital* 46 (1930): 98.

5. Simon Flexner and James Thomas Flexner, *William Henry Welch and the Heroic Age of American Medicine* (New York: Viking Press, 1941), 92–93; Nora Sigerist Beeson, ed., *Henry E. Sigerist: Autobiographical Writings* (Montreal: McGill University Press, 1966), 65.

6. William Henry Welch, Diary no. 37, May 31, 1931, Welch Papers.

7. *Autobiographical Writings,* Diary, October 31, 1931, 72.

8. Ibid., Diary, December 31, 1931, 75.

9. Henry E. Sigerist, *American Medicine* (New York: W. W. Norton, 1934), xvii.

10. *Autobiographical Writings,* 81.

11. Later developed in his Messenger lectures at Cornell and published as *Civilization and Disease* (Ithaca: Cornell University Press, 1943).

12. "Activities of the Institute of the History of Medicine," *Bulletin of the Institute of the History of Medicine* 1 (1933): 45–46.

13. Henry E. Sigerist to Arnold Klebs, May 19, 1933, Institute Papers.

14. *American Medicine* (New York: W. W. Norton, 1933).

15. *Socialized Medicine in the Soviet Union* (New York: W. W. Norton, 1937). A new, revised edition was published ten years later: *Medicine and Health in the Soviet Union* (New York: Citadel Press, 1947).

16. Henry E. Sigerist to Gilbert W. Rosenthal, February 9, 1934, Institute Papers.

17. Henry E. Sigerist to William W. Ricker, April 17, 1937, and Sigerist to D. R. Hooker, February 27, 1939, Institute Papers.

18. Genevieve Miller, personal memento.

19. Henry E. Sigerist to Genevieve Miller, August 20, 1943, Institute Papers.

20. His impact on these students is further discussed in the essay by Milton I. Roemer, Leslie A. Falk, and Theodore M. Brown in this volume.

21. *Bulletin of the History of Medicine* 6 (1938): 864–71; 7 (1939): 856–63; 12 (1942): 451–57.

22. Genevieve Miller, "The Missing Seal, or Highlights of the First Half Century of the American Association for the History of Medicine," *Bulletin of the History of Medicine* 50 (1976): 93–98, 106–8.

23. Henry E. Sigerist to G. Miller, July 14, 1941, Institute Papers.

24. He became a U.S. citizen on September 13, 1943. *Autobiographical Writings*, 184–85.

25. For an extended discussion of their activities, see the essay by Walter J. Lear in this volume.

26. He was especially interested in Yale. On July 24, 1944, he wrote to one of his students, "If I had a boy who intended to go into medicine, I would send him to Yale. In my opinion, Yale Medical School is much better than ours and the spirit is totally different. We are orientated toward the past while Yale is toward the future." Henry E. Sigerist to Nell Snow Talbot, July 24, 1944, Institute Papers. For further discussion of this phase in Sigerist's career, see the essay by Theodore M. Brown in this volume.

27. *Autobiographical Writings*, Diary, November 4, 1943, 185.

28. Ibid., Diary, July 15, 1945, 195.

29. "Transactions of the Nineteenth Annual Meeting of the American Association of the History of Medicine Held at Atlantic City, N.J., May 26 and 27, 1946," *Bulletin of the History of Medicine* 20 (1946): 95–385.

30. *Autobiographical Writings*, Diary, September 28, 1946, 201.

31. Ibid., Diary, January 23, 1947, 204.

32. For these papers, see *Bulletin of the History of Medicine* 22 (1948): 5–46.

33. Genevieve Miller and Henry E. Sigerist, compilers, "A Bibliography of the Publications of the Johns Hopkins Institute of the History of Medicine 1929 to 1947," *Bulletin of the History of Medicine* 22 (1948): 65–93.

34. "Medical History in the United States, Past—Present—Future," *Bulletin of the History of Medicine* 22 (1948): 62.

CHAPTER 4

Henry E. Sigerist: Orientalist

Ilza Veith

The vivid personality of Henry E. Sigerist was marked particularly by his unlimited interest in every facet of human endeavor, in every phase of history, and in every part of the world. His writings reflect this breadth of interest, but they do not reveal it to its full extent because one aspect of his studies, indeed the one that had occupied his interest longer than any other, has rarely found its way into print. This—his preoccupation with the culture, languages, and medicine of the peoples of Asia—attracted him long before he turned to the history of medicine, even before he undertook the study of medicine itself. His interest in the Far East never waned and probably formed the basis for my welcome on his part to the Institute of the History of Medicine.

Henry Sigerist's autobiographical accounts dwell lovingly on the period in which he pursued the studies of the Far East. In the introduction to the Heath Clark lectures, which he delivered at the London School of Hygiene and Tropical Medicine in 1952, he exclaimed, "It is with deep emotion that I am addressing an audience at the University of London, because this takes me back to my very early student days. In the summer of 1911—a coronation year—a summer full of sunshine, in a world that did not require passports—I came to London, a Swiss student from the University of Zurich, just twenty years old. I was not enrolled for a degree, but spent an all-too-short summer term here, attending courses. I was not a medical student then but was studying oriental languages and literature." [1]

Sigerist's involvement in oriental studies began while he was attending the gymnasium in Zurich. Soon realizing that "language is the key to the understanding of every civilization,"[2] he took private lessons in Arabic and enrolled in the Hebrew courses that were offered at the gymnasium for future theologians. Following graduation he enrolled as a student in the Philosophical Faculty of the University of Zurich, there continuing his Arabic and Hebrew studies and also taking up Sanskrit. His intellectual impatience, so familiar to all who knew him well, was even then in evidence, for since the course in Sanskrit "proceeded rather slowly I worked with a private tutor and at the end of the year we were reading the Panchatantra and similar texts."[3]

The reader of Sigerist's autobiographical notes must be amazed at the ambitious program that he had added to the normally exacting and crowded gymnasium curriculum. But Sigerist's desire and capacity for learning were so extraordinary that even the offerings of the University of Zurich could not satisfy his intellectual appetite. He tells us that:

> In those days the University of Zurich was rather weak in oriental studies and this determined me to spend most of the year 1911 in London. I had some excellent courses at University College, and since I was the only student attending them learned a great deal. With Mabel Bode I read the Meghaduta and with H. Hirschfeld the Fakhri and the Delectus Veterum Carminum Arabicorum of Noeldeke. At the same time I began the study of Chinese at King's College and devoted a great deal of time to it. My teachers were rather skeptical and repeatedly pointed out to me that it was impossible to embrace the whole Orient that I would have to specialize either on the Near East, on India, or on the Far East. But I refused to specialize. I was interested in the East as a whole, in comparative religion and comparative literature, in the migration and transmission of literary subjects and similar problems. And since I was very young I thought that nothing would be impossible to me.
>
> I worked very hard in those years and always had some grammar in my pocket and a notebook full of Chinese ideograms. But the time came when I had to admit that my teachers were right. It could not be done. The task became so big that quite physically I could not master it.[4]

It is futile to speculate whether a more rational program geared to a specific end might have kept Sigerist in the field of Indian or Far Eastern research. As it was, he abruptly ended his formal oriental studies and returned to Zurich. Nevertheless, although he turned from the humanities to the sciences, he continued, for a brief while at least, to read on Far Eastern subjects. In his native city he must have achieved the reputation of a specialist on China when he was not yet twenty years of age. On January 28, 1911, the *Neue Zürcher Zeitung,* one of the leading European newspapers, published a feuilleton by Sigerist entitled, "Neues vom Chinesischen Geistesleben" (News about Chinese Intellectual Life). It was an article reviewing Richard Wilhelm's *Kungfutse: Gespräche (Lun Yü)* (Conversations) and Wilhelm Grube's *Religion und Kultus der Chinesen* (Religion and Religious Life of the Chinese), both of which had been published in 1911.

Sigerist's discussion of these books, which have since become classics in their field, reveals his extensive knowledge of the subject matter and the maturity of his judgment. In spite of this successful publication, however, he was as firm in his decision to turn to another field of study as he was decided to continue to avoid specialization. He enrolled at the University of Zurich and spent a year studying science in general and only then began the study of medicine.

He was granted his doctorate in medicine in 1917 but while still a medical student decided upon a career in medical history, which could give him the latitude of interest he craved. From this point on and for decades, Sigerist's interest in the Orient seemed lost. His writings, though dealing with a vast variety of medicohistorical subjects, did not show the slightest trace of his early attraction to the Far East. It was therefore a complete surprise to me when I first met him in 1943 to see how close he was to the culture of the East.

At that time I had been engaged in translating and analyzing the "New Laws" of the Chinese political philosopher of the eleventh century Wang An-shih, whose suggested reforms included a government-controlled medical program. Having heard of Sigerist's concern with medical planning, I mentioned this early exotic example to him very shortly after we had been introduced at a meeting of the History of Ideas Club at the Johns Hopkins University. He immediately suggested that I show him the material, and when I brought it to the Institute of the History of Medicine a few days later, I had my first glimpse of Henry Sigerist's oriental side. He greeted me with a few Chinese words of welcome and then suggested that we have a cup of tea while he read my manuscript. The tea was *Hu-kwa*, a brand to which he was so partial that he had it sent from Boston when, years later, he was unable to obtain it in Switzerland. Sigerist prepared it ceremoniously and expertly, and served it in a tea set that had been imported from China. My article pleased him, and he accepted it for publication in the *Bulletin of the History of Medicine*. To him it represented a happy combination of a glance into the thinking of the Far East with an early health scheme; to me this event was much more portentous—it led to my first publication[5] and to my long and happy association with him.

Shortly after our first meeting Sigerist suggested that I make use of my reading knowledge of Chinese in the translation and analysis of the *Huang Ti Nei Ching Su Wĕn* (The Yellow Emperor's Classic of Internal Medicine), the oldest Chinese medical classic (which until then had never been available to Western readers). Following this suggestion, I later completed this work under a Rockefeller fellowship as a thesis for a doctorate in the history of medicine.

Sigerist was delighted to have a student of Far Eastern medicine as his first doctoral candidate at the Johns Hopkins Institute of the History of Medicine, which he had been heading for more than a decade. But he was also a little perturbed, for at that time the chances of finding an academic appointment for a graduate in the history of medicine seemed remote. In view of the subsequent burgeoning of our field, I find it amusing to recall that after having pointed out the dismal future of a medical historian, Sigerist's expression brightened and he said, "Well, you can always teach German or something else."

During the years I spent as a student at the Institute, we had many long conversations about the East that revealed to me the extent of his knowledge of India, China, and Japan. When he accepted an invitation from the Indian government in 1944 to study health problems and to make recommendations to the government about their solution, he arrived in India with an intellectual preparation that is generally found only among Western Indologists. He was thus able to recount the development of Indian medicine, discuss the medical classics and their philosophy, and appreciate the important role that *traditiongrube* played in the thinking of the Indian nationalists, particularly in view of the dearth of modern medical schools. Because of his familiarity with the culture and economic history of India, he could suggest, without hurting Indian feelings, that traditional medicine continue to be studied, but as part of the *history* of medicine rather than as a basis for medical practice: "Since India is confronted with the problem of indigenous medical systems and will be so for a long time an Institute of the History of Medicine could greatly help to clarify the situation."[6] Indeed, he was able to make concrete suggestions as to the academic program of such an institute:

An Institute of the History of Medicine in India will . . . investigate the medical heritage of the country dispassionately and critically, not in order to prove a point. It will endeavor to reconstruct and envisage the medical past of India from the perspective of history, in relation to and as part of the general civilization of the various periods.[7]

Sigerist specifically recommended that the institute arrange for critical editions and translations of the many Sanskrit, Pakrit, or Pali texts that had never been evaluated and that it should extend its attention to works written in Persian and Arabic as well as to those in the vernacular. It should serve not only as a humanistic center but also as a repository of background information for those who sought to spread health education and public health measures throughout the country.

Sigerist's suggestions must have been very much to the liking of his Indian hosts, for in the summer of 1949 when he had retired to the *Casa Serena* in Pura, Ticino, in Switzerland, he received a series of invitations urging him to help with the actual launching of an Institute of the History of Medicine in Bombay. But he decided that he could not then interrupt his work on his *History of Medicine*. The first volume had to be seen through the press, and he was then deeply immersed in the preparation for the second volume, which was to deal in equal proportions with ancient Greek and Indian medicine. He felt that the knowledge gained in the research would make his advice to the Indians much more significant. In July 1949 he wrote me:

> I greatly enjoy writing my second volume. After the evil spirits of Babylonia, the Greek atmosphere is very refreshing, and it is great fun to demonstrate that Ayurvedic medicine was just as advanced and just as effective as Hippocratic medicine. The parallelism in the development of the two countries is really striking. My Indian friends would like me to come over for a few months and help them in organizing an Institute of the History of Medicine in Bombay and in a few other projects, but so far I have resisted the temptation to accept as I wish to get further advanced in my work.

Sigerist had arrived at the decision to divide his second volume between Greece and India after considerable thought. He saw Indian civilization as having developed simultaneously with that of Greece, and he came to the conclusion that both civilizations and their medical accomplishments had followed a parallel course throughout antiquity and the Middle Ages. Correspondence with Indian friends and renewed study of the ancient Indian writings had convinced him that India shared the role of Greece as a precursor of modern medicine.[8]

In spite of his early familiarity with the Indian medical texts, the research on Indian medicine turned out to be complicated far beyond Sigerist's expectations. On December 4, 1951 he wrote me:

> I am working hard on Volume II of the *History* which is very difficult as it includes Greece, Rome, and India. The difficulty with Volume I was the scarcity

of sources while here you are drowning in texts, and I do not want the volumes to have more than 600 pages, so that I have to condense the material a good deal. I had also to brush up on Sanskrit as I like to read crucial passages in the original. Greek texts I am reading every day as a matter of course. The first three volumes are very slow as there is much philological work involved. From Volume IV on the task will be much easier, because all your sources will be either in Latin or in vernacular languages, and also you will be dealing with dated texts. The chronology of the Indian literature is perfectly hopeless.

Nevertheless, even these difficulties could not deflect Sigerist from his plan of treating Indian medicine in much detail, a plan that he considered a quite necessary innovation though rather daring. In the summer of the following year, volume II was still far from completed. In August of 1952 he wrote me:

> You enquire about Volume II and when it is to appear. Well, the book is not finished. . . . I have to cut down and condense left and right, without making the footnotes top heavy. Well, you know yourself how it is. If all goes well, and if the press does not delay the book once it has the manuscript, the volume could be out next spring. The third volume I am afraid will be slow also, as it contains Arabic medicine and Chinese medicine, about both of which we know so little. And here again I shall have to read an endless number of texts in difficult languages.
>
> When my second volume comes out, I am sure classicists will criticise that I gave India almost as much space as Greece. But I am just trying to get away from this one-sided approach which considers Europe (and America) as the navel of the world. It is strange how this old-fashioned concept is still prevalent in many places. In the otherwise excellent Historical Museum of Berne I found great Chinese, Japanese and Indian works of art in the division "Völkerkunde"; all that is not Europe is simply Völkerkunde (ethnology).
>
> At the moment I have much correspondence with Japan where one of my books will come out in September, and the translation of another is being considered. My translator keeps me supplied with the most delicious Japanese green tea, the one that is pulverized as finely as face powder, which you drink out of large bowls, after having whipped it.

Sigerist's decision not to accept the invitation to Bombay seems to have put a temporary end to the Indian planning for an institute. Sometime later, however, on March 24, 1953, the thought appears to have come alive again, for I received a very happy letter saying:

> Could you do me a great favour? I have vague plans of going to India for a year or two, of course without abandoning *The Book*. There are plans to estab-

lish a model medical school in Delhi with an Institute of the History of Medicine, such as I recommended in 1944. They would like to have me help them, but as you will know things move slowly in India and nothing may come of it. Still I am anxious to learn a modern Indian language and as you have very close connections with the Oriental Departments of the University of Chicago, I wish you would find out what the present situation is. In 1944, that is before the liberation, Hindustani was the main language, a blend of Hindi and Urdu. I have several text books of Hindustani here, but I understand that India is making Hindi more and more the national language for the Northern provinces, while Urdu is the language of Pakistan. Could you find out what Indian languages are being taught at the University of Chicago, and does your Press have a good text book of Hindi? I should be grateful for all the information your have on the subject.

Less than a month later he had translated his plan of preparing himself for the trip into action. In a letter dated April 12, 1953, he wrote:

I am very grateful to you for the information you gave me about Hindi, which confirms what I heard from other sides. I have just ordered a Hindi grammar of 600 pages from E. T. Brill in Leiden. You know how I approach a new language, first I am interested in the grammar of Hindi and then I want to know what its relation is to Sanskrit and how the words are derived and through what process the language went from early days to today. The pronunciation of course is a serious matter and unfortunately Linguaphone has records for Hindustani only and not for Hindi yet. Hindustani is a hybrid language, a mixture of Hindi and Urdu and it seems logical that Urdu will be the official language of Pakistan and Hindi of India. Of course there are endless other languages. In Madras alone, there are six of them but I am sure that Hindi will gradually become the national official language.

His extensive reading on India during the many years of preparation of his second volume reawakened in Sigerist all the excitement and interest that had led him to take up his Far Eastern studies in his youth. He avidly welcomed visitors from Asia, he was delighted by gifts from the Orient, and he even arranged the flowers from his beloved garden in Pura in Japanese style. During that time he wrote: "A Buddhist monk (of American birth and ancestry) was in Switzerland recently, and announced that he was coming back with a whole group of missionaries. He thinks that the Western World is ripe for Buddhism—maybe he is right." And then he went on to say,

I am also deeply immersed in Indian literature and am enthralled by it. My early days in London come awake and again I feel drawn to Buddhism much more than to Christianity which seems forbidding with all its logic and justice. In Buddhism one is master of one's own fate and one's fate is determined by one's own deeds. There are no gods and no saints that can help one. Buddhist texts deal gently with disease, with old age, and with death, and Buddhist compassion led to the foundation of hospitals for men and even for animals many many centuries before there were such institutions founded in the West.

As so many years earlier in London, Sigerist again refused to limit himself to the study of one Far Eastern civilization. Partly because he planned to discuss China extensively in his third volume and partly because that country fell heir to much Buddhist and Indian thinking, Sigerist extended his studies to include China as well. He was generous in sharing his wide reading experience on China and always recommended those books that had impressed him most. In August 1948 he wrote:

> I just read Lauterbach's *Danger from the East*. If you have not read it yet, do not miss it. It is an excellent account of recent developments in Japan, Korea, and China, and at the same time a terrific indictment of U.S. Policy. And just now I am reading with infinite delight Robert Payne's *China Awake*. He is a brilliant writer, who knows China very well and loves the country. He had a touch of tuberculosis and this undoubtedly has added a great deal of color to his writing.

Early in October of the same year his interest in China had reached the point where he began to revive his knowledge of the language:

> You may be amused to hear that I have resumed my study of Chinese and that I am memorizing three new characters every morning while shaving, quite apart from deciphering texts. It is great fun, and I am increasingly interested in China. Have you read Robert Payne's *China Awake* (New York, Dodd, Mead, 1947) which I mentioned before? If not, get it by all means, because it is a delightful book. Payne was teaching English literature in Kunming during the war, and his book is an abstract from his diary of the years 1944–46. It is beautifully written and gives a superb picture of present-day China, particularly of its young generation. Just now I am reading or rather re-reading *The Dream of the Red Chamber* in the German translation of Kuhn. You probably have it. Payne considers it one of the three greatest novels of world literature, and I am sure he is right. The other two by the way are, according to him, Genji Monogatari and Marcel Proust, *A la Recherche du Temps Perdu,* both of which I have here also.
>
> I think it is very wise of you to take courses in Chinese, Japanese, Russian, because you should remain fluent in those three languages, and as you very

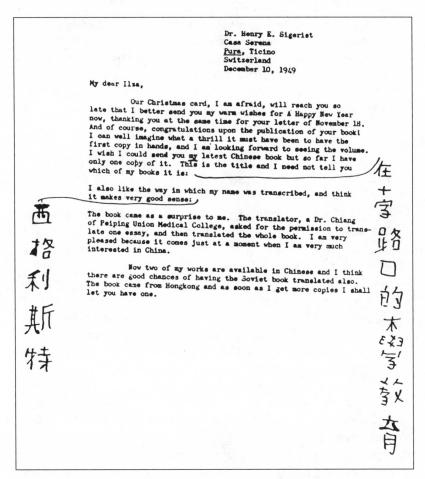

Dr. Henry E. Sigerist
Casa Serena
Pura, Ticino
Switzerland
December 10, 1949

My dear Ilza,

Our Christmas card, I am afraid, will reach you so late that I better send you my warm wishes for A Happy New Year now, thanking you at the same time for your letter of November 18. And of course, congratulations upon the publication of your book! I can well imagine what a thrill it must have been to have the first copy in hands, and I am looking forward to seeing the volume. I wish I could send you my latest Chinese book but so far I have only one copy of it. This is the title and I need not tell you which of my books it is:

I also like the way in which my name was transcribed, and think it makes very good sense:

The book came as a surprise to me. The translator, a Dr. Chiang of Peiping Union Medical College, asked for the permission to translate one essay, and then translated the whole book. I am very pleased because it comes just at a moment when I am very much interested in China.

Now two of my works are available in Chinese and I think there are good chances of having the Soviet book translated also. The book came from Hongkong and as soon as I get more copies I shall let you have one.

16. Letter from Henry Sigerist to Ilza Veith, December 10, 1949.

justly say one gets rusty very quickly. Although it is not so difficult to revive what you have once known thoroughly, as I find now with Chinese characters.

A year later he announced to me in Chinese writing the publication of the Chinese translation of his *University at the Crossroads,* and he was delighted with the Chinese transliteration of his name, which was pronounced Hsi-Ko-Li-Ssu-T'ĕ. Sigerist's "latest Chinese book" coincided with the publication of my book, the *Huang Ti Nei Ching Su Wĕn,* whose writing he had inspired. His preface to this book reveals his knowledge about Chinese medicine and his ability to see analogies in all medical systems. The following passages of the introduction are characteristic of him:

In all early civilizations . . . medical theory had a strongly philosophical character. Hence medical books are important sources of philosophical thought and their study presents an additional key to the understanding of civilizations of the past.

China is no exception to the rule. The country has some excellent modern physicians and scientists trained in very good schools, but they are only a handful for a population of four hundred millions. The overwhelming majority of the people therefore is still served by indigenous practitioners who feel the pulse, examine the patient, reason about his symptoms, and treat him exactly as their ancestors did many centuries ago.

The *Nei Ching*, the Classic of Internal Medicine, attributed to Huang Ti, the Yellow Emperor, is indeed a very important if not *the* most important early Chinese medical book, particularly its first part, *Su Wĕn* "Familiar Conversations" between the Emperor and his physician Ch'i Pai. It is important because it develops in a lucid and attractive way a theory of man in health and disease and a theory of medicine. It does this in very much the same way as did the physicians of India who wrote the classic books of Ayurvedic medicine, or the Hippocratic physicians of Greece; that is, by using the philosophic concepts of the time and picturing man as a microcosm that reflects the macrocosm of the universe. The theory expounded in the *Nei Ching Su Wĕn* has remained the dominating theory of Chinese indigenous medicine to the present day.[9]

Perhaps again, as in his youth in London, Sigerist found it impossible to cope simultaneously for any length of time with both the Indian and the Chinese civilizations and languages, for his letters ceased to contain further mention of his study of the Chinese language, although he continued to report on his reading about the country. He was particularly gratified, early in 1951, to hear that "medical history is now a required subject in all medical schools of the People's Republic and the minimum is a 20-hour course. From all the letters I get I feel that there is a tremendous impetus in the country and very great enthusiasm, particularly among students."

In the summer of 1952 he again resumed his study of the Chinese language. He wrote:

Have you read George N. Kates, *The Years That Were Fat, Peking: 1933–1940,* N.Y.: Harper, 1952? If not, get hold of the book: I just finished reading it and loved it: It is one of the finest books on China I have ever seen. It inspired me to resume my Chinese studies, and like a good school-boy I am re-reading the *San Tzu Ching*.[10] A former student of mine has just translated "Civilization and Disease" in Chinese but it is not out yet. At the moment I am writing a new preface for the Japanese edition of the Soviet book.

A month later, in response to my letter he wrote:

> I was sure that you would like *The Years That Were Fat*. Gunther Stein was here recently and gave me a copy of his book *Challenge of Red China*, published in New York in 1945. There could not possibly be a greater contrast than between these two books, one that talks of the old way of life as much as was left of it in those years, and the other of the new China that was being prepared. Gunther Stein was in China for ten years as correspondent of the *Christian Science Monitor*, and in my opinion is one of the ablest foreign correspondents. Unfortunately his sympathy for Red China makes it impossible for him to write for American papers today, and at the moment he lives in Geneva and is writing books.

It is obvious from the foregoing quotation that Sigerist's interest in the Orient was more than that of a historian. He felt equally drawn to all Eastern thought, be it of the past or of the present; and the political changes in China, Japan's readjustment to postwar conditions, and the intellectual renaissance of India occupied his thoughts as much as the many ancient Buddhist texts that he read "because Buddhism played a very important part in the formation of Hindu medicine." He even attempted the study of certain Buddhist sects and reported in 1949 that "I recently read Suzuki's introduction to Zen Buddhism but I must say, that this is a sect that I find difficult to understand."

In the last years of his life, when his illness cast a frequent shadow over his old *joie de vivre*, Sigerist's imagination dwelt more and more on Asian philosophy. The predominance of fate in Indian thinking, the freedom from passion and the absence of material desires in the Buddhist religion struck him as eminently more desirable than the Western striving for technical advances and material comfort. More than once he expressed his hope that the Orient would resist the technical advances of the West, and he pointed to Japan as a warning example, which as the only really westernized country had been drawn to war and into defeat largely because of its own industrialization. Doubtless, many of his ideas on Asia and particularly on India found their way into the unfinished manuscript of his second volume. But there are still so many more thoughts touched upon in his magnificent letters, which have never found their way into any manuscript. Years before his death many of his letters conveyed an awareness of his measured span of life, and even this was often couched in oriental wording that hints at emotions rarely fully expressed. We shall never know whether it was the autumn of the year or his consciousness of the autumn of his life that led him to conclude one of his last long letters to me as follows:

It is autumn, the garden is still full of flowers and grapes and the trees just begin to discolor; and I remember Tu Fu:

"As in a dream I look upon the shrubbery
Aglow in the full moon on the sloping rock—
And my entire life passes before me like a vision.

The islands far below in the dim light of dusk
surrounded by the pale autumnal reeds.
This, then, is autumn, oh my soul!"

Notes

My paper was originally published in the *Journal of the History of Medicine and Allied Sciences* 13 (1958): 200–211. This version has been slightly updated.

1. Henry E. Sigerist, *Landmarks in the History of Hygiene* (London: Oxford University Press, 1956), v.

2. Henry E. Sigerist, "University Education" (address delivered at Selborne Hall in Johannesburg on November 15, 1939, on the occasion of the conferring of doctor of literature *honoris causa* by the University of the Witwatersrand), *Bulletin of the History of Medicine* 8 (1940): 5.

3. Ibid., 6.

4. Ibid.

5. Ilza Veith, "Government Control and Medicine in Eleventh Century China," *Bulletin of the History of Medicine* 14 (1943): 159–72.

6. Henry E. Sigerist, "The Need for an Institute of the History of Medicine in India," *Bulletin of the History of Medicine* 17 (1945): 120.

7. Ibid., 121.

8. For another perspective on Sigerist's treatment of India in the second volume of his *History of Medicine,* see Heinrich von Staden's essay.

9. *Huang Ti Nei Ching Su Wěn* (The Yellow Emperor's Classic of Internal Medicine), chaps. 1–34 translated from the Chinese with an introductory study by Ilza Veith (Baltimore: Williams & Wilkins, 1949; reprinted, Berkeley and Los Angeles: University of California Press, 1966), v–vi.

10. In the original letter, Sigerist wrote this title in Chinese characters. The *San Tzu Ching* or "Trimetrical Classic" was formerly used as the first primer in Chinese schools.

CHAPTER 5

My Father, H.E.S.: A Photo Essay

Nora Sigerist Beeson

Zurich Days

From the many photographs in my possession of my father's life and time, I have endeavored to reconstruct some details that may not be known to many and which may complete the biographical picture found in the other essays of this volume. Of course much will be based on my own perceptions as a child growing up for her first twenty years in a vibrant intellectual home.

My parents' wedding pictures from 1916 are proper: my mother, Emmy Escher, a very beautiful bride, a friend and classmate of my father's sister; and my father, rather solemn at age twenty-five (fig. 17). Being a physician (he had received his medical degree in 1917), my father saw to it that my birth six years later occurred in a hospital and not at home. And as the new member of a good bourgeois family in Switzerland, I was accompanied home by a *Kinderschwester* (a baby nurse), who stayed with mother and child for a good period of time. My sister Erica was my older sibling, born in 1918. Other servants saw to the household and the garden of our very comfortable house in the Dolder (fig. 18), still today a fine residential section of Zurich overlooking Lake Zurich.

In my father's life, the serious scholar-scientist always prevailed, and although his father had been a religious man, Henry must have had doubts. The Greek philosophers were surely more important to him than

93

17. A wedding photograph of Emmy and Henry Sigerist.

the Christian saints or church fathers. And so, when I was born, perhaps a struggle of religious conformism arose. Should I be baptized, as was the Protestant custom, or not? In the end, my father bowed to the dictates of Zurich society. Instead of being carried as an infant to the nearby Kreuz Kirche, I was happily marched to church for baptism at the age of two, in a beautiful white dress with a stylish matching white hat. Later, my father was an avowed agnostic, at times espousing the Marxist credo that "religion is the opium of the masses." No one in our family attended church; religion to my father was a philosophical concept, which he studied in all civilizations, and which was of interest to him as part of a society's fabric, and not as a "prop" to living (as he used to say).

But to go back a bit. Many of my father's habits and interests were formed in his teens in Zurich. He began to keep records in an orderly fashion even before he had the historian's penchant for preserving events for himself or posterity. A few little handwritten notebooks were early diaries in which he described what he had seen and read, how school affected him, which aunt had come to tea, and above all where he had traveled. He continued keeping diaries throughout his life: in words, most extensively from 1931 to 1947, with a page generally written every day; in scrapbooks, where programs and announcements of concerts, conferences, lectures, and medical and cultural events were carefully positioned on pages of thick books; and in photographs, most of them taken by himself, some pasted in albums, others mounted on gray cardboard cards and then filed by subject, country, and so forth.

A stack of postcards in my possession also gives a glimpse of the Zurich days. Some are carefully dated and annotated: the Roman ruins of Vindonissa, June 7, 1906; the Count Zeppelin dirigible passing over Zurich on July 1, 1908, between 2 and 3 P.M. Another treasure trove of postcards illuminates fun in Zurich and the beginning of one of my father's many collections: portraits of marvelously costumed opera singers were interlaced with literary figures, scantily clad dancers, and coyly posing actors and actresses in various roles. Zurich has always been a thriving cultural center, and evidently the young Sigerist enjoyed what it had to offer.

Not to forget the pleasure of writing: My father wrote for himself, and for the general public, or for anyone who would read about his thoughts, books, or places that had excited him as a young student. So as early as 1910, the conservative *Neue Zürcher Zeitung,* still today a power in the news, printed one of his essays, brief to be sure, in the August 30 issue; others followed in the next few years.[1] The writing impulse never left Sigerist: sometimes urgent, sometimes diminished, sometimes frivolous,

18. The house in Zurich, where Henry and Emmy lived from 1919 to 1925. Emmy is on the balcony.

as much in letters (the huge correspondence is measured in many shelf feet in the archives of his papers at the Sterling Memorial Library at Yale University and the Alan Mason Chesney Archives at Johns Hopkins) as in papers, books, book reviews, articles, tributes, obituaries, and so forth.

There is little doubt that books, aside from human interrelationships, were the basic ingredients necessary to fuel my father's energy. He wrote: "I was a bookworm and my mother often worried about it. Even in the summer holidays which we regularly spent in the mountains, I took piles of books and my Greek grammar along. . . . Books were my passion."

There is an amusing book in my library. It is hard to imagine a more inappropriate method, in 1913, of wooing Emmy Escher, a pretty twenty-year-old girl interested in music and the theater, than by giving her a slim volume (one of the lovely Insel Verlag editions) of an Icelandic saga, translated from the Old Norse into German: *Die Saga von Freysgoden Hrafnkel*. It was a memento of their trip together to Fideris in the mountainous Grison canton. A flaming poem by my father is on the flyleaf, in his typical bold handwriting, invoking Siegfried and Brünhilde and other primeval beings. Perhaps it is Henry's only rhymed poem.[2] As translated from the original German by Jürgen Riehle, it reads:

> As we were resting on lofty meadows
> Northern magic like sudden shadows
> Struck our minds and filled our eyes
> With awe at nature's mightiest guise:
> We felt the ancient powers call
> The mountains like warriors to Valhall's hall.
> They came alive and seemed to rise
> As dark, swift clouds obscured the skies.
> And Siegfried came, the valiant knight,
> To wed in fire Brünhilde, the bride.
> Then we descended to gentler heights
> And you sang songs of nature's delights.
> And our tempestuous, wild ascent
> Mellowed to peaceful, quiet content.
>
> In remembrance of a Nordic mood
> From your Henry E. Sigerist
> June 30, 1913

Yet this "historical" approach must have been not ineffective, for Emmy and Henry were married three years later.

My mother came from the distinguished Escher family, which traces its roots to the late fourteenth century and over the years has contributed many of the leading politicians, bankers, judges, architects, doctors, and businessmen to Zurich. When she was four years old, her mother died of cancer; her father, in the textile business, moved from Milan back home to Zurich. They were well-to-do, but it was her grandparents who had the finest villa, with coaches and horses, on what is now Zurich's most elegant street, the Bahnhofstrasse. Their beautiful china, silver, furniture, splendid dresses, and paintings are even today enjoyed by family members.

After schooling in Zurich, my mother attended what was then deemed necessary—a kind of home-economics finishing course. I suppose it served her in good stead for running a constantly changing home life, which she did with much grace and love. Never an intellectual, she found it difficult later on to keep up with my father and took refuge in her music. During the war, she was proud to do nurses' aid work in a Baltimore hospital, enjoying the status it gave her. Compassionate, generous, and ever patient, she was a warm friend to many.

In general, my father's acquiring and collecting of books was systematic, and the subjects covered were enormous. While Greek, Arabic, Latin, and Hebrew books were partly for study purposes, the English, German, and French classics were also considered a must. All books from the Zurich days were carefully numbered in the upper right-hand corners of the inside covers, and the numbers, titles, and authors were entered in a handsome register. (The three well-bound catalogues of this "Bibliothek Sigerist-Escher" are now in the University of Zurich medical history collection.) The bookplate, undoubtedly designed by himself, was pasted inside the book's cover: an ornamental goblet with the Sigerist family crest of three slanting spearheads on one side and the Eschers' crest of a bulbous cup surmounted with a star on the other side. "Ex Libris Sigerist-Escher" sealed the book's ownership.

When my father's research library of some six thousand volumes was sold to the University of Zurich after his death, I kept what I thought might be of greater interest to me than to the university. The seven-volume set of Arthur Schnitzler's collected works (Berlin 1913) is numbered 593, while the five-volume set of Byron's works, in English of course, is numbered 786. And I was touched to rediscover recently that my father's fifteen-volume Goethe set, numbered 508 and signed "Henry Sigerist, 25, 12, 08," has the following inscription: "passed on to Nora Sigerist Beeson 41 years later, Dec. 25, 1949." This set traveled across the Atlantic Ocean three times. Books were treasured possessions and were treated like members of the family.

I am not certain when my father began his fine collection of books by the Swiss eighteenth-century physiologist and writer Albrecht von Haller. It became his most concentrated book hunt, a passion that extended over his lifetime, bringing him in touch with medical booksellers and knowledgeable persons all over the world. As a *Privatdozent* in Zurich, Sigerist had become interested in Haller. Much later, I shared his excitement whenever a new Haller book entered his library and his sorrow when he felt that the valuable collection should be in a safer haven than in his Swiss house in Pura. In 1955–56 Yale University acquired his Haller collection.

Leipzig, 1925 to 1932

Our move to Leipzig in late 1925 was the first of three major changes. The handsome Swiss furniture was made to last a lifetime, even outliving its owners, despite being crated, loaded, and unloaded numerous times. And the books had a lifetime of their own. Never forsaken, they ended up sharing a woodshed with a family of tame hedgehogs when space was tight during the last ten years in Switzerland. Mold bothered the books, hardly the resident animals. In Leipzig began my conscious knowledge of what would, for the next twenty-two years, become the center of our household—THE INSTITUTE.

But first the house (fig. 19). Situated in what was then named Oetzsch, a village and a kind of suburb of Leipzig, it derived its name from the nearby enclave of Slavic Sorbs (or Wends). In fact, our favorite cookies were in the shape of Cyrillic letters—*Russische Buchstaben*. The house was large, or so it seemed to me. My father's study was completely booklined from floor to ceiling, with custom-made shelves. The desk was the centerpiece. The drawers held his papers, pads, pencils, fountain pens, and the special large blue books he always used for writing. On the surface, there was never any disorder—a few framed photographs and a copy of an ancient Egyptian head of Nefertite. And of course ash trays, lots of them, for most of his life my father was a chain smoker of cigarettes (pipes and cigars occasionally), a habit that certainly contributed to his early death at age sixty-five.

The household was tuned to his life. Next to the study was the living room with the Bechstein grand piano, where I had welcome music lessons, but only when he was away, so as not to disturb him. Yet music was an important aspect of my father's life. Although his cello was still in the closet, I never heard him use it, since he had stopped playing much earlier for "lack of time." Records appeared, and on the wind-up Victrola we played the newest releases of the famous tenor Richard Tauber, of favorite Franz Lehar operettas, and of the latest *Schlager* (hits), which we soon

19. The house in the Leipzig suburbs, where the Sigerist family lived from 1925 to 1932. It was sold hurriedly, at a loss, and Sigerist vowed never to buy a house again.

knew by heart. My mother had a beautiful soprano voice and continued studying most of her life. Only at Christmas—that magical event with many surprises—did my father join the singing, in a good true baritone. Once or twice I was taken to the Thomaskirche, famous for its choir boys and for the fact that J. S. Bach had worked there for the last twenty-seven years of his life.

Mealtimes were punctual, geared to my father's schedule. There were dinner parties with colleagues from the university, with friends, and with frequent out-of-town visitors. Sparkling with silver and fine glass, the dining room was sometimes out of bounds for us two children, and we happily ate on the veranda accompanied by the resident dog or cat. Later, in Baltimore, my father often fussed about the "tyranny" of the household, its ironbound rhythm. Yet without a well-regulated "outer" life, his "inner" life could not have encompassed his many activities. Indeed, one of his few "practical" obligations—maintaining the early Ford car in which he drove to work every day—threw him into anger and anxiety. Like most European intellectuals, *Herr Professor* was to be spared all manual exertion.

20. Karl Sudhoff, director of the Leipzig Institute of the History of Medicine.

Being asked to be the director of the Institute of the History of Medicine in Leipzig was a great honor for the thirty-four-year-old Sigerist, especially as he was taking over what the famous Karl Sudhoff had begun (fig. 20). I was only dimly aware, at the dinner table conversations, how exciting he found his teaching, publishing, organizing, and socializing life. On the few occasions I was taken to see the Institute, the rooms seemed drab to me, but of course I was more pleasantly involved with my school, music, and the company of my friends.

The Institute was obviously the pinnacle of my father's life, and his work was pleasure until, in the early 1930s, budget cuts and a threatening political situation marred his scholarly pursuits. But there was also fun, especially the elaborate costume balls (fig. 21), where the students sparkled with their fantastic, original getups. On Sundays, we sometimes went for a drive, one of the few relaxations, but Saxony was flat and uninteresting compared with Switzerland, unless we went to see the huge impressive monument to Napoleon's defeat at the Battle of Nations in 1813, the *Völkerschlachtdenkmal*.

I much preferred staying in the large garden, my mother's domain. It was well planned: splendid dahlias in a row by the house, tree roses of all colors planted at the edge of the lawn, raspberry plants in a line, and white narcissus along the wall to the neighboring house. My father paid admiring visits but rarely joined us there, staying indoors with his books. Sports also were not considered "serious."

Whenever possible, we returned to Switzerland during school and university vacations. Coming from the drab countryside of northern Germany, the Swiss mountains and lakeside resorts offered a fabulous variety of terrain. After a serious bout of pneumonia, my father (and we) recuperated at a rented chalet in Beatenberg. And of course the annual stay in Basel with my grandmother was a delightful interlude with the family. Henry was devoted to his mother, Emma Sigerist-Wiskemann, an indomitable woman who had provided him with a superb education. Of course she was immensely proud of her only son, who could do no wrong in her eyes, though neither she nor other close family members accepted his growing "socialist" ideas—as she called them. It did not spoil their relationship. When an offer for a position in Baltimore was extended to him, one of the prerequisites for acceptance was the granting of a four-month summer period in Europe, partly to track down medieval manuscripts in European libraries and partly to enjoy the company of his many relatives, young and old. For the five war years, from 1940 to 1945, when he could

21. Members of the Leipzig Institute and other faculty members at a costume ball held at *Fasching* (carnival) time, 1929.

no longer journey abroad from the United States, he worried constantly about a Nazi attack on Switzerland, Basel on the border being especially vulnerable. Ironically, it was the British who dumped some bombs on the city; "they were never good at geography," my father wrote. His mother's death in 1954 was a great sorrow and may have precipitated his stroke in that year.

One circumstance marred my otherwise blissful seven years in Germany, the threat of surgery. My father was remarkably calm, I thought. When visiting me in the hospital, it was plain that he *enjoyed* being back among doctors. Medical history had replaced practical medicine as he had experienced it in medical school and in the Swiss army. But medicine remained at the basis of his belief that the human animal, a social being, should benefit from medical knowledge and its applications. This included all humans, an idealistic vision that propelled him later to become a political-medical activist as well as a scholar, a change that offended many of his colleagues.

I knew immediately that something important was about to happen when one day my sister and I were called into my father's study—a room mostly closed to us. The announcement that we were going to move and settle "in America" is still crystal clear in my memory, especially my concern over whether my nanny and dog could accompany us. With a positive *NO* as an answer, the prospect became less glamorous and romantic than it was made out to be. It was also made clear to us that we were in "some danger"; Raschwitz, the stretch of dark forest we had to pass through when driven to school in Leipzig, was the scene of fights between citizens and brown-shirted Nazis. That sinister threat was ever present, though its exact explanation escaped me at the time.

Sigerist was always acutely aware of politics, even as a student. A humanist, passionately supporting liberal democracy and the Weimar Republic, he was absolutely certain that fascism was on the rise in Germany and that it would gain in strength and become a European danger. He often remarked that anyone reading Hitler's *Mein Kampf* (published in 1925 to 1927) who did not heed the inevitable was an idiot. No one believed him. Perhaps he remembered "l'Affaire Dreyfus," the hot topic in Paris when he was growing up, which caused his mother to say, when entertaining friends at dinner, "on ne parle pas de l'Affaire" (we do not mention the Affair), fearing that the party might end in fist fights.

Looking back, Dr. Welch's offer was most fortuitous. So many of his German friends in the medical field, both Jews and non-Jews, including his devoted publisher Bruno Hauff, came to a bitter end.

In the fall of 1932 I entered school in Baltimore, not knowing a word of English.

Baltimore, 1932 to 1947

Once again, the Institute became the center of Sigerist's work, but now I was old enough to enjoy some of it. Much larger than in Leipzig, the Johns Hopkins venue in Baltimore encompassed the world, or so it seemed to me. Only years later did I realize that medical history is a comparatively small field. But here was an imposing building, the Welch Medical Library, a famous medical school, tangible past "greats"—such as in the oil painting by J. S. Sargent of William H. Welch, William Osler, William S. Halsted, and Howard A. Kelly—and roomy bright offices for my father and his staff. In fact, there was enough room for a number of separate desks for his various activities: one for attending to his huge correspondence and for developing Institute events, exhibits, seminars, and lectures was situated in his main office, where he received the many foreign visitors and listened to his colleagues; another desk was piled with work on medieval medical manuscripts, a continuation of his philological interests; still another one was for his ongoing personal projects—the writing of books, book reviews, introductions, papers, editorial work on journals, obituaries, and so forth. He usually skipped lunch so as to find time for his research, while pursuing his daily ritual of brewing tea from his vast tea collection, a much discussed hobby.

Of course, Sigerist's prime responsibility and intense interest were his students. At first few in number, they increased greatly over the years as his reputation as a fascinating, not to say controversial, lecturer spread from the medical school to the School of Public Health, and to the outside world. As a teenager, I occasionally attended a lecture or seminar. His talks were clear and organized and never, never read. The key points he wished to make were written down in a few notes, but the delivery was spontaneous, free, and emphatic. To bolster his arguments and explanations, he used slides, films, and once even musical illustrations with a live string quartet (fig. 22).

Sigerist was in great demand as a public speaker, and this led to a widening circle of acquaintances and also to more and more commitments. Among those asking for his services were medical student organizations, medical and public health societies of all sorts, colleges and universities, private clubs, even ladies' groups—"we so love to hear you speak—now just what was your subject?" Fees were small, and travel ex-

22. The performers at a concert held during the Institute's first Graduate Week, 1938. All the music played had some relationship to medical history. Sargent's famous portrait of the Hopkins "greats" (Welch, Halsted, Osler, and Kelly) frames the concert's participants: Emmy at the *center* with the four student musicians, and Sigerist on the *right*.

penses often erased the gains. But he hardly ever refused, and at home he agonized about preparing yet another talk, sometimes locking himself into his hotel room a few hours before the event, to complete his notes and thoughts. He even gave radio broadcasts about the urgent issues of the time, especially national health insurance, then called "socialized medicine." I remember well my own debate on that subject with the debating society in my high school, and how terrified I was that I might lose to my opponents on the "wrong" side. Fortunately, my team, the "right" side, won.

As teacher, lecturer, and medical activist, my father was a great success, yet the frustrations mounted. At home, he would ask himself why he had accepted yet another speaking engagement; why he was not left in peace to do his own writing; why he had not warded off yet another visitor or another student seeking advice. And we asked why he was not able to say a simple *no*. Clearly, he sought and enjoyed his public recognition, which went far beyond the usual limits of an academic career.

By carefully scheduling and organizing his time, he attempted to coordinate his many activities. Every day he drove to the downtown medical school, returning for dinner at six. Before eating, he concocted his own cocktail and read the French, Italian, German, and other newspapers. Often a stray guest had been brought along or invited, sometimes unexpectedly, and we became quite adept at FHB (family hold back) so as to accommodate the visitor, who was always welcome. At dinner, we shared our daily happenings—his accounts endlessly fascinating and opinionated. Over the years, his political views became less and less tolerant, and he grumbled and fumed about idiotic presidents, idiotic policies, idiotic AMA decisions, and so on. Enamored of the Soviet experiment, he was unwilling to see or believe the hideous purges, which he dismissed as part of a necessary transition period. He only saw the positive features of a socialized organization of medicine. As always, his research was based on an immersion in his field of study—here intense Russian language preparation and three long trips to the Soviet Union (figs. 23 and 24).

23. Tartar children at a school in the Crimea, photographed by Sigerist during one of his study trips to the Soviet Union in the 1930s.

After dinner, there was an hour or so of listening to records, with animated discussions about new soloists or conductors, as well as a perpetual battle with the fireplace and damp smoldering logs. Then we dispersed. His best working hours, my father always insisted, were between 8 P.M. and 1 or 2 A.M., when he wrote his books and essays undisturbed. The few hours of sleep at night were often interrupted by his rhinitis, which I am now convinced he aggravated by overusing the available nasal sprays, and by his hypertension and incipient cardiac difficulties—problems he described in his essay "Living under the Shadow" (1952).

In keeping with his obsessive work habits, my father kept detailed daily, monthly, and yearly schedules carefully recorded in longhand in blue copybooks. Each volume was started at the beginning of the academic year and listed what was to be accomplished. As the year progressed, completed work was crossed out and new projects were added.

The year 1939–40, for instance, was divided as follows:

1. Writing
   Books: finished, dictate, prepare
   Papers [14 listed by titles]
   Reviews
   Prefaces [2 listed]
   In print [10 listed by title, when and where published]
   Out [12 listed]
2. Editorial programme
   Bulletin of the History of Medicine
      Volumes VII and VIII
      Special numbers
   Publications of the Institute
      Series 1, 2, 3, 4
3. Institute projects [4 listed]
4. Teaching
   Regular classes
   Study groups
   Courses planned for 1940-1941
   Lectures and addresses [13 listed with dates and locations]
5. Johns Hopkins Medical History Club [3 meetings with dates]
6. Committee work
   University [4 listed]
   History [6 listed]
   Sociology [such as Committee on Suicide]
   Various [such as Council on Soviet Relations, Maryland State Planning
   Commission]
7. Conventions [name, place, date]
8. Travels
9. Various events [honorary memberships, D. Litt from Witwatersrand]

For the daily schedules, there was a specially printed pad, with headings, days, and hours given.

Unknown to most were his exasperated remarks muttered to us or inscribed in his diary, such as "Again too many visitors kept me from completing a book or paper," "am behind in my work again because of too much other work," "the publishers are damn slave drivers, always after me to finish," or "got sidetracked by silly ideas about waterclosets or food." It was surprising that he was able, much of the time, to stick to his daily quota of writing five finished pages a day, including research. So at the end of two months, he had some three hundred final pages.

During my teenage years in Baltimore, I formed a close relationship with H.E.S. Naturally, I was swept along by his whirlwind intellectual ideas, though often I differed with his outspoken opinions. But it was his many nonmedical interests as well as our mutual European stays that fostered a close kinship. Music was a great bond. There were subscriptions to excellent concert series. More exciting to me was the *Hausmusik*—monthly chamber music events in our house on Cloverhill Road (figs. 25 and 26), where good amateurs played quartets, trios, and so forth—my mother, nervous before an "audience," sang German lieder. Many musicians became our close friends, all of this fueling my own musical education as a violinist.

Another abiding interest was my father's hobby of photography. He developed his films himself and enjoyed his experiments with enlargements and different kinds of paper. It was fun to see the results—or failures. His Leica camera was used to document trips, people, meetings, and animals. His good friend, the psychiatrist Gregory Zilboorg (fig. 27), was always a jump ahead of Sigerist, with more and more outrageous equipment. It was a cheerful rivalry. To this day I have kept my dislike of posing as the

25. Emmy in front of the house rented by the Sigerist family on Cloverhill Road, Baltimore, in 1942.

26. The Sigerist girls, Erica (*left*) and Nora (*right*) playing music at home, Cloverhill Road, Baltimore, Christmas 1936.

27. The psychiatrist Gregory Zilboorg, one of Sigerist's closest friends.

foreground or background to something, while H.E.S. endlessly adjusted filters, lenses, light, and distance.

I think I learned how *not* to cook while assisting him in another one of his hobbies—*la cuisine française.* The feast day, whether it was a birthday, graduation, or simply the arrival of some visitor, began with an *ordre de bataille*: a battle plan listing all necessary ingredients and the timing of preparations. Our long-suffering Alice was asked to leave the kitchen to him, and then it began. He used every implement in our possession, often over and over again as I cleaned up in between. Cheer and jokes flew, aided by "necessary" nips of sherry or wine to spur along the hours needed to perfect his meals. Relying on Escoffier's cookbook, he spared no amount of cream, butter, and other rich ingredients. The end results were superb: *canard à l'orange,* lobster Newburgh, *coquille Saint Jacques, dinde truffé, trippe à la mode de Caen,* and perhaps a risky zabaglione desert, which might curdle if the temperature was not just right (fig. 28).

28. The chef at work during a summer vacation at Bolton Landing.

*Baby's Birthday
Dinner
Feb. 22. 1939
MENU
champignons farcis
Poulet cocotte Bonne-Femme
Mousse au chocolat
Gateau Noisettes
Champagne Mumm Extra-Dry
Café — Liqueurs
Many happy returns...*

Choice wines accompanied the meals and often handmade menus, illustrated with appropriate photos (fig. 29). Oh my! It taught me to cook simply when faced with preparing everyday meals after my marriage.

On weekends, we sometimes visited neighbors. Adolf Meyer, a fellow Swiss, was the famous psychiatrist and director of the Johns Hopkins Psychiatric Clinic, who lived in a pretty house nearby. Being extraordinarily taciturn, he made few pronouncements, which we eagerly awaited. I was most impressed by Atkins, his marvelous black cook and butler. Fielding Garrison was just across the street, as was Allen Freeman. There were some great cookouts with the Institute's colleagues—Erwin Ackerknecht, San Larkey, Owsei Temkin, Ludwig Edelstein, Genevieve Miller, and Hope Trebing. And to initiate the weekend, every Friday evening on my father's return home, he would stop at a corner of University Parkway to buy us bunches of flowers from the "flowerman," as we called him.

Best of all were the trips abroad every summer. I was taken out of school early and returned again in the fall, after school had started.

Equipped with long reading lists for the summer, I and my education were surely not shortchanged. For seven years we enjoyed Atlantic ocean liner crossings, always stopping off first in Paris, my father's birthplace. He adored the city. And it was to my advantage that he was "available" after working mornings in the Bibliothèque Nationale. Patiently explaining, he introduced me to the Louvre's paintings. Even more fun were the visits to the theater. His whispered plot explanations caused many irate "shushes," I'm afraid. Memorable also were the opera performances at the Palais Garnier, the opera house where the building itself made me marvel as much as the colossal performances.

We continued on to Switzerland. My father was a nervous traveler, arriving at the station long before departure time. He especially dreaded passing through customs, but partly at fault, I'm sure, were the innumerable pieces of luggage that accompanied us. I remember having to keep track of as many as thirty-five to forty different receptacles, including the Gladstone, the plaid, the slide box, the special trunk he had built to hold his books, which could be made into a traveling desk (it took three men to carry it), the various steamer trunks for clothes, my mother's hatbox, my own violin, and many more. Fortunately, for six summers (1934–39) we ended in a handsome patrician house on the Lake of Lucerne. Kastanienbaum, with few chestnut trees left (hence the name), was an idyll (fig. 30). After his own study travels in France, Italy, the Soviet Union, and South Africa, my father would join us there for four or five weeks. Since no public transportation connected this village with Lucerne, the paddle-wheel boats were the only means of arrival and departure. We had no car, but bread was delivered every morning early, vegetables later, and sometimes meat on certain days. Most fun was the beer wagon, drawn by two superb large horses; to us, its delivery of blocks of ice for the metal icebox, which did great service without any power of any sort, was more important than the cases of beer. And the weekly shopping trips, by boat, were infinitely more pleasant than a run behind a smelly gasoline engine.

With a number of guest rooms, the house welcomed all our friends, family, and even our dog, Tippi. Luise cooked up a storm, and the Monopoly craze hit us teenagers. Henry liked fishing best and joined us as we swam and boated on the lake, the house being set in large grounds and woods bordering the water. Most of the time he would retreat to his study to read proofs, fuming at the deadlines imposed by his publishers. I think it was there that he taught me to play chess; other games he found silly and a waste of time. To him, these summer respites were a refueling for the winter months as much as a vacation of sorts.

Political tensions clouded our summers. In the second half of the 1930s,

30. The splendid house in Kastanienbaum, with its flaming black-and-yellow shutters. Its garden reached down to the shores of Lake Lucerne.

my father was convinced that war would break out—it was just a matter of time. He was very worried about returning to Baltimore, and one fall we waited anxiously lest the *Queen Mary* would fail to pick us up on the French shore, rumor being that all transportation had been canceled. A great shout went up as the illumined hulk appeared in the dark night, and once more we would return to our "winter quarters."

In 1939 we were indeed caught by the outbreak of the war. Within twenty-four to thirty-six hours, Switzerland mobilized its army, since every man had his uniform and rifle at home, ready to defend the borders. We had elegant army officers quartered in our house, and I'm afraid I found it all very exciting. Henry was on an extended lecture tour in South Africa, and we had to somehow make our way back to the States. With refugees sleeping in all the public rooms, a boat finally left for New York; it did not hit mines. Henry wrote in his diary:

> And so the year [1939] has come to an end. The war, long expected, long delayed, is on and soon will be an open war against the USSR and socialism.
>
> In a few days I shall be home and back at the Institute, after seven months of travelling. I have enough of it. I can hardly wait to see the family again. But

I am afraid of the Institute, of the terrific amount of work, of stupid administrative work that is expecting me. It is getting so much more every year that I do not know where this will end, and how I shall escape. I wish I could live in Kastanienbaum and write my six volumes in peace.[3]

For my father, the war years and particularly the postwar times were extraordinarily difficult. Exasperated by staff cuts and by ever increasing administrative work, he came home one day, yelling, "I even had to take care of the window blinds." His publishing work was pushed into the background. He suffered from the ghastly toll of life the war was taking— "our generation is to blame," he always remarked and wrote. In addition, loyalty investigations were affecting many of his friends and colleagues, and to him the shadow of former fascist dangers was still vivid. Aside from that, his liberal pronouncements on political events, often ill-timed and wrongly considered, made him a thorn in the side of the university's administration. I'll never forget how the FBI came to question him at home; their file on him was growing. For years, he had hatched the plan of writing a multivolume history and sociology of medicine, and with failing health and failing university support, he felt the need to change his life radically.

He agonized for many, many months over the decision to leave Johns Hopkins, but once he had made up his mind, he did not look back. Often he talked about the country retreat he was searching for in Switzerland, with only a donkey to connect him to the outside world. Well, that much-talked-about donkey turned into a small Volkswagen, which my mother, at age fifty-four, learned to drive.

She was delighted to return to her home country and Swiss family, never having fully accepted American life. In the European fashion, money was not much talked about in our family, and I was unsure just how the new existence, with another huge move of furniture and books, was to come about. Fortunately, Yale University made my father a research associate (with professorial rank); a cashed-in life insurance policy took care of the move.

The Last Ten Years in Pura, Switzerland

Delightfully situated above the Lake of Lugano, in the canton Ticino, the house in the village of Pura was comfortable, set in a beautiful strip of garden (figs. 31 and 32). The vineyard just below produced a sour red wine but looked marvelous. Better, Pura was still unspoiled, keeping its

31. Casa Serena, Pura, Ticino, Switzerland, where Henry and Emmy lived from 1947 to 1957.

32. Henry and Emmy in the garden at Casa Serena.

Italianate character, complete with a communal baking oven and an outdoor stone trough for washing clothes.

Living in Rome off and on for some years, my husband and I visited frequently, though we could not afford the long trip north very often.

I think the dilemma of my father's dramatic change became quite obvious after a while. He adored the countryside; loved his garden, especially the camellia bushes and small palm trees; spoiled his two cats, Babyface and Agamemnon; and made friends with some of the local Pura residents. Sciolli *falegname* was an excellent carpenter, known by that name because there were many Sciollis. Fortunately, he was more adept at his trade than at winemaking, a skill he taught my father, with explosive results when all the corks popped one night in the cellar. Another friend raised trout, which were lovingly transported alive to fancy hotels and restaurants. Since Roman days, pottery was a much practiced craft in that canton. Delightfully near, the local *ceramica* produced fine hand-painted ware. Our friends there made us many, many *boccalini*, which were given as presents to all visitors. Thus, "Casa Serena" on these little drinking jugs traveled all over the world.

Another charming friend was the local doctor in Lugano, Dr. Achille Piotti, who took superb care of Henry for the ten years that he lived in Pura. Piotti knew all the local chapels, fine altarpieces, and wayside stations in this Catholic canton, and these my father photographed and annotated carefully.

Without admitting it, Henry missed the university life in which he had been active for some thirty-seven years. Oh, there were very many visitors. All were welcome. Always the organizer, he brought together medical historians in seven Pura Conferences, where serious papers were interlaced with splendid meals and excursions. With an enormous correspondence, he kept in touch with his colleagues all over the world. And there were offers of chairs in the history of medicine (in London, Zurich, Berlin, Berne, Basel, and Jena), all of which he refused.

Mornings were spent with his assistant-typist, but progress on his planned volumes was slow. Pura was, after all, still an isolated environment. In these last ten years, he completed one and one-half volumes of the history. I think he was split in many directions, guilt ridden when not working, and finally severely impaired in health. Once or twice I visited from New York with the grandchildren, Christopher Sigerist (1950–76), and Miranda, born in 1953.

Saying goodbye in Pura in 1955 to take an early flight back to New York, my father gave me one of his camellias. I embraced him—we both knew it was to be the last time. He died peacefully in his beloved Casa Serena on March 17, 1957, a few weeks before his sixty-sixth birthday.

Notes

1. My father's early publications, both scholarly and more popular, are well described by my cousin Marcel Bickel in his essay in this volume.

2. The original text of the poem is as follows:

Wir sassen einst auf bergigen Matten,
Da überkam uns wie ein Schatten
Des Nordens Zauber, als wir schauten
Der hohen Naturgewaltige Bauten:
Wir fühlten der Urdinge Wesen und Walten.
Die Felsen wurden zu Riesengestalten,
Und dichte Wolkenmassen zogen
Zu Walhalls Burg in dunkeln Bogen.
Und Siegfried kam, der Recke traut
Zu freien im Feuer, Brünhilde, die Braut.
Dann zogen wir nieder zu milderer Flur,
Und Du sangst Lieder an die Natur.
Und unser gewaltig stürmisches Streben
Wandelte sich zu sanftem Erleben.

Zur Erinnerung an eine nordische Stimmung
von Ihrem Henry E. Sigerist
30 Juni 1913

3. Nora Sigerist Beeson, ed., *Henry E. Sigerist: Autobiographical Writings* (Montreal: McGill University Press, 1966), Diary, December 31, 1939, 159.

PART 2

Sigerist as
Medical Historian

CHAPTER 6

Henry E. Sigerist and Aspects of Medical Historiography

Owsei Temkin

It is now over a year since Dr. Sigerist died. The time for giving expression to one's immediate distress over his departure has passed. The time to evaluate his many contributions objectively has, in my opinion, not yet come. Considerations such as these made me hesitate to accede to the suggestion of our program committee to talk on aspects of Dr. Sigerist's historiographical work. It seemed inappropriate to me that I talk about a man to whom I owed much, with whom I had been associated for twenty-one years, but with whom I had also disagreed on many points. When our committee pointed out to me that I was not expected to talk about the man but his work, I reconsidered. In doing so I was guided by the thought that Dr. Sigerist's death confronted us with the necessity of taking stock. It is not a matter of praising him or blaming him, nor is it a matter of passing definite judgment on what he has written, said, and done. Rather, we are forced to ask what he has done that needs no repeating, where should we follow him, and where should we go a different way? And it was understood that I would confine myself to his historiography, which means that I would not speak about his sociological ideas nor his activities as editor, organizer, and teacher.

With this resolve I entered upon the preparation of my talk and began to reread his publications, starting with the articles of his early Zurich days. But when I came near his Leipzig period and the time when I first met him, about half a year after his arrival, the picture of my former teacher appeared before me, and I found myself living through old memories and engaged in new disputes. Clearly that made it impossible for me to interpret Dr. Sigerist's words as if he were an author from a remote past whom I had never met. Thus I yielded to the unavoidable, and though I am speaking about the man's thoughts and not about the man himself, I shall speak about his ideas as I remember them extending over the time of our association, which came to an end in 1947 when Dr. Sigerist left Johns Hopkins. For this reason I shall not go beyond the first volume of his projected *History*.[1] This book virtually belongs to the Baltimore phase, since the bulk of the manuscript was written by 1947. And though here and there I have refreshed my memory by reference to his printed statements, especially the introductory chapter to the volume just mentioned, I must yet warn you that you are dealing with personal impressions as they now stand out in my mind. Others will study Dr. Sigerist's writings and may arrive at conclusions contradicting what I have to say. Moreover, there are already articles available by others who also knew him well and may have seen sides that I overlooked, or misjudged, or which time does not allow me to mention.

Henry E. Sigerist was a pupil of Karl Sudhoff, the undisputed master of medical historians in Germany at the end of the First World War. This pupilage showed itself in the choice of subject, as well as interpretation of the task, of medical history. The other leading historian at the time was Max Neuburger in Vienna; Neuburger's approach to medical history was philosophical. The two volumes of his *History of Medicine* that appeared in 1906 and 1911, respectively, largely dealt with the ideas behind the activities of men and schools. But Neuburger's most creative years were over, and his sensitive personality, unable to assert itself against Sudhoff's domineering nature, was not likely to attract Sigerist. There were of course some younger scholars. But neither Diepgen, nor Charles Singer, nor Garrison, nor Castiglioni, to mention but four names, were at the time so situated as to guide a young aspiring scholar. Thus he turned to Leipzig, where Sudhoff was the director of the Institute for the History of Medicine, which he had organized as a great research center.

Sigerist's turning to Sudhoff is understandable. Sudhoff stands out as the great archivist who made text after text of medieval material available. Sudhoff had begun his scientific career with an investigation of the genuineness of Paracelsian books and manuscripts and had ended it with a new edition of Paracelsus's scientific works. Since Paracelsus could not be understood without a knowledge of his medieval presuppositions, medieval medicine had filled most of Sudhoff's work in between. From Sudhoff Sigerist accepted the task of devoting himself to the medical literature of the early Middle Ages. Like every historian, he needed a period in which he felt at home and to which his detailed research work could be devoted. Medieval scholarship, in medicine no less than in other fields, is largely a matter of manuscript study, because so many sources have not yet been printed. On the other hand, the large number of authors and texts sometimes demands different methods from those of the classical philologist.

Sigerist liked to expatiate on these differences. He compared the medievalist, especially the Arabist, with the Renaissance scholar. The latter, when suddenly confronted with a large mass of newly discovered ancient texts, brought them out in editions that were far from ideal. Often just a single manuscript was printed; the task was to acquaint the world with the new content. Critical methods and editions came later, when the details began to matter. The medievalist often was in a similar position. Better fifty works made known in a faulty manner, than one text edited painstakingly and the rest ignored. This was the attitude of a historian to whom texts are source material, rather than that of a philologist for whom texts are literature. Yet Sigerist had been imbued with philological training; before turning to medicine he had studied oriental languages. In a way his dedication to the early Middle Ages was a resumption of his linguistic interests. And in his own work he did not sacrifice the exactness of the classical scholar.

Quite a number of early medieval medical texts were made public by Sigerist and his pupils, beginning with the "Cirurgia Eliodori" in 1920.[2] He conceived the plan of preparing a large-scale survey of all early medieval texts, describing them and analyzing them as to content, time, place, and authorship, in short, a *catalogue raisonné,* as he liked to refer to it. The catalogue proper was to be followed by two volumes, one containing editions and the other a history of early medieval medicine.[3] He was very much occupied with this idea in the early years in Baltimore. He traveled to Italy and France, inspecting and photographing texts and ordering photostats where necessary. He described his activity in "A summer of research,"[4] and he built up in the Johns Hopkins Institute a considerable collection of photostats. In the late thirties, he gave up his ambitious plan. He described some of his findings in the *Bulletin,*[5] but fundamentally it was a "cleaning up" job. Whether he was discouraged by the knowledge that others were engaged in similar work, or whether his interests had shifted too far away from the subject, need not concern us here. A catalogue of the "Presalernitan medical manuscripts" appeared in 1956 from the pen of Beccaria, a survey, rather than a *catalogue raisonné* of early medieval texts. Beccaria may be right in his belief that Sigerist's plan was conceived on too vast a plane to allow realization.[6]

An evaluation of the single contributions in this field will largely be left to specialists. But we have to ask ourselves what the occupation with early medieval medicine meant within the total context of Sigerist's work and what it means to us. Let us take a concrete example, the *Studien und Texte zur frühmittelalterlichen Rezeptliteratur,* which Sigerist wrote as his *Habilitationsschrift,* and which Sudhoff published in 1923. As the title indicates, the book is a study of early medieval antidotaries (i.e., works containing prescriptions for all kinds of diseases), and it investigates not just the details but the whole genre of this kind of medical literature. In the first part, Sigerist gives an outline of the history of pharmacology to the end of antiquity. The second, and main, part offers *in extenso* a number of Latin antidotaries from about 900 A.D. The concluding part studies questions of authorship, influences, and the historical setting within the ancient past and the later, arabicizing, Middle Ages.

Even the most enthusiastic defender of the value of historical studies will be hard pressed to recognize any direct contribution to modern medical thought in this book. It is a historical piece of work in which the medical content is of secondary significance. Nowhere does it evince a sign of its author's having hoped for a startling discovery of a highly efficient drug within this mass of prescriptions. The fascination of doing such work lies in the deciphering of a difficult text, in identifying names, tracing influences, reconstituting the time and circumstances under which this literature could flourish. I remember Sigerist's having often referred to the book in connection with the so-called *Antidotarium Nicolai.* He was, rightly, proud of having shown the latter to be a post-Constantinian edition of the old Salernitan antidotary, which itself was under strong Arabic influence.

When Sigerist started upon his career, the tasks of a medical historian were relatively simple. He had to have a medical education and must direct his historical interests to medical subjects. The aim of all this was simply the elucidation of the medical past. The medical historian differed from other historians in the ability to understand the medical meaning of his sources. This point of view is clearly implicit in Sigerist's earliest programmatic article, "Tasks and Aims of Medical History" of 1922,[7] belonging to the same period as the above-mentioned book. The task is formulated largely in terms of textual historical research. Medical history needs "strict historical philological method." Sudhoff is quite clearly the acknowledged master. As to the aims, they are viewed in a more or less traditional way too. Medical history enhances our modesty; it is a warning against the dangers of specialization, and an integral part of epidemiology. A bridge between sciences and humanities, it has a great educational value, leaning toward a new humanism and strengthened idealism.

One cannot help wondering how the tasks thus defined are to implement the aims. The latter are valid enough, but they appear as a mere rationalization of the right to indulge in historical research. Thus it is understandable that a reaction set in against Sudhoff's position, and Sigerist himself, more than anybody else, encouraged a wider approach to medical history. And yet, he never lost interest in the early Middle Ages, one of the most arid periods of medicine, and he never renounced the philological textual method. I think that Sigerist simply expressed the need felt by a serious medical historian to cultivate historical research, i.e., the establishment of facts, of their chronological order, of the persons involved, and so on. Whether it be the early Middle Ages or any other period is irrelevant. What matters is the historical dedication, once a subject has been chosen. Let us not dismiss this as antiquarianism. Nobody could have been further removed from antiquarianism than Sigerist was. But he always stated that the methods of medical history must be historical, and that implies that what he learned from Sudhoff should not be forgotten by us.

It did not take long for Sigerist to shake off the limitations of Sudhoff's approach and to begin viewing the history of medicine in a universal context. To do this he needed a philosophical framework, and not being a systematic philosopher, he found the framework in various philosophical tendencies of the day. Toward the end of his Zurich years and at the beginning of his Leipzig period, he was influenced by Spengler's ideas of cultural morphology. The difference between antiquity and the Occident became, to Sigerist, a difference between ancient humoral medicine and modern medicine based on "the anatomical idea." A comparison between Galen and Virchow shows that there is much truth in the estimate of the relative role of anatomy. But Sigerist's claim that ancient medicine was without anatomical basis aroused the opposition of scholars who found the statement irreconcilable with the anatomical efforts of the Alexandrians and of Galen. Here we have an early example of the friction that Sigerist's general ideas so often aroused. The framework was taken over while the medical content was sometimes adapted to it in a drastic manner. I think that Sigerist was aware of it; he liked to say that to make a point clear you must not mind overstating it. It may have been the very exaggeration of Sigerist's formulation that proved stimulating. Exaggeration or not, here were given perspectives and connections that made medicine an intellectual adventure of mankind.

Again the framework changed. Spengler's morphology of culture soon gave way to a more flexible relativism that viewed all the cultural manifestations of a period as expressions of its style. This philosophy, in which the influence of the art historian Wölfflin is unmistakable, dominated the most fruitful years in Leipzig. Its best product is Sigerist's article on Harvey and the baroque.[8] Here he shows that Harvey's work on the circulation of the blood and on embryology exhibits the same preoccupation with movement as does baroque art from the late sixteenth century on. Just as the baroque is thereby distinguished from the more static art of the Renaissance, so Harvey stands in contrast to the anatomists of the sixteenth century who studied the dead form of the human body.

The Harvey article seemed to demonstrate that medical history itself could be beautiful, because it could be approached with the esthete's eye. Art in medicine, or medicine in art, had been studied before. But in these older studies, the two had no organic relation. Sigerist saw them as expressing the same spirit. Of course, Sigerist did for medicine what had been done for other disciplines before him. But he did it in a manner supported by his own esthetic nature. This personal element has to be mentioned because it explains his love for esthetic themes. The interpretation of St. Sebastian, the patron saint of the plague, as a reincarnation of Apollo[9] thus belongs not only to the same period but to the same type of work. The evidence for the thesis lies mainly in one's ability to see Apollo in the Renaissance paintings of the youthful St. Sebastian.

The esthetic nature of the subjects treated concealed the danger of this approach. This danger manifested itself in a short article "Kultur und Krankheit" (Culture and Disease)[10] in which the very appearance and manifestation of diseases was related to the cultural style of a period. If at heart Sigerist had been a romantic, he might have adhered to this thesis and tried to develop its possibilities. *Civilization and Disease* reverts to the theme; but this book, published in 1943, is pervaded by a different spirit. It retains some of the old ideas but also indicates Sigerist's growing preoccupation with social, economic, and political interpretations. The change from a more idealistic to a more materialistic orientation in the history of medicine was paralleled by Sigerist's heightened interest in medical sociology, with which I am not concerned here. It is, of course, this new vista that in a maturer form underlies the first volume of Sigerist's *History*, but

since it was his sociological work that exhibited the more extreme formulations of it, I can forgo further comment at this point.

One element was preserved through all the metamorphoses of Sigerist's
philosophy. Medicine must be understood within a broader context, be it
cultural, social, economic, or all of these. This emphasis marks Sigerist's
position within medical historiography. Others before him had seen the
association between medicine and philosophy. Nor had people been blind
ťo the fact that medicine represents part of a civilization. But I do not
think that anybody before 1925 had insisted quite as outspokenly on the
fact that medical research and practice are conditioned by their time and
cannot be understood otherwise; and I believe this to be one of Sigerist's
lasting achievements. Those of us who remember the near hostility that
this point of view encountered in the late 1920s will also know that it was
not self-evident. Whatever way medical history may go in the next years,
I do not believe that it will return to the older isolationist outlook.

Three times did Sigerist attempt major historical syntheses of medicine, the first in his *Einführung in die Medizin* (1931), or *Man and Medicine,* as the English title has it. This book grew out of lectures to medical
freshmen in Leipzig. The historical method was used to explain the present day structure of medicine. But in contrast to a history of medicine,
it starts from the present and utilizes history as a tool for explanation.
Course and book were extremely successful in Germany, more so than in
this country, for reasons that may lie in differences in medical education.

Man and Medicine was followed soon afterward by *The Great Doctors.*[11] This is a history of medicine and, in spite of the title, not a biographical one. The book reflects the interrelation of general trends and
conditions with the work and contributions of great individuals. The great
doctor is not made to spring from a historical vacuum; nor is the development of history attributed to abstract forces of which the individual is
a mere point of intersection.

The third attempt at a synthesis was to be on a much larger scale; it was
to be a history of medicine in eight volumes. The first volume appeared
in 1951 and contains a long chapter entitled "The Historical Approach to
Medicine." The title of this chapter is significant because medicine, not
history, is made the object. This harmonizes with Sigerist's definition of
the medical historian: "The historian of medicine is a physician, trained
in the research methods of history, who takes an active part in the life
of his time and is in close touch with the medical problems of his time"
(p. 31). Such words can be said without being meant, and I therefore has-
ten to affirm that Sigerist considered himself a physician, far removed

from any medical practice though he was and even little interested in the progress of the medical sciences. He included his own social interests within the concept of the physician. Thus he could say that the historian of medicine "never is a narrow specialist who perceives only limited aspects of medicine, but he tries to see medicine as a whole, not only from the point of view of the medical profession but of society as well. Driven by a contemporary living interest he sets out to consult and re-create the past of medicine" (p. 31).

The last sentence makes it clear that Sigerist was a decided follower of the school represented by Benedetto Croce, whose dictum that "every true history is contemporary history" he quoted with approval (p. 30 f.). In as far as this is a proposition in the philosophy of history in general, it is outside our scope. But it is of concern to us in as far as Sigerist expected the medical historian to be a medical man. For Sigerist, the historian to whom medicine meant no more than a special area of historical investigation was not a medical historian. This attitude was traditional in Europe, where medical history had always been a medical discipline.[12] But such a tradition is not ours or is no longer ours. Thus we are confronted with the problem of whether or not to accept Sigerist's definition.

Before attempting an answer, it may be good to broaden our quest. We just heard that the medical historian "tries to see medicine as a whole, not only from the point of view of the medical profession but of society as well." The introductory chapter is supposed to tell us how this is to be done, and the rest of the volume should be a lesson in application.

This introductory chapter constitutes a synthesis of all of Sigerist's approaches to medical history. If we compare it with his earlier *Man and Medicine,* we become immediately aware of a great difference. In *Man and Medicine,* the main divisions ("Man, the Patient," "Signs of Disease," "Disease," "Causes of Disease," "Medical Help, the Physician") are based on the traditional concept of medicine as a relation between man as the subject of disease, disease itself, and the physician as the healer. But in the introductory chapter to his *History,* Sigerist outlines the task of medicine under the following four headings: "1. Promotion of health, 2. Prevention of illness, 3. Restoration of health, 4. Rehabilitation" (p. 7). Consequently, the medical historian "will first endeavor to find out what health conditions were in a given society at a given time" (p. 8). This in turn is dependent upon geography and economic and political history. To understand what was done "to maintain and promote health and to prevent illness" one has to know the history of religion and the history of education (p. 8). The study of the physician's thought comes later. It is here, in the history of medical theories, which "always represent one aspect of the general civilization of a period," that Sigerist now finds the place for "style" as a common denominator (p. 11). Also it is at this place, where he turns to the physician, that Sigerist discusses the role of "the great doctor."

Thus, there seem to emerge what Dr. Rosen so aptly called levels of integration.[13] The geographic and, in the widest sense, social factors determining health and disease embrace, so to speak, the more specific factors of cultural life, which in turn modify the thought and practices of laymen, the medical profession, and its outstanding representatives. This is a much wider approach than in the previous books and is based on a much wider concept of medicine.

The main element added to the older concept of medicine is public health. Public health is no invention of the last decades; nor can it be said that Sigerist was the first to pay attention to the history of public health. But whereas formerly public health appeared as something loosely connected with medicine or as an application of medical knowledge, it is now not only an integral part of medicine but a fundamental part. Promotion of health and prevention of disease are direct objects of public health policy, while the practicing physician contributes to them but indirectly through attention to individual patients. Nothing characterizes the role Sigerist assigned to public health better than his evaluation of the parts that history plays in the work of the practitioner and medical planner.

> It is obvious that a doctor can treat a patient suffering from pneumonia or syphilis or any other disease successfully without any knowledge of general or medical history. The only history he must know is that of his patient. The moment, however, when we plan an anti-venereal disease or anti-tuberculosis campaign, or medical services for rural districts, or whatever it may be—the moment, in other words, when we address our efforts not to a single individual but to a group—we need more historical knowledge. The success or failure of our efforts may well depend on whether we have a correct appreciation of the many social, economic, political, religious, philosophical, and other non-medical factors that determine the situation, an appreciation that we may acquire only as the result of historical analysis (p. 32).

Few will read Sigerist's first volume without being deeply impressed by the forcefulness of his vision, by the wide sweep combined with great learning with which he treats the medicine of such civilizations as Egypt and Mesopotamia, and the clarity of his diction. Even those who disagree violently with his views thereby testify to the impression he made. Sigerist was a great historian, not only a clever popularizer or a good medievalist. Therefore it must be a matter of regret to all of us that his *History* was not completed.

I cannot help asking myself what it would have been like if Dr. Sigerist had been able to complete it. Whatever the details might have been, as a whole it would have represented a grandiose vision of medicine. I say vision because this word indicates the personal note that I am sure would have pervaded the whole as it pervades the first volume. Sigerist is not understandable as a historiographer if one disregards his strong artistic proclivities. Apart from the attention given to art, which I mentioned before, he was an artist *qua* writer of history. As he himself said, "The historical investigator becomes a writer of history, and the writing of history is a creative process, is art" (p. 30). And when he added, "Like every artistic creation a book of history has a strong personal note," he was actually characterizing his own book.

I can perhaps illustrate best what I have in mind by citing our repeated arguments over primitive medicine. I objected to placing a chapter on primitive medicine at the beginning of any history of medicine. Primitive medicine, I contended, as a study of medicine among so-called primitive peoples, is a matter for anthropologists and must not be presented as a substitute for the origins of medicine, about which we know next to nothing. Historians, in my opinion, should go back in history as far as the material carries them, and should stop where the material stops. But whether right or wrong, such a view could not and never did satisfy Sigerist. A piece of art needs a beginning and an end. The chapter on primitive medicine served him as a beginning just because it permitted him to introduce the ideas that he needed for scaffolding the structure of his history. I have no doubt that there would also have been an end, an outlook into the future, telling us where the possible development led and giving us marching orders, for according to Sigerist:

> It is a sheer waste of effort to oppose powerful social trends. Historical analysis reveals that these trends are not accidental but the result of the whole economic and social structure of a given society. We can influence developments and can take an active part in shaping the future—there is no reason for fatalism—but we can do so only in certain directions. And history tells us what these directions are (p. 32).

There is room for legitimate doubt that history fulfills the function of prophecy. If I may be permitted to set belief against belief, I would say that the past tells us little about the directions in which the future will go.

Rather, by wrestling with historical facts and thinking about them, we find ourselves and what is possible and desirable for us.

Sigerist's history would have presented a vision of medicine, not just of what medicine has been, but of what it is and should be. In his way, Sigerist would have fulfilled the historian's mission to reshape the very object he is dealing with. It is not unlikely that the idea of Germany as a powerful political concept in the minds of men was in part due to the German historians of the nineteenth century.[14] But even where the historian need not create, he will at least define. Any great history will have this effect, and for this reason, and not just because it needs literary skill, is the writing of history rightly called an art. In this sense Sigerist's *History* would have been great history even if we disagreed with the vision.

But we are recalled to earth by the fact that Sigerist's *History* was not completed. Mingled with this reminder is the nagging doubt in my mind that it could ever have been completed as planned. My doubts refer to the possibility of capturing in a few volumes the kind of history of medicine we have just imagined. This, you will agree, is a very pertinent question for all of us, which should be discussed without reflection on whether to continue Sigerist's volumes or not.

Let us first of all be clear about the distinction between a textbook of the history of medicine and a history of medicine. The two are not necessarily identical. A textbook sets forth what its authors and others teaching medical history expect a student to know about the subject. There are textbooks of varying length according to the teachers' point of view, and we need good textbooks. But Sigerist did not set out to write a textbook. He wanted to present a work "which was to be at once a synthesis and a starting point for further research, and with which [he] would try to set a new pattern of medical historiography." [15]

In looking for models for Sigerist's historiography one must not think of Haeser, Garrison, and Neuburger. Rather one must think of the great French historians of the last century, men like Michelet. It was Sigerist's aim to write history in the grand style, history that recreated the past and thus *was* the past for everybody to see. For everybody to see, and not just for students and scholars. In the terminology of today, this means popular history.

The indisputable fact that Sigerist was an eminently successful popular author is not to be explained by mere facility of writing. As we all know, he possessed this facility to a very high degree. But this popularizing was of a distinct kind, which had little to do with the popular productions that are mushrooming around us. His popular style grew out of the French literary tradition of historiography, for which clarity of writing and composition were primary postulates, and dullness an unforgivable sin. As a scholar, Sigerist was a pupil of Sudhoff; as an author he was not. Sudhoff was not only a professor but a *Geheimrat,* who was at his best when writing for other professors and graduate students. Sigerist, although a professor, was a man of the world. The audience to which he addressed himself was composed of educated physicians or educated laymen interested in medicine. Sigerist usually did not explain medical terms; however he used them sparingly. He never talked down to his readers, and he did not try to make everything understandable to everybody. It would be a mistake to interpret his simplicity of diction as an attempt to write "for the millions." This simplicity was an expression of his inner conviction that the world was constructed in a simple, explicable fashion. Sigerist was what the French call a *simpliste;* as to "the millions," he was much too fastidious in his taste to think of them as his readers. If he reconstructed the past for everybody to see, everybody meant all persons who mattered.

But such a wide audience was not to be taken for granted in the twenties. It would be going too far to say that Sigerist created it. Especially in the Anglo-Saxon countries, others, like Osler, had exerted their influence in the same direction. But Sigerist certainly helped to shape this audience all over the world. Medical history might still remain an object of serious study for a woefully small number, but it became a matter of discussion for wide circles. Thus we come back to Sigerist's *History:* it was to recreate the past for all educated and interested persons to see. But what about this recreation, this synthesis of which Sigerist spoke?

When I reread the chapter on the historical approach to medicine, I was once again impressed by its many-sidedness. But I was also beset by the feeling that it was not the program for a book, but for research. Sigerist himself partly intended it that way; he was expressing his views as to how one ought to study and write history. One may disagree with him in philosophical principles, and I have indicated my own disagreement in certain respects. One may also add to, or omit, some of the details. Nevertheless, it remains a noteworthy memorandum of the methodology of medical history. But could any single work, whether written by a single individual or a group, fulfill all his demands and present a history of medicine in the sense in which Sprengel's *History,* written about 150 years ago, was such a history, a summing up and mirror of the entire past? Even eight volumes would hardly suffice to do for all periods what Sigerist wanted to do. More importantly, with the progress of the history, its basis would have become insufficient. We have not reached the point where we can satisfactorily deal with the history of a particular science within the overall scheme of medicine as a great social institution. Even the ramifications that Sigerist put under the common denominator of style are not enough. A physiologist, for instance, can demand a historical treatment of his discipline that will throw light on the problem on which he works in the laboratory. He may be awed, but will hardly be helped, by a demonstration that he is a child of his time, just as Harvey was a child of his period, the baroque.

Many of you may disagree with me. I myself am aware of treating an unfinished work as if it had been finished—which seems hardly fair. If Sigerist had lived and composed his *History,* he might have confounded all my doubts. But since this was not to be, I had to act the way I did to meet his expectation that his *History* be "a starting point for future research." What will this further research be like, and how will it compare with Sigerist's endeavor?

During his active life, Sigerist wrote much and contributed much. If we merely look at those articles and books that he completed, we find our knowledge enriched and ourselves stimulated to undertake fruitful tasks. There is no going back to the generation before him, neither to the polished charm of Osler, nor to the learned positivism of Sudhoff. Sigerist's work stands out by itself, to instruct, to stimulate, to provoke. He has spoken clearly and needs neither me nor anybody else to make him known.

What then is our task in medical historiography now? I sincerely hope that you do not expect an answer to this question, because I believe that the question itself reflects a dangerous attitude. Dangerous, because it presupposes that there is some kind of "we" to be let loose upon some "task" that has been set by some mysterious authority. There are many tasks, and Sigerist more than anybody else has made us aware of new ones. There is something for everybody to do according to individual taste and ability, provided only that it represents good scholarship, which is the only authority I would recognize because it stands for the honest wish to find what is true. Here again I think we can find contact with the Sigerist who wrote: "History must be true. True history is always fruitful while pseudo-history is destructive" (p. 33). And just as Sigerist in one person combined historian and medical man, so "we" should include both historians and physicians, regardless of whether attracted by the joy of historical investigation, intrigued by a medical problem, or impelled by the desire to do something useful for medicine and to elevate medical education. Out of this melting pot there may emerge a race of medical historians who have overcome the dichotomy of history and medicine. Until then let us find ourselves through teaching and research. For the rest, let us have many histories, and let us not pin our hopes on a single history that will be for future historians what Aristotle's *Physics* was for medieval scientists.

A distinguished British scholar quite recently wrote: "Some historians even seem to have given up the study of history, and study their fellow-historians instead, or historiography as they call it." [16] I believe I discern a note of criticism in this remark, and I would agree that an overoccupation with problems of historiography is not healthy. For this reason, I have put emphasis on good work rather than on plans, which, as you know, so often go agley. Dr. Sigerist liked an audience; he would not have minded being the object of study, even though he might have winced at some of the things I have said. But I know that he would have agreed with me that the medical historian's main virtue is to do work that his own conscience will approve.

Notes

This essay represents a paper read at the thirty-first annual meeting of the American Association for the History of Medicine, New York, May 24, 1958 and published in the *Bulletin of the History of Medicine* 32, 1958, pp. 485–99. Although more than thirty years have since passed, my views have changed so little that I have no reason to make any substantive changes.

1. By Dr. Sigerist's *History* I refer to his *A History of Medicine,* vol. 1: *Primitive and Archaic Medicine* (New York: Oxford University Press, 1951).
2. "Die 'Cirurgia Eliodori,'" *Archiv für Geschichte der Medizin* 12 (1920): 1–9.
3. The plan was expounded at length in "The Medical Literature of the Early Middle Ages. A Program—and Report of a Summer of Research in Italy," *Bulletin of the History of Medicine* 2 (1934): 26–50.
4. See above reference and *Bulletin of the History of Medicine* 2 (1934): 559–610.
5. *Bulletin of the History of Medicine* 10 (1941): 27–47; 11 (1942): 292–303; 14 (1943): 68–113.
6. Augusto Beccaria, *I Codici di Medicina del Periodo Presalernitano* (Rome: Edizioni di Storia e Letteratura, 1956), 11.
7. "Aufgaben und Ziele der Medizingeschichte," *Schweizerische Medizinische Wochenschrift* 13 (1922): 318–22.
8. "William Harvey's Stellung in der Europäischen Geistesgeschichte," *Archiv für Kulturgeschichte* 19 (1928): 158–68.
9. "Sebastian-Apollo," *Archiv für Geschichte der Medizin* 19 (1927): 301–17.
10. "Kultur und Krankheit," *Kyklos* 1 (1928): 60–63.
11. The original German edition of *Grosse Ärzte* appeared in 1932, i.e., one year after the *Einführung in die Medizin.*

12. However, this did not necessarily prevent a one-sided historical orientation in research as pointed out above.

13. George Rosen, "Levels of Integration in Medical Historiography: a Review," *Journal of the History of Medicine and Allied Sciences* 4 (1949): 460–67.

14. See G. P. Gooch, *History and Historians in the Nineteenth Century* (London: Longmans, Green, and Co., 1913), passim.

15. *History,* foreword, xviii.

16. W. K. C. Guthrie, *In the Beginning* (Ithaca, N.Y.: Cornell University Press, ·1957), 12.

CHAPTER 7

"Hard Realism" and "A Few Romantic Moves": Henry Sigerist's Versions of Ancient Greece

Heinrich von Staden

> After a life of hard realism one must be
> allowed a few romantic moves.
> *Henry E. Sigerist*

For all his preoccupation with revolutionizing twentieth-century medicine, Henry Sigerist from his earliest writings to his latest made ancient Greece a central point of historical, ideological, and autobiographical reference. His versions of ancient Greece are marked by complex dynamics, by tensions between divergent emphases, and by both substantive constants over decades and substantial change over time. Four conspicuous features of these complex, rich relations seem particularly noteworthy: (1) the central place of ancient Greece in Sigerist's understanding of modern "genealogy" (collective and individual), (2) his advocacy of contextual history, (3) his accommodation of the agonal heterogeneity characteristic of Greek culture, and (4) his programmatic deployment of comparative cultural perspectives in the interpretation of ancient Greek medicine.

Ancient Greece as Genealogy

Despite his comparative studies of medical cultures (ancient and modern), despite his aspiration to reform modern consciousness and modern practice, and despite his oft-stated commitment to eschew a Eurocentric historiographic bias, Sigerist to the end passionately reiterated historico-genealogical themes that resonate with neoclassical and romantic phil-hellenism. The Greeks, he explains to an American audience in 1937, are "our medical ancestors;"[1] the Mediterranean, he writes in 1951, is "our great mother who gave birth to our entire Western civilization;"[2] Attica, he observes late in life in his unfinished autobiography (ca. 1954), is "the mother of us all,"[3] indeed, "the civilizations of Greece and Rome [are] the foundations of our Western world."[4] And in the posthumously pub-lished second volume of *A History of Medicine* he reaffirms that "the Greek method paved the way for modern Western science" and "Greek science and medicine . . . laid the solid foundations upon which our mod-ern systems of medicine and science are erected."[5] Such "genealogical" invocations of Greece are repeated many times. Sigerist, many of whose writings originated in the oral context of public lectures, did not hesitate to repeat the same themes, sentences, and paragraphs in different works, and the result is a thick texture of allusion to the ancient Greek lineage of much of modern culture throughout his oeuvre.

Constructions of collective cultural or professional genealogy—of "mothers," "ancestors," "pavers of the way," "foundations," and "influence"—usually are, of course, not free of ideological valorizations, and Sigerist's versions are no exception. As in eighteenth- and nineteenth-century philhellenism,[6] Sigerist's genealogical reconstructions tend to go hand in hand with the theme of loss, notably of a loss of all that was good in ancient Greece. As in German romanticism in particular, so too in Sigerist's versions of Greece there are therefore strong recuperative and nostalgic strains, perhaps most conspicuously in the earlier decades of his scholarly work. In *Antike Heilkunde* (Ancient Medicine) (1927), for ex-ample, Sigerist argues that ancient Greece has given us "immortal ideals which unfold their power over millennia" and which, being immortal, still retain their validity and authority for us.[7] Moreover, despite mod-ern advances in the understanding of pathogens and in anatomy, physics, and chemistry, in practice "we nevertheless have not become better physi-cians."[8] A return to the Greek past therefore is a moral and pragmatic imperative: "the great ideals of the [Greek] past should help us find the right way again."[9] This "right way" includes, centrally, a restorative re-discovery of nothing other than the very goal of medicine itself:

The ancient Greeks also gave us the ideal of the healthy person, of the person who, being in balance physically and mentally, is beautiful and noble. With this ideal, medicine has been given its highest goal. And especially now that

33. Sigerist working at his Institute desk.

we are beginning to wake up from the previous century's intoxication with the natural sciences, now that the ground that seemed so firm is beginning to wobble, now that we have become uncertain and are looking for a pillar, let us cling more closely than ever to these [Greek] ideals.[10]

The "father of the social history of medicine," the fervid proponent of socialized medicine (which, one might add, was not the norm in classical Greece[11]), the partisan of social progress, here is advocating salvation from the malaise of twentieth-century medicine by means of a recuperative reanimation of a lost Greek past, notably of an aestheticomoral version of ideal bodily existence. The ancient Greeks, Sigerist argues, recognized that the way to beauty passes through physical as well as mental health, which in turn depends on perfect harmony and balance effected by exercise and moderation. In a variety of modulations, this theme recurs especially in Sigerist's works of the 1930s and 1940s, and it reflects the aesthetic historicism of much of nineteenth-century German and Swiss historiography.[12]

Furthermore, Sigerist defines not only the bodily ideal that modern physicians should strive to realize in their patients but also the ideal twentieth-century "political" physician in ancient Greek terms. In the final section of *Einführung in die Medizin* (Man and Medicine) (1931), for example, Sigerist argues that "if ever, then certainly today the physician may become a statesman, the *Asklepios politikos* (political Asclepius) envisioned by Plato."[13] Classical antiquity, moreover, provides modern medicine with an epistemological model. In discussing three of his own incurable conditions in the *Atlantic Monthly* ("Living under the Shadow," 1952), Sigerist traces his epistemological valuation of medicine to a Hellenistic tradition of stochasticism also adopted by some Romans: "Of course we must keep in mind that in medicine there is no truth with a capital T, that medicine is what Celsus aptly called it, an *ars coniecturalis* (conjectural art)."[14]

The loss sensed by Sigerist, like the loss felt by many nineteenth- and early twentieth-century philhellenists, is, however, not only the loss of the distant Greek past but also of a more recent European past; his nostalgia is not only for classical Athens or for Hippocratics of the fifth and fourth centuries B.C.E. but also for a time within reach of personal memory. Sigerist, who paradoxically wrote eloquently on *Heimweh* (homesickness) as a culture-bound disease,[15] comparable to tarantism, displays no small amount of nostalgia for a time when the study of Greek and Latin still flourished. He vigorously defends the traditional *humanistisches*

Gymnasium (humanistic gymnasium) with its strong curricular focus on Greco-Roman antiquity, and he deplores the recent decline of Greek and Latin in secondary education. In the second chapter of his unfinished autobiography, for example, he comments nostalgically on a very recent cultural past that still enjoyed the social, political, and human benefits of what nowadays might be called "the canon":

> In the nineteenth century and at the beginning of our century many people in Europe and America had this same type of classical education. This created a common ground on which people met and understood one another. When I made a study of the beginnings of social insurance in Germany in the eighteen eighties, I had to read volumes of minutes of the meetings of the German Reichstag and was amazed to see on what a high level the discussions were carried on. Conservatives, liberals, and socialists argued while quoting Plato and Aristotle. At international diplomatic conferences the participants were always courteous because they all had a common educational background. Today they have nothing in common. They insult one another, their manners are bad, their speech vulgar . . . and the result is poor politics.[16]

Here the latent tension between Sigerist's avid advocacy of a multicultural, non-Eurocentric approach to history (see below), and his passionately positive valorization of our collective Greek heritage is not far below the surface.

At issue in Sigerist's numerous references to Greece is, however, not only collective genealogy and loss—i.e., not only Attica as "the [lost] mother of us all"—but also an individual lineage, a personal intellectual and professional pedigree: Sigerist's own. "The classical education my old Gymnasium gave me," he writes in later life in the autobiographical fragment, "became the foundation upon which I built my whole life, and the Greek and Roman classics remained a constant source of inspiration and happiness. Even today I hardly ever travel without having the poems of Horace in my pocket."[17] Elsewhere it is the Homeric *Odyssey* that is thus privileged ("I never travel in the Mediterranean without having my old school edition of the *Odyssey* with me"[18]), but of significance here is Sigerist's characterization of his training in Greek and Latin as an enduring foundation and inspiration.

Autobiography is a notoriously suspect genre of historiography, but Sigerist's tendency to grant a position of centrality to ancient Greece within his own genealogical self-understanding should not be taken lightly. By all accounts blessed with an extraordinary gift for languages, Sigerist never tired of stressing his command of the classical languages and their effect on his personal and professional life. In the somewhat in-congruous context of Johannesburg, South Africa, 1939, after more than two months of witnessing the misery entailed by inadequate health care for the disenfranchised majority of the South African population, Sigerist in a public address vividly recalls his teenage years at a Swiss classical Gymnasium (the *Zürcher kantonales Gymnasium*), pointedly praising his own training in Greek and Latin.[19] As a schoolboy, he later recalls, he was so thoroughly captivated by Greek that he took his Greek grammar along on summer holidays,[20] and "every day I got up an hour earlier than nec-essary to review my Greek and to read books on the subjects we studied, and this was very early because in the summer classes began at seven in the morning."[21]

Such passages do not merely represent nostalgic autobiographical reconstructions. Rather, they are crucial to his professional self-understanding.[22] In fact, Sigerist actively planned in 1933 to write and publish a new Latin grammar, between his books on American and Soviet medicine.[23] Furthermore, long after he had articulated his commitment to social history, and well after he had become a protagonist in the poli-tics of social progress, Sigerist continued to allude to the supreme joy he derived from working on Greek and Latin texts. In his first diary entry of 1943, for example, Sigerist writes: "There is nothing I like more than philological work and it is my bad luck that I have not more time for it."[24] Sigerist may never have returned to pure philology, but his return to "mother Greece" never ceased, and the last years of his life were largely devoted to writing about ancient Greece.

Sigerist's Greece was, however, far more than a collective and indi-vidual ancestor whose "great ideals" we, to our detriment, have lost and ignorance of whom has resulted in modern cultural fragmentation, in social vulgarity, and in poor politics. His genealogical consciousness also manifests itself in his lively, omnipresent vision of Greece as a world full of brilliant specific achievements, both theoretical and practical—a vision often conveyed by value terms in the superlative form. In the realm of the observation and comprehension of symptoms, for example, Greek medi-cine represents the "highest achievement."[25] The Greeks followed the way that is methodologically "most correct" when they described case histo-ries, recording "without any bias whatsoever" the course of diseases and the subsidiary antecedent and concomitant circumstances, and they did this "in exemplary manner."[26] The Greeks' attentiveness not only to all symptoms but to all external and environmental factors was "something incredibly innovative," and the ancients thereby succeeded in composing a large number of "classic disease descriptions," among which that of consumption is "masterful."[27] Aretaeus's account of diphtheria is not merely "excellent" but "in today's medical literature one would have to search far and wide to find such a vivid description."[28] The Hippocratic *Prognostic* is "one of the most valuable books of the world's medical literature of all times."[29] With reference to the Greeks' operations for tumors (and particularly to the use of radical mastectomy by a Greek surgeon, Leonides, to treat breast cancer), Sigerist observes: "The principles we are following today, namely the elimination of the tumor as radically as possible, were discovered in far remote antiquity. . . . We have not found any new principle yet."[30] Similarly, "when we speak of the foundation of human anatomy, we immediately remember the names of two great Greek physicians—Herophilus and Erasistratus."[31] In etiology the Hippocratic *Airs, Waters, Places* "achieved everything that could possibly be achieved without modern aids."[32]

None of these judgments is revolutionary; they reflect the mainstream of nineteenth- and early twentieth-century scholarship, even if many of Sigerist's contemporaries eschewed his exuberant superlatives (and though many a current historian might find his generalizations impressionistic, overstated, and in need of qualification or of more nuanced differentiation, even when they seem partly valid). Also where Greeks went wrong, as in their humoral theories, Sigerist is unstinting in his use of positive terms: "The humoral theory was the result of many brilliant and correct observations. It was logical, explained many phenomena of health and disease, and gave valuable guidance to the medical practitioner."[33]

In Sigerist's view, the noble Greeks more often than not also were right and hence efficacious in realms such as regimen and hygiene. Here, too, his claims—again teeming with superlative value terms—are in need of qualification or complication. Greek dietetics, he claims, was "a most efficacious treatment,"[34] and "diets devised by Hippocratic physicians for the sick are still used today in basically the same composition . . . and throughout the centuries patients were benefited by them."[35] Current historians are more likely to accept his judgments that it was the Greeks who invented a large number of operations that have become "classic" and still are performed,[36] and that Hippocrates "made the greatest discovery that medicine could ever make: . . . that nature heals."[37] Likely to give pause, by contrast, is his claim that the Greeks brought personal hygiene to its "highest perfection" and that Greece hence is "a world of the healthy and sound."[38] Through their attitude to the human body, Sigerist argues, "the Greeks . . . created a system of hygiene which set an example for all time. . . . Health appeared as the highest good. . . . The ideal man is healthy and beautiful. The aesthetic ideal was at the same time a hygienic ideal. Greek education tended to develop man into a harmonious being."[39]

For this multitude of particular achievements too, but above all because of the great Greek aesthetic, moral, and hygienic ideal of the healthy-beautiful-noble-harmonious-balanced person,[40] today as "science is about to suffocate the art of medicine, we look back, searching for help . . . back to Hippocrates. . . . The wheel of history cannot and should not be turned back, but the great ideals of the past should help us to find the right way again."[41]

Sigerist does not offer references to ancient texts to substantiate his historically problematic, oft reiterated characterization of these "great ideals" of the Greeks that are to serve as a lodestar for modern medicine. Nor does he cite any ancient Greek text that describes the closely related Greek "ideal person" who is to serve as the aesthetic-hygienic goal of twentieth century medicine, and who in ancient Greece supposedly was a fundamental feature of the Greek *Lebensanschauung* (outlook on life).[42] It is not unlikely that Sigerist held these problematic generalizations to be so self-evident or so universally shared by his readers that he saw no need to substantiate them, not even in works that, unlike *Antike Heilkunde* (1927), *Einführung in die Medizin* (1931), and *Grosse Ärzte* (Great Doctors) (1932), offer some indication of his ancient and modern sources (e.g., *Civilization and Disease*, 1943). He probably had encountered these general ideas in his fondly, vividly remembered classical training in Zurich, in German philosophy, in romanticism, and notably in cultural historians such as the most influential Swiss historian of the nineteenth century, Jacob Burckhardt (on whom see below). Indeed, in their reception of Greek antiquity, other revolutionary "fathers of modernity" and reformers of consciousness, such as Karl Marx, Friedrich Nietzsche, and Sigmund Freud, likewise did not succeed in escaping the residual pressures of romantic philhellenism.[43]

Strong though the hold of such valorizations of Greek antiquity was on Sigerist throughout his life, he was too discerning a scholar to remain unaware for long of some less than noble-beautiful-healthy-harmonious aspects of his beloved Greece, and this too generates tensions within his version of ancient Greece. This awareness surfaces relatively early, but it becomes more conspicuous in later works, as his goal of doing contextual history becomes more of a reality. In *Einführung in die Medizin* he already juxtaposes the Greek ideal of the noble and beautiful healthy person with the social reality of being ill in classical antiquity. In ancient Greece, disease renders one inferior. The ill person, the cripple, the weakling are inferior persons and can count on consideration on the part of society only to the extent that their condition is capable of improvement. Most expedient is to destroy a weak human being. Antiquity did not know an organized care of cripples. To count as a full and equal human being, the ill had to become healthy again. . . . Thus the ill person in Greek society also found himself burdened with an odium, not that of sin but of inferiority.[44]

Sigerist's explicit awareness of darker sides of Greek culture is further attested by his recognition in 1931 that the "highly refined personal hygiene" developed by the Greeks "was not general. It affected only the upper social strata. The great mass of the common people, the slaves, farmers, and laborers, had no part in it."[45] Similarly, in 1936 he observes:

We admire the graceful Greek bronze statuettes that fill our museums, but we do not think of the copper miners providing material for these works of art, or the coal miners digging for coal to make the bronze, working ten hours in narrow galleries suffocated by heat and smoke. They were prisoners of war or convicts as a rule. The ancient physicians, keen observers as they were, noticed the influence of certain occupations on the worker's health. . . . A case of lead poisoning was correctly described by Hippocrates. . . . But nothing was done to protect the workers.[46]

In his Messenger lectures of 1940, published as *Civilization and Disease,* Sigerist repeats these words, and in his unfinished final work he offers a vivid description of the harsh conditions under which slaves worked in the Athenians' silver mines at Laurium (although, with reference to slaves outside the mines, he insists that "the Athenians were humane to slaves").[47]

Even as Sigerist's positive valorization of Greek antiquity continues to be given frequent expression, it therefore is on a tacit collision course with his increasing attentiveness to the historical contexts of Greek medicine—contexts that include social and other realities that in part undermine the claims of romantic philhellenism.

Contextualizing Greek History

Sigerist was a contextual historian of Greek medicine in a richer, more complex sense than most of his precursors or successors. Not only was he attentive to the relevance of divergent changing social environments, of economic formations, and of political structures for the history of ancient

Greek medicine; in addition, the generous reach of his erudition and of his intellect allowed him to draw on European classical scholarship of the nineteenth and early twentieth centuries to accommodate among his contextual strands the physical geography of ancient Greece; Indo-European linguistics; the history of Greek dialects; the development of literacy and of literary genres in early Greece; Greek religion, philosophy, and art; the development of early Greek mathematics; and many other features of Greek cultural history.[48]

A *History of Medicine* might be his most mature, extensive, and sophisticated exercise in contextual history, but Sigerist's fundamental commitment to such an approach already manifests itself in his earlier years. In fact, it probably can be traced to a powerful encounter during his secondary education. Of none of his teachers does he speak as warmly as of Otto Markwart (1861–1919), a pupil of the famous Swiss art historian and historian of Greek and Renaissance culture Jacob Burckhardt (1818–97). Markwart, who himself published on history and on art history, revered his great teacher and wrote a well-known biography of Burckhardt.[49] Significantly, as a teacher of history at Sigerist's secondary school, Otto Markwart became an ersatz-Burckhardt to his young pupils, as Sigerist fondly and graphically recalls in an early chapter of his unfinished autobiography:

> he [Markwart] had been a student of Jakob Burckhardt, that great humanist, and the spirit of the master was alive in the disciple who was able to convey to us some of its sparks. . . . He also saw to it that our classroom had good large photographs of classical sites on the wall, so that the Forum Romanum and the [Greek] temples of Paestum were as familiar to us as the monuments of Zurich. His teaching was inspiring. . . . From Markwart I learned that history is not a dead subject but a living force that determines our life. He taught us to think in terms of historic forces and developments. In his broad approach to history that embraced all aspects of civilization he passed on to us boys the teachings of his master, Jakob Burckhardt, whose works we devoured.[50]

Jacob Burckhardt's famous *Griechische Kulturgeschichte* (The Cultural History of Greece), published from his manuscript legacy in several volumes (1898–1902) shortly after his death, was in all probability among these "devoured works," and it would have reinforced the young Sigerist's interest in contextual history. Although Burckhardt was much more interested than Sigerist in Greek myth, cult, and religion and was much less sympathetic to Greek—or any—democracy, his "cultural history" included extensive discussions of the historical development of the *polis* (city-state), subject populations, slavery, economic and class differences, constitutional developments (also outside Athens), heterogeneous forms of government, characteristics of urban and rural populations, popular values, politicians, internecine Greek warfare, the Greeks' views of "barbarians," their attitudes to women, their *Naturgefühl* (feeling for nature), and so on. These and other features in turn served as a basis for Burckhardt's discussions of Greek science, medicine, sculpture, painting, architecture, poetry, music, philosophy, oratory, historiography, and ethnography, and, finally, for his lengthy account of *der hellenische Mensch in seiner zeitlichen Entwicklung* (the Hellenic human being in chronological development), which includes an account of "Hellenic health" and "beauty" that resonates with Sigerist's views on the "healthy Greeks" and their aesthetic-hygienic bodily ideals.[51]

This then is the approach transmitted to Sigerist and his fellow-pupils by the inspired teaching of Otto Markwart. Shortly after Markwart's death in 1919, Hermann Scher characterized the close affinity between Markwart and Burckhardt as including the following elements: a profound concern with, and grasp of, the real problems of human beings in history; the integration of political history into general cultural history; impregnating the subject matter with a strong dosage of personal convictions; the absence of any nationalistically conditioned sensibility; a reticence in religious matters; a frequent expression of pessimism, particularly concerning present conditions; a love of the visual arts; and a lack of pedantry and regimentation in teaching.[52] Add to this the deep love of France, of Italy, and of ancient Greece shared by Burckhardt and Markwart, and it becomes evident that Markwart endorsed, taught, and—in the classroom too—lived Jacob Burckhardt's approach to history. The impact of this animated, multidimensional approach to history on the young Sigerist endured to the end of his days, as Sigerist's own words attest.

Throughout his professional life, Sigerist seems to have selectively transposed this strong heritage of Jacob Burckhardt and Otto Markwart into the history of Greek medicine. Late in life Sigerist still praises the method of Burckhardt and Markwart as a "broad approach to history that embraced all aspects of civilization,"[53] and in a lecture given in London in 1953, he still sounds Burckhardtian tones, with specific reference to ancient Greece: "If we wish to understand correctly a new scientific development, we must study it within the framework of the general civilization of the period, studying that civilization in all its aspects, economic, social, literary, artistic, etc."[54]

In much of Sigerist's scholarly production, early and late, this fundamental legacy is visible: for example, in his active integration of political history into his version of ancient Greek medicine, in the deeply personal moral sensibility that he often brings to bear on the history of Greek medicine, in his anationalistic approach, in his easy, habitual identification of paradigms for the future within a distant past, and in his active accommodation of the visual arts in medical history.[55] As Sigerist himself acknowledged in 1939, "the old Gymnasium in Zurich was a great school to which I owe infinitely more than I was aware at the time."[56] Perhaps more than he ever realized.

However, influence and resistance, like reception and revision, often go hand in hand. This was true of Burckhardt himself who, though powerfully influenced by romantic philhellenism, more than once expresses his moral outrage at the Greeks, for example, for killing fellow Greeks and for developing democracy.[57] And it is true of Sigerist who, while transformatively transposing the Burckhardt-Markwart heritage of multidimensional contextual history into medical history, increasingly liberates this heritage from many a tether of romanticism—from a *Sehnsucht* (nostalgic yearning) rich in affective expressiveness, from a deep distrust of the present, from a fear of the future, from a concomitant *Flucht in die Vergangenheit* (escape into the past), from looking for a *wahre Heimat* (true home) only in another time and place, and from a wistful preoccupation with a personal "mythopoetic youth" that recapitulated the myth-filled "youth" of Greek culture. Yet residual traces of such elements remain visible even later in his life: in 1950, Sigerist describes himself as still torn between "ideals of my youth of a life in beauty, and my career as a fighter for social progress."[58]

Some of Sigerist's contextual interests, notably in the geographic determinants of Greek medicine, might reach back beyond his momentous adolescent encounter with Otto Markwart to his three years (1901–4, i.e., from the age of ten to thirteen) in a progressive private school with "a very international student body" in Zurich.[59] The school was run by an atheist, socialist, and botanist, Dr. Fritz von Beust. Von Beust had his young charges construct complicated relief maps of various ruggedly mountainous regions of Switzerland,[60] and he used field excursions to teach them the importance of personal observation of geography for understanding botany.[61] Sigerist later made geographic features of Greece similar to those of Switzerland—mountains and valleys that separate regions and communities from one another—a crucial feature of his interpretation of the development of ancient Greek political structures and of the heterogeneous traditions that characterize ancient Greek culture (see below).[62] He likewise made geography a centerpiece of his comparison of Greek and Indian medicine. In his late forties and again in his early sixties, Sigerist admiringly recalls von Beust as "an educator of genius," who "opened up for me the realm of nature."[63] A good forty years after these experiences, when recalling his first visit (1931) to Greece, Sigerist still stresses the importance of a personal observation of physical geography for the practice of a contextual history of medicine, "I have a visual mind, I like to see things. The moment I see a landscape I understand what happened in it. . . . One understands Greek individualism and particularism seeing the small valleys, the rivers and brooks, dry in the summer, torrents in the spring draining the water into lovely creeks."[64]

"Social history" often is associated with Sigerist's later works, but he himself stresses that in his early years in Zurich, when reading the proofs of Karl Sudhoff's *Kurzes Handbuch der Geschichte der Medizin* (Short Handbook of the History of Medicine) (1922), he "had missed the sociological approach" and had asked himself, "Who benefitted from the great medical discoveries? All population strata or only the wealthy?"[65] Such personal recollections suggest that at least in Sigerist's retrospective self-understanding, "social history" had already explicitly animated his historiographic consciousness in the early 1920s. This self-understanding would seem to be verifiable in part in Sigerist's work, at least from *Einführung in die Medizin* (1931) on. Here Sigerist not only emphasizes the philosophical contexts and contents of medicine but also the importance of bringing sociological, environmental, psychological, and anthropological perspectives to bear upon medicine. "The physician," he argues, "always has to do with the whole human being, with the totality of conditions of life," and only through a "philosophical" investigation ("philosophical" here seems to include all aspects enumerated) can one obtain a picture of human beings in this "totality"—as recognized, says Sigerist, by a Hippocratic who said, "the physician who is a philosopher is equal to the gods."[66]

In *Einführung*, Sigerist is already attentive to the social and economic status of the Greek physician, to his work spaces and travels, to his relations to patients, to the role of medical associations in antiquity, and to the relevance of the Greek doctor's insecure place within the social order for understanding the distinctively Greek preoccupation with prognosis.[67] Similarly, in 1931 he explains the difference between the Greek emphasis on personal hygiene and the Roman emphasis on public hygiene in sociopolitical terms.[68]

In 1937 Sigerist gives further explicit expression to this feature of his self-understanding—i.e., continuity of methodological commitment—by emphasizing the continuity between his early work on ancient or medieval medicine and his later work on Soviet medicine:

> All my life has been devoted to the study of developments in the medical field and I have approached the problems of Soviet medicine as a historian from the perspective of history, studying and analyzing it as a historical phenomenon, in the same way as I approached the problems of ancient and medieval medical history before.[69]

Similarly, in 1943, seven years after perhaps first recording his intention of writing a *Sociology of Medicine* that "will establish a new medical field" and a *History of Medicine* that "will be quite different from all existing books" by virtue of giving "a picture of medicine as one aspect of civilization, as a social institution,"[70] Sigerist writes: "For thirty years I have been preparing two books—a History and Sociology of Medicine," again implying continuity of purpose, vision, and method ever since his days at the University of Zurich.[71]

Continuity between his early and late work can readily be substantiated in the case of two contextual strands emphasized in Sigerist's accounts of ancient Greece, namely, the philosophical and religious ambience in which Greek medicine developed its distinctive traits. As early as *Antike Heilkunde* (1927) he emphasizes the importance of cosmology for Greek humoral theories and of Greek intellectual culture for medical theory generally.[72] In *Einführung in die Medizin* he argues that "Hippocratic medicine arises out of Presocratic philosophy," a view repeated in *Grosse Ärzte* (1932) and *Civilization and Disease* (1943) and developed at great length in *A History of Medicine*.[73] Similarly, in *Einführung in die Medizin* he already argues that Greek theories and practices of hygiene have religious roots.[74] He draws attention in particular to the special religious status of the parturient, who is regarded as impure and hence as a source of pollution, and who therefore is excluded from religious sanctuaries and from civic-religious activities for a specified period, which in turn affords her time for convalescence. *Civilization and Disease* (1943) contains a chapter "Disease and Religion," much of it devoted to Greek religion (notably to religious conceptions and treatments of disease), and in *A History of Medicine* a lengthy chapter is devoted to religious medicine in ancient Greece.[75]

Notably, in *Civilization and Disease* (1943) and in *A History of Medicine* Sigerist introduces further social and cultural factors into his contextual study of medicine in classical antiquity. These include ancient clothing, architecture, housing, city planning, lighting, eating habits, sewage treatment, and water supplies. Economic factors, occupational hazards in Greece, ancient laws pertaining to diseases, the consequences of the Greek slave economy both for disease and for science and technology are likewise within Sigerist's purview. While he does not repeat his early view that medical theory is culture bound whereas medical technology is not (the latter being more easily transportable from one culture to another), he nevertheless continues to stress the relation of Greek medical practice to the technology of its time.[76]

Sigerist is also attentive to cultural context as a factor that inhibits the doing of science in antiquity. In *Einführung* and elsewhere he argues, for example, that Erasistratus' introduction of anatomical pathology, like Aristarchus' heliocentric model of the universe, did not find acceptance among the ancient Greeks because "certain forms of thought are not possible in certain cultures," and "if they do surface, they meet with no response."[77] Above all, he increasingly underscores the complexity of the phenomenon called "civilization"—"it has both material and spiritual aspects"[78]—and the need to accommodate this complexity on the horizon of the contextual understanding one brings to bear upon ancient Greek medicine.

Approaches displaying kinship with Sigerist's broad contextual history of ancient medicine again are at the forefront of scholarship today and so are two of his further emphases: the pluralism of Greek medical traditions and the value of comparative cultural studies.

Pluralism and Rivalry in Greek Medicine

What I have labeled the "agonal heterogeneity" both of Greek culture in general and of Greek medicine in particular,[79] is often, though not consistently, recognized by Sigerist. Like Jacob Burckhardt and others, Sigerist at times rightly stresses that there is no such thing as "*the* Greek view" on any given issue nor "*the* (universal) Greek practice" in any matter. Greek geography, Sigerist argues (as have many historians), fostered the development of small warring city-states, which in turn favored the formation of a rich variety of political, social, and economic arrangements. In Greek medicine too, there is no central authority and hence no "codification" of theory or practice. Rather, there are many divergent theories, also within individual medical "schools," and these frequently enter into rivalry with one another. As has often been pointed out, the *agon* (contest and contestation) within Greek medicine and science has counterparts in numerous Greek political, oratorical, philosophical, religious, legal, athletic, poetic, and other competitions, contests, and rivalries. Jacob Burckhardt also stresses this feature in his extended discussions of *der agonale Mensch* (the agonistic human being) and of *das Agonale als Triebkraft* (the agonistic as a driving force) in Greek culture.[80]

Sigerist actively deploys these perspectives in his accounts of ancient Greece. In *A History of Medicine*, for example, elaborating upon a theme already present in his earlier works, he stresses the political and social differences between Dorians, Ionians, and other Greeks. In 1941, for example, he had observed:

> In ancient Greece the social position of women varied a great deal according to tribes. Among the Dorians of Sparta, girls took an active part in the physical exercises of boys. They were trained to be mothers of soldiers. Conditions were different among the Ionians, where the girl grew up in the house, was veiled in the streets, and was married by her parents.[81]

Despite many a lapse, notably in *Antike Heilkunde* (1927)—which announces as its agenda a depiction of the single unchanging "essential nature *(Wesen)* and achievement" of Greek medicine, rather than its "development" *(Entwicklung)* over a thousand years[82]—Sigerist displays increasing awareness that there is not one single Greek medical tradition (nor a single "rationalist" tradition), let alone a single Greek theory of the humors or a uniform Greek treatment for disease x or for disorder y, but a plurality of all of these. In his article "On Hippocrates" (1934), but particularly in *A History of Medicine* he already recognizes, for example, that the Hippocratic works are "as different as possible [from one another] in character and content."[83]

A recognition of the rich pluralism accommodated and fostered by Greek culture also extends to Sigerist's discussions of "religious medicine." Not only does Sigerist correctly portray the therapeutic practices of Greek cults as actively coexisting with Greek "scientific" medicine until late antiquity, but he also recognizes the pluralism within Greek religious medicine itself. This allows him to steer clear of the common but misleading tendency to discuss Greek religious healing practices only in terms of the cult of Asclepius. Instead, he offers a differentiating though brief account of more than two dozen Greek healing divinities.[84]

Certain features of Sigerist's version of the pluralism of Greek medicine have become controversial in recent years, and others inevitably have become outdated. The traditional distinction between rival Coan and Cnidian school traditions within the Hippocratic Corpus, for example, is accepted by Sigerist but has been sharply challenged in recent years (although practically all experts would still agree with Sigerist that treatises in the Corpus were written by different authors with divergent theoretical commitments, in different places and, to some degree, at different times). On the whole, however, recent scholarship has strongly reaffirmed that a profoundly agonal heterogeneity is a fundamental feature of ancient Greek medicine and indeed of most of Greek culture.

Comparative Cultural Studies

In addition to stressing the dynamic pluralism internal to Greek medicine, Sigerist introduces comparative sociocultural perspectives. This approach, while not original with Sigerist, anticipated the current questioning of Eurocentrism, and particularly of Eurocentric presentism, in the interpretation of ancient cultures. It is most prominent in the unfinished second volume of *A History of Medicine,* where Greek, Hindu, and Persian medicine are juxtaposed. In particular, Sigerist finds "the parallelism in the development of Greek and Indian medicine . . . striking, both in chronology and in content." [85] Ancient Persia, by contrast, "did not in any way contribute to the advancement of medicine," because its "medicine . . . remained primitive" [86] (i.e., it was, according to Sigerist's oft repeated definition of "primitive" medicine, "a blend of religious, magical, and empirically grounded rational views and practices" [87]). He is aware of the comparative opportunities offered by Greek and Chinese medicine too, but China is relegated to a later volume (which death prevented Sigerist from writing).[88] The main agenda of the posthumous second volume accordingly is "to study the development of Greek and Indian medicine in the West and East within the framework of the general culture of Greece and India." [89] Sigerist aspires thereby to offer a corrective to the "utterly naïve and viciously wrong" approach to history that is inclined to "consult the history of medicine . . . from our present Western point of view, going backward, looking for precursors and ancestors." [90] Both Eurocentrism and presentism therefore are simultaneously at issue. The right course is to "study ancient medicine in the various countries as if it never had any successors, and if we do this, we soon find that Western and Indian medicine were closely related and equally effective not only in antiquity but also in the Middle Ages." [91]

Sigerist's interest in India, also in the context of comparative historical studies, dates back at least to his first year at university as a student of oriental philology.[92] Whether the influence of Jacob Burckhardt, who draws freely on oriental material in his discussions of Greek culture and notably in his accounts of Greek science and philosophy, was at play here too is unclear.[93] But it is evident that not only Greece but also India, and not only a multidimensional approach to Greek history but also a comparative cultural perspective are prominent in Sigerist's autobiographical reconstructions of his youth.

There is considerable discrepancy between design and execution—between Sigerist's programmatic formulations of the enormous comparative task he set himself and its incomplete performance. The bulk of *A History of Medicine,* II, consists of the two framing sections devoted to ancient Greece: "I. Archaic Medicine in Greece" (pp. 10-117) and "IV. The Golden Age of Greek Medicine" (pp. 211-335). In these lengthy sections there is scant reference to India or Persia,[94] let alone any sustained comparative analysis of sameness and difference. As a consequence, the sections on Greece are mostly a broadly based contextual account of the archaic and classical periods of Greek culture, with particular emphasis on Greek medicine; here the comparative crystallization of the "striking parallelism in the development of Greek and Indian medicine" promised at the outset[95] is never realized.

By contrast, Sigerist refers fairly often to Greece in the two shorter middle sections on non-Greek cultures ("II. Hindu Medicine," pp. 119-93, and "III. Medicine in Ancient Persia," pp. 195-209). In part this is because of the structure of the work, in part perhaps because, as he himself concedes, "Greek medicine . . . is closer to a Western historian whose education was in the Greek humanistic tradition,"[96] and Greece therefore is a constant point of orientation when he is writing on India and Persia. Even in these sections, however, there is no sustained effort at a comparative analysis and little reflection on the daunting methodological problems posed by comparative cultural studies. It nevertheless is Sigerist's great merit not only to have advocated a comparative approach to the history of medicine and, at least since the 1920s, to have stressed the importance of intercultural exchange in antiquity,[97] but also to have tried to implement such an approach on a large scale in this late work.

The spectrum of Sigerist's specific comparative references—most of them regrettably introduced only in passing—offers a hint of the rich potential that lurks in his approach; had he lived to complete the *History,* more of this potential might have been actualized. A strikingly consistent feature of these references is, however, that they tend to stress differences between ancient India and ancient Greece, rather than the "parallel development" envisioned by Sigerist in 1949.[98] Whether his comparisons concern geography, politics, "mentality," material and spiritual values, philosophy, religion, or magic, the dominant theme is "difference." Thus the Indian subcontinent is "in every respect different from the Balkan peninsula. . . . Greece . . . is small, and has a great variety of landscapes with its mountains, valleys, creeks, and highly indented shoreline. Here man dominates the landscape. India, on the other hand, is a large country . . . in which man feels very small."[99]

Geography in turn has political consequences: to "small Greece" the aggressive expansive policy of the Persians was a question of life and death, and "not until the Persian peril had been averted could Greek culture develop freely and produce its most beautiful creations," whereas India was "a large country that could develop its culture even while some border regions were occupied by a foreign power."[100] Furthermore, "the Indians never became a seafaring nation like the Greeks" and "the Indians never possessed the aggressive spirit of the Greeks, who were frequently forced by economic pressure to settle abroad. . . . India never felt the urge to subjugate her neighbors."[101]

Sigerist also emphasizes religious differences as well as dissimilarities in cultural "valuations of material goods"; in this respect, he claims, "there could be no greater difference than that between the ancient Greeks and the Indians."[102] He argues that the Greeks "as a whole" cherished the good life on this earth, regarding health and wealth as desirable goods, whereas the Indians believed that the quest for material goods was vain and that real freedom was the freedom that the spirit achieved from passions and from things material.[103] "As a whole" is a qualifier perhaps prompted by his awareness of similarities between the Buddhist theory of the transmigration of immortal souls and its Pythagorean, Orphic, and Platonic counterparts. But here Sigerist does not make this important point explicit.

He further argues that the Indian belief in reincarnation is responsible for their "lack of historical sense" and for the "un-Greek" blending of fact and fiction in Indian historiography: "There is no Indian Thucydides, Tacitus, or Sze Ma-chien. Why write history when the past is still alive, when the heroes of a bygone age are still with us?"[104] In philosophy, too, Sigerist sees mainly difference: "The ways of Indian philosophy were different from those of Greece, and . . . medicine always reflects the philosophy of its time."[105] Characteristic of most of these comparative judgments is that they offer little more than generalizations that, at least in the case of Greece, often are in need of complication and substantiation.

Physical, social, and cultural differences between Greece and India, then, dominate Sigerist's comparative references. Occasionally, however, he introduces historical, religious, philosophical, and therapeutic similarities, such as the Greeks' assimilation of Cretan culture after their conquest of Crete, and the Indo-Iranians' assimilation of an earlier civilization when they conquered the Indus Valley,[106] the cross-cultural ancient custom of tracing the origin of medicine to a divinity, and, of course, the Greek and Indian beliefs in metempsychosis.[107] Moreover, there are "great similarities in the procedures and achievements of Greek and Indian doctors," since "like problems call for like . . . solutions" and "the great Indian medical collections of Charaka, Susruta, and Vagbhata . . . correspond to the Hippocratic writings." [108] Likewise, the role of Hippocrates in Greek medical lore is said to be comparable to Charaka's in India.[109] On the whole, however, the distinctive peculiarities of each of the two cultures, rather than such parallels, fill the foreground when Sigerist — usually with tormenting brevity, generality, and allusiveness — takes a comparative turn.

Despite its fragmentary nature, its inaccuracies of fact, its lack of particularities to substantiate many generalities, its at times superseded views, and its ideological tensions, Sigerist's work is marked by emphases that, although not all original, today once again inform some of the more provocative work on ancient Greek medicine: multidimensional contextual history, awareness of the pluralistic rival tendencies that energetically coexisted within Greek medicine, and a comparative sociocultural approach. Many of the passages introduced above offer tantalizing glimpses of the interpretative harvest that could be reaped by means of a fusion of the contextual and comparative approaches, in particular. The promise of the fusion envisioned by Sigerist has never been realized. But similar strategies, recently deployed with more secure methodological safeguards, with greater historiographic subtlety, and with a conceptual precision lacking in earlier work on Greek medicine, have yielded illustrations of the hermeneutic potential of Sigerist's methodological visions.[110]

Notes

I am grateful to Theodore M. Brown and to Susan P. Mattern for helpful comments on earlier versions of this paper.

1. Nora Sigerist Beeson, ed., *Henry E. Sigerist: Autobiographical Writings* (Montreal: McGill University Press, 1966), Diary, February 6, 1937, 120.
2. Ibid., Diary, March 7, 1951, 235.
3. Ibid., 49.
4. Ibid., 43.
5. *A History of Medicine,* vol. II (New York: Oxford University Press, 1961), 14, 111.
6. See, e.g., E. M. Butler, *The Tyranny of Greece over Germany* (Cambridge

University Press, 1935); Walter Rehm, *Griechentum und Goethezeit* (Leipzig: Dietrich, 1936; 4th ed., Bern: Franke, 1968); Henry Hatfield, *Aesthetic Paganism in German Literature from Winckelmann to the Death of Goethe* (Cambridge, Mass.: Harvard University Press, 1964); S. Prawer, ed., *The Romantic Period in Germany* (London: Weidenfeld and Nicholson, 1970). See also Heinrich von Staden, "Nietzsche and Marx on Greek Art and Literature," *Daedalus* (winter, 1976): 79–96; id., "Greek Art and Literature in Marx's Aesthetics," *Arethusa* 8.1 (1975): 119–44.

7. *Antike Heilkunde* (Munich: Ernst Heimeran, 1927), 47. All translations from the German are my own. Whenever a text by Sigerist was first published in German, I have tried to use the German original.

8. Ibid., 46.

9. Ibid., 47.

10. Ibid., 47–48.

11. See F. Kudlien, *Der griechische Arzt im Zeitalter des Hellenismus: seine Stellung in Staat und Gesellschaft* (Wiesbaden: Steiner, 1979); id., *Die Sklaven in der griechischen Medizin der klassischen und hellenistischen Zeit* (Wiesbaden: Steiner, 1968); L. Cohn-Haft, *Public Physicians of Ancient Greece* (Northampton, Mass.: Smith College, 1956); R. Pohl, *De Graecorum medicis publicis* (Leipzig, 1905).

12. *Antike Heilkunde*, 42–43; cf. *Civilization and Disease* (Ithaca, N.Y.: Cornell University Press, 1943), 68. See Hannelore Schlaffer, *Studien zum ästhetischen Historismus* (Frankfurt am Main: Suhrkamp, 1975), who focuses on Jacob Burckhardt and Friedrich Hebbel as representatives of aesthetic historicism. See also J. Burckhardt, *Griechische Kulturgeschichte,* vols. I–IV, in *Gesammelte Werke* (Basel: Benno Schwabe, 1956), vols. V–VIII [a reprint of Jacob Oeri's edition of 1898–1902]. Cf. Egon Flaig, *Angeschaute Geschichte. Zu Jacob Burckhardts "Griechische Kulturgeschichte"* (Rheinfelden: Schäuble, 1987), and E. M. Janssen, *Jacob Burckhardt und die Griechen* (Assen: Van Gorcum, 1979).

13. *Einführung in die Medizin* (Leipzig: Georg Thieme, 1931), 391 (*Man and Medicine* [New York: W. W. Norton, 1932]; henceforth *Einführung*). Sigerist later reiterated this Platonic–political ideal for the modern physician, e.g., in his lecture (October 18, 1933) "The Physician's Profession Through the Ages," in *Henry E. Sigerist On the History of Medicine* [henceforth, *On History*], ed. Felix Marti-Ibañez (New York: MD Publications, 1960), 15. It would appear that Sigerist here badly misappropriates Plato (*Republic* III. 405–8, especially 407e3): Plato envisions eugenics and a refusal to treat the weak and the good-for-nothing as specialities of this "political Asclepius."

14. Ibid., 274. For examples of Hellenistic definitions of diagnosis and therapeutics as conjectural or stochastic, see Ps.-Galen, *Introductio sive medicus* 5, in C. G. Kühn, ed., *Claudii Galeni Opera Omnia*, vol. XIV (Leipzig: Cnobloch, 1827), 684; K. Deichgräber, *Die griechische Empirikerschule*, 2nd ed. (Berlin: Weidmann, 1965), 93.20–25, 143.14–30, 150.28–33, 152.1–7, 161.28. Sigerist is probably referring to Celsus, *De medicina,* prooemium 48; Celsus draws on these Hellenistic debates.

15. "Science and History" (1954), in *On History*, 82–84.

16. *Autobiographical Writings,* 43–44.

17. Ibid., 50–51.

18. Ibid., 43.

19. "University Education," in *On History*, 252: "I was in the humanistic division, where for six and a half years we had eight hours of Latin and for five and a half eight hours of Greek, so that at the end of the course most of us could read Latin and some of us also Greek fluently." This observation is reiterated with some discrepancies (e.g., "*seven* hours of Greek . . . and *seven* hours of Latin") in *Autobiographical Writings*, 52, where Sigerist likewise passionately defends the institution of the traditional *humanistisches Gymnasium*.

20. *Autobiographical Writings*, 44.

21. Ibid. A diary entry of February 3, 1947, shortly after Sigerist, now in his mid-fifties, had resigned his chair at Johns Hopkins, confirms that this childhood "Greek habit" was deeply inscribed in his self-understanding; ibid., Diary, 204–5.

22. E.g., ibid., 43: "And there are a number of subjects that one never learns unless one starts early. . . . In my own profession I must read Latin books of up to five hundred pages all the time and also Greek books, and this I could never do unless I had the solid foundation that my old Gymnasium gave me."

23. Ibid., January 1, 1933 and October 3, 1933, 82, 89.

24. Ibid., January 2, 1943, 178.

25. *Antike Heilkunde*, 8; so too *Einführung*, 116.

26. *Antike Heilkunde*, 14.

27. Ibid., 17.

28. Ibid., 18–19.

29. Ibid., 11.

30. "The Historical Development of the Pathology and Therapy of Cancer" (1932), in *On History*, 61–62.

31. "The Foundation of Human Anatomy in the Renaissance" (1934), in *On History*, 155. Cf. "Ambroise Paré's Onion Treatment of Burns" (1944), in *On History*, 177 (on Galen).

32. *Antike Heilkunde*, 21.

33. *Civilization and Disease*, 153.

34. *Antike Heilkunde*, 33.

35. *Civilization and Disease*, 231.

36. *Antike Heilkunde*, 39.

37. *Antike Heilkunde*, 31; cf. *Einführung*, 130; *Grosse Ärzte. Eine Geschichte der Heilkunde in Lebensbildern* (Munich: J. F. Lehmanns, 1932; 6th ed., 1970), 28 (*The Great Doctors. A Biographical History of Medicine* [New York: W. W. Norton, 1933]; henceforth, *Grosse Ärzte*).

38. Ibid., 42; "The Physician's Profession," in *On History*, 6; "The Philosophy of Hygiene" (1931), ibid., 19; "The Social History of Medicine" (1940), ibid., 27.

39. "The Philosophy of Hygiene," in *On History*, 19.

40. Ibid., 19; "The Physician's Profession," ibid., 6; "The Social History of Medicine," ibid., 27; *Antike Heilkunde*, 47; *Einführung*, 93, 333; *Civilization and Disease*, 68.

41. *Antike Heilkunde*, 47. In virtually every chapter of general works such as *Einführung in die Medizin* and *Civilization and Disease*, Sigerist conspicuously introduces ancient Greek theories and practices to interpret and analyze the origins of modern developments. In *Grosse Ärzte* he devotes no less than eight chap-

ters to Greek physicians, including less known figures of the Hellenistic age such as Herophilus, Erasistratus, and Heraclides of Tarentum (but no Roman physicians). Along with books devoted exclusively to ancient medicine, such as his early *Antike Heilkunde* and the posthumously published second volume of *A History of Medicine,* not to mention numerous articles and lectures that deal exclusively or in part with ancient Greece, these general works thus confirm ancient Greece as a dominant point of both general and specific orientation in Sigerist's understanding of the genealogy of modern culture, including modern medicine.

42. *Einführung, 333.*

43. See von Staden, "Nietzsche and Marx" and "Greek Art and Literature."

44. *Einführung,* 93–94. Sigerist often repeats these observations (at times verbatim), for example in "The Physician's Profession," in *On History,* 6; "The Social History of Medicine," ibid., 27; *Civilization and Disease,* 68–69; and near the end of his last work, *A History of Medicine,* vol. II, 299. For a different approach to the Greeks' attitudes toward incurable patients see von Staden, "Incurability and Hopelessness: The Hippocratic Corpus," in *La maladie et les maladies dans la Collection hippocratique. Actes du VIᵉ colloque international hippocratique,* ed. P. Potter, G. Maloney, J. Desautels (Quebec: Les Éditions du Sphinx, 1990), 75–112.

45. "The Philosophy of Hygiene," in *On History,* 19–20.

46. "Historical Background of Industrial and Occupational Disease," ibid., 47–48.

47. *Civilization and Disease,* 45–46; *History of Medicine,* II: 224–26.

48. *History of Medicine,* II: passim (e.g., 11–18, 40–117, 213–59, 298–316); for the scholarly sources used by Sigerist see his footnotes to the pages cited.

49. O. Markwart, *Jacob Burckhardt. Persönlichkeit und Jugendjahre* (Basel: Benno Schwabe, 1920).

50. *Autobiographical Writings,* 46–47.

51. J. Burckhardt, *Griechische Kulturgeschichte, Gesammelte Werke,* e.g., I: 51–260 (historical development of the polis), I: 290–305 (Greeks and barbarians), III: 3–53 (art and architecture), III: 55–274 (poetry and music), III: 302–38 (oratory), III: 379–92 (philosophy and science, comparisons with the Orient), IV: 59–80 (the role of colonization); IV: 1–604 ("der hellenische Mensch in seiner zeitlichen Entwicklung," especially 206 and 582 on medicine; 4, 6–7, 82–84, 90–91, on health and beauty; 47, 138–42, 224–35, 385–88, 561–66 on women). Cf. Egon Flaig, *Angeschaute Geschichte* and E. M. Janssen, *Jacob Burckhardt und die Griechen* (Assen: Van Gorcum, 1979), who emphasizes *inter alia* Burckhardt's synthesis of a "realism" derived from August Böck and an "idealisation" inspired by Friedrich Schiller. Both Flaig and Janssen also underscore Burckhardt's aesthetic historicism.

52. See Markwart, *Jacob Burckhardt,* VIII–IX (preface by Hermann Scher).

53. *Autobiographical Writings,* 47.

54. "Science and History," in *On History,* 86. Nora Sigerist Beeson, *Autobiographical Writings,* ix, alludes to Sigerist's indebtedness to Burckhardt: "Sigerist's concept of history like that of Jakob Burckhardt included all facets of culture as well." Elisabeth Berg-Schorn, *Henry E. Sigerist (1891–1957): Medizinhistoriker in Leipzig und Baltimore. Standpunkt und Wirkung* (Cologne: Kölner Medizinhis-

torische Beiträge, Band 9, Med. diss. 1978), 16, 19, likewise acknowledges the importance of Burckhardt's influence upon Sigerist. See also *Autobiographical Writings,* Diary, September 24, 1933, 88: "My bible just now is Jakob Burckhardt's *Welthistorische Betrachtungen* (Reflections on world history). . . . It is extraordinary how much he anticipated."

55. E.g., *Civilization and Disease,* chap. X (pp. 196–211); *History of Medicine,* II: 40–43, 72, 80–83, 252–59, 296–97, 313–16. Even Sigerist's teaching style seems to have been influenced by the Burckhardt-Markwart model; his students ·in Leipzig, in particular, recall that Sigerist's pedagogic style was unpedantic, informal, unorthodox, and inspiring; see Berg-Schorn, *Henry E. Sigerist,* 57–59; Erwin H. Ackerknecht, "Recollections of a Former Leipzig Student," *Journal of the History of Medicine and Allied Sciences* 13 (1958): 147–50.

56. "University Education," in *On History,* 253.

57. See Markwart, *Jacob Burckhardt,* 152: "Burckhardt hasste die Demokratie, so wie sie sich in der griechischen Polis entwickelte; er hasste sie, wo sie ihm im Leben entgegentrat"; cf. ibid., 84, on Burckhardt's moral outrage at internecine Greek warfare. See Flaig, *Angeschaute Geschichte,* 88–98.

58. *Autobiographical Writings,* Diary, May 7, 1950, 232.

59. Ibid., 41.

60. Ibid., 42.

61. "University Education," in *On History,* 252. See Marianne Christine Wäspi, *Die Anfänge des Medizinhistorikers Henry E. Sigerist in Zürich* (Zürcher medizingeschichtliche Abhandlungen 206, 1989), 11.

62. *History of Medicine,* II: 11–14, 121–23. See *Autobiographical Writings,* Diary, June 20, 1949, 227.

63. "University Education," in *On History,* 252; *Autobiographical Writings,* 41–42.

64. *Autobiographical Writings,* 50.

65. "Erinnerungen an meine Leipziger Tätigkeit" (1955/56), in *Autobiographical Writings,* 63–64.

66. *Einführung,* 78–79. The Hippocratic saying is from a late accretion (perhaps first or second century) to the Hippocratic Corpus: *De decenti habitu* 5 (IX, p. 232.10 Littré). On its date see U. Fleischer, *Untersuchungen zu den pseudohippokratischen Schriften Parangeliai, Peri Ietrou,* und *Peri euschemosynes* (Neue deutsche Forschungen 10, 1939), 108.

67. *Einführung,* 356–58. For similar emphases in Sigerist's subsequent writings see "The Physician's Profession," in *On History,* 6; "The Social History of Medicine," ibid., 28–29, 31; *History of Medicine,* II: 298–311.

68. *On History,* 19–20.

69. *Socialized Medicine in the Soviet Union* (New York: W. W. Norton, 1937), 23.

70. *Autobiographical Writings,* Diary, January 1, 1936, 115–16.

71. Ibid., Diary, September 11, 1943, 184.

72. *Antike Heilkunde,* 26–27.

73. *Einführung,* 129 (see also 77–78); *Grosse Ärzte,* 26; *Civilization and Disease,* 148–54; *History of Medicine,* II: 87–111.

74. *Einführung*, 332-33. See also "Developments and Trends in Gynecology" (1941), in *On History*, 36. Cf. von Staden, "Women and Dirt," *Helios* 19 (1992): 7-30.

75. *Civilization and Disease*, 131-47; *History of Medicine*, II: 44-83.

76. *Civilization and Disease*, 231-32. On the cultural transferability of medical technology and techniques see *Einführung*, 312.

77. *Einführung*, 143-44; *On History*, 157 (see ibid., 84-85); cf. *Grosse Ärzte*, 231.

78. *Civilization and Disease*, 232. This, too, is a Burckhardtian theme: see Markwart, *Jacob Burckhardt*, 121, on Burckhardt's turn to the classical past as a home "aus wirklich Irdischem und aus Geistigem und Fernem wundersam gemischt."

79. See G. E. R. Lloyd, *The Revolutions of Wisdom: Studies in the Claims and Practice of Ancient Greek Science* (Berkeley: University of California Press, 1987), especially 50-108; von Staden, "Affinities and Elisions: Helen and Hellenocentrism," *Isis* 83 (1992): 578-95.

80. Burckhardt, *Gesammelte Werke*, IV: 59, 84-89, 94 f., 109-10, 113-17, 201 ff., 368.

81. "Developments and Trends in Gynecology," in *On History*, 37-38. So too *History of Medicine*, II: 215.

82. *Antike Heilkunde*, 5.

83. *On History*, 105, 111; *History of Medicine*, II: 277, 291.

84. *History of Medicine*, II: 45-51.

85. Ibid., II: 3.

86. Ibid., II: 206.

87. Ibid., II: 204. For Sigerist's unchanging definition of "primitive medicine" see, for example, *Einführung*, 128, 355; "The Physician's Profession," in *On History*, 3-5; "The Social History of Medicine," ibid., 28-29; *Civilization and Disease*, 131-32; and especially *History of Medicine*, vol. I: *Primitive and Archaic Medicine*. See also Temkin's essay in this volume.

88. *History of Medicine*, II: 7 n.1. See *Autobiographical Writings*, Diary, August 30, 1953, 243: "The first of January I would like to be able to begin volume III of my History—the Middle Ages, but it will still be the Orient, the Arabs, the Persians, India, and China."

89. Ibid., II: 7.

90. Ibid., II: 4. See also *Autobiographical Writings*, Diary, January 17, 1949, 224: "While I read [an address by an Indian colleague] I was always thinking of my second volume [of *A History of Medicine*]. It was to be on Greco-Roman medicine but now I find that this is a very one-sided Western point of view. Hindu civilization was as high as the Greek and at the same time. Indian medicine was certainly equal to Hippocratic medicine."

91. Ibid.

92. See "University Education," in *On History*, 253-54 and *Autobiographical Writings*, 52. See also Veith's essay in this volume.

93. E.g., Burckhardt, *Gesammelte Werke*, III: 382, 384, 393-94; IV: 407 ff., 417-19. As a student in Basel (1837-39) Burckhardt himself took no less than ten courses on Hebrew language and literature and on "Hebrew archaeology," as well

as a course on the history of polytheistic religions, and in Berlin (1841) he took a course on comparative ethnography (see Markwart, *Jacob Burckhardt*, 396–98). Burckhardt's formal education, in other words, extended considerably beyond Greco-Roman culture and its European sequels to include non-Indo-European comparative perspectives.

94. Typical are brief passing undocumented references such as: "The magic of [Hippocrates'] name for the Western medical world can be compared only to Charaka's for India" (*History of Medicine*, II: 260), or "Pythagoras and Buddha were contemporaries, and the Orphic movement was undoubtedly inspired by the East" (II: 96).

95. *History of Medicine*, II: 3.

96. Ibid., II: 7.

97. E.g., *Antike Heilkunde*, 37; *Grosse Ärzte*, 32, 33; *Einführung*, 312.

98. *Autobiographical Writings*, Diary, January 17, 1949, 224: "Indian medicine was certainly equal to Hippocratic medicine. The task therefore would be to picture the parallel development of Greek and Indian medicine." Had Sigerist not been prevented by death from writing the projected section (in *A History of Medicine*) on the "Golden Age" of Indian medicine, the reader might have seen more of what he meant by "parallel development."

99. *History of Medicine*, II: 121; see also II: 123, 135.

100. Ibid., II: 197.

101. Ibid., II: 122.

102. Ibid., II: 125.

103. Ibid., II: 126. A consideration of the "magico-religious system" of Vedic medicine, which, he believes, has counterparts in Egyptian and Mesopotamian medicine, likewise leads Sigerist to see only differences between Greece and India; ibid., II: 161–62.

104. Ibid., cf. II: 149.

105. Ibid., II: 182.

106. Ibid., II: 137.

107. Ibid., II: 96 (reincarnation); II: 183 (divine inventors of medicine).

108. Ibid., II: 182.

109. Ibid., II: 260.

110. See notably G. E. R. Lloyd, *Demystifying Mentalities* (Cambridge: Cambridge University Press, 1990), for a comparative contextual approach to Greek and Chinese science and medicine. For a contextual approach that emphasizes, in particular, sociopolitical context, see G. E. R. Lloyd, *Revolutions of Wisdom; Science, Folklore, and Ideology: Studies in the Life Sciences in Ancient Greece* (Cambridge: Cambridge University Press, 1983); *Magic, Reason, and Experience* (Cambridge: Cambridge University Press, 1979). For slightly different contextual emphases in the interpretation of Greek science cf., e.g., Heinrich von Staden, "Affinities and Elisions: Helen and Hellenocentrism," *Isis* 83 (1992): 578–95; "Women and Dirt," *Helios* 19 (1992): 7–30; "The Discovery of the Body: Human Dissection and its Cultural Contexts in Ancient Greece," *Yale Journal of Biology and Medicine* 65 (1992): 223–41; "Spiderwoman and the Chaste Tree: The Semantics of Matter," *Configurations* 1 (1992): 23–56.

CHAPTER 8

"I Always Wish I Could Go Back":
Sigerist the Medievalist

Michael R. McVaugh

From Pura in 1951, three years before the stroke that ended his work as a historian, Henry Sigerist prepared an appreciation of Julius Pagel to mark the hundredth anniversary of the latter's birth: calling Pagel "one of the foremost . . . of . . . the second generation of modern medical historians," Sigerist suggested that "forty years after his death we may be justified in asking what his work has meant to us, historians of the third generation who did not know him personally but were young students . . . at the time of his death."[1] It has seemed natural to take Sigerist's reflections as a starting point for this essay, because circumstances have repeated themselves; a hundred years after Sigerist's birth in 1891, almost forty years after his death, a fourth generation of medical historians is assessing *his* work. Moreover, Julius Pagel's principal historical interest was the Middle Ages, and it is all the more appropriate to consider Sigerist as a medievalist in the light of his assessment of Pagel's achievement, for it is hard not to imagine that Sigerist was silently reflecting on his own career in medical history as he wrote.

A scholar's published work, Sigerist suggested in his remarks on Pagel, falls into three broad categories: one of occasional essays, newspaper articles and the like, essentially ephemeral by nature; another of textbooks, which are valuable in their day but inevitably serve that day and are supplanted; and finally a third "of research materials and tools, of texts made available, described and analysed, of bibliographies and other reference books. This is usually the part of a historian's work that lives the longest," and it was also the aspect of Pagel's scholarship on which Sigerist dwelt most carefully: "A distinguished Latinist and mediaevalist, he published, himself and through his students, a number of medieval medical texts from the manuscripts and today no one can work on such physicians and surgeons as Henricus de Mondeville, Wilhelmus de Congeina, Johannes de Sancto Amando, Gualterius Agulinus, or Mesue and others without consulting Pagel's and his school's editions and translations"[2] — an appraisal of Julius Pagel's contributions that remains just as true in the 1990s as it was in the 1950s.

This final side of a historian's scholarship, about which Sigerist wrote so feelingly, was the one to which he had committed himself at the beginning of his own career. He came to Leipzig from Switzerland in 1919 to visit Karl Sudhoff's Institut für Geschichte der Medizin, with a medical degree but an avocation for philological study.[3] He had hoped to work on the great Swiss physiologist Haller, but Sudhoff the medievalist had no intention of wasting his young disciple's gifts and instead immediately encouraged him to investigate the medical texts of the Middle Ages — thrusting heaps of photostats of manuscripts on him, as Sigerist remembered his brief stay in Leipzig.[4] It was a career, Sudhoff explained, that could still engage him in Swiss materials and lead back to Haller in the end: "Your program, it seems to me, could be the classical foundations of medicine and their medieval-modern superstructure in its Swiss style; or, to speak less figuratively, Swiss medicine from Carolingian times to Haller, with a strong emphasis on the Middle Ages and Renaissance — a rich field for a life's work!"[5]

After returning to Zurich — eventually becoming *Privatdozent* (1921) and professor (1924) there — Sigerist launched upon that very program, editing and publishing three short texts from the early Middle Ages in Sudhoff's *Archiv für Geschichte der Medizin*.[6] As it proved, the program allowed him immediately to begin to investigate the Swiss medical tradition. The library of the former abbey of St. Gall, south of Lake Constance, possessed several early medical codices of particular importance, and one of these — MS 44 — Sigerist used in preparing his *Habilitationsschrift*, published at Zurich in 1923 as *Studien und Texte zur frühmittelalterlichen Rezeptliteratur* in his master's *Studien zur Geschichte der Medizin*.[7] Here he edited seven important pre-Salernitan *antidotaria* found in manuscripts of the seventh to eleventh centuries and offered some generalizations about their form, content, and sources. He argued that in many respects these early medieval collections revealed far greater continuity with the *antidotaria* of antiquity than with the *antidotaria* of Salerno that followed them, which he concluded were strongly influenced by Arabic material communicated through the eleventh-century translations of Constantine the African.

Sudhoff had pressed quantities of photocopies on Sigerist when he returned to Zurich, as well as copies of all the institute's publications still available, "and he generously allowed me to make prints of negatives in its photographic collection. Zurich had no institute, and my task would be gradually to build up there a kind of younger Leipzig."[8] As it happened, the library of St. Gall was amenable to sending its manuscripts to Sigerist in Zurich for study and photographic reproduction. The St. Gall manuscript Sigerist had employed for his edition of *antidotaria* proved also to contain two recipe collections of a different sort, often incorporating popular remedies from folk medicine rather than ones that could be traced back to a Greek progenitor. Under Sigerist's supervision, a Zurich medical student, Julius Jörimann, edited these two texts for his dissertation from Sigerist's photographs (together with a third found in a ninth/tenth-century Bamberg manuscript, photographs of which were loaned by Sudhoff).[9] Another student, Hermann Leisinger, edited a medley of pseudo-Galenic treatises on urines from St. Gall MS 751 and a number of others.[10] No doubt consciously, Sigerist was working toward making himself and his students at Zurich a task force that would identify and publish the medical literature of the early Middle Ages, working outward from Swiss codices.

A further step toward this was the collaboration Sigerist undertook with his Zurich colleague Ernst Howald (professor of Greek language and literature) on a critical edition of the *Herbarius* ascribed to Apuleius as well as of some connected texts. Working generally from photographs (though Sigerist spent a week in Monte Cassino studying one manuscript and traveled to London to examine others), occasionally from transcripts provided from others, the two prepared their edition—of the text as well as of the plant drawings that are generally associated with it—from eighteen principal manuscripts and as many more of lesser value. Publication was held up by the need to raise extra money for the reproduction of the drawings, but the edition finally appeared in 1927, two years after Sigerist had been called back to Leipzig to succeed Sudhoff as the head of the institute.[11]

Sigerist's Zurich work is the part of his achievement as a medievalist that, as he must have known by 1951, would "live the longest." The individual works transcribed in his *Studien and Texte,* and the much more intricate critical edition of pseudo-Apuleius prepared in cooperation with Howald, are texts that students of early medieval medicine still depend on today and will no doubt continue to do so far beyond the foreseeable future; they correspond to Littré's Hippocrates or to Pagel's Henri de Mondeville. No doubt most of the broader historical conclusions Sigerist drew from them would still be generally accepted, but that is not why they matter, for the interests of modern scholarship in the field have inevitably deepened and become more sophisticated. As Sigerist recognized, the edited text itself outlives any particular attempt at historical interpretation.[12]

One last medieval project was conceived at Zurich, an ambitious program "to publish a catalogue of all the medical manuscripts preserved in Swiss libraries. It was to be in three parts—one describing the early medieval Latin manuscripts, the second devoted to the Latin manuscripts of the scholastic period, while the third part was to contain all the manuscript texts written in vernacular language."[13] The finding tools that historians of medieval science now take for granted did not exist in 1925—Thorndike and Kibre's *Catalogue of Incipits* was still a dozen years away—and Sigerist had recognized at the very beginning of his work that the selection of texts to edit required a prior sense of what existed and what was important. "We cannot depend on critical philological editions of these medieval texts until we know what materials exist, which are important and which are not, and how they are related," he wrote in his foreword to the *Studien,* adding: "here Sudhoff has shown us the way."[14] His vision of a catalogue of the Swiss medical manuscripts began to take shape with his close study of the St. Gall codices, and he allowed Jörimann to cite it as "in preparation."[15]

But the move to Leipzig altered all these plans, though it did not affect his commitment to the Middle Ages. Sudhoff had amassed in Leipzig ten thousand photographs from manuscripts in libraries throughout Europe, but they were uncatalogued, and only Sudhoff really had known what was there.[16] To Sigerist, exploring this collection—to which he himself added nearly fifteen hundred more—encouraged dreaming about projects on a scale much larger than merely Switzerland, and he now began to plan instead the elucidation of the entire body of medical literature surviving from the early Middle Ages. He had more students at the Leipzig institute than at Zurich, and between 1928 and 1932, under his direction, they produced a half-dozen editions of early texts that Sigerist had come upon in the St. Gall manuscripts, texts that they published either in Sudhoff's *Archiv* or in *Kyklos*.[17] But it was not merely editions that they undertook. One student, Jesaja Muschel, translated the Hebrew version of the *Capsula eburnea* (The Ivory Box), an early prognostic treatise, and compared it with the Latin one, arguing for their common descent from a Greek original (in the case of the Hebrew, via Arabic).[18] Another, Walter Puhlmann, assembled a typology and bibliography of published editions of Latin texts composed in the pre-Salernitan period.[19]

As the new director of the institute and professor of medical history at Leipzig, Sigerist found his own time for detailed "analytical" research of a narrowly defined character severely curtailed: he found time only to publish three brief studies of material he had already examined.[20] Besides, his new role tempted him to indulge more fully his enormous breadth of interests, as it freed him to leave analysis for synthesis—to develop Sudhoff's work "organically," as he put it, by imbedding history of medicine within a sociological approach.[21] Even at Zurich it is not clear that he had ever been content with the single-mindedness of the committed textual scholar, something that eventually Sudhoff himself may have come reluctantly to recognize.[22]

When he crossed the Atlantic in 1932, Sigerist had had no intention of renouncing his study of the early medieval literature; he expected, if anything, that his new position and its attached resources would make it easier for him to continue his work. Indeed, he now visualized with increasing clarity the outline that his results would eventually take. In its final form, it would consist of three parts or volumes. The first of these was planned as "a catalogue of all manuscripts containing early mediaeval texts. It will be arranged geographically, according to countries, cities, libraries. Each manuscript will be described as to its physical appearance, and to its content," and the works contained were to be identified by long incipits and explicits. Full-page plates were to be included to illustrate every manuscript written before the twelfth century, for manuscripts from the late Middle Ages and even the Renaissance were also to be included in the survey if they included texts originally composed in the earlier period.[23]

The second of the three volumes would be "a collection of texts. All treatises heretofore unknown, or such as need a new critical edition, will be published there." In cases where incessant alterations over the centuries had made critical editions impracticable, or where well-known texts had undergone such abridgement and rearrangement as to warrant speaking of a new composition, Sigerist saw no alternative to printing each of these versions.[24] Then, when the first two volumes were completed, a third volume could be prepared tracing the history of medicine and medical literature in the early Middle Ages. This final volume

> will give the synthesis, while the first two volumes are analytical in character. The first part of the third volume will picture the general development, will study the medical centers, the influence of the monasteries and the general characteristics of early mediaeval medicine. The second part, then, will discuss the Latin translations of Greek medical classics, the works of mediaeval writers, and finally the anonymous and pseudonymous literature. In each treatise, I will give a list of the manuscripts preserved, a list of the principal editions and of the literature on this text, and I will endeavor to trace the history of each text down to our day. There will be consistent cross-references from one volume to the other, and it is needless to say that numerous indices will be required in order to give this study its full value. Indices not only of proper names, but also of *incipits* and *explicits,* will be given, and eventually of rare words that seem to me to be important from a point of view of linguistics.[25]

"If I succeed," Sigerist wrote in his diary, "this will be a piece of work that will last a century, just as we still consult Angelo Mari [*sic*] and Fabricius. My other books are written for the day and will not survive me long." [26]

It is hard not to catch one's breath at the audacity of these plans. They reveal enthusiasm, optimism, self-confidence—and an utter lack of realism as well, both about the magnitude and technical difficulties of the project he had laid out and about the likelihood that, given its scope and his own responsibilities and other perennially competing interests, he would ever complete it. Nevertheless he immersed himself in it enthusiastically in the spring of 1933, as his first year at Hopkins came to an end: "the medieval studies are in swing again," he told himself happily, "and if everything goes well should be terminated in a few years." [27] He visited Europe that summer, spending much of it in libraries in Bologna and Florence, and boarded ship for his return to the United States in September with a somewhat chastened appreciation of the task he had set himself.

> I hoped that I would be able to get through with the Italian libraries. I did not. I worked in 10 libraries, examined 22 manuscripts, ordered 646 photostats, and 58 ordinary photos. But I still have to visit, in Italy, the libraries of Naples, Monte Cassino, Rome, Arezzo, Pisa, Lodi. This will have to be done next year. The reason why I didn't fulfil my programme is that the preparation wasn't quite accurate enough, that there was too much material, too scattered. Time

was too short for such an enormous mass of material. Still the results are not bad. I have very important material on which I can work the whole winter and I learned the technique of doing such work. Next year it will be much easier and require much less time.[28]

He still told himself the three volumes could be completed by 1937.[29]

For his second research trip, in the summer of 1934, he set himself the goal of studying 502 manuscripts (twenty-five times as many as he had managed the previous year!) in Italy, France, Belgium, Holland, and Switzerland and took a camera with him to make his own photographs; but although the trip was indeed more productive than that in 1933, he fell far short of his objective: "43 medieval manuscripts were examined in 18 libraries. Ordinary photos were made of 30 manuscript pages with miniatures, 814 pages were photostated and 310 photographed with the Leica, so that I have photographical records of 1,154 manuscript pages—enough to keep me busy for the whole winter."[30]

Sigerist might put a good face on it and call it "a good summer," but he must have decided that he could not realize his goals as easily as he had once dreamed and that he would do better to redirect his energies into other projects. He talked as though the redirection would only delay his medieval studies—"I would hate to interrupt them entirely"—but in fact it effectively ensured their abandonment. Russia had to be visited in the summers of 1935 and 1936 and a book written on the subject; then another book had to be finished by 1937. Sigerist briefly dreamed that then the medieval volumes could be taken up and completed, perhaps by 1939. But distraction followed distraction, and by the beginning of 1937 he had implicitly abandoned the three-volume medieval study and was instead looking ahead to a synthetic five-volume history and sociology of medicine as his magnum opus.[31]

If Sigerist had persisted in his program, ambitious as it was, some at least of his project would undoubtedly have been realized; as it is, however, sixty years later even the first two analytic volumes seem impossible of realization. Sigerist's first planned volume, a complete catalogue of all early medieval medical texts, has been partly achieved in Augusto Beccaria's *I codici di medicina del periodo presalernitano* (Medical Codices of the Pre-Salernitan Period), (published in 1956, but begun in 1935, just as Sigerist's researches were effectively ending); but "Beccaria," though organized geographically as Sigerist had wanted, does not include something else he had insisted upon: identification of later manuscripts containing copies of early writings. To be sure, other finding guides have

34. Sigerist photographing manuscripts with his Leica camera, 1934.

been produced in the interim that help fill part of this gap: Thorndike and Kibre, now in its second edition; Pearl Kibre on Hippocrates;[32] and Richard Durling on Galen;[33] but it has not been dealt with systematically. Nor did Beccaria give a complete analysis of a codex's contents, only of the medical texts it held; nor, for that matter, did he provide plates of any of the manuscripts he described.[34] "Beccaria" will long remain an utterly indispensable tool for the study of early medicine; yet if "Sigerist" had been completed, we would have had no need for a "Beccaria," and as Sigerist anticipated, his name would have been secure for a century and more.

In the early 1940s Sigerist did publish two articles in the *Bulletin of the History of Medicine* that gave a sample of his researches in this phase, describing the pre-Salernitan material he had encountered in five manuscripts from Montpellier and Vendôme.[35] His accounts of these codices give a good sense of what he had once hoped to produce for all such European manuscripts — the codicological information and contents-catalogue that Beccaria's work now supplies, but with much fuller excerpts to identify them and with cross-references to other manuscripts where the individual texts could be found, with illustration of at least one leaf. Another feature of these articles is their incorporation of long excerpts or complete short texts transcribed from the manuscripts, which, if Sigerist had not by this time abandoned his original plans, would presumably have been reserved for the second volume of Latin texts.

On the other hand, even had Sigerist continued to put philology ahead of all his other interests, it is doubtful that that second volume would ever have appeared. Beccaria's own judgment on Sigerist's dream — *"Il disegno, a quanto si può concepire, era assai vasto e compiuto e forse per ciò anche questa volta finì col restare senza effetto"* (His plans, as far as they can be understood, were vast and ambitious and perhaps for that reason were never realized)[36] — is truest here. Wonderful though it would be to have a single volume holding all the pre-Salernitan medical literature of the Latin Middle Ages, there is so much of it, as indeed Beccaria has now made us aware, that it would take a team of scholars several decades to prepare the critical editions Sigerist dreamed of. Perhaps unfortunately, medical historians since Sigerist have tended to be absorbed by the thought and practice of the later rather than the early Middle Ages and have tended to study the impact of translations from the Arabic on the Latin tradition and on the growth of medical learning in the medieval universities; when they have edited medieval texts, they have been more likely to pick material from the Renaissance side of the watershed marked by Salerno, not from that of late antiquity.

Sigerist's effective abandonment of his medieval project after 1935–36 no doubt owes most to his growing intellectual engagement with other fields and to the increasingly obvious impracticality of his vision, but it cannot have been entirely unaffected by the appearance of publications by other scholars in his adopted United States who were pursuing similar goals. George W. Corner published an account of early Salernitan surgery and its western antecedents in the *Bulletin* in 1937, following up his publication ten years before of early Latin anatomical texts.[37] Thorndike and Kibre's *Catalogue of Incipits* appeared in that same year and immediately became the finding guide that Sigerist's cross-references would have provided on a smaller scale. But one might speculate that Loren MacKinney's work did most to free Sigerist from any possible sense of guilt about putting aside the early Middle Ages. MacKinney, a young professor of history at the University of North Carolina, had traveled to France in the early 1930s to examine early medieval medical manuscripts in libraries there and had paid particular attention to the rich holdings of Paris's Bibliothèque Nationale and of the cathedral of Chartres, which Sigerist had not yet investigated. The photostats that MacKinney made of portions of the Chartres manuscripts are in many cases all that survives of them today, for the cathedral library was destroyed in 1944.[38] MacKinney had published some of his results (on a literary source for tenth-century medicine) in the Institute's *Bulletin* in 1934[39] and was invited to Baltimore in 1936 to give the Hideyo Noguchi lectures on early medieval medicine, surely at Sigerist's behest; the three talks offered a synthetic view of early medicine, stressing, as Sigerist had done, its positive role in preserving elements of the classical tradition. The Institute published MacKinney's lectures the next year, in a sense thereby forestalling Sigerist's own planned third volume.[40] Although MacKinney dealt essentially with developments in France alone, within that context he provided very much what Sigerist had projected, a general account of early medieval medicine as revealed not only by an examination of the manuscripts surviving from the period but by historical and literary sources as well, evidence of a sort that Sigerist had not yet fully exploited.

In the late thirties and forties, therefore, Sigerist could feel easier about turning definitively aside from his original path. During this last phase of his career, his work on the Middle Ages was almost entirely confined to writing up his visits to Montpellier and Vendôme for the *Bulletin* and to preparing a few short essays, ones tending typically to focus on a curious passage or brief text that could be discussed entertainingly for the general reader. These occasional pieces were not driven by the needs of a narrowly defined program of systematic investigation, but were triggered by Sigerist's broad appreciation of the timeless social and cultural implications of medicine, which he was now free to indulge. As a result, they sometimes anticipate themes that today's historians of medicine have only recently rediscovered. Of these essays, the last Sigerist wrote—in the *Quarterly Bulletin* of Northwestern's school of medicine—is perhaps the most suggestive.[41] Though it is little more than an English translation of the *De cautelis medicorum* (On the Precautions that Physicians Must Observe) published among the works of Arnald of Villanova—Sigerist also looked at the structure and sources of the Latin text and discussed its authorship—the choice of a text shows a typical perceptiveness, for the *De cautelis* is remarkable in including candid instructions to physicians who must convince skeptical patients of their expertise before being allowed to take charge of a case. It is a fascinating and revealing picture of the doctor-patient relationship as it was in the Middle Ages before the invention of the university allowed unquestioned medical authority to inhere in the academic degrees of *licentiatus* and *magister,* and it was Sigerist's sensitivity to such issues that let him identify in a Gothic edition a little work of potential significance for historians as well as the clinicians who were its immediate audience.[42]

Pieces like these teased but could not satisfy a longing for the detailed textual studies that Sigerist had had to defer. More satisfying to him had been his publication, in 1943, of an English translation of Arnald of Villanova's *De vinis*—more accurately, of the *De vinis* as rendered into German in the late fifteenth century and published in 1478.[43] Three years before, Henry Schuman had approached him about this volume, "the earliest printed book on wine"; Schuman wanted to publish a facsimile of the original edition and asked Sigerist for an introduction and translation. Initially Sigerist refused: "I probably felt unconsciously as a result of my past philological training that people who cannot read Latin do not deserve such texts anyway." Undiscouraged, Schuman sent him a photostatic copy of the German edition. Sigerist read this with increasing delight, recognizing that the German version was a different book that went far beyond Arnald's text on medicinal wines to discuss "wine at large, real wines that you drink for the joy of it," and he undertook the assignment.[44]

The task involved no manuscript study, but the obscure German kept Sigerist returning to Arnald's Latin again and again. He was able to demonstrate that at some point Arnald's text had been conflated with another (which he managed to identify) and that the whole had then been given Arnald's name; it was this conflation that had been translated into German.[45] Relatively remote in character from his original scholarship, the project nevertheless was deeply satisfying and awoke in him regrets for the kind of work he had once done and done so well.

> Wrote twenty-one pages—a record—and finished the Arnald. I think I hit the right tone. It is scholarly in the beginning and ends in the light vein which should be about correct for this kind of book. It was a great pleasure writing it. There is nothing I like more than philological work and it is my bad luck that I have not more time for it. Circumstances have driven me into so many other fields but I always wish I could go back to pure philology.[46]

But of course that was impossible. Sigerist finally acknowledged this in 1950 in his James Bryce lecture at Oxford, though here he spoke as if he had abandoned his plans only recently: "[they] unfortunately fell a victim to the war and the post-war period when the libraries were disrupted and it was impossible to travel, and afterwards I found myself engaged in other projects."[47] He summarized the results of his research and the character of the early Latin medical literature as he conceived of it, expressing the hope that "some day some future research worker will undertake the job that circumstances prevented me from achieving." His lecture distinguished between the works of late antiquity, either Latin translations from Greek or compilations by Latin authors, and the anonymous or pseudonymous constructions of the Middle Ages that covered all branches of medical literature, many of which he exemplified by works he and his students had studied. Indeed, examined closely, the very structure as well as the content of the lecture proves to derive from Sigerist's Leipzig period; much of it is no more than a very thinly fleshed-out version of Walter Puhlmann's 1930 typology of the pre-Salernitan literature. In a sense, the Bryce lecture was Sigerist's testament as a medievalist—it was the last publication to appear under his name, its notes still incomplete at his death—but it was a testament he had drafted twenty years before.

Sigerist's final appraisal of the significance of early medieval medicine—that "the greatest achievement of these anonymous compilers was that they kept the torch alight for almost eight hundred years"—was also essentially unchanged from that with which he had begun his research into medieval history thirty years before.[48] It is the view of a philologist, and of a Latin philologist; a student of vernacular writings might have found more room for contributions from folk medicine. The organic approach one might have expected from Sigerist, looking closely at the wider world in which monastic medicine was practiced—the approach that MacKinney had adopted in his studies of early medieval France—was one he had never been able to pursue systematically.

The medievalist in me is bound to regret Sigerist's abandonment of the realm of "philology" and to share his own undoubted sadness that he had not been able to accomplish more in it. If he had chosen to continue on that course first marked out for him by Sudhoff, the medical literature of the early Middle Ages would unquestionably be far more accessible to us today than it is—or than it is likely to be in the foreseeable future.

And yet the historian of medicine in me cannot really complain. It was as a medievalist disciple of Sudhoff that Victor Robinson viewed the young Sigerist in 1922, three years after he had made his first visit to the Leipzig institute.

> Doctor Sigerist! We greet you at the threshold of a brilliant career. . . . Perhaps in the Congress that may be held in New York in 1955, after you have spoken and are hailed as a savant, we may explain to some novice: "That's the venerable Professor Sigerist. When we first met him in London, in the summer of 1922, he was a young man, but full of zeal for medical history. Scholarship sat lightly upon him, and he wore his honors easily. In an age when the majority of young men devoted themselves to Commerce, Henry Sigerist lit his brand at Sudhoff's torch and carried on the master's work. After the session, come to our study and look over the shelf of Sigerist's books—contributions to culture." [49]

Today that is a poignant tribute—by 1955 Sigerist was incapacitated—and yet of course prophetic as well, for by then the shelf of "contributions to culture" that Robinson had foretold was there; and there are those who would see them as richer contributions than texts in the Sudhoff tradition would have been. But what would Sigerist himself have felt?

Sigerist concluded his 1951 assessment of Julius Pagel's achievement by recognizing that beyond essays, textbooks, and research materials, "there is a fourth category of contributions that the historian who is an academic teacher passes on to posterity, one that cannot be expressed in figures and cannot be listed in bibliographies, but is very real, very tangible nevertheless, namely the inspiration he gives his students and the enthusiasm he arouses in them." [50] Here once more I think Sigerist must inevitably have been reflecting on his own career as he wrote, and if so, he must have been clear-sighted enough to recognize that he himself had exemplified this ideal. If he had not achieved the scholarly immortality of a three-volume "Sigerist," he had certainly achieved a different kind of immortality in the thought and careers of those he inspired. Whether Sigerist *himself* was satisfied with that much will remain, for me, an open question.

Notes

I am deeply grateful to Dr. Owsei Temkin for reading and commenting upon an earlier version of this paper.

1. Henry E. Sigerist, "On the Hundredth Anniversary of Julius Pagel's Birth," *Bulletin of the History of Medicine* 25 (1951): 203.

2. Ibid., 204–5.

3. Henry E. Sigerist, *Autobiographical Writings* (Montreal: McGill University Press, 1966), 42–44, 47, 50–52, 55–56.

4. Henry E. Sigerist, "The Medical Literature of the Early Middle Ages: A Program—and a Report of a Summer of Research in Italy," *Bulletin of the Institute of the History of Medicine* 2 (1934): 27.

5. " 'Ihr Weg wäre dann, wie mir scheint, der gewiesene klassisch-medizinischer Unterbau und mittelalterlich-moderne Aufbau im Schweizer Stil oder weniger bildlich gesprochen, Schweizer Medizin von der karolinger-Zeit bis zu Haller mit starkem Nachdruck auf dem Mittelalter und der Zeit der sog. Renaissance— ein reiches Feld für eine Lebensarbeit!' " Quoted by Sigerist in "Erinnerungen an Karl Sudhoff," *Sudhoffs Archiv für Geschichte der Medizin* 37 (1953): 97.

6. "Die cirurgia Eliodori," *Archiv für Geschichte der Medizin* 12 (1920): 1–9 [based on Paris BN lat. 11219]; "Die Lecciones Heliodori," *Archiv für Geschichte der Medizin* 13 (1921): 145–56 [based on Glasgow, Hunter T. 4. 13]; "Die Prognostica Democriti," *Archiv für Geschichte der Medizin* 13 (1921): 157–59 [from the same Hunterian MS.].

7. Henry E. Sigerist, *Studien und Texte zur frühmittelalterlichen Rezeptliteratur*, Studien zur Geschichte der Medizin, vol. 13 (Leipzig: Johann Ambrosius Barth, 1923; rpt. Vaduz: Topos, 1977). See Elisabeth Berg-Schorn, *Henry E. Sigerist (1891–1957): Medizinhistoriker in Leipzig und Baltimore. Standpunkt und Wirkung* (Cologne: Kölner Medizinhistorische Beiträge, Band 9, Med. diss. 1978), 48–49.

8. "Und erlaubte mir in grosszügiger Weise, Abzüge von photographischen Platten der Bildersammlung herstellen zu lassen. Zürich hatte kein Institut, und es sollte meine Aufgabe sein, dort allmählich eine Art Leipziger filiale aufzubauen." "Errinerungen," 98.

9. Julius Jörimann, *Frühmittelalterliche Rezeptarien*, Inaug. diss. (Zurich: Dr. Carl Hoenn, 1925).

10. Hermann Leisinger, "Die lateinischen Harnschriften Pseudo-Galens," *Beiträge zur Geschichte der Medizin*, h. 2, Zurich/Leipzig: Füssli, 1925. The other MSS consulted were Vat. Barb. 160; Glasgow, Hunter T. 4. 13; Munich CLM 505 and 11343; BM Harley 4346 and Sloane 1313. The last four MSS were of the twelfth century or later.

11. *Antonii Musae de herba vettonica liber; Pseudoapulei Herbarius*, eds. Ernes-

tus Howald et Henricus E. Sigerist; Corpus Medicorum Latinorum, IV (Leipzig and Berlin: Teubner, 1927). For the circumstances of its appearance see the introduction to the edition as well as "Medical Literature," 29-30.

12. Walter Artelt, *Einführung in die Medizinhistorik* (Stuttgart: Ferdinand Enke, 1949), 110-11, cited the Howald-Sigerist edition as still exemplifying the technique of stemmatic analysis at its most sophisticated as a tool in editing ancient or medieval texts. For examples of more recent scholarship in this area still dependent on this edition see Dietlinde Goltz, *Mittelalterliche Pharmazie und Medizin dargestellt an Geschichte und Inhalt des Antidotarium Nicolai; Veröffentlichungen der Internationalen Gesellschaft für Geschichte der Pharmazie e.V.*, n. f. 44 (1976), esp. 36-38; and Linda Ehrsam Voigts, "The Significance of the Name Apuleius to the *Herbarium Apulei,*" *Bulletin of the History of Medicine* 52 (1978): 214-27.

13. "Medical Literature," 28.

14. "Auf philologisch-kritische Editionen solcher mittelalterlichen Texte kann es uns noch nicht ankommen, bevor wir wissen, was für Material überhaupt vorliegt, was wertvoll, was wertlos ist, was für Zusammenhänge bestehen. Sudhoff hat uns hier den Weg gewiesen." *Studien,* iv.

15. Jörimann, 1, n. 1: "Über diese ganze Literatur [Rezeptsammlungen] s. H. E. Sigerist, 'Die medizinischen Handschriften der Schweiz,' Bd. I: Die lateinische Literatur des frühen Mittelalters. (In Vorbereitung)." Leisinger also alluded to its forthcoming publication (5, n. 1).

16. "Erinnerungen," 99.

17. Erhard Landgraf, "Ein frühmittelalterlicher Botanicus," *Kyklos* 1 (1928): 3-36 [based on St. Gall 217]; M. Wlaschky, "Sapientia Artis Medicine; Ein frühmittelalterliches Kompendium der Medizin," *Kyklos* 1 (1928): 103-13 [based on St. Gall 44 and 751; Glasgow, Hunter T. 4. 13; and Vatican Angelicus N. 1502]; Ernst Hirschfeld, "Deontologische Texte des frühen Mittelalters," *Sudhoffs Archiv für Geschichte der Medizin* 20 (1928): 353-71 [three short texts found in St. Gall 751 and a number of other manuscripts]; Werner Bernfeld, "Eine Beschwörung der Gebärmutter aus dem frühen Mittelalter," *Kyklos* 2 (1929): 272-74 [from St. Gall 752]; Rudolf Laux, "Ars Medicinae, ein frühmittelalterliches Kompendium der Medizin," *Kyklos* 3 (1930): 417-34 [from St. Gall 751; Glasgow, Hunter T. 4. 13; Bruxelles 1342-50, Turic. C128/32; Paris BN lat. 11219; and Bamberg L. III. 8]; Herbert Normann, "Disputatio Platonis et Aristotelis. Ein apokrypher Dialog aus dem frühen Mittelalter," *Sudhoffs Archiv für Geschichte der Medizin* 23 (1930): 68-86 [from St. Gall 751 and Bruxelles 3701].

18. Jesaja Muschel, "Die pseudohippokratische Todesprognostik und die Capsula Eburnea in hebräischer Überlieferung," *Sudhoffs Archiv für Geschichte der Medizin* 25 (1932): 43-61. On the *Capsula,* see Pearl Kibre, *Hippocrates Latinus* (New York: Fordham University Press, 1985), 110-11.

19. Walter Puhlmann, "Die lateinische medizinische Literatur des frühen Mittelalters," *Kyklos* 3 (1930): 395-416.

20. "Fragment einer unbekannten lateinischen Übersetzung des hippokratischen Prognostikon," *Sudhoffs Archiv für Geschichte der Medizin* 23 (1930): 87-90 [based on St. Gall 44]; "Zum Herbarius Pseudo-Apulei," *Sudhoffs Archiv für Geschichte der Medizin* 23 (1930): 197-204 [a footnote to his and Howald's

edition]; "Masse und Gewichte in den medizinischen Texten des frühen Mittelalters," *Kyklos* 3 (1930): 439–44 [using St. Gall 751].

21. *Autobiographical Writings,* 64; translated from "Erinnerungen," 17.

22. "[Sudhoff] regards him [Sigerist] perhaps as more brilliant and stirring and full of ideas about organization than as a solid, steady, thorough investigator"; the passage is from William Welch's diary for August 26, 1928, quoted in Berg-Schorn, *Henry E. Sigerist,* 165—though see also Sudhoff's remarks in a letter of 1929 quoted by her on p. 52. Cf. the assessment of his philological studies by Owsei Temkin: "This side of his work to which we owe much new knowledge represents the professional historian and it may be the reason why he is sometimes considered a medievalist. I doubt that such a designation was to his heart. Early medieval medicine to him was a field of special interest, not a specialization. The mere recital of titles referring to detailed work in other periods, for instance his edition of Haller's letters to Gesner [published in 1923], would suffice to prove my contention." "In Memory of Henry E. Sigerist," *Bulletin of the History of Medicine* 31 (1957): 287.

23. "Medical Literature," 35.

24. Ibid., 35–36.

25. Ibid., 37.

26. *Autobiographical Writings,* Diary, July 10, 1933, 86. "Angelo Mari" must be a transcriber's error for Angelo Mai (1782–1854), successively librarian of the Ambrosian and Vatican libraries, who edited a series of previously lost or unknown classical works that he had discovered in medieval palimpsests, most importantly perhaps Cicero's *De republica* (1822). (I am grateful to Dr. Owsei Temkin for proposing this identification to me.) Johann Albert Fabricius (1668–1736) was famous for his compilations of classical literature, his *Bibliotheca Latina* (1697) and especially his *Bibliotheca Graeca* (1705–28), "maximus antiquae eruditionis thesaurus."

27. *Autobiographical Writings,* Diary, May 31, 1933, 84.

28. Ibid., Diary, September 30, 1933, 88–89.

29. Ibid., Diary, October 3, 1933, 89.

30. Ibid., Diary, no date given but probably late September or early October 1934, 101.

31. Ibid., Diary, January 1, 1937, 119.

32. Pearl Kibre, *Hippocrates Latinus.*

33. Richard J. Durling, "A Chronological Census of Renaissance Editions and Translations of Galen," *Journal of the Warburg and Courtauld Institutes* 24 (1961): 230–305; id., "Corrigenda and Addenda to Diels' Galenica," *Traditio* 23 (1967): 461–76, and 37 (1981): 373–81.

34. In my view, Ernest Wickersheimer, *Les manuscrits latins de médecine du haut moyen âge dans les bibliothèques de France* (Paris: C.N.R.S., 1966), approaches Sigerist's vision more closely (it includes plates of many though not all the manuscripts it describes), but it deals exclusively with France.

35. "Early Mediaeval Medical Texts in Manuscripts of Montpellier," *Bulletin of the History of Medicine* 10 (1941): 27–47; "Early Mediaeval Medical Texts in Manuscripts of Vendôme," *Bulletin of the History of Medicine* 14 (1943): 68–113.

Sigerist's original plan of research is obvious in that while the manuscripts he described are not themselves all from the pre-Salernitan period, all do contain texts of the eleventh century or before.

36. Augusto Beccaria, *I codici di medicina del periodo presalernitano* (Rome: Edizioni di storia e letteratura, 1956), 11.

37. George W. Corner, "On Early Salernitan Surgery and Especially the 'Bamberg Surgery,'" *Bulletin of the Institute of the History of Medicine* 5 (1937): 1–27; id., *Anatomical Texts of the Earlier Middle Ages* (Washington, D.C.: Carnegie Institution, 1927).

38. Frederick Behrends, "Two Poems by Fulbert among Photographs of Chartres MSS in the University of North Carolina Library," *Scriptorium* 31 (1977): 295–96.

39. Loren C. MacKinney, "Tenth-Century Medicine as Seen in the *Historia* of Richer of Rheims," *Bulletin of the Institute of the History of Medicine* 2 (1934): 347–75.

40. Loren C. MacKinney, *Early Medieval Medicine with Special Reference to France and Chartres* (Baltimore: Johns Hopkins Press, 1937) — a "splendid book," said Sigerist ("The Latin Medical Literature of the Early Middle Ages," *Journal of the History of Medicine and Allied Sciences* 13 (1958): 138, n. 58).

41. "Bedside Manners in the Middle Ages," *Quarterly Bulletin of the Northwestern University Medical School* 20 (1946): 136–43; reprinted in *Henry E. Sigerist on the History of Medicine,* ed. Felix Marti-Ibañez (New York: MD Publications, 1960), 131–40.

42. The text may first have attracted his attention because a portion of it strongly resembled the deontological fragments that Ernst Hirschfeld had published in *Sudhoffs Archiv* in 1928.

43. Arnald of Villanova, *The Earliest Printed Book on Wine* (New York: Schuman's, 1943).

44. Ibid., 19.

45. See further Henry E. Sigerist, "A Fifteenth-Century Treatise on Wine," *Bulletin of the History of Medicine* 15 (1944): 189–200.

46. *Autobiographical Writings,* Diary, January 2, 1943, 178.

47. Published as Henry E. Sigerist, "The Latin Medical Literature of the Early Middle Ages," *Journal of the History of Medicine and Allied Sciences* 13 (1958): 127–46.

48. Cf. his appraisal of the period as expressed before the Medical Society of Zurich in 1921: "[The monks] watched faithfully during the worst period over the spark of the ancient spirit which though buried under a mountain of ashes continued to glimmer until a fresh breeze fanned it into flame." Henry Sigerist, "Tradition and Nature Observation in Medieval Medicine," *Medical Life* 30 (1923): 287.

49. [Victor Robinson], "Henry Sigerist: An Appreciation," *Medical Life* 30 (1923): 126.

50. "Hundredth Anniversary," 205.

CHAPTER 9

Intellectual Legacy and Political Quest: The Shaping of a Historical Ambition

Elizabeth Fee and Theodore M. Brown

A crucial failure haunts attempts to assess Henry Sigerist's achievement as a historian. He dreamed of writing a comprehensive and truly innovative history of medicine that would integrate social and political perspectives with traditional learning, thus bringing together the several fields of medicohistorical scholarship in a culminating synthesis. He first articulated that desire in 1936 but, after postponing the project numerous times, did not actually start writing until July 1945. He wrote substantial portions of the first volume of his *History of Medicine* before leaving the United States in 1947 and finished it after settling into his new home in Switzerland. Volume I was published in 1951, but Sigerist died before completing the second volume. Six other volumes, often projected, were apparently never begun. This huge gap between aspiration and achievement necessarily becomes the touchstone of any review of Sigerist's historiographic contributions.

Those warmly disposed to Sigerist have blamed external circumstances for his inability to complete the grand project. He had been weighed down by administrative burdens, enervated by the assaults of a hostile medical profession, depressed by the increasingly reactionary political climate of postwar America, and debilitated by failing physical health. Those more critically disposed have blamed Sigerist's flaws and personal deficiencies:

his underestimation of the difficulties of his project, his distractibility by the affairs of the moment, his excessive political enthusiasms, and perhaps his insufficient scholarly dedication. Sigerist failed to finish—indeed he barely started—his *History,* according to this latter view, because the task was so extravagantly ambitious.

After attempting to sympathize with all aspects of Sigerist's oftentimes contradictory career, we see matters somewhat differently. We recognize that he was inspired by a desire to give medical history clear contemporary relevance and struggled to achieve a fresh social-historical synthesis by reinterpreting historical scholarship in the light of his politics. But he did not always appreciate how difficult and daunting this would be to achieve. Increasingly, Sigerist understood that he wanted, and needed, to bridge history, sociology, and economics, but he long continued to oscillate between these areas, oftentimes still perceiving them as separate and largely unconnected. Indeed, in retreat or when depressed, he would long nostalgically for some earlier version of himself or for a simpler and more conventional project. When he finally discovered the connections he sought, he was at last able to overcome his self-imposed barriers, accomplish what he had long attempted, and succeed in writing volume I. Although he ran out of time and energy and was unable to complete the other volumes as planned, we would argue that volume I is in itself a significant realization of Sigerist's aspirations; it articulates a new historiographic program and demonstrates its application to the concrete details of Egyptian and Mesopotamian medicine. He had finally brought together his central passions: his scholarship and his politics. This essay outlines the quest that, we believe, shaped Sigerist's career as a historian in the last two decades of his professional life.

Sigerist's Early Career in Medical History

As has been abundantly demonstrated in the earlier essays in this volume, Sigerist did not initially set out to write an innovative and synthetic social history. His first interests and training were in philology and medieval studies. He was strongly directed by his mentor, Karl Sudhoff, to track down manuscript medical texts, establish their authenticity, and fit authors and contents into an orthodox intellectualist and iatrocentric framework. To Sudhoff's occasional dismay, Sigerist was also interested in a wide variety of other topics. But it was not until he left the relatively restricted intellectual world of Zurich for the greater openness and ferment of Leipzig in Weimar Germany that Sigerist really came into his own. In

Leipzig he cultivated his rapidly expanding interests in cultural history, pursued historical themes bearing on contemporary clinical practice, and began to explore the political and economic aspects of medicine. These latter interests—characteristic of Sigerist's Weimar period—became so engrossing that even in his Leipzig study of classical Greek medicine, he began to shift to more social perspectives.

Two books conceived and written in Leipzig capture Sigerist's new interests most clearly—*Einführung in die Medizin* (Man and Medicine) and *Grosse Ärzte* (The Great Doctors). These books made him famous well beyond Germany and the field of medical history. Both—*Einführung* (written in 1929–30 and published in 1931)[1] and *Grosse Ärzte* (written in 1931 and published in 1932)[2]—show clear traces of the old Sigerist, Sudhoff's student, protégé, and hand-picked scholarly successor. But both also exhibit the new Sigerist as he had developed independently of his mentor's interests. In *Grosse Ärzte,* for example, Sigerist included a capsule account of Harvey as the ideal representative of the baroque era, a passionate defense of Paracelsus as a prototypical German physician of rebellious and romantic style, and a sympathetic biography of Virchow as the courageous mid-nineteenth century proponent of social and medical reform.[3] These Weimar portraits are blended with more conventional ones that could easily have fit into Sudhoff's *Kurzes Handbuch* (Short Handbook) in its celebration of the evolutionary unfolding of the mainstream Western medical tradition.[4]

In *Einführung,* Sigerist's Weimar interpolations are more striking. Thus he exemplifies *Kulturgeschichte* in arguing that "in every epoch certain diseases are in the foreground . . . [and] are characteristic of this epoch."[5] He likewise probes various "philosophical-borderline" questions and a host of foundational medical issues.[6] Finally, he explores at some length the ideas of psychoanalysis; the complex reciprocal relationships between physician, patient, and society; and such contemporary social questions as health insurance and social hygiene legislation.[7] These interpolations made the *Einführung* a very current book but also indicated that Sigerist was now carrying a complex and perhaps unwieldy intellectual load. He had retained the ideas and methods he had learned from Sudhoff and was trying to balance them against his eclectic Weimar additions.

By the time the *Einführung* was published, Sigerist had already received an invitation to lecture in the United States during the 1931–32 academic year. Since he had become quite disaffected with life in Depression-era Germany, he readily accepted; America beckoned as an exciting new country full of possibilities. The interaction between his new American environment and his European heritage would be central to the next stage in his development as a medical historian.

Sigerist Discovers America

Sigerist landed in New York in September 1931, spent two months at Johns Hopkins, and then began a six-month tour across the continent. Delighted with almost everything he saw, he shared the conviction of many Americans that theirs was the country of the future. He visualized American history as a Homeric epic and promptly cast himself as an American Homer, who would not only interpret America to the Americans but also help solve its present problems. He also cast himself as an American Freud—one who could interpret the unconscious forces of history and thus help the country heal itself.[8]

Sigerist started writing his next book, *Amerika und die Medizin* (American Medicine), the day after his return to Germany and finished it during his first winter (1932–33) as director of the Johns Hopkins Institute of the History of Medicine. Its tone is relentlessly upbeat and optimistic: the overarching themes are the progressive nature of American medicine, the tremendous speed of its development, and its brilliant prospects. As Sigerist described his rush to publish the volume: "I was so overflowingly full of what I had experienced that I had to share my impressions, to trace a picture of American medicine, as it had become alive for me."[9]

While he was in the United States, Sigerist's first period of delight with America was followed by a second, equally uncritical, period of enthusiasm for the Soviet Union. *Amerika und die Medizin* had initially been written in German, for a European audience. In October 1934, two years after his move to America, Sigerist finished his epilogue to the English translation, *American Medicine,* with reference to a proposed volume on medicine in the Soviet Union:

> The United States of America and the Union of Soviet Socialist Republics today are the two countries that are experimenting in the medical field and are seeking new forms of medical service. . . . A book on Russian medicine will integrate this study on American medicine, and both together will make evident what the actual course of medicine is.[10]

Sigerist Turns toward the Soviet Union

Each New Year's Day, Sigerist carefully wrote out his plan for the year ahead on the first page of his diary. On January 1, 1933, he had recorded his still private idea of writing a book on Russian medicine; he also planned a three-volume work on medieval manuscripts, some translations, and a Latin grammar for the edification of struggling American students.[11] Over the next couple of years, he would complete the American volume, finish only a small part of the proposed work on medieval manuscripts, abandon the Latin grammar, and enthusiastically devote himself to the study of Soviet medicine.

In June 1933, Sigerist arrived in Europe for a long-planned summer of research on medieval manuscripts but, while meeting exiled German friends in France, was distracted from his archival explorations by urgent political discussions.[12] He was tempted by the idea of becoming politically active in European affairs, but told himself that as a Swiss national and a scholar, he should remain objective and detached.[13] But as the threat of fascism grew, as friends and acquaintances returned from the Soviet Union full of news about revolutionary developments, and as the political issues became more sharply framed and more compelling, Sigerist gave up any claim to detachment and threw himself into the great social and political issues of the day. After some anxious soul-searching, he decided to rededicate two of his precious summers—previously devoted to medieval studies—and spend them instead in studying the Soviet Union.[14] Sigerist had fully engaged the thirties.

Sigerist still referred to his work on medieval manuscripts as his "real work" but now seems to have regarded it with considerably less enthusiasm than before. In his diary, he noted with puzzlement that he felt little excitement about his planned summer research in the Italian archives.[15] Once in Europe in the summer of 1934—his last dedicated to medieval studies—Sigerist's diary accounts are mixed with reports of strikes in San Francisco, troubling news from Germany and Austria, reactions to left-wing books, and discussions of politics and economics.

Throughout early 1935, Sigerist was busy planning his first Soviet trip. In February, he confided to his diary: "It isn't spring yet but already I feel restless. . . . I am afraid that there will be no time for medieval studies. Well, they will have to wait." [16] He then spent the summer of 1935 in the Soviet Union. Weary of his administrative burdens at Hopkins, feeling less committed to traditional scholarly studies, and despairing of the future of Europe, he was ready to discover a new society based on equality and social justice.[17] Although Sigerist did not keep his diary as such during the Soviet tour, his reactions to the trip are detailed in his enthusiastic and extravagantly optimistic account, *Socialized Medicine in the Soviet Union*.[18] After visits to health facilities across the country, he had persuaded himself that his hopes for that nation were either already realized or in process of becoming true.[19] He returned to America inspired and affirmed in his conviction that the Soviet Union had ushered in a new era in medicine, a new civilization, and a new man.[20]

Sigerist spent two months in the summer of 1936 in the Soviet Union and two months in Switzerland, where he started writing *Socialized Medicine in the Soviet Union*. Conceived as a primer on the Soviet medical system and an introduction to socialism for young medical workers, the book provided a brief history of the revolution, an outline of the principles of Soviet medicine, and a general picture of social welfare measures and public health initiatives.[21] It is breathless in its endorsement of everything Soviet. Sigerist explained that he had not "wasted time" in describing the inadequacies and inefficiencies of Soviet institutions; as in the case of his American book, he had chosen to stress only "positive achievements," convinced that only these would "enrich the world."[22]

When he returned to Baltimore, Sigerist was ready, he thought, to begin his *History,* an intention first declared in his diary in January 1936.[23] But he was now aware of a dissonance between his newly acquired Marxist categories of analysis and his older historiographic principles, and after months of struggling to conceptualize and organize the project, he confided to his diary: "I have terrific gaps. My knowledge of economic history is most superficial and I should be able to devote at least a year to studying it. I must ask for a leave of absence soon."[24] Economic history had been irrelevant to the history of medicine conceived exclusively in terms of philological scholarship or cultural history, but it would be essential for a major reinterpretation informed by Marxist ideas. Sigerist was searching for a new historiographic framework consistent with his political convictions and social vision.[25]

Constructing a new framework would take time, thought, and concentration. Sigerist's favorite mode of learning was by travel—both his American and Soviet books had been the results of long tours in which he soaked up information by looking, by talking to people, by asking questions and observing. He had started each of these books immediately on his return from a trip abroad, writing at high speed in an attempt to capture the experience intact. But what had worked for his American and Soviet books would not work for the projected *History of Medicine*. Sigerist needed time for digestion and reflection—time to learn new analytical approaches and time to break down the inhibiting conceptual barriers that in his mind still separated contemporary comparative "medical sociology" from "real history." "What I need," he told himself, "is a whole year devoted to research—without any lectures."[26]

Yet Sigerist did not have, or did not take, the necessary time, instead continuing his old patterns of incessant activity. He was in constant demand: as a teacher who loved the energy he absorbed from working with students, as a public speaker who delighted in responsive audiences, and as an effective administrator who, despite his repeated complaints, derived satisfaction from being attentive to institutional needs. Instead of creating the contemplative space he needed, Sigerist acceded to (yet resented) the pressures, demands, and satisfactions of the moment. Within a few weeks of promising yet again to commit himself fully to research, he agreed to serve for a two-year term as president of the History of Science Society and even decided to make a movie, never finished, called "Baltimore: Profile of a City." [27]

Sigerist's Writing Blocks and "Inhibitions"

On New Year's Day 1939, Sigerist again resolved to begin his "great work—the History and Sociology." [28] Yet at the same time, he planned a lecture tour in South Africa and scheduled an exhausting round of talks, lectures, seminars, and conferences in America. As time passed, his unwritten "great work" became even bigger: the "History and Sociology" grew into an eight-volume "History" and a four-volume "Sociology"— but there were still no chapters on paper and no time in which to focus on the work. [29]

When Sigerist returned to the United States from South Africa in January 1940, he found that the mood of the country had changed. Feeling no longer welcome in America, he began to fantasize about escaping to scholarly isolation: "I have only one desire; to return to Switzerland, to hide in a village and to work, to write my book." [30] In this period, he undertook small projects of historical reinterpretation: in "The People's Misery," he presented Johann Peter Frank—portrayed in *The Great Doctors* as a bureaucratic rationalizer—as a populist, calling upon the ruling elite to commit itself to the needs of the peasants. [31] Similarly, he reinvented Max von Pettenkofer—once the scientist of hygiene—now as a humanitarian, bringing nutritious meals to the poor. [32] In these small pieces, Sigerist tried to bring his politics into the rewriting of history, but if his efforts were well intended, the results were modest.

When Sigerist faced a bigger assignment—the 1938 Terry lectures at Yale (finally published in 1941 as *Medicine and Human Welfare*) [33] or the 1940 Messenger lectures at Cornell (ultimately published in 1943 as *Civilization and Disease*), [34] larger problems surfaced. Acutely unhappy, he struggled to break through to a new historiography consistent with his social vision and his politics. But because he could not yet see clearly how to do this, he remained blocked for long periods. He would recycle old material and pull together bits and pieces, some of it new, but some of it quite stale. In *Civilization and Disease,* he began with two fresh chapters on the material and economic determinants of disease but then relapsed into nine chapters on cultural factors that could have been—and probably were—largely written in Leipzig.

Sigerist had promised himself to begin writing the *History of Medicine* in 1941, on his fiftieth birthday. He did not, however, begin the book in 1941 or, for that matter, in 1942. In November 1942, he wrote in his diary: "I suffer from lack of sleep and in spite of working 14 hours a day achieve very little." [35] For comfort, he retreated to medieval studies and translations. [36] Still teaching, editing, and writing reviews, translations, and reports, his black moods became more frequent as he contemplated his inability to write his projected masterwork, the often-promised *History of Medicine.* [37] In late 1943, he wrote in his diary: "Of course it is hard to work and work day in and day out and to feel that what you do is insignificant, mere odds and ends, that your real work, the one you have been preparing all your life is lost forever." [38]

Sigerist increasingly dreamt of escape. If he could only get away, he insisted, he would be able to accomplish the work that would give his life and career true meaning. [39] In the spring of 1944, he was greatly cheered by the idea that Yale might offer him a research chair. He began again to think about writing his *History* and *Sociology* and even planned a lecture tour of Canada: "Now that I *do* think of writing the Sociology these tours have meaning again. On such tours I gather the materials and the experience for the book." [40] He became increasingly worried when he heard no more from Yale and started to work at a frantic pace, sleeping only a few hours a night and drafting a new book of contemporary essays, *The University at the Crossroads.* [41] Feeling alone, unappreciated, and unsupported, he contrasted his own loneliness with the imagined happiness of his counterparts under socialism. [42]

Looking at Sigerist's schedule, it seems reasonable to suggest that his most time-consuming responsibilities were those he had willingly, even eagerly, assumed. A week after complaining about the imposed demands of his Hopkins job, for example, he left for Canada, spent almost five weeks conducting a health survey of Saskatchewan, then touched down in Baltimore for two weeks and promptly left again for a seven-week tour of India. [43] These tours, rationalized as ways of preparing to write his

Sociology, were simultaneously welcome distractions from his blocked efforts at writing his *History.* They were also energizers—times when he slept and ate heartily, felt better about himself, took pleasure in a job well done, and enjoyed his celebrity status and the appreciative audience responses to his lectures and reports. But the trips had another, unrecognized purpose. All the while he was in motion, and although he didn't realize it himself at the time, he was absorbing important lessons for his *History.*

The *History,* Volume One, and Sigerist's Return to Europe

At last, in July 1945, Sigerist began writing. Within two months, he had completed 225 pages of the first volume. In 1946, he was still writing, and still dreaming of escape, this time to a village in the Alps: "I would like a garden with camellias and mimosas and a lemon tree. It would be the monastery that I would enter and never leave." [44] He resolved to leave America and, in late June 1947, moved to the Ticino region of Switzerland near the Italian border. [45]

Once relocated in Europe and allowing himself time for work and reflection, Sigerist was able to finish the first volume of his *History.* He now realized that his medical sociology and health care reform efforts were not useless distractions from proper scholarship but the very key to integrating his scholarly and political selves. As he wrote in the foreword, "Field work in social medicine . . . [at an earlier time] seemed to have no connection whatever with my historical studies; yet after every such tour I knew that I had a deeper understanding of the workings of history." [46]

Finally published in 1951, volume I begins with a long introduction, a "statement of policy" as he calls it, in which he traces the outlines of "a new pattern of medical historiography." Sigerist had been struggling to define the essence of this new historiography since the mid-thirties, when, as we have suggested, he had moved clearly in the direction of political engagement, comparative medical sociology, and efforts to construct a materialist understanding of health and disease. In 1936 he told George Sarton that the history of medicine, like medicine itself, must be grounded in an analysis of the social and economic realities of society. [47] From 1936 on, in his essays, lectures, and books, Sigerist had introduced recognizable if sometimes adulterated fragments of a new methodological approach in which he took geographic, demographic, socioeconomic, occupational, and organizational factors as fundamental agencies in the causation and distribution of disease. He used a similar method to analyze professional and societal responses to those patterns of health and disease.[48] In volume I these earlier fragments, largely purified of their *Kulturgeschichte* residues, are finally fused into a more unified historiographic structure.

Sigerist derived his new historiography from the insights and findings of his earlier-developed comparative medical sociology, now used systematically to explore the material foundations and social relations of medicine in past societies. Generalizing on the basis of his knowledge of the contemporary world, he mapped the economic structures and class frameworks of past societies; building his analysis on the basis of a critical sociology, he proposed to follow these social structures diachronically rather than synchronically. By thus dissolving the compartmental barriers between "medical history" and "medical sociology," Sigerist allowed the lessons learned through field work to be transformed into a novel historical approach that displaced earlier, more conventional, methods and assumptions. The end result was to be a new social history of medicine that could identify powerful trends deriving from "the whole economic and social structure of a given society" and make these central in understanding the historical dynamics of health and medicine.[49]

Sigerist argued that the historian must first consider the prevailing health conditions in any society, by examining the dominant diseases to which rich and poor were subject. Historical epidemiology should clearly include analysis of the class relations of health and disease. The historian should study the material conditions of the society, starting with the geographical, physical, and socioeconomic environment. This study should include analysis of the economic structure of society, of the means of production of food and commodities, and of the conditions of work and recreation, housing and nutrition. One needed to know what methods were used to maintain health and prevent illness and how such hygienic measures were distributed by class: did rich and poor have different possibilities for protecting their health? A study of therapeutic responses was needed to understand the various kinds of health practitioners and the services they delivered to the different sectors of the population. The historian must explore the social history of the patient, the relationship of patients to doctors, and the relationship of illness to social structure. In addition, it was important to understand the impact of sickness, medical care, and medical institutions on people's lives and to consider the level of development of a sense of collective social obligation, social welfare measures, and public health.

Sigerist illustrated his new approach in a detailed study of ancient Egypt.[50] Moving from a description of the geographic setting to an analysis of social and economic conditions, he noted that the hierarchically layered and fundamentally inequitable Egyptian socioeconomic order led to perverse health consequences. Therapeutic responses to illness were likewise stratified and inequitable. Different systems of magicoreligious and empiricorational medicine coexisted, but the most highly specialized and presumably most effective empiricorational practitioners were available only to the elite, who seemed, if anything, to suffer from an oversupply of medical attendants.[51]

This new description contrasted sharply with the portrait of Egyptian medicine that Sudhoff had presented in his *Kurzes Handbuch* or that Sigerist himself had outlined in *Grosse Ärzte*.[52] In the latter book, Sigerist had recounted the tale of Imhotep's elevation from ancient Egyptian high official to god of healing, to illustrate the point that throughout the course of history, most of the sick had sought aid from faith rather than from scientific medicine—suggesting that their troubles owed more to superstition than to economic inequity. In volume I of his *History of Medicine*, twenty years later, Sigerist had completely revised the medical history of ancient Egypt and placed it on a materialist foundation. He had clearly begun the task he had set himself of reinterpreting the entire history of medicine.

Sigerist's quest was at last successful. He had demonstrated the possibility of a new interpretation that drew its central inspiration from Marxist theory, infused with a rich sense of cultural complexity that he carried over from his earlier historiographic training and experience. Although he was unable to finish his *History*, he had written enough to serve as a model that others might be able to follow. To the end, Sigerist hoped that other scholars would complete the work he had started. In October 1954 he suffered a severe stroke, which caused considerable disability and from which he never fully recovered.[53] In 1961, four years after his death, Oxford University Press published the incomplete draft of the second volume of Sigerist's *History*, edited by his former Hopkins associate, Ludwig Edelstein.[54]

It is of course sad that Sigerist was unable to finish the enormous task he had set himself. From one perspective, the task was simply too large—no one person could realistically expect to rewrite the entire history of world health and medicine in the kind of depth and detail that Sigerist desired. He had wanted to bring together economics and medicine, sociology and science, in one grand synthesis, unified by a single vision. The quest was an admirable one, and even its partial realization represents a triumph of historical scholarship and imagination.

Today, historians of medicine tend to write monographs. Many share at least some of Sigerist's ideas but generally select a more limited canvas, being content to present aspects of a larger, still unwritten whole. Broad synthetic histories remain radically unfashionable in an age of cautious specialization.

Yet there is much to be said in favor of adopting a larger canvas, a broader perspective. Medicine is but one of many factors contributing to health; the overwhelming importance of social and economic conditions in determining broad population patterns of health and disease is well established.[55] As a historian, Sigerist was searching for ways of addressing these issues—including in his synthetic work a specific focus on medicine but also going well beyond the limits of medical thought and practice. He was both inspired and constrained by his inheritance of European historiography and his classical training.[56] This entire tradition of scholarship with its emphasis on intellectual lineage and cultural context was challenged by the implications of Sigerist's new-found politics, his passion for the Soviet Union, and his discovery of Marxist materialism. It was Sigerist's quest, the central struggle of his career, and his final achievement to bring together these disparate, apparently contradictory elements and to create a new program for the history of medicine.

Notes

1. Henry E. Sigerist, *Einführung in die Medizin* (Leipzig: Georg Thieme Verlag, 1931). Translated by Margaret Galt Boise as *Man and Medicine. An Introduction to Medical Knowledge* (New York: W. W. Norton, 1932); citations are to this edition.

2. Henry E. Sigerist, *Grosse Ärzte. Eine Geschichte der Heilkunde in Lebensbildern* (Munich: J. F. Lehmanns Verlag, 1932). Translated by Eden and Cedar Paul as *Great Doctors. A Biographical History of Medicine,* in several British and American editions; citations will be to the 1958 Doubleday Anchor Book edition, *The Great Doctors* (Garden City, N.Y.: Doubleday, 1958).

3. Henry E. Sigerist, *The Great Doctors,* 101, 124–25, 139, 322–25.

4. Karl Sudhoff, *Kurzes Handbuch der Geschichte der Medizin* (Berlin: Verlag von S. Karger, 1922).

5. Henry E. Sigerist, *Man and Medicine,* 180.

6. *Ibid.,* 51–71, 213–20, 233–75.

7. *Ibid.* 53–67, 271–74, 289–316.

8. Henry E. Sigerist, *Amerika und die Medizin* (Leipzig: Georg Thieme Verlag, 1933). Translated by Hildegard Nagel as *American Medicine* (New York: W. W. Norton, 1934); citation to the English edition, xvi–xvii.

9. He continues: "An artist, after a great experience, a deep emotion, will be urged to put into tangible form what he has felt. In the same way, the historian who has felt the pulse of history will be bound to recreate the process he has witnessed." *American Medicine,* xviii.

10. *American Medicine,* 288.

11. Henry E. Sigerist, Diary, January 1, 1933. Yale University Library, Henry E. Sigerist Papers, Addition (June 1987), Biographical Data and Memorabilia, group 788, box 1 (hereafter cited as Diary); partially excerpted in Nora Sigerist Beeson, ed., *Henry E. Sigerist: Autobiographical Writings* (Montreal: McGill University Press, 1966), 82. In the following references, where specific manuscript diary entries are included in the selection published by Nora Sigerist Beeson, both the manuscript and published references are given; where diary entries were not included in that volume, only the manuscript diary entry is cited.

12. Without doubt, Sigerist's observation of the social conditions and contradictions of the depression and the hungry thirties influenced his perceptions of American reality. He saw, in ever starker terms, the contrast between agricultural plenty and hunger, between the wealth of the fortunate few and the growing desperation of the unemployed. But a close reading of Sigerist's diaries suggests that the experiences of his summers in Europe and his horrified observations of the rise of fascism in Germany and Italy were more important in bringing him to a new and sharpened political perspective.

13. Henry E. Sigerist, Diary, July 20, 1933.

14. Sigerist was especially eager to visit the Soviet Union, the country in which he now believed history was being made. "There is no doubt that Russia is a unique opportunity. There are new ideas, new trends in all fields and while we talk they act there. . . . I must go there, see and study a world *in statu nascendi.*" Diary, July 22, 1933.

15. In February 1934, Sigerist made his reservations for the summer trip to Europe and reflected, "Last year I was looking forward to the summer trip. This year I'm not, I don't know why." Diary, February 21, 1934.

16. Henry E. Sigerist, Diary, February 5, 1935.

17. En route to Russia, he wrote: "I am sailing full of enthusiasm for that new world about which I read so much. Will I find what I am looking for, hopes realized, the promise of a better future, a world built on rational foundations with justice for all?" Henry E. Sigerist, Diary, June 8, 1935; *Autobiographical Writings,* 109.

18. Henry E. Sigerist, *Socialized Medicine in the Soviet Union* (New York: W. W. Norton, 1937).

19. For details and critical analysis, see John Hutchinson's essay in this volume.

20. In a fairly typical passage, Sigerist exults: "With us it has become a maxim that human nature can not be changed, that man will always remain the same selfish brute. The Soviet Union has proved that human nature can be changed. It has been changed. A new social order has been established. A new civilization has been created with boundless possibilities of development." *Socialized Medicine,* 63.

21. "I wished I could have written what I felt: that the book was written primarily for young medical [workers] as an introduction to socialism." Henry E. Sigerist, Diary, May 20, 1937.

22. *Socialized Medicine,* 308.

23. Henry E. Sigerist, Diary, January 1, 1936.

24. Ibid., November 17, 1937; see also November 30, 1937.

25. In his exploration of Marxist economic history, Sigerist had been much impressed by the work of the British writer, John Strachey, and especially by his

The Coming Struggle for Power (London: Gollancz, 1932). It is significant that there were few American theorists upon whom Sigerist could draw in attempting to construct a new historiography. For the weaknesses of American Marxism in this period, see Christopher Phelps, "The Poverty of Marxist Crisis Theory During the Great Depression," University of Rochester seminar paper, May 1994.

26. Henry E. Sigerist, Diary, November 4, 1938.

27. Ibid., December 20, 1938; December 29, 1938.

28. Ibid., January 1, 1939.

29. Ibid., January 4, 1939. For Sigerist's discussions of these proposed works and his outline of the *Sociology,* see the essays in this volume by Brown and Fee and by Roemer, Falk, and Brown.

30. Henry E. Sigerist, Diary, February 1, 1940; *Autobiographical Writings,* 163.

31. Henry E. Sigerist, "The People's Misery: Mother of Diseases. An address, delivered in 1790 by Johann Peter Frank. Translated from the Latin, with an introduction," *Bulletin of the History of Medicine* 9 (1941): 81–100. For Sigerist's earlier view of Frank, see *The Great Doctors,* 243–57.

32. Henry E. Sigerist, "The Value of Health to a City. Two lectures delivered in 1873 by Max von Pettenkofer. Translated from the German," *Bulletin of the History of Medicine* 10 (1941): 437–503; 593–613. For Sigerist's earlier view of Pettenkofer, see *The Great Doctors,* 389–93.

33. Henry E. Sigerist, *Medicine and Human Welfare* (New Haven: Yale University Press, 1941).

34. Henry E. Sigerist, *Civilization and Disease* (Ithaca, N.Y.: Cornell University Press, 1943).

35. Henry E. Sigerist, Diary, November 19, 1942; *Autobiographical Writings,* 177.

36. In this period, for example, he published Arnald of Villanova, *The Earliest Printed Book on Wine* (New York: Schuman's, 1943); see Michael McVaugh's essay in this volume.

37. "Few people," he said in a gloomy mood, "read what I write, particularly my historical papers." Henry E. Sigerist, Diary, August 4, 1943.

38. Henry E. Sigerist, Diary, November 26, 1943; February 25, 1944. See also *Autobiographical Writings,* 184.

39. Henry E. Sigerist, Diary, April 10, 1944. See also Theodore M. Brown's essay in this volume.

40. Ibid., May 3, 1944.

41. Henry E. Sigerist, *The University at the Crossroads. Addresses and Essays* (New York: Henry Schuman, 1946).

42. "The Soviet researcher," he said, "feels very close to the people because they appreciate his work. He feels carried and constantly stimulated by their sympathetic understanding." Diary, July 29, 1944.

43. Jacalyn Duffin's "The Guru and the Godfather: Henry Sigerist, Hugh Mac-Lean, and the Politics of Health Reform in 1940s Canada," *Canadian Bulletin of Medical History/ Bulletin canadien d'histoire de la médecine* 9 (1992): 191–218, provides a useful perspective on Sigerist's relationship to the health reform process in Canada; Ilza Veith's essay in this volume discusses his interest in India.

44. Henry E. Sigerist, Diary, November 25, 1946; *Autobiographical Writings,* 202.

45. See Nora Sigerist Beeson's essay and the accompanying photographs.

46. Henry E. Sigerist, *A History of Medicine,* vol. I (New York: Oxford University Press, 1951), xvii.

47. Henry E. Sigerist, "The History of Medicine and the History of Science," *Bulletin of the History of Medicine* 4 (1936): 1–13.

48. See, in addition to *Medicine and Human Welfare* (1941) and *Civilization and Disease* (1943), "Historical Background of Industrial and Occupational Diseases," *Bulletin of the New York Academy of Medicine,* 2nd series, 12 (1936): 597–609 and "The Social History of Medicine," *Western Journal of Surgery* 48 (1940): 715–22.

49. Henry E. Sigerist, *A History of Medicine,* vol. I, 32.

50. Ibid., 217–373.

51. Ibid., 320–21.

52. Karl Sudhoff, *Kurzes Handbuch der Geschichte der Medizin,* 1–2, 7–8; Henry E. Sigerist, "Imhotep and Aesculapius," in *The Great Doctors,* 21–28.

53. *Autobiographical Writings,* 247.

54. Henry E. Sigerist, *A History of Medicine,* vol. II (New York: Oxford University Press, 1961), v–x.

55. See also Elizabeth Fee, "Public Health Past and Present: A Shared Social Vision," introductory essay to the expanded edition of George Rosen, *A History of Public Health* (Baltimore: Johns Hopkins University Press, 1993), lx–lxvii.

56. See also Heinrich von Staden's essay in this volume.

PART 3

Sigerist and
American Politics

The Pleasures and Perils of Prophetic Advocacy: Socialized Medicine and the Politics of American Medical Reform

Elizabeth Fee

As a European immigrant and as a historian, Henry E. Sigerist played a surprisingly important and visible role in American medical politics. In the 1930s and early 1940s, he became a leading proponent of national health insurance and the country's chief advocate of socialized medicine. He turned his potential handicaps to advantage: he used his familiarity with European and especially the German health insurance system to speak with authority on international variations in medical care organization. As a historian, he was persuaded—and persuasive in arguing— that the history of medicine was a story of social and scientific progress.[1] According to his historical account, individualized medical practice was based on relatively primitive science and technology; this must gradually be superseded by state-run and state-financed health services capable of deriving maximum benefit from an increasingly sophisticated scientific and technological base. National health insurance was but one step in this historical progression. Sigerist thus lent the weight of history to the cause of medical reform.

In America in the 1930s, Henry Sigerist's message about the need for increasing state intervention in health care was compatible with the views

● WHAT IS THE STATE OF THE NATION'S HEALTH?

Is the People's Health
A Government Responsibility?

DR. HENRY E. SIGERIST

How can the people get better medical care?

Should the poor be thrown upon the private charity of the doctor for treatment?

●

"A NATIONAL HEALTH PROGRAM"

Will be discussed by

Dr. Henry E. Sigerist

Director, Institute of the History of Medicine at the Johns Hopkins University; world renowned authority on the history of medicine. Author of "Man and Medicine", "The Great Doctors", "American Medicine", "Socialized Medicine in the Soviet Union". Dr. Sigerist's works are translated into many languages, including Chinese.

●

Sunday, February 19th, 1939, 8.15 P.M.

PEOPLES FORUM

120 N. 18th Street 6 Subscription 25c

Questions and Discussion.

COMING—Feb. 26. Leo Huberman. Mar. 5. Ruth McKenney. Mar. 12. Dr. Ch'ao-ting Chi. Mar. 19. Sam Adams Darcy. April 2. Harry Gannes.

and interests of medical liberals. These included representatives of some of the most powerful private foundations and influential professors at the nation's leading medical schools who believed that medical care should be more efficiently and rationally organized, but without challenging the political and economic foundations of American society. Between 1935 and 1939, Sigerist belonged to this charmed circle of liberal leaders and, at the same time, emerged as a spokesman for the left wing of the medical profession, an impassioned advocate of socialized medicine, an enthusiastic supporter of socialism and the Soviet Union, and a popular hero in an overlapping network of antifascist and progressive groups that were continuously organizing, debating, and preparing statements and manifestos on the political issues of the day.[2]

But by 1940, after the Nazi-Soviet pact and the Soviet invasion of Finland, Sigerist became vulnerable to attack. Most of the assaults came from conservative physicians angered by his activism in medical politics and his advocacy of national health insurance. In the context of rapidly spreading anti-Soviet public feeling, they used his book *Socialized Medicine in the Soviet Union* as a weapon against him.[3] Hurt and upset by the violence of these attacks, Sigerist continued to be active in medical politics, although now displaying increasing ambivalence. He continued to speak out forcefully on public platforms across the country but, at the same time, began emotionally to disengage from political activities and ultimately from America.

This essay examines the shifts and turns in Sigerist's relationship to medical politics and medical reform. The main focus is his years in America: from his early period as a rapidly rising star in the world of medical politics, through the 1930s to the war years, when his luster was dimmed, to the postwar years when he chose to leave the country as the winds of anticommunism were gathering force. For this decade and a half, Sigerist was an inspirational force for the students, interns, physicians, and public health professionals whose lives he touched and whose efforts to organize he encouraged and promoted.[4]

The Leipzig Years: 1925–1932

In his autobiographical writings, Sigerist traced his interest in the social and political organization of medicine to his time at the Leipzig Institute

35. (*facing page*) Flyer advertising Sigerist's talk "A National Health Program" at the People's Forum, Philadelphia, February 19, 1939.

of the History of Medicine.[5] Although still engaged in intense scholarly studies, he was already exploring a wide range of social, cultural, and philosophical problems and calling on scholars to derive their fundamental questions from contemporary concerns. The political and economic crisis of Germany in the late 1920s also directed his attention to practical problems in the organization of medical care. As social welfare expenditures were cut and physicians' incomes fell, many doctors saw the health insurance system as the source of their problems.[6]

In this context, Sigerist not only defended the German insurance system but argued that the state must take broadened responsibility for medical care.[7] As Germany's political and economic crisis deepened, he focused increasing attention on these controversial issues and ended his volume of introductory lectures to medical students, *Einführung in die Medizin* (Man and Medicine), by lauding the German social insurance system as "an epoch-making world event."[8] He warned physicians against nostalgia for a long-dead era of individual private practice. The physician who "obstructs progress and clings to yesterday's ideals" would, he declared, be pushed aside.[9]

Erwin Ackerknecht, a student member of the Leipzig Institute and himself a Trotskyist in the 1920s, later claimed to have introduced Sigerist to Marxism.[10] Whatever their origins, Sigerist's early political views were shaped both by his defense of German health and welfare measures and by his antagonism to the rising power of German fascism; in the Leipzig period, he had definite socialist leanings but was not yet strongly influenced by Marxism.

In America: From the Depression to the New Deal, 1931–1935

When Sigerist arrived in the United States in 1931 for an extended lecture tour, the country was in the midst of depression. The economic boom and unbridled financial speculation of the 1920s had ended with the stock market crash of 1929; Franklin D. Roosevelt was running for president; and millions of people were unemployed or underemployed. Health care costs were but one of the country's many problems as the Committee on the Costs of Medical Care (CCMC), funded by eight major foundations, prepared its final and most famous report.[11] The CCMC had already published, over a period of five years, twenty-six research volumes and fifteen smaller reports on the organization and financing of health care; the total representing, as one of its supporters declared, "the most complete body of information on medical care and medical economics ever available in this country." [12] These reports detailed the difficulties people faced in meeting the costs of illness and showed how the economic depression had exacerbated longer-term problems of financing medical and hospital care.[13] Despite its rather mild proposals for medical care reform, the American Medical Association attacked the final report as an "incitement to revolution." [14]

Immediately on his arrival in America, Sigerist read an article in *Harper's* magazine entitled "The Crisis of Medical Service"; he promptly endorsed the work of the CCMC but balanced his cautious criticisms of medical financing with a lively enthusiasm for all things American.[15] *American Medicine,* the book he began immediately after his return to Germany, was full of admiration for American dynamism, experimentation, and fluidity as well as for its sophisticated science and technology.[16] But, cautioned Sigerist, although American medicine was technically brilliant, it was delivered through an outdated, irrational, and disorganized system of individualistic fee-for-service practice.[17] Instead, he argued, medical services should be rationally organized and managed on a local and national level to provide patients with comprehensive and affordable care: "The organization of medical care is built everywhere on presuppositions that belong to the past. . . . The physician has not yet found his place in modern society." [18]

Sigerist's contempt for fee-for-service medicine resonated with the attitudes of critics of American medicine. It may also have been expressive of an aristocratic European distaste for money making: "It is unworthy of his professional standing for the physician to be forced to express the value of each individual service in terms of money, as if he were a storekeeper," he said. "It is an insult to their profession. . . . Are physicians really supposed to be inferior to professors, judges, or clergymen? Those whose minds are on riches had better join the stock exchange." [19] In an amusing and caustic series of remarks, he expressed amazement at the widespread resistance to health insurance "since America is the promised land of insurance companies. People insure themselves against every possible risk, and insurance agents swarm like mosquitoes in August." He ended, rather more diplomatically, by suggesting that the states should experiment with a variety of approaches to medical care organization and financing, and with the hope that the American Medical Association would adopt a responsible position with regard to reform.[20]

During his early years in America, Sigerist was welcomed and applauded by the leaders of American academic medicine and by representatives of the liberal philanthropies. Men such as Harvey Cushing at Harvard, John Fulton at Yale, and William Henry Welch at Hopkins were delighted with Sigerist's engaging lectures, his obvious erudition, and his personal charm. It was a sign of his reputation and acceptance when Harvey Cushing, who had become ill, chose Sigerist to speak in his place at the 150th anniversary of the New Haven County Medical Association in 1933.[21] Cushing suggested he talk about the history of medical societies and consult Morris Fishbein—the acerbic, talented, urbane, and conservative editor of the *Journal of the American Medical Association*.[22] Cushing was perhaps not yet aware that Sigerist and Fishbein represented polar positions on the great medical political issues of the day. Sigerist ignored the advice to consult Fishbein and, after some anguished soul-searching, produced an appropriately innocuous paper on the history of medical societies.[23]

By this time, Sigerist had already begun to develop a friendship with a very different figure in American medicine, John A. Kingsbury of the Milbank Memorial Fund. In 1932, when Sigerist heard that Kingsbury was coming to Baltimore to speak about his recent trip to the Soviet Union, he was alarmed to discover that Kingsbury and Sir Arthur Newsholme were planning to publish a book on Soviet medicine—one possibly competitive with his own projected volume. He was however soon reassured by Kingsbury's friendly encouragement and later recalled this first meeting as the beginning of an important friendship.[24] Sigerist found in Kingsbury an ally who shared his interest in the Soviet Union and his enthusiasm for the more wide-ranging versions of medical care reform; he also found an excellent guide to progressive medical politics.[25] Kingsbury invited Sigerist to participate in Milbank Memorial Fund conferences and join the forces working for national health insurance. As Sigerist warmed to Kingsbury, his relationship to the more conservative kingmaker, Harvey Cushing, cooled.

In 1933, Sigerist's private political views were becoming more distinctly socialist. He was completing *American Medicine* and eager to begin his book on Soviet medicine. Horrified by the growth of fascism in Europe, he was fascinated by the Soviet Union. "Socialism is rational," he decided, and "therefore scientific. It would appeal to America much more than any mystic [fascistic] conception of the state."[26] Returning from a summer in Europe, he assured a *New York Times* reporter that socialized medicine was "the answer to over-specialization."[27]

Nationally, the burning health policy question in 1934–35 was whether President Roosevelt would include health insurance in the social security bill he recommended to Congress.[28] In 1934, Roosevelt established a cabinet-level Committee on Economic Security under the chairmanship of the secretary of labor, Frances Perkins, with authority to recommend social welfare policy. Preparatory work was done by a series of technical committees; Edgar Sydenstricker, a leading proponent of national health insurance, was director of the Technical Committee on Medical Care. Roosevelt and Perkins were concerned about the potential medical opposition to health insurance and wondered whether to omit it from the reform proposals presented to Congress. Sydenstricker and his assistant, Isidore S. Falk, tried to enlist the aid of progressive physicians to argue in favor of national health insurance, but theirs was an uphill battle.

By the time Sigerist became involved with the struggle over national health insurance in 1934, the more conservative physicians were already well organized in opposition. In January that year, Sigerist had his first public confrontation with Morris Fishbein at a conference in Philadelphia, "The Medical Profession and the Public."[29] Sigerist spoke on the history of European medical care systems and health insurance; like several of the other speakers, he noted in his diary, he emphasized the "socialistic trends" while Fishbein rejected all innovation.[30] A couple of months later, in March 1934, Sigerist was invited by Kingsbury to speak at the Annual Conference of the Milbank Memorial Fund. About one hundred distinguished participants and guests gathered at the Academy of Medicine in New York; the speakers included Surgeon General Hugh S. Cumming, Edgar Sydenstricker, Charles-Edward A. Winslow, Harry L. Hopkins, Thomas Parran, and Lillian Wald, among others; the attendees included Michael Davis, Jean Downes, Louis Dublin, Iago Galdston, George St. J. Perrott, and G. Canby Robinson—virtually everybody who was anybody in the medical care liberal reform circuit at that time.[31] The participants attended workshops on different aspects of health policy, and Sigerist participated in one on health planning and medical care with Isidore S. Falk, who greatly impressed him.[32] He was also delighted with Fiorello La Guardia, the mayor of New York, "a little man but an energetic devil" who gave what he described as "a very good speech, very progressive."[33] After an opulent dinner, Sigerist, Harry L. Hopkins, and C.-E. A. Winslow spoke on the need to reorganize medical care. Sigerist was in good company: Hopkins was head of the federal relief programs (first the Civil Works Administration and later the Works Progress Administration) and Winslow was professor of public health at Yale and chairman of the Executive Committee of the Committee on the Costs of Medical Care.[34]

In his talk "Trends toward Socialized Medicine," Sigerist argued—much as he had done earlier in Leipzig—that as society became more complex, states could no longer leave medicine to the individual physician-patient relationship; they needed to intervene in the social sphere, to encourage cooperation, and to distribute risk in the organization of medical care.[35] Visionary and by no means inflammatory, Sigerist's speech delivered exactly the message those at the meeting wanted to hear: that historical trends supported moves in the direction of more structured and rational forms of medical care delivery.

Sigerist was more impressed, stimulated, and energized by this meeting than by any other event in his American experience to date. The combined weight of medical care experts such as Michael M. Davis, foundation officials such as John A. Kingsbury, university presidents such as Livingston Farrand of Cornell, government officials such as Thomas Parran, and not least, the enthusiasm of Mayor La Guardia, convinced him that America might really be ready for national health insurance. "After this very inspiring meeting I have the firm conviction that sickness insurance is not far," he concluded. "The responsible politicians are in favor of it and the opposition of the profession is not of a valid kind." [36]

Inspired by the discovery that national medical care reform was more strongly supported, better organized, and more respectable than he had realized, Sigerist decided to broaden the scope of the Institute of the History of Medicine, appoint a sociologist, and establish a special division for the social aspects of medicine. With increasing frequency, he began to use the term "medical sociology" (or variants thereof) to designate his growing interest in contemporary and comparative studies of medical care organization and financing.[37]

At this point, Sigerist's public positions were generally in line with those of the dominant forces of health reform; many liberal academics, foundation representatives, and federal officials within the New Deal agencies shared his distaste for the entrenched positions of organized medicine. They were warmly receptive to his presentations of the historical inevitability and current necessity of change. When, for example, Michael M. Davis, director for medical services of the Julius Rosenwald Fund, outlined a program of needed research in 1935, he called for sociological and historical studies of medical care in terms that clearly reflected Sigerist's interests.[38]

In 1934 and 1935, John Kingsbury provoked the wrath of the organized medical profession by his outspoken support for national health insurance; the physicians responded with a threatened boycott against the

Borden Company—the milk and baby food company whose profits provided the Milbank Memorial Fund's endowment.[39] Through these tactics, they were successful in having Kingsbury fired from his position. Such a demonstration of power tended to make other foundation officials cautious. They did, however, support limited experiments in medical care delivery.[40]

But while these liberal experiments continued, the prospects for national health insurance were fading at the federal level. The Roosevelt administration postponed consideration of a national health program, giving the medical profession, hospitals, and the insurance industry additional time to mobilize against reform.[41] As anti-insurance forces within the American Medical Association mounted a propaganda and letter-writing campaign, Harvey Cushing was running for president of that organization. Cushing wrote to Perkins's Committee on Economic Security and to President Roosevelt that national health insurance would "lead to the deterioration of the doctor, the demoralization of his professional code and the placing of the profession under a bureaucracy." [42] Responding to the cresting wave of medical opposition—of which Cushing's letter was but one sign—Roosevelt quietly dropped any reference to national health insurance from the social security legislation presented to Congress in 1935. The Social Security Act of 1935 thus included old age and unemployment insurance but failed to provide medical coverage.

In the absence of a national health program at the federal level, progressive physicians developed a variety of local medical care plans in the 1930s. Medical cooperatives multiplied, many sponsored by the Farm Security Administration.[43] Some were created at the initiative of individual doctors with the support of farmers and/or union groups; in Elk City, Oklahoma, for example, Dr. Michael M. Shadid and the Oklahoma Farmers' Union built the Farmers' Union Cooperative Hospital and ran it successfully, despite bitter opposition from the local medical society.[44] Under cooperative plans, the annual fees of participating members supported the medical and nursing personnel and paid for building and administrative costs. Kingsley Roberts, as director of the Bureau of Cooperative Medicine, provided advice and assistance to the entire medical cooperative movement. At one point, Sigerist himself helped Roberts establish a small local experiment in cooperative medicine in Greenbelt, Prince George's County, Maryland, in a new town built in 1935–37 as a relief project of the Resettlement Administration.[45] The major problem for most of these plans was the power of the American Medical Association to control hospital appointments, deny rebellious physicians ad-

36. Sigerist lecturing on innovations in health care organization at the Greenbelt Health Association, March 22, 1941.

mitting privileges, and therefore deprive their patients of hospital care.[46] When one of the more powerful cooperatives, the Group Health Association of Washington, D.C., provoked the antagonism of the American Medical Association, the resulting struggle ultimately ended in a successful antitrust suit against organized medicine.[47]

Encouraged by the success of many of these local efforts, Sigerist and

37. The students of Sigerist's health economics seminar, visiting the Greenbelt Health Association and Medical Center, March 22, 1941.

other progressive reformers considered the defeat of national health insurance at the federal level to be merely a temporary setback. They intended to continue the struggle until they were successful—believing that attainment of their goal would not be long postponed. But Sigerist's main focus was now elsewhere. In the summer of 1935, he sailed—full of high hopes—for his first visit to the Soviet Union. He would return convinced that he had seen how an ideal medical and public health system should be organized.

National Health Insurance and "Socialized Medicine," 1935–1939

After 1935, supporters of national health insurance at the federal level focused their attention on the Interdepartmental Committee for the Coordination of Health and Welfare Activities, chaired by Josephine Roche, assistant secretary of the treasury. Sigerist expressed "tremendous admiration" for Roche: "She is the most energetic and intelligent woman I have ever met and charming in addition."[48] Under her leadership, the Interdepartmental Committee decided to survey the "health needs of the nation," and on the basis of the National Health Survey, to develop a national health program.[49] Roche established a Technical Committee on Medical Care, staffed by I. S. Falk, Martha May Eliot, Joseph Mountin, George St. J. Perrott, and Clifford Waller, all respected representatives of federal health agencies and experienced veterans of earlier reform efforts. They designed a National Health Program to include public health, maternal and child health, hospital construction, tax-supported medical care, temporary disability insurance, and compulsory health insurance.[50] Breaking with the American Medical Association, 430 liberal and progressive doctors formed the Committee of Physicians for the Improvement of Medical Care, led by such prominent figures as John P. Peters, the Ely Professor of Medicine at Yale, and James Howard Means, the Jackson Professor of Clinical Medicine at Harvard. A small but prestigious group, it included a Nobel laureate, deans of medical schools, and the surgeon general of the United States.[51] They supported the principles of the National Health Program and advocated cooperation between the government and the medical profession in designing a national system of medical care.[52] With President Roosevelt's consent, the government's Interdepartmental Committee organized a major national conference in Washington, D.C., in July 1938, to mobilize public support for the National Health Program. At this conference, representatives of labor, farmers, business, and government expressed overwhelming enthusiasm for the program, while representatives of the American Medical Association were adamantly opposed.[53]

Senator Robert Wagner of New York now offered to introduce national health insurance legislation to Congress. Alarmed, the American Medical Association promised to support the other provisions of the National Health Program if reference to national health insurance were dropped. The Interdepartmental Committee, perhaps too optimistic about the prospects of success, rejected the offer. President Roosevelt expressed cautious support for the National Health Program and urged Congress to study the issue. In the meantime, the American Medical Association and local medical societies organized a massive and well-financed publicity campaign against the National Health Program, compulsory health insurance, and "socialized medicine."

Although many physicians considered national health insurance a radical, even socialistic measure, Sigerist characterized it as a first, relatively conservative step. In 1937, his most controversial book, *Socialized Medicine in the Soviet Union,* made apparent his admiration for the Soviet system of state-run health services. In 1938, Sigerist summarized his position in an article "Socialized Medicine" for the *Yale Review.*[54] In a strong and straightforward argument, he asserted that people had a right to health care and that society had a responsibility to take care of its members. An ideal medical care system would be organized around health centers, each with a hospital and a public health department and connected to smaller local health stations staffed by general practitioners, nurses, and technicians. Doctors in the local health stations would in turn organize committees of citizens to conduct health surveys, carry out health education, and arrange a variety of social and health activities. Every citizen would be entitled to free medical care; physicians, like other health workers, would be salaried.

Sigerist asserted that such a system was already operating successfully in the Soviet Union. In the United States, however, doctors were "afraid of government competition" because government services were "obviously more efficient."[55] An efficient medical service was simply a matter of using existing resources more rationally, with the government paying premiums for the indigent. Sigerist admitted that his ideal system was not yet politically possible: "There is no chance in the world of having such a system adopted in America at the present time but it is good to have a definite goal in mind."[56] His widely discussed essay on socialized medicine was named the first of ten outstanding magazine articles of the month.[57]

Now regularly paired with Morris Fishbein on the medical lecture circuit, Sigerist expressed grudging admiration for his opponent's style of oratory but regarded his political positions as "stupid" and "reactionary."[58] In his kinder (if still condescending) moments, Sigerist attributed the American Medical Association's stand to doctors' social and economic ignorance—to be cured by an appropriate application of historical and sociological knowledge.[59] But as the struggle over national policy intensified, Sigerist found himself roundly attacked: "I am the target of conservative physicians. . . . a former president of the A.M.A. describes me as a foreign communist who tries to impose the Russian system on America."[60]

Until August 1939 and the Nazi-Soviet pact, many audiences regarded the Soviet Union with more curiosity than antagonism, and Sigerist received dozens of invitations to talk about Soviet medicine from such groups as the Goucher College Alumni, the Baltimore District Child Study Association, the Association of Medical Students, and the Engineers' Club.[61] Beginning in 1935 and throughout the later 1930s, he had been involved in organizations providing support and medical aid to the Spanish Republic and had participated in antifascist organizations. Sigerist became the darling of left-wing intellectuals, the dinner companion of Owen Lattimore and Lillian Hellman, and the idol of student radicals. He was clearly identified as a spokesman for the Soviet Union, socialized medicine, and indeed, for communism itself.

From 1935 through 1939, during the period of its Popular Front strategy, the Communist Party helped build a string of organizations in which communists, liberals, and "progressives" could make common cause.[62] But although Sigerist became close to the Communist Party in this period, he never became a formal member.[63] Instead, he took on many speaking engagements as part of his sense of political responsibility and served as catalyst to organizations of medical students and interns; he enjoyed his role as a public speaker, and as he once described his impact on an audience, he "put dynamite into the crowd."[64]

January 1939 probably represented the peak of Sigerist's influence in American medical politics. That month, he was interviewed by *Time* magazine and by the New York *Daily News* and photographed "from all sides."[65] On January 23, President Roosevelt read a message to the U.S. Congress, giving general support to the National Health Program, suggesting that a medical care program be funded by federal grants and administered by states and localities, and asking Congress to study the issues.[66] The next day, the *Daily News* published an article by Sigerist advocating compulsory health insurance and suggesting that the premiums be used to finance health centers and promote group practice.[67] On January 30, *Time* magazine published a flattering article about him and his influential role in the debate over "socialized medicine," and placed his photograph on the cover.[68] Sigerist was amused to note that he had received almost as much attention as did President Roosevelt.[69]

He was now deluged with speaking requests from such diverse organizations as the Junior Chamber of Commerce; the Colonial Dames of America, in Omaha; and the Progressive Arts League of Indiana.[70] His scholarly research program was put on hold as he gave dozens of talks to promote the National Health Program and the cause of compulsory health insurance. "The issue," he told himself somewhat grandly, "is so vitally important for the people that I feel obliged to sacrifice much of my research and to throw in my entire personality."[71] He summarized his public position in a paper, "The Realities of Socialized Medicine," for the *Atlantic Monthly*, in a calm reasoned exposition that he hoped would be "so stringent in its logic" that people would be forced to accept his views.[72] This article was promptly reprinted as a pamphlet and widely distributed by organizations supporting national health insurance.

While thus active in the national debate over compulsory health insurance, Sigerist also aided the local Maryland campaign. He spoke on socialized medicine to an audience of over five hundred at the home of Elisabeth Gilman, daughter of the first Johns Hopkins University president, Daniel Coit Gilman.[73] He also joined Kingsley Roberts and John Kingsbury—both well-known supporters of national health insurance—on the lecture circuit. Sigerist considered himself an "amateur" in the field of social insurance, perhaps by contrast to the expert health economists in several foundations and government agencies, but he reassured himself that the amateur often had "more imagination and less inhibition than the specialist who is inclined to think along traditional lines, and who, being aware of difficulties, often lacks courage."[74]

During the spring of 1939 at Hopkins, Sigerist devoted his sociological seminar to a practical exercise in health planning, one that *Time* magazine termed "the first course in practical socialized medicine ever held in the U.S."[75] Students were instructed to make a thorough survey of health conditions in each of the Maryland counties; to study various population groups, their incomes, occupations, and health problems; and then to develop "an ideal plan that would guarantee to every individual the best possible medical care"—and also to calculate the costs of this care.[76]

This seminar was excellent preparation for the First All-Maryland Health Conference in May 1939, when delegates from labor unions, farm organizations, and local communities gathered to support the National Health Program. According to Sigerist's account, a delegate from the local medical society, the Medical Chirurgical Faculty, presented "the usual reactionary stuff" and "a number of stuffed shirts presented official views."[77] Sigerist and Isidore S. Falk defended health insurance and dissected their opponents' arguments. In a bitter debate, the three delegates of the American Medical Association faced the almost unanimous opposition of 350 delegates from 120 organizations: "It was the doctors against the people," concluded Sigerist, "a shocking performance."[78]

The Wagner Health Bill of 1939 (S. 1620) reflected the National Health Program of 1938, modified in response to medical society protests. It was essentially an amendment to the Social Security Act, broadening its health powers and authorizing the states to provide medical care. The bill allowed the states broad discretion in determining the form of care and in deciding who might receive it. The entire medical care program was

38. Sigerist giving one of his many radio talks.

to depend on voluntary state participation. Despite such concessions, intended to appease organized medicine, the Wagner Bill aroused the physicians' unrelenting antagonism. Faced with avid medical hostility, lukewarm public support, and the disinterest of a conservative Congress, the bill was allowed to die in committee.[79] President Roosevelt, now preoccupied with the prospects of war in Europe, lost interest in comprehensive health legislation.

In January 1940, Sigerist participated in a radio program "Does America Need Compulsory Health Insurance?" in the series *Town Hall Meeting of the Air*. In a debate format, C.-E. A. Winslow of Yale supported voluntary health insurance programs, Terry Townsend of the New York State Medical Society represented organized medicine and argued for the status quo, while Sigerist advocated "socialized medicine."[80] Broadcast by seventy-eight stations, the program had an estimated listening audience of several million people and provided Sigerist with the single largest audience he had ever had for his ideas. He presented familiar themes: compulsory health insurance was a moderate reform, he said, a method of assuring the availability of health services to all. It was important to go further and to reorganize medical care around health centers with physicians—both general practitioners and specialists—on salary. The entire system should ideally be centrally financed through taxation and provide free services to patients.[81]

Sigerist also gave a press conference during which he talked about his recent visit to South Africa and the European war situation and made some ill-considered remarks seeming to justify the Russian invasion of Finland; he then found himself violently attacked in the newspapers. One newspaper article by a "Hopkins man," argued—in Sigerist's summary—that "since Russia has invaded Finland, health insurance cannot be any good in America."[82] Finding himself assailed on all sides, Sigerist began to regret taking so prominent a role in medical politics.[83] But for better or worse, he had now become a national symbol of socialized medicine, and it was difficult to retreat. One day, he was startled but pleased to hear about a play in New York, *Medicine Show*, in which every night on the stage an actor cried, "What we need now are men like Dr. Sigerist of Hopkins and Peters of Yale. That's what we need!"[84]

Local Medical Care Plans and Medical Cooperatives, 1940

In 1940, when the war prevented Sigerist from undertaking his usual summer research in Europe, he decided to spend several months traveling across the United States visiting cooperatives, prepaid medical care programs, and other innovative medical care plans. He reported his observations during this "unforgettable" and "beautiful" trip in a long series of articles for the progressive New York newspaper *PM*. He originally planned to compile these articles into a book, "Medical Service Plans in the United States," but this project was never completed.[85] These newspaper articles do, however, offer an excellent glimpse of the progressive medical care programs of the period. They also leave no doubt about Sigerist's preferences among the practical options then available for American health care.

Sigerist's articles discussed medical plans in Maryland, New York, Massachusetts, Michigan, Illinois, Wisconsin, Minnesota, Oklahoma, and California. He applauded the plans that placed physicians on salary because "there is nothing to interfere with the relationship between them and their patients."[86] He dismissed the vaunted "free choice of physicians" offered by medical insurance systems: "in other words, [such a plan] permits the patient to consult incompetent doctors if he so desires."[87] He complained that the plans organized by physician groups rarely promoted preventive medicine: "They are not health insurance but fee insurance plans, and merely serve to finance part of the haphazard services people are receiving today."[88]

Sigerist commended local efforts to deliver comprehensive medical and preventive care, although he warned that it would be difficult for many small groups to survive.[89] The real solution lay with compulsory national health insurance, which would permit the organization and staffing of group health centers across the country, even in rural and depressed urban areas.[90] Praising public health efforts, he argued that preventive activities must be made available to the entire population and not be restricted to the indigent.[91] He applauded Joseph DeLee's Chicago Maternity Center for providing services to poor women but argued that such programs should be publicly funded and not dependent on charitable donations.[92]

Across the Midwest and in California, Sigerist found thriving prepaid medical care plans, variously supported by labor unions, consumer cooperatives, church societies, and farmers' unions. All, to one degree or another, were violently opposed by their local medical societies. At each stop, Sigerist emphasized the importance of pooling resources, providing comprehensive services, and involving local communities in the organization of health care and health education.[93] He was delighted with the "socialized medicine" experiment of the health care plans in northern California offering medical care that was affordable, comprehensive, and oriented to prevention, with access to first-class hospital service when needed.[94] Such successes, said Sigerist, could readily be extended to the whole country, if compulsory health insurance obtained through employment were supplemented by public insurance funds to cover the costs of care for the poor.

A Season of Declining Popularity, 1940–1947

By the summer of 1940, Sigerist had put considerable distance between himself and many of the academic and philanthropic medical elite. Some remained loyal friends and supporters: John Fulton and John Kingsbury, among others. But the qualities that made Sigerist so inspiring to his students and younger colleagues also earned him enemies. Johns Hopkins University administrators became uncomfortable with Sigerist's increasing notoriety, especially when letters arrived from conservative medical alumni, deeply offended that their alma mater was sheltering a "radical communist" who might poison the minds of young physicians.[95]

Retreating from the intensity of his political involvements, Sigerist now spent more time writing—in 1941 publishing *Medicine and Human Welfare,* and in 1943, *Civilization and Disease.*[96] Also in 1943, one of his most insightful essays, "From Bismarck to Beveridge," proved an excellent guide to understanding the success—and failure—of campaigns for national health insurance.[97] Sigerist intended this essay to be the first of a projected series of historical studies on health and social policy.

In 1943, the Wagner-Murray-Dingell Bill, proposing a national system of health insurance similar to the old age insurance of the Social Security Act, was introduced into Congress with support from organized labor.[98] The bill would cover physicians' fees—subject to a rate limitation set by the federal government—and hospital services for up to sixty days a year, with the costs being paid by a federal fund based on payroll taxes. Sigerist outlined and explained the legislation in his paper "Medical Care for All the People." [99] Opposing the bill were such organizations as the National Physicians' Committee for the Extension of Medical Service, a lobbying group funded by pharmaceutical and drug corporations, medical supply companies, and conservative physicians, aided by the considerable political force of the American Medical Association and its constituent state and local medical societies.

To coordinate the effort to build support for the bill, Senator Wagner held a meeting in his office on February 5, 1944, with representatives of farmers, organized labor, and liberal physicians. Senators James Murray and John Dingell were present, as were Ernst Boas, the head of Physicians Forum, Michael M. Davis, Kingsley Roberts, and Sigerist. To guide the health reform process, the group created an organization with Michael M. Davis as chairman.[100] "I am sure a strong organization will result," said Sigerist, "We shall probably lose but at least not without a fight."[101] As the Committee for the Nation's Health, the group would later function as the chief lobby for President Truman's national health program.

A few months after the February meeting with Senators Wagner, Murray, and Dingell, Sigerist received a letter from the Civil Service Commission telling him that his eligibility for government service had been canceled, as of April 19, 1944, because he did "not measure up to the general standards of suitability and fitness maintained for government employees."[102] He stood accused of belonging to "Communist front" organizations and of displaying too much interest in the political and economic theories of Communism.[103] At the hearing, Sigerist defended himself from the charges with some vigor, but the decision against him marked a turning point in his American career; he now became increasingly sour on America and its prospects.

Rejected by his own government, Sigerist was nonetheless pleased to accept high-level invitations first to head a health survey of Saskatchewan, Canada, and then to be a member of the Health Survey and Development Committee chaired by Sir Joseph Bhore, charged with long-term medical and public health planning for India.[104] In 1944, he thus spent virtually the entire fall in Canada and India as an international consultant. During this period, he often commented that he was more honored and respected abroad than in the United States: "here I am considered a crackpot."[105]

In 1945, any immediate prospect of medical reform in the United States seemed to collapse with the death of President Franklin D. Roosevelt in April. Harry S. Truman picked up Roosevelt's medical reform program and announced it to Congress and the nation in November 1945 but failed to follow through with effective presidential leadership.[106] In Senate hearings, national health insurance was energetically opposed by the American Medical Association, the American Hospital Association, the American Dental Association, the American Bar Association, and the United States Chamber of Commerce, among other organizations, and the reform project fizzled.[107] By now, Sigerist was fully engaged in writing his long-delayed *History of Medicine*.[108]

Between 1945 and 1947, his role in medical care reform was peripheral.[109] He was preoccupied with his historical writing and his efforts to leave Johns Hopkins; the negotiations over his future funding and the specific arrangements for his move to Switzerland demanded considerable attention. In these years, he kept his main energy in reserve for his grand scholarly project, the *History of Medicine*.[110] In the summer of 1947, he left the United States for good, never to return.

Medical Politics and the Final Years in Switzerland, 1947–1957

Even from his retirement in Switzerland, Sigerist maintained an interest in American health politics and encouraged his many friends and former students who were still centrally involved in struggles over medical care reform. Their hopes were rapidly crushed in the McCarthy era.[111] Within a year of President Truman's Loyalty Order of October, 1947, left-leaning members of the federal government were being pursued by the FBI as "disloyal."[112] Many of Sigerist's friends and former students suffered from these anti-Communist witch hunts.[113]

Sigerist now paid more attention to developments in Europe, Latin America, and Asia and maintained warm relationships with several European leaders in social medicine.[114] One of the men he most admired was Andrija Štampar, a courageous public health leader from Yugoslavia who became, after the war, the first director of the World Health Organization.[115] Another was René Sand, a pioneer of European social medicine.[116] Štampar and Sand shared Sigerist's broad European culture and many of his political interests; like him, they were senior statesmen of progressive medicine. When Milton Roemer arrived in Geneva in 1951 to work for the World Health Organization, he promptly invited Sigerist and Sand to serve as consultants in preparing recommendations on the future organization and financing of medical care in Europe.[117]

While in Switzerland, Sigerist maintained a voluminous correspondence and happily received a constant stream of visitors. Many of his former students and friends in the United States were active within the American Public Health Association (APHA). Even in the dark days of McCarthyism, they focused on organizing a Medical Care Section within the APHA to serve as a national meeting ground for those committed to medical care reform.[118] After the annual APHA meeting of 1954, Roemer wrote to Sigerist: "You know all the social medicine enthusiasts and former students of yours who were there—Leslie Falk, George Rosen, Cy Axelrod, Milton Terris, Len Rosenfeld, Cecil Sheps and Mindel [Sheps], Fred Mott, Henry Makover, Franz Goldmann, Charlotte Silverman, Lorin Kerr, Paul Lembcke, and many others. Jerry Morris was over from London. The 'Medical Care Section' . . . has been an enormous success, and it is a real pleasure to see so many of our colleagues—who for years have been fighting an insurgent, minority battle—now in positions of respect and some influence." [119] When Sigerist died in March 1957, these were some of the men and women who would be carrying on his ideas in medical politics, public health, and medical care reform. Many among this group of activists would themselves become influential on the national scene, deeply involved in continuing efforts to reform the health care system. For many, Sigerist served as a prophet and guide; his words and ideas provided the inspiration for a loosely organized and often fractured movement that would nonetheless provide energetic leadership for many decades in the still uncompleted attempt to implement his vision.

Notes

1. Elizabeth Fee, "Henry E. Sigerist: From the Social Production of Disease to Medical Management and Scientific Socialism," *Milbank Quarterly* 67, suppl. 1 (1989): 127–50.

2. Sigerist was active in and/or lent his name and prestige to such organizations as the North American Committee to Aid Spanish Democracy, American Friends of Spanish Democracy, Medical Bureau to Aid Spanish Democracy, Russian War Relief, Inc., the National Council of American-Soviet Friendship, the American Committee for Democracy and Intellectual Freedom (ACDIF), and the American Association of Scientific Workers (AASW). As their names suggest, the first three organizations promoted the cause of the Spanish Republic and provided aid to those fighting in Spain; the second two promoted understanding of and aid to the Soviet Union. The ACDIF was a national antifascist organization of scientists and educators; the AASW was a group of radical and progressive scientists and academics. See Peter J. Kuznick, "Scientists, 1920–1950," in *Encyclopedia of the American Left,* eds. Mari Jo Buhle, Paul Buhle, and Dan Georgakas (Urbana: University of Illinois Press, 1990), 680–84; Peter J. Kuznick, *Beyond the Laboratory: Scientists as Political Activists in 1930s America* (Chicago: University of Chicago Press, 1987).

3. Henry E. Sigerist, *Socialized Medicine in the Soviet Union* (New York: W. W. Norton, 1937).

4. George A. Silver speaks of Sigerist's charismatic role in the 1930s in "Social Medicine and Social Policy," *Yale Journal of Biology and Medicine* 57 (1984): 851–64.

5. Nora Sigerist Beeson, ed., *Henry E. Sigerist: Autobiographical Writings* (Montreal: McGill University Press, 1966), 60.

6. See Ingrid Kästner's essay in this volume, and Michael H. Kater, *Doctors Under Hitler* (Chapel Hill: University of North Carolina Press, 1989) for a discussion of the German physicians' bitterness toward the health insurance system.

7. His 1929 defense appeared in his paper, "Die Sonderstellung des Kranken,"

Kyklos 2 (1929): 11–20. Another important paper of this period was his "Der Arzt und die Umwelt," *Deutsche Medizinische Wochenschrift* 25 (1931): 1049–51.

8. Henry E. Sigerist, *Einführung in die Medizin* (Leipzig: Georg Thieme, 1931); translated as *Man and Medicine: An Introduction to Medical Knowledge* (New York: W. W. Norton, 1932), 307–16 (quotation, 311).

9. Ibid., 327–28.

10. Erwin H. Ackerknecht, *Medicine and Ethnology: Selected Essays,* eds. H. H. Walser and H. M. Koelbing (Stuttgart: Hans Huber, 1971), 10. See also Erwin H. Ackerknecht, "Recollections of a Former Leipzig Student," *Journal of the History of Medicine and Allied Sciences* 13 (1958): 147–50.

11. For the final report of the Committee on the Costs of Medical Care, see *Medical Care for the American People* (Chicago: University of Chicago Press, 1932); Forrest A. Walker, "Americanism versus Sovietism: A Study of the Reactions to the Committee on the Costs of Medical Care," *Bulletin of the History of Medicine* 53 (1979): 489–504; and the essay by Roemer, Falk, and Brown in this volume.

12. John A. Kingsbury, *Health in Handcuffs: The National Health Crisis and What Can Be Done* (New York: Modern Age Books, 1939), 34.

13. The CCMC's final recommendations were split into a majority and several minority reports; the majority report advocated hierarchically and regionally organized group practice, the extension of public health services, and group payment for medical services through insurance, taxation, or a combination of both. A minority report, representing the position of the American Medical Association, rejected any fundamental changes in the organization of medical care and any voluntary or compulsory health insurance system.

14. See James Rorty, *American Medicine Mobilizes* (New York: W. W. Norton, 1939); James G. Burrow, *AMA: Voice of American Medicine* (Baltimore: Johns Hopkins Press, 1963). Daniel M. Fox's reading of the controversy is considerably less sympathetic to the reformers; he notes that medical practitioners were offended by the reformers' oft-stated conviction that most practitioners lagged behind the best standards of scientific medicine: *Health Policies, Health Politics: The British and American Experience, 1911–1965* (Princeton: Princeton University Press, 1986), 47–51. Sigerist certainly shared the reformers' low opinion of the average standard of medical practice.

15. R. L. Duffus, "The Crisis in Medical Service," *Harper's Monthly Magazine,* n. 163 (September 1931): 468–77; Henry E. Sigerist, unpublished diary, September 17, 1931. Yale University Library, Henry E. Sigerist Papers, Addition (June 1987), Biographical Data and Memorabilia, group 788, box 1 (hereafter cited as Diary); partially excerpted in Nora Sigerist Beeson, ed., *Autobiographical Writings,* 70. In the following references, where specific manuscript diary entries are included in the selection published by Nora Sigerist Beeson, both the manuscript and published references are given; where diary entries were not included in that volume, only the manuscript diary entry is cited.

16. Henry E. Sigerist, *American Medicine* (New York: W. W. Norton, 1934).

17. Leslie A. Falk, "Medical Sociology: The Contributions of Dr. Henry E. Sigerist," *Journal of the History of Medicine and Allied Sciences* 13 (1958): 214–28.

18. Sigerist, *American Medicine,* 187.

19. Ibid., 184.

20. Ibid., 192–95.

21. John Fulton to Henry E. Sigerist, November 30, 1933. Yale University Library, Henry E. Sigerist Papers (hereafter cited as Sigerist Papers/Yale), General Correspondence, 1931–46, group 788, series I, box 1.

22. Harvey Cushing to Henry E. Sigerist, December 2, 1933; Henry E. Sigerist to Harvey Cushing, December 6, 1933. Sigerist Papers/Yale, General Correspondence, 1931–46, group 788, series I, box 1.

23. Henry E. Sigerist, "Medical Societies, Past and Present," *Yale Journal of Biology and Medicine* 6 (1934): 351–62.

24. Sir Arthur Newsholme and John A. Kingsbury, *Red Medicine: Socialized Health in Soviet Russia* (New York: Doubleday, Doran, 1933). Henry E. Sigerist to Mabel Kingsbury, August 14, 1956, Sigerist Papers/Yale, General Correspondence, 1947–57, group 788, series I, box 15. But see also Sigerist's initial reactions as reported in the chapter by John Hutchinson in this volume.

25. Kingsbury was a strong advocate of national health insurance. With his support, the Milbank Memorial Fund had been one of the eight foundations funding the CCMC; Kingsbury himself had urged the "mutualization" (or socialization) of medical costs. For Kingsbury's views, see "Health Insurance Menaced by Medical Politics," *American Labor Legislation Review* 26 (1936): 30–34; John A. Kingsbury, *Health Security for the Nation* (New York: League for Industrial Democracy, 1938); John A. Kingsbury, *Health in Handcuffs: The National Health Crisis and What Can Be Done* (New York: Modern Age Books, 1939).

26. Henry E. Sigerist, Diary, August 7, 1933.

27. "Sigerist Predicts Socialized Medicine: Calls It Answer to Overspecialization," *New York Times,* October 19, 1933, 22.

28. For details of this effort, see Daniel S. Hirshfield, *The Lost Reform: The Campaign for Compulsory Health Insurance in the United States from 1932 to 1943* (Cambridge: Harvard University Press, 1970), 42–70.

29. Henry E. Sigerist, Diary, January 25, 1934.

30. Ibid., February 7, 1934.

31. "Twelfth Annual Conference of the Advisory Council of the Milbank Memorial Fund, held March 14th and 15th, 1934, at the New York Academy of Medicine." Sigerist Papers/Yale, Professional Activities, group 788, series II, box 32.

32. I. S. Falk, "Progress Report on Studies of Medical Care," in the session "Round Table on National Health Planning and Medical Care" of the Twelfth Annual Conference of the Advisory Council of the Milbank Memorial Fund, held March 14th and 15th, 1934, at the New York Academy of Medicine. Sigerist Papers/Yale, Professional Activities, group 788, series II, box 32; Henry E. Sigerist, Diary, March 14, 1934. For Falk's views in this period, see Isidore S. Falk, *Security Against Sickness: A Study of Health Insurance* (Garden City, N.Y.: Doubleday, Doran, 1936).

33. Fiorello La Guardia, the reform-minded mayor of New York City, would later introduce the Health Insurance Plan of Greater New York (HIP), a comprehensive prepaid health and medical care program that its more optimistic supporters considered a demonstration project for a national health system.

34. Henry E. Sigerist, Diary, March 15, 1934. For Winslow, see Arthur Visel-tear, "C.-E. A. Winslow: His Era and His Contribution to Medical Care," in Charles E. Rosenberg, ed., *Healing and History* (New York: Science History Publications, 1979), 205-28; for a good general account of the New Deal, see Roger Biles, *A New Deal for the American People* (DeKalb: Northern Illinois University Press, 1991).

35. Henry E. Sigerist, "Trends towards Socialized Medicine," *Problems of Health Conservation* (New York: Milbank Memorial Fund, 1934), 78-83.

36. Henry E. Sigerist, Diary, March 16, 1934.

37. Immediately after the Milbank conference, Sigerist started a new seminar, "Social Aspects of Medicine," and began to think about writing a book on the subject. His diary entries note his delight at the students' growing enthusiasm for such studies. Henry E. Sigerist, Diary, April 2, 9, 16, 23, 30, 1934; May 7, 28, 1934. See the essay by Roemer, Falk, and Brown in this volume.

38. Michael M. Davis, "Wanted: Research in the Economic and Social Aspects of Medicine," *Milbank Memorial Fund Quarterly* 13 (1935): 339-46.

39. James Rorty, *American Medicine Mobilizes* (New York: W. W. Norton, 1939), 112-30.

40. The Milbank Memorial Fund, for example, now under the direction of Edgar Sydenstricker, sponsored local and regional plans for the reorganization and prepayment of medical care. See Franz Goldmann, *Prepayment Plans for Medical Care* (New York: Joint Committee of the Twentieth Century Fund and the Good Will Fund and Medical Administration Service, Inc., 1941). For Sydenstricker, see Richard V. Kasius, ed., *The Challenge of Facts: Selected Public Health Papers of Edgar Sydenstricker* (New York: Prodist, 1974); Edgar Sydenstricker, *Health and Environment* (New York: McGraw Hill, 1933). The Julius Rosenwald Fund under Michael M. Davis, who like Sydenstricker had earlier worked with the CCMC, supported group hospitalization insurance and various cooperative medical experiments. See Michael M. Davis, *Eight Years' Work in Medical Economics* (New York: The Julius Rosenwald Fund, 1937); Michael M. Davis, "Change Comes to the Doctor," in the American Academy of Political and Social Science, *The Medical Profession and the Public: Currents and Counter-Currents* (Philadelphia: American Academy of Political and Social Science, 1934), 63-74; Michael M. Davis, *America Organizes Medicine* (New York: Harper and Brothers, 1941); Michael M. Davis, *Medical Care for Tomorrow* (New York: Harper and Brothers, 1955). The work of the medical economists is discussed in Daniel M. Fox, *Economists and Health Care: From Reform to Relativism* (New York: Prodist, 1979).

41. For various accounts of these struggles, see Oliver Garceau, *The Political Life of the American Medical Association* (Cambridge: Harvard University Press, 1941); James G. Burrow, *AMA: Voice of American Medicine* (Baltimore: Johns Hopkins Press, 1963); and, for a lively popular version, Richard Harris, *A Sacred Trust* (New York: New American Library, 1966).

42. Harvey Cushing, as quoted by Daniel S. Hirshfield, *The Lost Reform*, 55.

43. Michael R. Grey, "Poverty, Politics, and Health: The Farm Security Administration Medical Care Programs, 1935-45," *Journal of the History of Medicine and Allied Sciences* 44 (1989): 320-50; Michael R. Grey, "Dustbowls, Disease,

and the New Deal: The Farm Security Administration Migrant Health Programs, 1935–1947," *Journal of the History of Medicine and Allied Sciences* 48 (1993): 3–39.

44. Michael M. Shadid, *A Doctor for the People: The Autobiography of the Founder of America's First Cooperative Hospital* (New York: Vanguard Press, 1939); Sigerist's two reports on the Elk City Cooperative Hospital are reprinted under the title "Group Health Plans in the United States," in Milton I. Roemer, ed., *Henry E. Sigerist on the Sociology of Medicine* (New York: MD Publications, 1960), 197–202.

45. "Dr. Sigerist Finds Greenbelt Health Plan Excellent But Project Group Too Small for Complete Treatment," *PM*, July 22, 1940, 27.

46. See Paul Starr, *The Social Transformation of American Medicine* (New York: Basic Books, 1982), 299–310 for a discussion of AMA tactics in the 1930s.

47. This interesting series of events is discussed in detail in Patricia Spain Ward, "*United States versus American Medical Association et al.* The Medical Anti-Trust Case of 1938–1943," *American Studies* 30 (1989): 123–53.

48. Henry E. Sigerist, Diary, October 12, 1938.

49. The work of the Committee is described in Hirshfield, *The Lost Reform*, 100–134.

50. Josephine Roche, "The Worker's Stake in a National Health Program," *American Labor Legislation Review* 28 (1938): 125–30; Hirshfield, *The Lost Reform*, 105–8.

51. For the members of the Committee of 430 and their affiliations, see "The Committee of Physicians for the Presentation of Certain Principles and Proposals on the Provision of Medical Care," *New England Journal of Medicine* 217 (November 11, 1937): 798–800.

52. See Rorty, *American Medicine Mobilizes*, 81–83; Kingsbury, *Health in Handcuffs*, 72–73; Daniel M. Fox, *Health Policies, Health Politics*, 87–89.

53. The speakers included Kingsley Roberts (director of the Bureau of Cooperative Medicine), Michael M. Davis, Edwin Witte (staff director of the Committee on Economic Security), and C.-E. A. Winslow, all in favor of the National Health Program, and Morris Fishbein, against. Interdepartmental Committee to Coordinate Health and Welfare Activities, *Proceedings of the National Health Conference, July 18, 19, 20, 1938* (Washington, D.C.: Government Printing Office, 1938).

54. Henry E. Sigerist, "Socialized Medicine," *The Yale Review* (spring, 1938): 463–81. Reprinted in *Henry E. Sigerist on the Sociology of Medicine*, 39–53.

55. Ibid., 475.

56. Henry E. Sigerist, Diary, February 4, 1938.

57. The choice of the best articles each month was made by a committee of librarians. Hope Trebing to Henry E. Sigerist, June 11, 1938. Sigerist Papers/Yale, General Correspondence, 1931–46, group 788, series I, box 4.

58. After one dinner in Philadelphia, he wrote: "Many speeches, Fishbein's by far the best. That's the trouble with this fellow that he speaks so well." Henry E. Sigerist, Diary, March 4, 1938.

59. Ibid., October 19, 1938; *Autobiographical Writings*, 137–38.

60. Ibid., November 11, 1938.

61. Dorothy Healey and Maurice Isserman, *Dorothy Healey Remembers: A Life in the American Communist Party* (New York: Oxford University Press, 1990), 82; see also Harvey Klehr, *The Heyday of American Communism: The Depression Decade* (New York: Basic Books, 1984), 386–409.

62. See Mark Naison, "Remaking America: Communists and Liberals in the Popular Front," and other essays in Michael E. Brown, Randy Martin, Frank Rosengarten, and George Snedeker, eds., *New Studies in the Politics and Culture of U.S. Communism* (New York: Monthly Review Press, 1993).

63. Some years later, in Switzerland, Sigerist refused many invitations to lecture in the United States and wrote to Hope Trebing: "How I would wish to see America again, but I don't wish to expose myself to the humiliation of being refused a visa to visit the States. Although I have never been a member of the Communist Party, I certainly would be branded as a fellow traveller as I was a member of many organizations which are listed as Communist front organizations." Henry E. Sigerist to Hope Trebing, June 1, 1955, Sigerist Papers/Yale, Professional Activities, group 788, series I, box 9. As Oshinsky says, the "Communist front" organizations "appealed to people who admired the Soviet achievement or feared the rise of fascism, but who were left cold by the rigidity of Party life." David M. Oshinsky, *A Conspiracy So Immense: The World of Joe McCarthy* (New York: The Free Press, 1983), 91.

64. Sigerist's description of his lecture at the Third Eastern Medical Students Conference in New Haven, Connecticut. Henry E. Sigerist, Diary, March 15, 1936. This lecture was published as Henry E. Sigerist, "The Medical Student and the Social Problems Confronting Medicine Today," *Bulletin of the Institute of the History of Medicine* 4 (1936): 411–22; also published in the *Medical Bulletin* (Student Association, New York University College of Medicine) 1 (April 1936): 3–10.

65. Henry E. Sigerist, Diary, January 13, 1939.

66. Ibid., January [Monday] 23, 1939.

67. Ibid., January 16, 1938; *Autobiographical Writings,* 143.

68. "History in a Tea Wagon," *Time* 33 (January 30, 1939): 51–53. (The "tea wagon" of the title was Sigerist's wheeled filing cabinet containing the notes for his projected *History of Medicine* and his *Sociology of Medicine.*) The *Time* cover photo caption reads: "Johns Hopkins' Sigerist. His Philosophy: History Spirals Toward Socialization." *Time* published another admiring story about Sigerist, "the world's greatest living medical historian" and "the nation's ablest, and most respected, champion of socialized medicine," when he was getting ready to leave the country in 1947: see "Doctor's Project," *Time* 49 (March 10, 1947): 50–52.

69. Henry E. Sigerist, Diary, January 23, 1939; *Autobiographical Writings,* 144.

70. Henry E. Sigerist to Hope Trebing, June 19, 1939. Sigerist Papers/Yale, General Correspondence, 1931–46, group 788, series I, box 4.

71. Henry E. Sigerist, Diary, May 24, 1939.

72. Ibid., April 3, 1939; Henry E. Sigerist, "The Realities of Socialized Medicine," *Atlantic Monthly* 163 (June 1939): 794–804. Also issued as a pamphlet by the People's National Health Committee, *A Health Program for the American People: The Wagner Health Bill and the National Health Program,* 1940, and reprinted in *Henry E. Sigerist on the Sociology of Medicine,* 180–96.

73. Henry E. Sigerist, Diary, December 11, 1938. Elisabeth Gilman was a prominent socialist who ran for Governor of Maryland and for the U.S. Senate on the Socialist Party ticket. See Elizabeth Fee, Linda Shopes, and Linda Zeidman, eds., *The Baltimore Book: New Views of Local History* (Philadelphia: Temple University Press, 1991), 32.

74. Henry E. Sigerist, Diary, January 8, 1938; *Autobiographical Writings*, 143.

75. "History in a Tea Wagon," *Time* 33 (January 30, 1939): 52.

76. Henry E. Sigerist, Diary, February 14, 1939.

77. Ibid., May 27, 1939.

78. Ibid., May 28, 1939.

79. Hirshfield, *The Lost Reform*, 135–59.

80. Telegram to Henry E. Sigerist in Cape Town, August 2, 1939, from Marion Carter, director, Town Hall Radio Forum, New York City, in cooperation with the National Broadcasting Company (NBC). A letter from Marion Carter to Henry E. Sigerist, August 9, 1939, gives more details about the planned program, "Does America Need Compulsory Health Insurance?" Sigerist Papers/Yale, Professional Activities, series II, box 31.

81. Henry E. Sigerist, "Remarks," *Town Meeting* 5 (1940): 4–8.

82. Henry E. Sigerist, Diary, January 15, 1940; *Autobiographical Writings*, 161. Guy L. Hunter, "Russia, Socialized Medicine and the Views of Dr. Sigerist," *Baltimore Sun*, January 15, 1940, 8.

83. "It was a serious sacrifice that I devoted so much time to improving the people's health and what I got for it was hatred. I have enough. I'm through." Henry E. Sigerist, Diary, [2-page entry] January 16–17, 1940; *Autobiographical Writings*, 162.

84. Henry E. Sigerist, Diary, May 2, 1940; *Autobiographical Writings*, 167.

85. Sigerist had also planned to write a book to be called *An Introduction to the Economic Problems of Medicine*, using the material gathered from his trip. This project, too, remained unfinished. See Henry Sigerist, "The Johns Hopkins Institute of the History of Medicine During the Academic Year 1941–1942," *Bulletin of the History of Medicine* 12 (1942): 446. Milton I. Roemer published Sigerist's planned introduction to that volume in *Henry E. Sigerist on the Sociology of Medicine*, 54–64.

86. "Dr. Sigerist Surveys the Health Plan at the Endicott–Johnson Shoe Factory: Staff of 100, Three Medical Centers Care for 50,000 Workers and Their Families," *PM*, July 15, 1940, 25; "'Ideal Rural Hospital' Discovered at Cooperstown, N.Y., by Dr. Sigerist: He Says Local Health Plan Similar to That of Bassett Hospital Is Workable for Others," *PM*, July 22, 1940, 27.

87. "Dr. Sigerist Compares and Analyzes Three Upstate Group Health Plans: Visits Industrial Plants in Binghamton . . . Reports Results of Survey in Detail," *PM*, July 17, 1940, 27.

88. "Dr. Sigerist Finds Utica Health Plan Costly to Members for What It Gives: He Views Similar Plans as Fee Insurance Rather Than Health Insurance," *PM*, July 19, 1940, 27.

89. "Dr. Sigerist Finds Greenbelt Health Plan Excellent but Project Group Too Small for Complete Treatment," *PM*, July 22, 1940, 27.

90. "Dr. Sigerist Examines Health Plan Set Up by CIO Detroit Auto Workers,"

PM, July 26, 1940, 27. Sigerist especially criticized a plan by Paul de Kruif, *Health is Wealth* (New York: Harcourt Brace, 1940), to provide public health services and medical care for the indigent, fund medical education and research, and construct hospitals throughout the states. Sigerist said that the plan, developed as a compromise position after the defeat of the Wagner Bill in 1939, was really a capitulation to organized medicine's demands because one "undemocratic and highly controversial" clause made it impossible for any state to experiment with compulsory health insurance. See "Dr. Sigerist Analyzes the Background of Paul de Kruif's Mass Health Plan," *PM*, July 30, 1940, 27.

91. "Dr. Sigerist Examines Failure of Anti-TB Campaign in Detroit," *PM*, August 19, 1940, 11.

92. "Dr. Sigerist Cites America's Need for More Adequate Maternity Care," *PM*, August 2, 1940, 27.

93. "Dr. Sigerist Studies Health Plan Based on Car Insurance Principle," *PM*, August 23, 1940, 11; "Dr. Sigerist Finds Much That's Good at the Chicago Civic Medical Center," *PM*, August 26, 1940; 11; "Dr. Sigerist Surveys Budget Plan Aiding Health of Union Groups," *PM*, August 30, 1940, 11; "Dr. Sigerist Calls Local Units Good in Minnesota Health Plan," *PM*, September 16, 1940; "Farm Health Plan in Oklahoma is Commended by Dr. Sigerist," *PM*, September 20, 1940; "Oklahoma Farmers' Health Plan Worth Copying, Dr. Sigerist Says," *PM*, September 23, 1940; "Dr. Sigerist, in Los Angeles, Studies Ross–Loos Health Plan," *PM*, September 30, 1940; "Ross–Loos Branch Clinic Plan is Explained by Dr. Sigerist," *PM*, October 4, 1940; "Dr. Sigerist Finds Ross–Loos Health Plan 'Basically Sound,'" *PM*, October 8, 1940. Sigerist's three reports on the Ross–Loos Health Plan are reprinted under the title "Group Health Plans in the United States," in *Henry E. Sigerist on the Sociology of Medicine*, 202–8.

94. Henry E. Sigerist, "California Socialized Medicine Experiment Has 16,000 Beneficiaries, $2.50 a Month Top," *PM*, November 8, 1940; "The California Physicians' Service," *PM*, November 11, 1940; "Dr. Sigerist Discusses San Francisco's Health Service System," *PM*, November 12, 1940; "Dr. Sigerist on Coast Health Plan" *PM*, November 13, 1940. See also Ricky Hendricks, *A Model for National Health Care: The History of Kaiser Permanente* (New Brunswick, N.J.: Rutgers University Press, 1993).

95. See, for example, Arthur M. Shipley to Isaiah Bowman, May 29, 1939; Isaiah Bowman to Arthur Shipley, June 2, 1939; Laurence Wharton to Isaiah Bowman, January 19, 1940; D. Luke Hopkins to Laurence R. Wharton, January 24, 1940; Jas. K. Anderson to Isaiah Bowman, February 1, 1940; Wallace M. Yater to Board of Trustees, January 25, 1941; Marshall Winchester to Isaiah Bowman, April 7, 1942. The Ferdinand Hamburger Jr. Archives of the Johns Hopkins University, Records of the Office of the President, 1903–63, file 28.9 (Institute of the History of Medicine).

96. Henry E. Sigerist, *Medicine and Human Welfare* (New Haven: Yale University Press, 1941); *Civilization and Disease* (Ithaca, N.Y.: Cornell University Press, 1943). Other wartime essays were published in *The University at the Crossroads: Addresses and Essays* (New York: Henry Schuman, 1946).

97. Sigerist articulated a class analysis of the politics of health insurance in "From Bismarck to Beveridge: Developments and Trends in Social Security Legis-

lation. I. The Period of Bismarck," *Bulletin of the History of Medicine* 13 (1943): 365–88, written while the Wagner-Murray-Dingell Bill for national health insurance was before the U.S. Congress. As Milton Terris, then a student at Johns Hopkins, notes, Sigerist's analysis of the political balance of forces in the United States—given the lack of a strong Socialist Party or a sufficiently powerful labor movement—suggested that the Wagner-Murray-Dingell Bill would fail. Sigerist's pessimistic analysis proved correct. See Milton I. Terris, "The Contributions of Henry E. Sigerist to Health Service Organization," *Milbank Memorial Fund Quarterly* 53 (1975): 503.

98. For details, see Monte M. Poen, *Harry S. Truman Versus the Medical Lobby: The Genesis of Medicare* (Columbia: University of Missouri Press, 1979), 33–41.

99. Henry E. Sigerist, "Medical Care for All the People," *Canadian Journal of Public Health* 35 (July 1944): 253–67. Reprinted in *Henry E. Sigerist on the Sociology of Medicine,* 229–47.

100. Monte M. Poen, *Harry S. Truman Versus the Medical Lobby,* 42.

101. Henry E. Sigerist, Diary, February 5, 1944; *Autobiographical Writings,* 186.

102. United States Civil Service Commission to Henry E. Sigerist, June 3, 1944. Sigerist Papers/Yale, Professional Activities, group 788, series II, box 31.

103. Fourth United States Civil Service Region Investigations Division, "Report of Partial Hearing and Special Hearing," November 15, 1943. Sigerist Papers/ Yale, Professional Activities, group 788, series II, box 31.

104. Henry E. Sigerist, "Saskatchewan Health Services Survey Commission," "The Need for an Institute of the History of Medicine in India," and "Report on India," in *Henry E. Sigerist on the Sociology of Medicine,* 209–28, 273–87, and 288–96.

105. Henry E. Sigerist, Diary, August 5, 1943; August 16, 1944; July 26, 1945; September 28, 1946; *Autobiographical Writings,* 184, 189, 196, 201.

106. Monte M. Poen, *Harry S. Truman Versus the Medical Lobby,* 55–75.

107. Ibid., 89–92.

108. See "Intellectual Legacy and Political Quest," by Elizabeth Fee and Theodore M. Brown in this volume.

109. When John B. Grant visited Baltimore in September 1945, he was surprised to find that Sigerist was "excluded from local deliberations" and no longer much involved with local medical or public health activities outside of the Institute and his own students. John B. Grant, Diary, September 24–28, 1945, Baltimore. Rockefeller Foundation Archives, Rockefeller Archive Center, North Tarrytown, N.Y., Record Group 12, series 1, Diaries.

110. Sigerist wrote about his health problems in "Living under the Shadow," *Atlantic Monthly* 189 (January 1952): 25–30.

111. See Alan Gregg to Henry E. Sigerist, November 5, 1948. Sigerist Papers/ Yale, General Correspondence, 1947–57, group 788, series I, box 13; Monte M. Poen, "The Truman Legacy: Retreat to Medicare," in *Compulsory Health Insurance: The Continuing American Debate,* ed. Ronald L. Numbers (Westport, Conn.: Greenwood Press, 1982), 97–113.

112. Milton I. Roemer to Henry E. Sigerist, July 11, 1949. Sigerist Papers/Yale, General Correspondence, 1947–57, group 788, series I, box 20. See Milton I. Roemer and Fred Mott, *Rural Health and Medical Care* (New York: McGraw-Hill,

1948), a book that catalogued some of the positive achievements of the New Deal at a time when, as Sigerist wrote, "the New Deal is being slandered and smeared from all sides." Henry E. Sigerist to Milton I. Roemer, September 18, 1948. Sigerist Papers/Yale, General Correspondence, 1947–57, group 788, series I, box 20.

113. See the correspondence with Robert L. Leslie, the business manager of the *American Review of Soviet Medicine* and a long-time member of the Communist Party, USA. Robert Leslie to Henry E. Sigerist, January 25, 1949, Sigerist Papers/Yale, General Correspondence, 1947–57, group 788, series I, box 16. Sigerist's old friend, John A. Kingsbury, as chairman of the National Council of American-Soviet Friendship, battled the Subversive Activities Control Board (McCarran Committee), which was investigating the more than 260 organizations on the attorney general's "Subversive List." John A. Kingsbury to Henry E. Sigerist, January 18, 1952, 3–4; October 21, 1953; "Statement by Dr. John A. Kingsbury, National Chairman of the National Council of American-Soviet Friendship, prepared for submission at the Hearing before the Subversive Activities Control Board, 10 May 1954," Sigerist Papers/Yale, General Correspondence, 1947–57, group 788, series I, box 15.

114. Milton I. Roemer, "Henry Ernest Sigerist: Internationalist of Social Medicine," *Journal of the History of Medicine and Allied Sciences* 13 (1958): 229–43; Milton I. Roemer, "Medical Care Programs in Other Countries: Henry Sigerist and International Medicine," *American Journal of Public Health* 48 (1958): 425–27.

115. Mirko D. Grmek, ed., *Serving the Cause of Public Health: Selected Papers of Andrija Štampar*, trans. M. Halar (Zagreb, Yugoslavia: Skola narodnog zdravija, "Andrija Štampar," Medicinski facultet, 1988). See also the warm and admiring remarks about Andrija Štampar in Henry E. Sigerist, "Yugoslavia and the Eleventh International Congress of the History of Medicine," *Bulletin of the History of Medicine* 7 (1939): 99–147. Milton Terris has suggested that Štampar used Sigerist's ideas as the basis for the World Health Organization's widely cited definition of health. Milton I. Terris, "The Contributions of Henry E. Sigerist to Health Service Organization," *Milbank Memorial Fund Quarterly* 53 (1975): 489–530; Milton I. Terris, "What is Health Promotion?" (editorial), *Journal of Public Health Policy* 7 (1986): 147–51.

116. See the essay by Roemer, Falk, and Brown in this volume.

117. Milton I. Roemer to Henry E. Sigerist, August 19, 1951; Milton I. Roemer to Henry E. Sigerist, November 6, 1951. Sigerist Papers/Yale, General Correspondence, 1947–57, group 788, series I, box 20; World Health Organization, "Medical Aspects of Social Security: Statement of Consultant Group, prepared for consideration by the International Labour Organization in formulating its new Conventions on Social Security," December 19, 1951, 2–6; press release, World Health Organization, Geneva, "WHO Advises on Social Security Schemes—Specialists Make Recommendations on Medical Aspects of Proposed ILO Conventions," December 21, 1951. Sigerist Papers/Yale, General Correspondence, 1947–57, group 788, series I, box 20.

118. For the history and politics of the debates over medical care within the American Public Health Association, see Arthur J. Viseltear, *Emergence of the Medical Care Section of the American Public Health Association, 1926–1948* (Washington, D.C.: American Public Health Association, 1972); Arthur J. Viseltear,

"Compulsory Health Insurance and the Definition of Public Health," in *Compulsory Health Insurance: The Continuing American Debate*, 25–54; Milton I. Roemer, "The American Public Health Association as a Force for Change in Medical Care," *Medical Care* 11 (1973): 338–51.

119. Milton I. Roemer to Henry E. Sigerist, November 3, 1954. Sigerist Papers/Yale, General Correspondence, 1947–57, group 788, series I, box 20.

CHAPTER 11

Dances with Commissars:
Sigerist and Soviet Medicine

John F. Hutchinson

No book that Sigerist wrote brought him more notoriety than *Socialized Medicine in the Soviet Union,* which he published in 1937. Its consistently laudatory tone made him a hero among young radicals and a dupe or a fellow traveler among conservatives. Sigerist wrote it, so he said, for the next generation, for those who would become the leaders of medicine in the West. He was confident that these young people—"students, physicians, public health officers, nurses, and social workers who are deeply concerned with the future of medicine" would read his book and appreciate that traditional prejudices would have to be abandoned "in order to serve society more efficiently and improve the people's health."[1] For him, socialism was "the only possible solution of the medical problem";[2] hence his fascination with the Soviet medical system.

Reading these words now, amid the misery and wreckage left by the collapse of the Soviet Union, it is all too easy to forget that seventy years ago the Soviet experiment with socialism seemed full of promise. We need to be reminded that for the generation that lived through World War I, the traditional forms of social organization had lost much of their attraction. In the twenties and thirties, the west was full of intellectuals—and not only intellectuals—who sincerely believed that the Russian Revolution had opened a new era in world history. Henry Sigerist was one of them. He believed that, just as the revolution had replaced capitalism with socialism, so it also marked the beginning of a new medical epoch in which preventive medicine would replace therapeutic medicine. *Socialized Medicine* thus became a major part of the campaign that Sigerist waged during his fifteen years in America, not only to make Americans better informed about medicine and public health in Russia, but also to make them appreciate that only a socialized medical system could overcome the barriers that poverty inevitably imposes on health. Although he came to love the land and people of the Soviet Union, Sigerist was primarily interested in Soviet medicine because of what it could teach westerners about how to improve health care in their own countries and how to work toward better health in the poverty-stricken countries of Latin America, Africa, and Asia.

Sigerist's Interest in Soviet Russia

How did Sigerist, with his thoroughly bourgeois family background and education, come to hold such a sympathetic attitude toward the Soviet Union? As a mature adult, he attributed his social awakening to the effects of World War I. It was the war, he claimed in 1938, that had convinced him that "nothing but socialism could save the world."[3] His wartime experience with the medical corps of the Swiss army was a kind of awakening, not only to "practical public health work among the civilian population," but also to the real world of ordinary people, of peasants and factory workers who saw the Russian Revolution as a beacon of hope.[4]

Yet if these memories are accurate, it has to be said that his radicalism was a long time developing. In the first fifteen years after the 1917 revolution, there is nothing in Sigerist's work to suggest the development of an outspoken advocate of socialized medicine. He heard something about the Soviet reforms in medicine and health care in 1930 from one of the leading Bolshevik reformers, the social hygienist Ilya Davidovich Strashun.[5] There is, however, no indication that Sigerist wanted to visit the Soviet Union at this time, and indeed, it was not Russia but America that lured him away from Leipzig.

The years 1931–33 were pivotal in transforming Sigerist the scholar into Sigerist the scholar and social activist. His investigation of medicine in America persuaded him that its commercialism was morally repugnant because it had lengthened the economic distance that separated poor patients from needed therapeutic services and remedies. Convinced that substantial changes were urgently required, he aligned himself with the reform cause in *Amerika und die Medizin* (American Medicine), which he first published in 1933.[6]

While writing his book on American medicine, Sigerist heard a speech that had a profound impact on him. On December 6, 1932, he attended a dinner hosted by William H. Welch at the University Club in Baltimore. The guest speaker was John Kingsbury, secretary of the Milbank Memorial Fund, who had visited Russia the previous summer and was full of praise for the Soviet health reforms. "How Popsie Welch was thrilled when he heard it," Sigerist recalled long afterward in a letter to Kingsbury's widow.[7] Welch was not the only member of the audience to be moved by what he heard. Kingsbury's glowing description of the achievements of the Soviet reformers planted in the receptive soil of Sigerist's mind a vision of how medical care everywhere might be transformed for the better. Soon, even before he published *Amerika und die Medizin,* he was conceiving of a book on Soviet medicine as its logical sequel.[8] On April 17, 1933, he confided to his diary, "Today I realized that our public health is barbaric. Medicine is still in its first, the therapeutic, period. For the next, the preventive period, a social revolution is needed. Under the capitalist system—even less in a fascist state—preventive medicine is not possible. Russia therefore signifies the beginning of a new epoch in medicine also."[9] This is the moment when the basic theme of his Soviet book took shape in his mind; almost immediately he threw himself into the study of Russian and Soviet medicine.[10]

Planning the Soviet Book

Once he had decided to write about Russia, he set himself to the task with his customary vigor and application. He began teaching himself Russian, with the aid of a set of sixteen records purchased from the Linguaphone Institute of America. He also subscribed to "a good many" Russian periodicals, including *Moscow News*.[11] In late October, he wrote to Kingsbury, telling him of his plans and emphasizing his intention to stress the philosophical and sociological basis of Soviet medicine.[12]

Kingsbury replied:

> This is exactly what is needed. . . . I shall look forward with keen interest to what you will have to say. . . . I hope you will be able to elucidate the subject of "dialectical materialism," which I confess rather baffles me. Before I went to Russia, Dr. Welch told me that I should try to fathom this philosophy, although he modestly remarked that he didn't understand it himself.[13]

Buoyed up by this response, Sigerist attacked a daunting reading list that included the works of Spinoza, Hegel, Feuerbach, Marx, and Engels; the fifteen-volume edition of Lenin's collected works; a French translation of Platonov's *History of Russia;* and Pokrovsky's *A Brief History of Russia,* an English version of which was published in New York in 1933 by International Publishers.[14] In December, Kingsbury sent him a copy of *Red Medicine,* the book that he and Sir Arthur Newsholme had just written about their visit to Russia in the summer of 1932. Sigerist found it "so full of information that it rather discouraged me to go ahead with my Russian studies," or so he wrote to Kingsbury, who immediately replied, "by all means go on with your studies and plans, for our study was at best rather superficial."[15] Sigerist's plans were no more than momentarily delayed, and within weeks he was searching for a copy—in Russian—of Skorokhodov's *History of Russian Medicine.*[16]

By the autumn of 1934, Sigerist was planning to make two summer visits to Russia, in 1935 and 1936, and to write the book itself during the winter of 1936–37.[17] Characteristically, he was already one step ahead of himself, at least in his private thoughts: "When I'm through with my Russian work I will attack the field of Chinese medicine, will survey the country and start an Institute for the History of Chinese Medicine there."[18] For the Russian trip, however, he had several immediate needs, such as financial support, travel advice, and letters of introduction. To pay his expenses, he had intended to use part of a $10,000 grant from the Keystone Fund, but to his chagrin he learned in February 1935 that the grant had been withdrawn.[19] With a travel budget of only $1000, he had to find more money somewhere, but he hesitated to ask the Milbank Fund because, as he noted in his diary, "I am a poor beggar."[20] Nevertheless, he wrote to Kingsbury, asking for letters of introduction and enclosing a two-page description of the idea of the book, the preparation done so far, and his plans for the coming trip to Russia. Part of this document may be quoted at length:

> The idea to make a sociological study on medicine in the Soviet Union originated several years ago while I was writing my book on American medicine. . . .
> While I wrote the book, I asked myself constantly how the different problems were solved in the Soviet Union; and I found it extremely difficult to obtain information as your book on Red Medicine was not yet published. I felt that the future of medicine will depend largely on what is being done in this country and in the Soviet Union. Although the two countries have a different economic structure, the problems seem to me very similar. Both are gigantic territories;

both are young in civilization. In the beginning of the 20th Century, the great development of American medicine started, and in 1917 a new era began for Russia. I realized that the difference in the underlying philosophy must necessarily result in different ways of medical organization, and I decided to make a study of Soviet medicine similar to my study on American medicine. Both books together will show what the future trends of medicine will be.

I am not interested primarily in how many hospital beds there are in Moscow or any other city today, as this is merely a transitory stage. What interests me mostly is how a definite philosophy applied to life determines medicine and medical service.[21]

This passage is noteworthy for several reasons. First, it demonstrates clearly the close connection in his mind between the American and Russian books; secondly, it reveals his Tocquevillian assumptions about the impact of space and novelty on the future of America and Russia; thirdly, it shows plainly his preference for describing "things as they are planned to be" rather than "things as they are," a preference that was to bring him considerable criticism from friend and foe alike.

As part of preparing himself to write the Soviet book, Sigerist began teaching a new seminar, "The Social Aspects of Medicine," at Johns Hopkins.[22] The seminar provided him with a forum in which he could hold forth on subjects of contemporary as well as historical interest, including the true nature of capitalism, the evils of fascism, and the Soviet experiment with socialism. One may catch a glimpse of Sigerist's mood in his diary entry for February 20, 1935:

I am so full of that subject, have so much to say that I speak passionately and this carries the audience. I discussed capitalism today, its essence, rise, and influence on medicine, then the German social insurance. I had the people in my hands, by God. They may disagree with many points, but all of them will think differently and will have clearer conceptions at the end of the course.[23]

At a session of the seminar two weeks later, Sigerist had "just started condemning the [Italian fascist] regime" when he was attacked with "stupid arguments" by three Italian students who were sympathetic to the regime. "I had a hell of a time in the seminar today," he confided to his diary; however at the next session a week later, so many students came to hear him speak about Soviet medicine that the session had to be moved to a lecture hall.[24] Sigerist was beginning to sense a new role for himself as the apostle of socialism and of socialized medicine.

Nevertheless, the spring of 1935 was, on balance, a bad time for Sigerist.

As he prepared to leave Baltimore to spend the summer in the Soviet Union, events both public and private seemed to be conspiring against him and his most cherished hopes. In the first place, the American Medical Association unanimously rejected President Roosevelt's sickness insurance scheme.[25] A second blow was the news, made public on April 20, that his colleague Kingsbury had been unceremoniously dumped from his position at the Milbank Fund.[26] Then, a few weeks after Sigerist's stormy seminar session on fascism, Allen Freeman, dean of the School of Hygiene and Public Health at Johns Hopkins, reported rumors that he was a Communist. He confided his reaction to his diary: "It is perfectly absurd. I was never a member of any political party and never will be. . . . It seems that people begin to be hysterical."[27] Finally, on June 8, 1935, thoroughly soured with America and increasingly uneasy about the fascist threat in Europe, Sigerist boarded a Soviet ship, the M.V. *Sibir,* for the trip from London to Leningrad. He was more than ready to be impressed by the Soviet version of socialism.

Foreigner Observers and the Soviet Experiment

Sigerist was one of many foreign physicians and health care workers who flocked to the Soviet Union in the twenties and thirties. Already in 1928, two Americans had published separate accounts of the Soviet reforms in health care and medicine. One was the young physician Horsley Gantt, who had gone to Russia with the American Relief Administration in 1922–23 and returned to Leningrad in 1925 to work with Pavlov at the Institute of Experimental Medicine. After touring central Russia and the Caucasus in 1927–28, Gantt published *A Medical Review of Soviet Russia*.[28] The other account was the work of Anna Haines, a nurse who had gone to Russia as a relief worker in 1917 with the American Friends' Service Committee, and who returned there in 1920 and again in 1925.[29] Because of her protracted stays at intervals over a decade, Haines was able to convey to her readers a real sense both of the horrors of famine and disease during the civil war and of the constructive changes carried out since it ended in 1921.

Sigerist knew both these works and read them as part of his preparation, but their authors exerted little or no influence on him. He never met Anna Haines, while Gantt he thought "a queer fish. He has been so long in the Soviet Union, and yet does not understand at all what is going on there. He always judges from momentary happenings, from surface features. The typical attitude of a scientist who has no historical sense at all, no understanding for social developments."[30] Sigerist had a much higher opinion of *Red Medicine: Socialized Health in Soviet Russia,* which Kingsbury had written in conjunction with Sir Arthur Newsholme, the well-known English authority on comparative public health administration.[31] The origins of this book are complex. In the late 1920s, Newsholme had undertaken for the Milbank Fund an extensive review of the relationship between private practice, public health, and disease prevention in several countries and, in addition, had published his reflections on these subjects under the title *Medicine and the State.*[32] None of these investigations had included Russia, apparently because Newsholme thought that the West had nothing to learn from such a backward country.[33] The Milbank trustees must have thought otherwise, for they commissioned him and Kingsbury to carry out a full-scale enquiry into Soviet medicine. Together they visited Russia in the late summer of 1932, and completed the text of *Red Medicine* within a matter of months. The book appeared in late 1933.

A more unlikely pair of collaborators than Kingsbury and Newsholme could scarcely have been imagined. A social worker by training and an urban progressive by inclination, Kingsbury was "eager to see if they [the Soviets] really have by fiat solved some of the public health problems upon which we have been working for decades."[34] The aging Newsholme, on the other hand, was an Edwardian gentleman imbued with the principles of British liberalism, and thus more likely to regard the Bolsheviks as criminals and hooligans rather than pioneers and innovators. The contrast in their attitudes rapidly became apparent. While aboard the ship that took them to the Baltic Sea, Sir Arthur's unconcealed aversion for the marriage and divorce practices of the Soviets led one of their fellow passengers to comment to Kingsbury, "What an archaic mind!"[35] In Moscow, they attended Meyerhold's play, *The Next War with the West,* after which the cast led the audience in a spirited rendition of the "Internationale"; this display of class enmity and militarism was too much for Sir Arthur, who told Kingsbury that this was "conclusive evidence that we must arm at once against the Bolsheviks."[36] Worse was to come in Samara on the lower Volga when Newsholme, already upset by the Soviets' penchant for antiwestern cartoons, encountered an exhibit about abortion, the explicitness of which he found utterly shocking; not yet recovered from this outrage on his moral sensibility, he discovered that their new Intourist guide, a woman, expected to share their railway compartment![37]

The result of this collaboration, *Red Medicine,* was a genuine attempt to illuminate and evaluate both the merits and the shortcomings of the Soviet experiment in medical reform. Such balance was an outcome of their diverse perspectives: Newsholme was, naturally, anxious that the book should not make them appear biased in favor of the Soviet system, while Kingsbury, who hoped soon to revisit the country, was equally anxious that it not display a bias against it. One thing they had no difficulty agreeing on was the need to give their readers a sense both of the path that Russia traveled to the 1917 revolution and of the distinct periods that had characterized the life of the Soviet Union. Achieving this goal was, however, difficult in practice, and Kingsbury found himself toning down Sir Arthur's first draft in order to excise the latter's disapproving comments on class hatred and the cruel treatment of the kulaks.[38] Kingsbury also persuaded Newsholme that they ought to say something about Russia's "tradition of competent and distinguished medical leadership," because "many people in America think that such doctors as they have, have probably been created entirely out of the proletariat since the revolution."[39] For his part, Newsholme served as a rudder to keep Kingsbury from turning the book into a eulogy of the Soviet medical system.[40] He resisted Kingsbury's suggestion that they ask Sidney Webb to write a preface: "Would it not place us too obviously in the Soviet camp?"[41] And again: "We can do more justice to the Russian experience, by erring if at all on the side of understatement."[42]

When *Red Medicine* appeared, it drew praise from almost every quarter for its balanced and impartial judgments. The only notable exception was a highly critical review by a Russian émigré in the book supplement of the *New York Times*.[43] Furious at its anti-Bolshevik tone and obvious distortions, Kingsbury prepared a lengthy and detailed reply but was persuaded not to send it by Newsholme, Welch, and Sigerist, all of whom thought it pointless to answer what Welch had called this "perfectly stupid review"; Sigerist added, "When a man is convinced that Russia is hell, you can write as much as you like and yet will never succeed in changing his prejudiced view."[44] In a letter to Newsholme, Kingsbury expressed his regret that the *Times* had not sent their book to Sigerist, "who undoubtedly would have been willing to write a review."[45]

The Writing of *Socialized Medicine in the Soviet Union*

Sigerist approached the task of writing about Russia in a manner quite different from that of his predecessors. Where Gantt and Haines had written from long personal experience involving both work and residence, he made short visits, putting himself entirely in the hands of his hosts. Where Kingsbury and Newsholme each had the other to act as a kind of balance wheel, Sigerist formed his own opinions and became impatient with those who did not share them. On the one hand, he claimed for his work the legitimacy of scholarly detachment, writing in his introduction, "I have approached the problem of Soviet medicine as a historian from the perspective of history, studying and analysing it as a historical phenomenon, in the same way as I approached problems of ancient and mediaeval medical history before. . . . I have my sympathies as everybody has but they are the result of study, not of emotions."[46] In the light of what has already been said about Sigerist's growing admiration for Soviet medicine, this last claim will scarcely stand scrutiny. In the epilogue to *Socialized Medicine*, Sigerist states his "conclusion" that a new era, that of preventive medicine, has begun in the Soviet Union; a statement that repeats almost word for word his diary entry of April 17, 1933.[47]

Indeed, what one misses in Sigerist's work is precisely the fact that he *does not* approach his subject "from the perspective of history." He was considerably more candid about his objectives in a letter to John Strachey of Victor Gollancz Ltd., who he hoped would publish the British edition of the book:

> I am interested in the ideas and trends of Soviet medicine and the book is to be primarily an essay on socialist medicine. All previous books on the subject were out of date in a couple of years, naturally. My book, however, will discuss principles and developments and will describe the present conditions merely as illustrations, to show how the principles are applied in the Soviet Union. The book will be written from a Marxian point of view and will have a strong plea for socialism and socialised medicine. . . . I have some influence on the young medical people in America . . . people who, as a rule, are not familiar with Marxism but are quite eager to learn about it and will accept it more readily if it is presented to them in a medical book, in a language they understand.[48]

Perhaps because Sigerist began with his conclusion already formulated and his ideological stance firmly established, he was neither as thorough nor as critical as he might have been in preparing himself to write a book about Russia. There are, for example, some glaring bibliographical lapses in his research. One misses any reference to the multivolume Russian series of the *Economic and Social History of the World War,* edited by James T. Shotwell for the Carnegie Foundation for International Peace. By 1929 this series included any number of useful studies on the state of Russia on the eve of the 1917 revolution. True, there is none specifically devoted to medicine, but issues of public health and medical care loom large in at least two of the volumes in this series.[49] Use of these volumes would also have given Sigerist a different perspective on the relationship between the war and the revolution than the official Soviet version that he would receive in the mid-thirties. Given his liking for statistics, another standard source that Sigerist could have used with profit—once he had learned Russian—was the collection produced by the Central Statistical Administration in 1925, entitled *Russia in the First World War, 1914-18 (in figures).*[50] Edited by the Deputy Commissar of Health Protection, Z. P. Solov'ev, this collection thoroughly documented the cost of the war to civilian and military health and to Russian medical personnel. A third important source that Sigerist missed was Z. G. Frenkel's *Community Medicine and Social Hygiene* (1926);[51] this would have given him an insight into the debt that Soviet social hygiene in the twenties owed to the community medical tradition of prerevolutionary Russia. I cite these basic sources not to prove that Sigerist missed relatively obscure works—which one could easily forgive—but rather to show that he missed some of the most important and appropriate historical sources. To be sure, his predecessors also missed them, but they did not make such grandiose claims for the soundness of their work. Admittedly, his Soviet hosts were unlikely to have encouraged a more extensive research effort, but there is no evidence, either in the book itself or in his diary, that he was frustrated in any way in his search for information. On the contrary, he expresses only boundless gratitude to his Soviet hosts for their help in preparing the book and was content to employ uncritically the official version of Russian and Soviet history that they gave him.[52] One is forced to the conclusion that he might have dug more deeply.

Nor did Sigerist display the slightest skepticism about what he was being told and shown. Newsholme and Kingsbury, by contrast, had been alert to the possibility that they were being shown the best, rather than the typical; they suspected that ideological considerations might determine both what they were told and whom they met; they noted their concern that translated messages could well be colored by the translator. Yet this skepticism did not prevent them, despite Newsholme's reservations, from recording their admiration for what the Soviet reformers had already achieved and for much of what was planned. Sigerist, on the other hand, displayed no such sophistication. After his first full day in Moscow (June 19, 1935), he wrote in his diary:

> Here I am taken care of and everything is prepared for me and made so easy. In the afternoon I went to VOKS (the All-Union Society for Cultural Relations with Foreign Countries) and had an extremely pleasant hour there discussing

the American situation with two clever women, one of them a doctor. They are very helpful and will even give me a special guide. Things could not be better and I feel quite elated.[53]

This passage reveals two things about Sigerist's time in Russia. First, he was obviously astoundingly naive about how foreign visitors were managed by the regime. Secondly, and perhaps more importantly, it was the situation in *America*, rather than in the Soviet Union, that he and his hosts discussed. One suspects that Sigerist was at least as keen on telling his hosts what was the matter with American society and American medicine as he was to find out about the Soviet system. Disillusioned with capitalist society, he was full of instant enthusiasm for the Soviet health resorts because there were "no financial interests to interfere" in the planning process.[54] After visiting his first *Prophylactorium* (dispensary), he described it in his diary as "the ideal health center for complete medical service as it was recommended for America by the Commission on Costs of Medical Care."[55] In short, Sigerist was determined to find in the Soviet Union what he thought was lacking in America.

Some of his friends and colleagues tried to save him from himself. One was C.-E. A. Winslow of Yale, who had first been to Russia in 1917, and who returned in the summer of 1936, encountering there Sigerist, who was on his second summer visit. Although Winslow could appreciate the immense changes that had been made since 1917, his opinions regarding the progress of medicine were less than enthusiastic. What he saw in 1936 led him to conclude that *Red Medicine* had presented "a somewhat distorted view of the medical and health services of the Soviet Union."[56] When they met in Moscow, Winslow urged Sigerist to beware lest his forthcoming book be vulnerable to similar criticisms.

Back in America, Winslow let Kingsbury know what he thought of the accuracy of *Red Medicine* and expressed his fears about Sigerist's book. Kingsbury wrote at length to Sigerist, pleading with him to double-check his data and even urging him—as he himself had been urged by Newsholme—to "err on the side of understatement."[57] Sigerist's speedy reply revealed his impatience with this line of criticism:

I know Winslow's attitude; it makes me mad. He is, of course, not alone. His is the general attitude of most medical men in this country even of those who, like Winslow himself, are rather sympathetic to the Soviet Union. They absolutely fail to see that what is happening in the Soviet Union is a *dynamic process,* that it is not a static condition. If you photograph a horse while it is jumping a fence, you get a most untrue and ridiculous picture of an animal hanging in the air against all the laws of gravity. In the same way, you cannot picture the Soviet Union the way you happen to have seen it on a definite day because things change from day to day. What counts are the principles and trends. That such an ambitious program can not be fulfilled in such a tremendous territory over night is obvious.

I do not consider it my task to criticize local shortcomings that may have been corrected by the time the book comes from the press . . . the shortcomings are temporary matters that will be changed as soon as conditions permit it. . . . The quality of service has improved a great deal in the last few years and will improve steadily in the future there is no doubt about it.[58]

As to the matter of checking his data, Sigerist undertook to ensure that he had reproduced his Soviet sources correctly, but offered no further guarantees. "The book will be fully annotated and I am giving the source of every figure I quote. As I cannot possibly check the figures, the responsibility will lie on the sources." [59] In other words, if his information was wrong, then only his informants were to blame.

Soviet Medicine: Ideology and Reality, 1918–1928

In the decade after the Bolshevik Revolution, Russian medicine and public health were transformed on a scale unparalleled in the history of that country. The new regime set out to create a bold new system of health care that would be both free and universally accessible, and one that would give high priority to the prevention of disease. In July 1918, a new Commissariat of Health Protection (Narkomzdrav, or NKZ for short) was established under the leadership of N. A. Semashko and his deputy, Z. P. Solov'ev; their task was to provide the centralized direction and momentum necessary to implement the planned changes.[60] Until the end of the civil war in 1921, substantial changes and improvements had to take a back seat, because the regime's first priority was to combat the famine and epidemic diseases that were sweeping the country. By the late twenties, however, Narkomzdrav spokesmen were claiming successes in a number of areas: more physicians were being trained to provide better care in facilities that had been expanded considerably in size and availability; specialties such as dentistry and physiotherapy had been deliberately encouraged; and real efforts had been made to improve the quality of rural medical care. From the outset about one-quarter of the health budget was devoted to the prevention of disease. When funding for most medical facilities was transferred to local soviets in 1922, Narkomzdrav retained control over preventive work, and in the mid-twenties, it organized many campaigns to improve sanitation and reduce the incidence of social diseases. In 1928, Narkomzdrav sponsored the publication of several statistical studies, all of which claimed to show the remarkable progress that had been made since the fall of the tsarist regime.[61]

Yet despite some undoubted achievements, all was not smooth sailing for the reformers. In a recent study of Narkomzdrav in the twenties, Neil Weissman has argued that there was always a substantial gap between theory and practice, and hence there were as many shortcomings as there were achievements.[62] It was one thing to plan reforms in Moscow offices; it was quite another to implement them in other cities and towns, let alone in the countryside. By the end of the decade, several serious problems were apparent. The grand plans of Narkomzdrav were often thwarted by niggardly financial support from local soviets; initiative had been sapped by excessive bureaucratic control; labor officials were jealous of Narkomzdrav's jurisdiction over workers' medical insurance; rural medical services were getting worse rather than better, thanks in part to the continuing unwillingness of physicians to practice in the countryside. The regime's new emphasis on preventive medicine had also run into trouble at the local level, in urban as well as rural areas; low funding, personnel shortages, and professional antagonisms combined to weaken preventive medical work at the local level.

The more reality refused to conform to the reformers' vision, the more stridently they defended that vision. Refusing to admit that their plans and assumptions had been in any respect faulty, Narkomzdrav spokesmen reasserted both the historical uniqueness and the ideological correctness of Soviet medicine. They were particularly sensitive to charges that their emphasis on centralized direction, evoking memories of tsarist bureaucrats, flew in the face of the traditions of prerevolutionary "zemstvo medicine."[63] Commissar Semashko himself explicitly denounced appeals to zemstvo traditions of local self-government and medical autonomy in a 1928 article on the shortage of rural physicians. Medical services in a socialist society, he argued, are planned and carried out as a duty to the state, not because of some philanthropic impulse or perceived need to fulfill one's debt to the peasantry.[64] From this time onward, the defense of rational planning and the emphasis on duty to the state became dogmas that governed all of Narkomzdrav's propaganda about its own work and provided the basis for a predictably negative evaluation of most of Russian medical history prior to 1917.

Sigerist's Portrayal of Soviet Medicine

The unwary Sigerist absorbed these dogmas. He repeated the standard Narkomzdrav line on the weaknesses of zemstvo medicine; he dutifully ascribed the famines of the early twenties to the White armies and those of the early thirties to the "kulak" opponents of the collectivization of agriculture; he continually asserted the primacy of rational planning and preventive work in the Soviet medical system. Unfortunately, what is missing here is a genuinely historical perspective, not only on the years before the revolution of 1917, but also on the Soviet period itself. Sigerist seems to have had little appreciation for the revolutionary, even utopian, enthusiasm of the early twenties, let alone for the dynamics of social and political conflict in the years following the end of the civil war.[65] With no sense of the struggles among Bolsheviks over the meaning of socialism, or among workers over their rights in a workers' state, or even among physicians over their relationship to the Party, Sigerist's treatment of the twenties is a curiously old-fashioned social history with the politics left out; almost the exact opposite, in fact, of the sociological–historical analysis he imagined himself to be writing.

Most regrettable of all is the fact that Sigerist unquestioningly accepted the Stalinist version of events between 1928, when the first five-year plan was launched, and 1935–36, when he visited the Soviet Union. In practice this means that he regarded rapid industrialization and the forced collectivization of agriculture as overriding historical necessities; conceded that in the process some people's enthusiasm got out of hand, but implied that the kulaks brought their fate on themselves; and concluded that things were better under the second five-year plan because the breakneck pace of the years 1928–33 had been eased. What is missing here is any sense of what the Great Break meant for the lives and fate of industrial workers, the great mass of peasants, women, intellectuals, or even physicians. To be sure, our present understanding of the Stalin revolution and of the cultural revolution that was an essential part of it is vastly different from what contemporary observers—with the possible exception of Trotsky—perceived to be taking place.[66] Nevertheless, one might expect Sigerist to have acknowledged that some sort of transformation of the relationship between the Party and Soviet society was under way. He was, after all, in Moscow during the purge trials, the meaning of which one could hardly ignore (though he did his best!). He seems to have had no inkling of the significance of recent events such as the Shakhty trial of 1928, which betokened a new hostility toward the intelligentsia, or the creation in 1929 of VARNITSO, a Communist front organization whose purpose was to terrorize the scientific intelligentsia—including physicians and medical research workers—into supporting Stalin's brutal reconstruction of Soviet life.[67] Neither of these events was kept secret; if Sigerist had asked the right questions, he might have gleaned at least some sense of the context in which Soviet physicians were operating.

Nevertheless one must not be too hard on Sigerist. There were some subjects so taboo that only a fool would have risked discussing them with an uninformed stranger. Thus he could scarcely have known that Semashko's ouster in January 1930 and his replacement as commissar by the loyal Stalinist M. F. Vladimirsky was part of Stalin's assault on the "right opposition" group, to which Semashko was connected. Indeed, much more was involved in this one event than Sigerist ever suspected.[68] The removal of Semashko was a sign that Soviet health policy would not be unaffected by the Great Break; as Christopher Davis has shown, what was spent on health in the years 1930-32 was allocated according to increasingly rigid political and economic criteria.[69] Briefly stated, those regions and social groups deemed most crucial to the success of the first five-year plan naturally received the highest priority. Davis believes that as a result of this policy of differential treatment of the population, "it is possible that inequality in medical care distribution was greater by the end of the first five-year plan than it had been at the beginning."[70]

Semashko's removal also signaled a reordering of priorities in medical research and education. In the twenties, the commissar of public health had been closely identified with the emergence and growth of social hygiene as a field for teaching and research; indeed, he had even written the principal textbook on the subject. According to Susan Gross Solomon, Semashko acted as patron for the development, funding, and institutionalization of social hygiene within Soviet medical research, education, and public health work.[71] Social hygiene research focused especially on the relationship between health (or the lack of it) and the living and working conditions of the population. Naturally, the politically sensitive and potentially costly conclusions of such research could be expected to call into question, if not to subvert, the goals of the regime during industrialization and collectivization; not surprisingly, Semashko's ouster was followed by a deliberately orchestrated campaign to discredit the aims and methods of social hygiene research. Some of those who had lost their positions and former influence occupied themselves with writing about past achievements: Semashko published his study of *Health Protection in the USSR* in 1934, and Strashun—Sigerist's informant in Leipzig—began taking up the study of medical history in 1930.[72]

By the time Sigerist visited the USSR in 1935–36, the medical curriculum had been revised to reflect the new party line, and the previous emphasis on preventive medical work had been considerably reduced. Naturally his informants at Narkomzdrav—G. N. Kaminsky, who had recently succeeded Vladimirsky as commissar, and his senior staff (including Strashun, who was nominally in charge of medical schools, but was in fact already teaching medical history)—gave Sigerist a quite different explanation for the curriculum changes, one that he dutifully reproduced in *Socialized Medicine*.[73] Similarly, Sigerist's account of the importance of preventive medicine conveys to the reader the impression that in this area there had been continual improvements since the early twenties; he clearly had no sense whatever that he was being lied to with statistics.[74] To be sure, not all the statistics were lies; his informant on the campaigns against venereal disease and prostitution during the twenties, Professor V. Bronner, supplied him with enough good information that this section of the book stands out for its thoroughness and reliability.[75]

Even if Sigerist failed to grasp the significance of the Great Break and the implications of Semashko's removal, one might think that he would do better with those events that took place, as it were, before his very eyes. Yet if one takes two important events from the year 1936—the revival of feldsher schools and the new abortion law—and examines his treatment of the issues involved, one finds the same readiness to repeat what he was told by Stalinist bureaucrats. Thus he shared in their distortions of both the present and the recent past.

Here is Sigerist's version of the feldsher issue:

> After the Revolution there was a tendency to discontinue the institution of feldsher, to let it die out. . . . It was soon recognized, however, that the country needed feldshers and that the rural districts particularly could not do without them. With the inadequate number of physicians available it was impossible to protect the people's health successfully unless additional personnel was sought.[76]

This is almost a caricature of the truth. From 1918 onward, Narkomzdrav physicians did indeed lead a concerted attack on feldshers and independent feldsher practice. What Sigerist did not appreciate was that this attack originated with the rapprochement between the Bolsheviks and leading members of the prerevolutionary Pirogov Society of Russian

Physicians, which had always opposed independent feldsher practice.[77] In the wake of the revolution, feldshers who confidently expected Bolshevik support for an assault on professional privilege mounted a strong challenge to the status and autonomy of physicians by organizing a union of all medical workers (*Vsemediksantrud*) in which physicians would enjoy no special position.[78] However, they reckoned without Semashko and other Bolshevik physicians who resolutely protected the expertise of physicians and ensured that their organization would enjoy autonomous status within the union. Official attempts to eliminate feldsher practice in rural areas were doomed to failure, partly because in the wake of the civil war many villages were too poor to employ physicians, partly because the peasants preferred traditional healers to modern scientific medicine, and partly because throughout the twenties, physicians were reluctant to work in the countryside. According to Samuel C. Ramer, so strong was the fear of cultural isolation and miserable living conditions that even unemployed physicians refused to work in rural areas.[79] Sigerist believed what he was told about the overall shortage of physicians, but the truth is that from 1925 onward, the government had made great efforts to attract physicians into rural service and had finally been forced to concede defeat. Thus Sigerist failed to appreciate that the 1936 decision to revive feldsher schools was, in Ramer's opinion, "a genuine defeat" for those who had sought to improve rural medical care and a recognition that the Great Break had condemned the countryside to permanently second-rate health care.[80]

A similar degree of ignorance surrounds Sigerist's treatment of the 1936 law forbidding Soviet women from having abortions. According to him, the 1920 decree that legalized abortion was merely an emergency measure, a makeshift to reduce mortality from botched operations by clandestine abortionists; as soon as the decree was introduced, he writes, "both government and Party began to issue propaganda against abortion," and did "infinitely more" by making "tremendous efforts to remove the causes of abortion by endeavoring to raise wages, to improve living conditions, and to create maternity homes and nurseries."[81] Here again one has no sense of the ideological dimension of the 1920 decree or of the fact that Bolshevik activists such as Aleksandra Kollontai regarded legalized abortion as one of the rights of the "new Soviet woman."[82] Not surprisingly, the 1920 decree produced a veritable deluge of women wanting abortions; official backtracking, which began in the mid-twenties, had less to do with protecting maternal health than with the system's inability to cope with the massive numbers. Sigerist notes the introduction of fees but fails to point out that this simply ensured that those who could pay received priority treatment. His treatment of the Party's change in attitude in 1935–36 is naive in the extreme: instead of perceiving its relationship to the insatiable labor needs of Stalin's industrialization drive, Sigerist solemnly intoned the official line that the 1920 law was no longer necessary and that the new decree was "not a retreat but on the contrary a further advance in the protection of mother and child."[83]

Socialized Medicine and After

Sigerist began to write the book in Switzerland in the late summer of 1936, right after his second visit to the Soviet Union. Originally, he had planned to complete the introduction and the first five chapters, then he revised his target to three chapters.[84] In the event, however, he spent the entire time in Switzerland writing only the introduction on Marxism, the length of which he justified on the grounds that it was essential for a real understanding of Soviet medicine. The remainder of the book thus had to be completed during the academic year 1936–37, and Sigerist was very strict with himself about refusing speaking engagements so that he could write. All went well for the first few months, but in early February he ran out of steam, confiding to his diary, "I am stuck on my book. I don't know why I have inhibitions. It may be physical. I feel badly."[85] The "inhibitions" lasted until the middle of March, a delay that meant something of a scramble to complete the manuscript before the end of June, when he intended to sail for Europe. Fortunately, VOKS in Moscow kept sending him a steady supply of material on various subjects: social insurance, the second five-year plan, the new Soviet constitution, and health care for mothers and infants. All of this Sigerist rapidly digested and incorporated in the manuscript.

Some idea of the frantic atmosphere in which the book was finished may be gained from his diary entry for May 16:

> Two more weeks and the book must be finished. I still have two more chapters to dictate. Polly [typist] is retyping the entire manuscript. Hope [Trebing, his secretary] and Fruma [Wolfson, his Russian-speaking research assistant] are working on the Appendix. Genevieve [Miller] is helping out when additional typing is needed. Esther Brown, in New York, is reading and correcting. I spend my nights preparing the new chapters, reading the old ones, dictating figures and data. And every day the [Soviet] newspapers bring new facts that have to be included.[86]

On May 27, Sigerist dashed to New York to visit the Soviet Photo Agency (Sovfoto), to choose illustrations for the book. He was especially pleased "to find a photo very well suited for the jacket: a Red Cross airplane with three nurses. It has all the qualities required for such a picture: it is medical, modern, Russian and has nice girls on it (not the Hollywood type!)."[87] Finally, on June 1, the manuscript was sent to Norton in New York; Sigerist noted, "At five o'clock highballs were on the table and at seven we were actually through. What a relief! The book is good. I have re-read it in the last few days. It is honest and should convince many young medical workers."[88]

Leaving his staff to deal with the backlog of work at the Institute in Baltimore, Sigerist spent the summer in Kastanienbaum with his family. Good news soon arrived, in the form of a letter from Victor Gollancz, who pronounced the completed manuscript "really a magnificent piece of work" and expressed his desire to publish the British edition immediately. But even in the mountains of Switzerland, embarrassing Soviet realities could not be escaped. The purges were continuing and reaching again into Narkomzdrav. At the end of July Gollancz wrote, "May I suggest that it is absolutely *vital* to omit Kaminsky's photograph, not only from the English edition, but also from the American? Am I not right in thinking that Kaminsky has now been dismissed? If so, won't the inclusion of his photograph mean that the book is banned over there?"[89] Sigerist replied, "I quite agree. . . . Under the circumstances it would be very unwise to publish his picture. I will also change the paragraph that I wrote about him."[90] When they found additional errors in the Soviet statistics, Sigerist wrote to Gollancz, "As it looks perfectly silly . . . to have incorrect totals, I would suggest that we omit them," a response scarcely in accord with his earlier assurance to Kingsbury about double-checking his data, but it was now too late for last-minute delays.[91] VOKS was continuing to send him new material, but Norton had already sent him galley proofs of the American edition and Gollancz was setting the British edition in type.

On October 28, 1937, Sigerist received advance copies of the American edition of the book; greatly pleased, he wrote in his diary, "Now I am ready to be insulted by the conservative press. I think I can stand it."[92] Insults there would be, but first came the compliments. Naturally there was a warm response from the Soviet embassy: Ambassador Troianovskii invited Sigerist to the Revolution Day reception, and Counsellor Umanskii wrote to congratulate him on "a remarkable achievement . . . it will immediately assume the rank of leading and standard text about public health and medicine in the Soviet Union."[93] Many of Sigerist's colleagues were equally generous: Winslow, who confessed that he had been re-thinking his views on the gap between program and practice, called it "a bold and effective stroke for righteousness"; Richard Shryock found it "a most incisive and effective statement"; Kingsbury appreciated "the excellent quality of the work and courageous manner of presentation. I feel confident [he continued] that it will command higher respect and will have greater influence than any book on the Soviet Union that has yet appeared in English." The only sour note among this group came from W. B. McDaniel, librarian of the College of Physicians of Philadelphia, whose

> only disappointment in it derives from the feeling that a greater degree of objectivity might have saved a few more souls. . . . [I] tremble at the ammunition you put in the hands of a possible opposition. I very much wish that I had . . . the opportunity and . . . the influence with you to prevail upon you not to write as advocatus; but it's done and that's that . . . it represents the only tactical error I have known you to make.[94]

The sort of letter that Sigerist probably appreciated most came from Mary Prihodoff, apparently a student at Ohio State University:

> I have just finished reading it and am tingling with excitement and hope for the success of that colossal experiment. No effort is too much in such a cause. Your trust in the wisdom of the leaders and the ultimate success strengthens my own faith. If men who are able to observe and judge believe, then we need not doubt.[95]

By early December, he was receiving letters "from all over the country—from doctors in small towns who read it and shared my views. There must be more socialist physicians than you would expect. You do not hear of them because they have to be careful. Someday we may have a Socialist Medical Association."[96]

The response to *Socialized Medicine in the Soviet Union* was positive, even enthusiastic, in journals of academic sociology and current affairs.[97] Readers who shared his reservations about the direction of American medicine delighted in his portrayal of Soviet medicine because it held out the prospect of a better future in which both medicine and society would be more rationally managed. In the medical journals, on the other hand, the response was considerably less favorable. Morris Fishbein did not even do it the courtesy of a proper review in the *Journal of the American Medical Association;* instead, he poked fun at Sigerist by quoting his laudatory comments on Soviet medicine alongside quotations from another American author, whose wife had suffered dreadful experiences in Soviet hospitals.[98] Sigerist had expected a negative response from the pillars of the medical establishment.[99] He was, however, distressed to receive a three-page critique of *Socialized Medicine* from Sir Arthur Newsholme, for whom he had considerable respect.[100] Newsholme took issue with several of Sigerist's claims: that the Soviet health administration was broadly based rather than controlled by specialists; that western countries failed to support science as they should; that the Soviet Union was the first country in the world to attempt to socialize medicine; and that a new era of preventive medicine had begun in the Soviet Union.[101]

Newsholme's comments provoked Sigerist to send a three-page reply a few days later. After reiterating his views on the breadth of "the Soviet Health pyramid" and the connection between socialism and scientific research, Sigerist turned to Newsholme's claim that Great Britain had pioneered both socialized medicine and preventive medicine:

> it makes all the difference in the world [he wrote] whether in a given country certain aspects of medicine are "socialized" or whether it is the whole of medicine, including all the medical industries. In my mind, socialized medicine is medicine organized socialistically, that is to say, a system under which all medical services, preventive and curative, are public functions. . . . I am the last to deny that hygiene and sanitation have progressed tremendously in the last hundred years; the facts are evident. An era of preventive medicine, however, is a period in which prevention is in the foreground of all medical considerations, in which every medical worker tends to prevent disease first of all. Our students are still trained to be primarily interested in disease and not in health. Most people do not see a doctor unless they are sick. Russia is far from having reached its goal, but the idea to supervise man medically from the moment of conception to the moment of death and to concentrate all efforts on prevention of disease is undoubtedly very promising and impresses me as the beginning of a new era in medicine.[102]

Newsholme replied, but without giving an inch on any of these issues. "I do not think [he wrote] the position is materially changed by my or by your letter. We understand each other better. That is all." [103] However, he went on to make a more general comment, the thrust of which Sigerist had heard before:

> I had great hopes of your book and was disappointed to find that it was written in a missionary spirit. This will, I fear, minimize its convincingness. My feeling is that you have glorified U.S.S.R. in some paragraphs by belittling good work done in English speaking countries, though I am confident this was not your

intention. A volume from you, written objectively, and semi-judicially, would at this time have carried great weight in bringing before the world the Soviet Russia's great achievement in medicine.[104]

Newsholme might as well have saved his ink and paper. This was not the time to urge restraint upon Sigerist, who was already thinking of returning to the Soviet Union as the leader of a traveling seminar in the summer of 1938. (In this role he displaced Kingsbury, who had a prior claim, but who was good enough to stand aside.[105]) For a time, Sigerist feared that what he finally admitted to be a crisis in Russia would make the visit impossible, but in the end arrangements went ahead, marred not so much by the purges as by the impending international crisis.[106] Once he knew that the travel arrangements had been approved in Moscow, Sigerist was elated:

> I am most excited at the thought of seeing the Soviet Union again. I love the country. I love its socialism but I also love the people and the landscape, so much that I would have liked it even under Tsarism [!—JFH]. It will be a great joy to interpret the country to a group of people and especially to [his daughter] Erica. The group promises to be very pleasant—mostly young people. I was afraid to have a group of old doctors but as a matter of fact most of the members are students or have just graduated . . . . I will try to convince them and make them apostles of socialism.[107]

With Erica's help, Sigerist published a four-part serialized account of their 1938 trip in *Soviet Russia Today*.[108] Its tone was extravagant: "there is more of everything and . . . everything has been improved." [109] At the lavish new workers' sanitorium in Sochi, they met the legendary Aleksei Stakhanov, who allegedly asked them whether such facilities were provided for American workers.[110] He ended what was to be his last visit to the Soviet Union "more than ever convinced that the complete socialization of medicine offers possibilities that no other system can give." [111]

After World War II, Sigerist produced a second edition of *Socialized Medicine,* but it was far less than the total reworking he first contemplated. He wrote one completely new chapter, on Soviet military medicine.[112] The original introduction, with its strong Marxist flavor, was deleted. A temporary research assistant, Julia Older, revised some of the other chapters, incorporating much recent material; Sigerist decided to add her name to the title page, "since she deserves a great deal of credit." [113] However it was not easy to find a publisher for a book that was far less than a fresh new look at Soviet medicine in the postwar era.

39. Pioneer Camp Artek in the Crimea, which Sigerist visited in August 1935.

After several refusals from other houses, it was eventually published by the Citadel Press in 1947 under the title *Medicine and Health in the Soviet Union*. A year later, Sigerist wrote from Switzerland to Kingsbury, who had just reviewed it in *Soviet Russia Today:*

> Personally, I much preferred the first edition because it was much more spontaneously written, while this new edition is to a large extent a patched-up job. But it is all that could be done under the present circumstances. I had to sacrifice most of my introductory chapters because it would have scared the readers too much, and so I let the tremendous accomplishment of Soviet medicine speak for itself almost without commentary. I think, however, that even in this form the book will do some good if not in the United States then in a number of other countries.[114]

Only during the last years of Stalin's rule did Sigerist become disillusioned with the Soviet Union, occasionally expressing what was for him strong criticism of the revival of Russian nationalism, of aging party leaders obsessed with their own survival, and of the cultural wasteland that Stalin's Russia had become.[115] Surprisingly, there is no entry in his diary to mark Stalin's death in 1953. During the thaw that followed, Sigerist received an invitation from the new head of Narkomzdrav to spend six weeks in the USSR in February or March of 1954. He turned it down, preferring to stay in Pura to finish his books. Russia was now an old man's memory.

What made Sigerist such an uncritical admirer of Soviet medicine? To his distaste for the American version of "capitalist medicine," his loathing of fascism, and his intellectual's conviction that socialism was the wave of the future must surely be added his missionary temperament. Like Sidney and Beatrice Webb, he was convinced that he had seen the future and was absolutely sure that it worked. Marxism gave him the assurance of the true believer, while the Hopkins seminar gave him a liking for the saving of young souls. Moreover he positively reveled in the combative rhetoric of class warfare. "Our place," he once wrote—referring to his fellow academics—"is with the coal miners and stevedores, not with the bankers and industrialists." [116] While writing the publicity blurb for the Soviet book, he confessed to his diary that "I do not care a hang whether the bourgeois moron reads it or not." [117] Faced with the difficulty of explaining the purge trials, he raged, "What does it matter what all these sentimental liberals think of the Soviet Union? What they actually care for is the preservation of the capitalist system and nothing else." [118] Finally, Sigerist shared with the architects of Soviet health policy under Stalin an outlook best described as medical totalitarianism. He really believed that humanity would be better off if every individual were under the medical supervision of the state from the cradle to the grave. At the Soviet health resorts he enthused that "the Russians had the very correct idea that not only labor must be under medical control but that rest and recreation are much more successful if conducted under medical supervision." [119] Sigerist's belief in the necessity for state control over all aspects of medicine ultimately made him an apologist for state control over most aspects of human life, as his Stalinist hosts were the first to appreciate.

Notes

1. Henry E. Sigerist, *Socialized Medicine in the Soviet Union* (New York: W. W. Norton, 1937), 310.

2. Nora Sigerist Beeson, ed., *Henry E. Sigerist: Autobiographical Writings* (Montreal: McGill University Press, 1966), Diary, April 28, 1937, 123.

3. Ibid., Diary, November 27, 1938, 140.

4. From his essay, "University Education" in *The University at the Crossroads: Addresses and Other Essays* (New York: Henry Schuman, 1946), reprinted in *Autobiographical Writings*, 59–60.

5. Sigerist heard Strashun lecture on the development of Soviet medicine at the Koch Institute in Berlin, and immediately invited him to visit the Institute in Leipzig. On Strashun's visit to Berlin and Leipzig, see Achim Thom and Karl-Heinz Karbe, *Henry Ernest Sigerist (1891–1957). Ausgewählte Texte* (Leipzig: Johann Ambrosius Barth, 1981), 26; a brief biography of Strashun is appended at 140–41.

6. For a fuller discussion of these issues, see Elizabeth Fee's essay in this volume.

7. Henry E. Sigerist to Mabel G. Kingsbury, August 14, 1956. Yale University Library, Henry E. Sigerist Papers (hereafter cited as Sigerist Papers/Yale), General Correspondence, 1947–57, group 788, series I, box 15.

8. *Autobiographical Writings*, Diary, January 1, 1933, 82.

9. Ibid., April 17, 1933, 83.

10. Until he acquired a reading knowledge of Russian, he was confined to western-language works, of which there were then very few. Newsholme and Kingsbury's *Red Medicine* did not appear until the end of 1933; the English translation of Semashko's *Health Protection in the Soviet Union* appeared in 1934; Sidney and Beatrice Webb's monumental *Soviet Communism: A New Civilization?* appeared in 1936.

11. *Autobiographical Writings*, Diary, January 23, 1934, 92.

12. Henry E. Sigerist to J. A. Kingsbury, October 25, 1933. Johns Hopkins Medical Institutions, Alan Mason Chesney Archives, Henry E. Sigerist Papers (hereafter cited as Sigerist Papers/Hopkins), box 86.

13. J. A. Kingsbury to Henry E. Sigerist, October 27, 1933. Sigerist Papers/Hopkins, box 86.

14. Henry E. Sigerist to J. A. Kingsbury, November 1, 1933. Library of Congress, Division of Manuscripts, John Adams Kingsbury Papers (hereafter cited as Kingsbury Papers), box 19.

15. Henry E. Sigerist to J. A. Kingsbury, December 13, 1933; J. A. Kingsbury to Henry E. Sigerist, December 14, 1933. Sigerist Papers/Hopkins, box 86.

16. Henry E. Sigerist to W. Horsley Gantt, February 23, 1934. Sigerist Papers/Hopkins, box 43.

17. *Autobiographical Writings*, Diary, October 6, 1934, 101.

18. Ibid., February 3, 1934, 93.

19. Henry E. Sigerist to J. A. Kingsbury, February 26, 1935, 1. Kingsbury Papers, box 19.

20. Henry E. Sigerist, Diary, February 7, 8, and 26, 1935. Yale University Library, Henry E. Sigerist Papers, Addition (June 1987), Biographical Data and Memorabilia, group 788, box 1 (hereafter cited as Diary). In mid-April, he learned that the Rockefeller Foundation had renewed its $12,500 grant for three years; see Diary, April 17, 1935. For discussion of Sigerist's resentment of "begging" to the foundations, see the essays by Brown and Beeson in this volume.

21. Henry E. Sigerist to J. A. Kingsbury, February 26, 1935, 2. Kingsbury Papers, box 19.

22. *Autobiographical Writings,* Diary, April 9, 1934, 94. For this development in his teaching program and his developing interest in the sociology of medicine, see the essay by Roemer, Falk, and Brown in this volume.

23. Ibid., February 20, 1935, 106.

24. Ibid., March 13, 1935, 107.

25. This issue is discussed more fully in Elizabeth Fee's essay in this volume.

26. See copy of the press release of that date in Sigerist Papers/Yale, Collected Letters, series I, box 86. Kingsbury broke his silence about his enforced resignation with a letter to the New York *Herald-Tribune,* which was published May 19, 1935.

27. *Autobiographical Writings,* Diary, April 1, 1935, 107.

28. W. Horsley Gantt, *A Medical Review of Soviet Russia* (London: British Medical Association, 1928).

29. Anna J. Haines, *Health Work in Soviet Russia* (New York: Vanguard Press, 1928).

30. Henry E. Sigerist, Diary, March 9, 1936. When he made this comment, Sigerist had been in the Soviet Union for two months, while Gantt had spent several years there during the twenties and had returned to Leningrad in 1935 to visit the dying Pavlov.

31. Sir Arthur Newsholme and John A. Kingsbury, *Red Medicine: Socialized Health in Soviet Russia* (Garden City, N.Y.: Doubleday, Doran and Company, 1933).

32. Sir Arthur Newsholme, *Medicine and the State* (London: George Allen and Unwin, 1932). See also his *International Studies on the Relation Between the Private and Official Practice of Medicine, with Special Reference to the Prevention of Disease* (London: George Allen and Unwin; Baltimore: Williams and Wilkins, 1931), 3 vols.

33. Just before they left for Russia, Newsholme wrote to Kingsbury, "I don't think that advanced civilizations like those of the U.S., Germany and Great Britain can learn much from a country recently emerged from serfdom." Sir Arthur Newsholme to J. A. Kingsbury, July 5, 1932. Kingsbury Papers, box 79.

34. J. A. Kingsbury to (Senator) Frederick C. Walcott, July 15, 1932. Kingsbury Papers, box 67.

35. J. A. Kingsbury, Diary, August 2, 1932. Kingsbury Papers, box 67.

36. J. A. Kingsbury, Diary, August 14, 1932. Kingsbury Papers, box 67.

37. J. A. Kingsbury, Diary, August 16 and 22, 1932. Kingsbury Papers, box 67.

38. After some negotiation, they agreed "to the policy of avoiding, as far as possible, comments on morals, etc., and such other matters of administrative policy which have no direct bearing on our subject . . . since we are not writing about the revolution [Kingsbury wrote to Newsholme] I think it's better not to enter into an expression of opinion concerning these deplorable attributes of revolution." J. A. Kingsbury to Sir Arthur Newsholme, March 1, 1933. Kingsbury Papers, box 79.

39. Ibid.

40. "My difficulty is how far can we trust Russian statistics," he wrote to Kingsbury, because "If justice is regarded as a thing to be manipulated politically, why not also social statistics?" Sir Arthur Newsholme to J. A. Kingsbury, April 18, 1933. Kingsbury Papers, box 79.

41. Sir Arthur Newsholme to J. A. Kingsbury, May 27, 1933. Kingsbury Papers, box 79.

42. Sir Arthur Newsholme to J. A. Kingsbury, April 1, 1933. Kingsbury Papers, box 79. Newsholme also had doubts about the appropriateness of Kingsbury's choice, "Red Medicine," as a title for the book; in his opinion, it was misleading, since much of the book was not directly concerned with medical issues. His preference was a title that emphasized "the socialized idea"; the eventual subtitle, "Socialized Health in Soviet Russia" was a compromise acceptable to both of them. Sir Arthur Newsholme to (Kingsbury's assistant) Dr. Freeburg, May 9, 1933. Kingsbury Papers, box 79.

43. The review, by H. A. Koiransky, appeared in *New York Times,* January 21, 1934, 4.

44. Henry E. Sigerist to J. A. Kingsbury, January 30, 1934. Sigerist Papers/Hopkins, box 86.

45. J. A. Kingsbury to Sir Arthur Newsholme, January 22, 1934. Kingsbury Papers, box 79.

46. *Socialized Medicine,* 23.

47. Ibid., 308. This may be contrasted with the more cautious judgment reached by Newsholme and Kingsbury: "The USSR is still behind other countries which began preventive work much earlier and probably from an initially higher level." *Red Medicine,* 274.

48. Henry E. Sigerist to John Strachey (Victor Gollancz Ltd.), September 10, 1936. Sigerist Papers/Hopkins, box 120.

49. Paul P. Gronsky and Nicholas J. Astrov, *The War and the Russian Government* (New Haven: Yale University Press, 1929); Tikhon I. Polner, *Russian Local Government During the War and the All-Russian Union of Zemstvos* (New Haven: Yale University Press, 1930).

50. *Rossia v mirovoi voine 1914-1918 goda. (v tsifrakh)* (Moscow: Central State Statistical Administration—Division of Military Statistics, 1925).

51. Z. G. Frenkel, *Obshchestvennaia meditsina i sotsial'naia gigiena* (Leningrad: P.P. Soikin, 1926).

52. *Socialized Medicine,* 309.

53. *Autobiographical Writings,* Diary, June 19, 1935, 113.

54. Ibid., June 14, 1935, 111.

55. Ibid., June 16, 1935, 112.

56. Winslow wrote to Kingsbury that he had found a much greater lag between program and performance than they had indicated in *Red Medicine,* and that they had perhaps misled their readers by suggesting that Soviet efforts to control malaria, syphilis, and tuberculosis were adequate when, in Winslow's judgment, they were not. J. A. Kingsbury to Henry E. Sigerist, February 12, 1937. Sigerist Papers/Hopkins, box 68.

57. Ibid.

58. Henry E. Sigerist to J. A. Kingsbury, February 17, 1937. Sigerist Papers/Hopkins, box 68.

59. Ibid.

60. For a fuller discussion, see John F. Hutchinson, *Politics and Public Health in Revolutionary Russia 1890-1918* (Baltimore: Johns Hopkins University Press,

1990), 189–95 and Neil B. Weissman, "Origins of Soviet Health Administration: Narkomzdrav, 1918–1928," in *Health and Society in Revolutionary Russia*, eds. Susan Gross Solomon and John F. Hutchinson (Bloomington: Indiana University Press, 1990), 97–120.

61. The most important of these were used by N. A. Semashko in his *Health Protection in the U.S.S.R.* (London: Victor Gollancz, 1934), a work used extensively by Sigerist.

62. This paragraph summarizes the argument put forward by Weissman, "Origins of Soviet Health Administration," 110–16. See also Christopher Davis, "Economic Problems of the Soviet Health Service: 1917–1930," *Soviet Studies* 35 (1983): 343–61.

63. These issues are treated in greater detail in Nancy M. Frieden, *Russian Physicians in an Era of Reform and Revolution, 1856–1905* (Princeton, N.J.: Princeton University Press, 1981) and Hutchinson, *Politics and Public Health*. See also Samuel C. Ramer, "The Zemstvo and Public Health," in *The Zemstvo in Russia: An Experiment in Local Self-Government*, eds. Terence Emmons and Wayne S. Vucinich (Cambridge: Cambridge University Press, 1982).

64. Cited by Weissman, "Origins of Soviet Health Administration," 116–17.

65. In addition to the Weissman essay cited above, see Sally Ewing, "The Science and Politics of Soviet Insurance Medicine," in Solomon and Hutchinson, *Health and Society in Revolutionary Russia*, 69–96; for a general introduction, see Sheila Fitzpatrick, *The Russian Revolution, 1917–1932* (New York: Oxford University Press, 1984).

66. The fundamental work on this subject is *Cultural Revolution in Russia, 1928–1931*, ed. Sheila Fitzpatrick (Bloomington: Indiana University Press, 1978); for a sampling of the variety of opinion about Stalin's work, see *The Stalin Revolution. Foundations of the Totalitarian Era*, ed. Robert V. Daniels, 3rd. ed. (Lexington, Mass.: D. C. Heath, 1990).

67. On the significance of the Shakhty trial, see Kendall E. Bailes, *Technology and Society under Lenin and Stalin* (Princeton, N.J.: Princeton University Press, 1978); on VARNITSO, see David Joravsky, "The Construction of the Stalinist Psyche," in Fitzpatrick, *Cultural Revolution,* 112–15.

68. For his bland treatment, see *Socialized Medicine,* 114–15.

69. Christopher Davis, "Economics of Soviet Public Health, 1928–1932," in Solomon and Hutchinson, *Health and Society in Revolutionary Russia,* 160–67.

70. Davis, "Economics of Soviet Public Health," 163.

71. Susan Gross Solomon, "Social Hygiene and Soviet Public Health," in Solomon and Hutchinson, *Health and Society in Revolutionary Russia,* 177–80. See also her "Social Hygiene in Soviet Medical Education, 1922–1930," *Journal of the History of Medicine and Allied Sciences* 45 (1990): 607–43 and "The Limits of Government Patronage of Science: Social Hygiene and the Soviet State, 1920–1930," *Social History of Medicine* 3 (1990): 405–35.

72. Thom and Karbe, *Henry Ernest Sigerist,* 141.

73. See *Socialized Medicine,* 124–28.

74. Ibid., 95–98.

75. Ibid., 228–33.

76. Ibid., 144. For a useful introduction to the subject, see Samuel C. Ramer,

"Who Was the Russian Feldsher?" *Bulletin of the History of Medicine* 50 (1976): 213–25.

77. On the medical politics of the 1917 revolution see Hutchinson, *Politics and Public Health,* 143–95 and Peter F. Krug, "Russian Public Physicians and Revolution: The Pirogov Society, 1917–1920," unpublished Ph.D. diss., University of Wisconsin–Madison, 1979, 101–228.

78. On this see Samuel C. Ramer, "Feldshers and Rural Health Care in the Early Soviet Period," in Solomon and Hutchinson, *Health and Society in Revolutionary Russia,* 126–28, and Krug, "Russian Public Physicians," 229–67.

79. Ramer, "Feldshers and Rural Health Care," 136–37.

80. Ibid., 139.

81. *Socialized Medicine,* 247.

82. This subject has been exhaustively treated in Richard Stites, *The Women's Liberation Movement in Russia: Feminism, Nihilism and Bolshevism, 1860–1930* (Princeton, N.J.: Princeton University Press, 1978), 346–91.

83. *Socialized Medicine,* 253. A recent treatment of these issues concludes that "Women were to be both workers and reproducers, whatever the cost — and the cost to maternal and infant health, to the psychological and social well-being of the mother and child, in the 1930s was very high indeed." Elizabeth Waters, "The Modernisation of Russian Motherhood, 1917–1937," *Soviet Studies* 44 (1992): 131.

84. Henry E. Sigerist, Diary, March 3 and 24, 1936.

85. Ibid., February 9, 1937.

86. Ibid., May 16, 1937.

87. Ibid., May 27, 1937.

88. Ibid., June 1, 1937.

89. Victor Gollancz to Henry E. Sigerist, July 30, 1937. Sigerist Papers/Hopkins, box 120.

90. Henry E. Sigerist to Victor Gollancz, August 2, 1937. Sigerist Papers/Hopkins, box 120.

91. Henry E. Sigerist to Victor Gollancz, September 13, 1937. Sigerist Papers/Hopkins, box 120.

92. *Autobiographical Writings,* Diary, October 28, 1937, 28.

93. C. Oumansky [K. Umanskii] to Henry E. Sigerist, November 2, 1937. Sigerist Papers/Hopkins, box 120.

94. C.-E. A. Winslow to Henry E. Sigerist, November 1, 1937; Richard H. Shryock to Henry E. Sigerist, November 4, 1937; W. B. McDaniel to Henry E. Sigerist, November 19, 1937; Sigerist Papers/Hopkins, box 120. J. A. Kingsbury to Henry E. Sigerist, November 17, 1937, Kingsbury Papers, box 19.

95. M. Prihodoff to Henry E. Sigerist, January 14, 1938. Sigerist Papers/Hopkins, box 120.

96. Henry E. Sigerist, Diary, December 2, 1937.

97. See, for example, the reviews in *American Journal of Sociology* 44 (1938–39): 176; *American Sociological Review* 3 (1938): 143; *Social Forces* 17 (1939): 579. The British edition also received a predictably favorable review in *New Statesman & Nation* 14 (November 27, 1937): 886.

98. *Journal of the American Medical Association* 109 (1937): 1911. The other work was Eugene Lyons' *Assignment in Utopia* (New York: Harcourt, Brace,

1937), from which (p. 440) Fishbein selected the following passage: "Ever after, the glowing reports of socialized medicine in Russia in American books and magazines have been a source of amusement to us. Always we have wished their authors only one punishment—a week or so as patients in the second best hospital in Russia."

99. Henry E. Sigerist, Diary, December 18, 1937.

100. After a dinner with Newsholme in November 1937, Sigerist described him as "a grand old man, still very alert. . . . there was an excellent discussion on public health problems and socialized medicine. It is so infinitely more satisfactory to have discussion with public health people than with physicians." Henry E. Sigerist, Diary, November 19, 1937.

101. Sir Arthur Newsholme to Henry E. Sigerist, November 23, 1937. Kingsbury Papers, box 19.

102. Henry E. Sigerist to Sir Arthur Newsholme, December 3, 1937. Sigerist Papers/Hopkins, box 87. A copy of this letter may also be found in the Kingsbury Papers, box 19.

103. Sir Arthur Newsholme to Henry E. Sigerist, December 9, 1937. Kingsbury Papers, box 19.

104. Ibid.

105. See his letter on this subject to Kingsbury, dated November 15, 1937, in the Kingsbury Papers, box 19.

106. "If there is a crisis in Russia it does not mean that socialism does not work. It means that the Russians are unable to make it work and that we will have to do a better job. But it would be a pity—the first large-scale experiment. In 1935 and 1936 the conditions were so extraordinarily good. I am still hopeful, but cannot help being depressed at times." *Autobiographical Writings,* Diary, February 24, 1938, 132.

107. Henry E. Sigerist, Diary, May 8 and 13, 1938. A list of the participants in the seminar may be found in Henry E. Sigerist to C. Oumansky [K. Umanskii], May 14, 1938. Sigerist Papers/Hopkins, box 128.

108. These articles appeared in *Soviet Russia Today,* November 1938, 21, 64; December 1939, 24–26, 29; January 1940, 25–27, 34; and March 1940, 24–26, 34.

109. *Soviet Russia Today,* November 1938, 21.

110. Ibid., March 1940, 24.

111. Ibid., March 1940, 34.

112. Henry E. Sigerist to Robert L. Leslie, June 18, 1946. National Library of Medicine—History of Medicine Division. MSC 470: American-Soviet Medical Society Papers, series 4, box 5.

113. Ibid.

114. Henry E. Sigerist to J. A. Kingsbury, April 23, 1948. Kingsbury Papers, box 19.

115. See *Autobiographical Writings,* Diary, February 28, 1947, 206; February 16, 1949, 225; and January 23, 1950, 230.

116. Henry E. Sigerist, Diary, April 6, 1936.

117. Ibid., May 20, 1937.

118. Ibid., March 4, 1938.

119. *Soviet Russia Today,* January 1940, 26.

CHAPTER 12

Hot War Creation, Cold War Casualty: The American-Soviet Medical Society, 1943–1948

Walter J. Lear

The history of the American-Soviet Medical Society focuses on several singular events and unusual persons within the American health field and is framed by the contingencies of international politics.[1] The two themes emphasized in this version of the society's history are the tumultuous relations between the United States and the USSR in the 1940s and the role of the organizer extraordinaire, Henry E. Sigerist.

In 1943 the average American was urged to help in every way possible to defeat the aggressive totalitarian regimes of Germany and Japan. In that year, a special issue of *Life* magazine extolled the achievements and the people of the USSR;[2] Hollywood produced a major pro-Soviet film, *Mission to Moscow;*[3] Wendell Willkie issued a highly influential plea for peaceful coexistence with the USSR, *One World;*[4] and the American government sanctioned United States–USSR friendship activities. Despite decades of deep distrust and hostility between the United States and the USSR, good relationships were now the official policy of both nations, allies against the common enemy.[5]

In the United States, initial reports about the excellent performance of the Soviet army medical services stimulated considerable interest in

40. "1944," an editorial cartoon marking the alliance between the United States and USSR.

Soviet medicine. The most influential of these reports came from a three-week visit to the Soviet Union in July 1943 by a group of prestigious British, Canadian, and American surgeons invited by the Soviet government. Wilder Penfield, the Canadian member of the group, summarized their evaluation: "Russia is abreast of the times in the field of medicine, and, looking into the future, the excellent organization of her system of medical education and her lavish support of research institutes promises a leadership that will make us look to our laurels."[6] This visit, orchestrated by the USSR to exchange medical experience among the Allies, helped generate high-placed interest and respect among North American physicians.[7]

The individual central to galvanizing the United States side of Soviet-American medical exchanges was Henry E. Sigerist. In the 1930s, Sigerist was already convinced that "what is being done in the Soviet Union today is the beginning of a new period in the history of medicine."[8] In 1937 he had published *Socialized Medicine in the Soviet Union,* which, despite its unabashedly favorable bias, was immediately recognized by many in the health field and the general public as the most comprehensive English-language book on the subject. Sigerist decided that he should create a journal about medicine in the USSR, but this project was not to be realized for five years. On May 15, 1939, he described in his diary a conversation with Thomas Addis: "We had endless matters to discuss, among others the plan of an American Russian Medical Journal. It occurred to me that the best way to launch it might be the organization of an American-Russian Medical Society."[9]

But long before these plans could be carried out, Sigerist was active in a series of other organizations sending aid to the Soviet Union or sharing information about the Soviet war effort. In the summer of 1941, at the suggestion of Jessica Smith, the editor of *Soviet Russia Today,* Sigerist and John A. Kingsbury called the founding meeting of Russian War Relief.[10] Later Sigerist was designated the head of its medical committee. Russian War Relief was a popular organization with over fifty local committees, mainly in the Northeast. It had wealthy supporters who were not on the political left but believed it quite proper to provide nongovernmental aid to people suffering hardship in war-torn Russia.[11] Russian War Relief collected and bought clothing, food, household goods, and medical supplies and "was able to send $46 million in aid to Russia in 1943 and 1944 alone." It avoided overtly political positions, although its work undoubtedly contributed in those years to the friendly attitude of the United States toward the USSR.[12] Sigerist noted that "A large part of RWR's relief work has been, of course, medical, and every U.S. community of any size numbers a prominent local physician among its RWR members." [13]

Another organization that emerged about the same time was the National Council of American-Soviet Friendship (henceforth referred to as the council); its immediate origin was the first Congress of American-Soviet Friendship held in November 1942. This three-day celebration of the twenty-fifth anniversary of the founding of the USSR included a Madison Square Garden rally at which Vice President Henry A. Wallace was the main speaker. Sponsors of the congress included "several cabinet members, the diplomatic representatives of most of America's allies, the governors of twelve states, the mayors of many cities throughout the country, some forty college and university presidents, forty officials of large trade unions, clergymen from every faith in the country and representatives of many fields in industry and culture." [14]

The council's purpose was to "promote better understanding and strengthen friendly relations between the United States and the Soviet Union as essential to the winning of the war, and the establishment of world-wide democracy and enduring peace." [15] Its chairman was Corliss Lamont, a wealthy left activist well known for his unequivocal support of the Soviet Union. It had chapters in twenty-eight cities across the nation and vocational committees, e.g., of architects, musicians, and scientists.

Initially the council was considered noncontroversial, focusing on the USSR war effort and on cultural exchange. It published pamphlets and a newspaper, circulated photographic exhibits, and provided speakers to interested groups including American Legion posts and Masonic lodges. Its "high peak was reached in 1944 when a dinner was held to mark the twenty-sixth anniversary of the Red Army. Messages of congratulation were received from Generals Marshall, MacArthur, Eisenhower, Pershing and Clark," and the United States Army was officially represented by a general. [16]

In subsequent years, as the official friendship between the United States and the USSR died, the council shifted its focus to defense of the USSR — correcting misrepresentations, answering criticisms, and advocating restoration of the prior United States policy. It did this so energetically and single-mindedly that by July 1947, it had received the cold war stamp of disapproval from the House Committee on Un-American Activities and lost many of its centrist and liberal sponsors. By March 1948 it rated inclusion in the Communist section of the attorney general's list. [17]

The council's Science Committee was formally established at the Second Congress of American-Soviet Friendship in November 1943 but began functioning earlier in a preliminary fashion.[18] Its sponsors included eighteen prominent liberal and left physicians, including Sigerist and three others who were to have key roles in the story that follows.[19] It was chaired by the three Americans who had been elected to honorary membership in the USSR Academy of Science in May 1942, one of whom was Walter B. Cannon, recently retired as professor of physiology, Harvard Medical School.[20] At the second congress, Cannon presided at the panel "Public Health and Wartime Medicine in the USSR"; among the speakers were three of the nation's foremost liberal health experts: Hugh Cabot, Alice Hamilton, and C.-E. A. Winslow.[21]

Organizing for a Peaceful and Enlightened World

The progenitors of the American-Soviet Medical Society (henceforth referred to as the society) were the physicians, dentists, and other health professionals active in Russian War Relief, the National Council of American-Soviet Friendship, and the Communist Party–USA. (Curiously there was no involvement of the physicians active in the Physicians Forum, the only other liberal/left organization of physicians at that time.) They included liberals of Russian-Jewish backgrounds, academics committed to peace and social justice but politically independent, and some staunch supporters of the USSR's experiment in state communism.[22] Despite such disparity in their basic politics, they all had a strong commitment to the mission of sharing clinical experience and medical research findings between the medical professions of the two nations.

Sigerist had a key role in the society from the beginning. In his diary entry of November 14, 1942, he noted: "[Among the things I did in the preceding two months] was . . . develop a plan for an American Russian Medical Society."[23] On a December visit to New York City he explored interest in such an effort and was pleased with the support he found.[24] He actively encouraged Abraham Stone, whom he knew from Russian War Relief activity, and other interested New York City physicians to organize the society, promising to take editorial responsibility for a new journal on Soviet medicine.

Stone's clinical specialty was urology, and his major research interest was sterility and infertility. In 1931 he and his wife, Hannah Stone, set up the first marriage counseling center in the United States, and their 1935 *Marriage Manual* was considered by many to be the best book on the subject. He became a leader of the birth control movement and editor of *Human Fertility;* in recognition of these contributions he received the

1947 Lasker Award of the Planned Parenthood Federation of America.[25] Stone had come to the United States from Russia in 1902, when he was fifteen, and had visited the land of his birth several times since the revolution. Shortly before Sigerist approached him, he had helped establish a New York City physicians' committee for Russian War Relief.[26] Stone served as secretary of the American-Soviet Medical Society during its entire existence.

Two others were key in founding and managing the society, Robert L. Leslie and Gerald I. Shapiro. Leslie, born in 1885 on the lower East Side of Manhattan, was the owner and manager of a typographical and printing business. He often said he graduated from the Johns Hopkins Medical School, used an M.D. after his name, and was referred to as "Doctor," but there is no confirmation of his medical training.[27] He was married to a physician who was in active practice, and both were members of the Communist Party–USA (henceforth referred to as the CP). Shapiro was born in 1909, also on the lower East Side. He was a dentist in private practice in Manhattan; his office was in the building adjacent to Stone's office and home, and they were friends. Shapiro was active in the New York County Dental Society (later elected its president), headed the NYC dental branch of the CP, and chaired the West Side (Manhattan) Chapter of Russian War Relief.[28] Leslie and Shapiro became involved in the American-Soviet Medical Society after attending a small meeting in December 1942 in the home of a physician, a leader of the medical section of the CP; these CP physicians, typographer, and dentist decided to help organize the society. Neither Sigerist nor Stone were present at this first meeting. According to one recollection of that meeting, those present regarded getting Sigerist's support as the first essential.[29] The precise time sequence and possible interrelations between Sigerist's plan for a journal and the CP medical section's initiative is not clear from the available information.[30]

In response to Sigerist's entreaty to proceed, Stone arranged a meeting on February 4, 1943.[31] Sigerist described it in his diary: "Yesterday I had a very successful meeting in New York. I helped organize the American Russian Medical Society or whatever it may be called ultimately. Abraham Stone called the meeting, about twenty people [came] to his home, and we discussed matters from 7:30 to 1:30. The meeting was very well prepared so that there was hardly any opposition but on the contrary great enthusiasm."[32] This meeting identified the tasks needed to get the society and its journal off to a good start.

Sigerist personally undertook nine of the major tasks:

1. Recruiting prestigious physicians for the officers of the society. He invited Walter B. Cannon to be president and Leo Eloesser, clinical professor of surgery at Stanford University Medical School, to be vice president.[33] Both had reputations as outspoken antifascists and had played major roles in United States medical support for the Republican forces in the Spanish civil war.[34]

2. Drafting the prospectus of the society and its journal. The printed prospectus follows word for word Sigerist's longhand draft, which even includes the text of a return postcard.[35]

3. Organizing and editing the journal. In his diary, Sigerist noted: "I shall be editor of the new journal. . . . Of course, I had great hesitations to overcome before accepting the job because I already had such a full load. But I really do not know who else could do it."[36]

4. Establishing working relationships with the appropriate USSR agencies and individuals.[37]

5. Drafting the constitution of the society.[38]

6. Promoting nationwide memberships and chapters.[39]

7. Raising money.[40]

8. Initiating the donation of Soviet medical books and journals to the society's library.[41]

9. Assisting with general organizational work. Sigerist notified Stone of his impending trips to New York City so that he could arrange meetings of the New York City organizing group that Sigerist could attend. Sigerist also provided much advice by mail on a variety of topics.[42]

The prospectus contains the society's constitution and briefly mentions the proposed activities in addition to the journal, namely, the library and the exchange of medical workers between the two countries. The final paragraph of the prospectus in its global humanitarian perspective anticipates by seven months the Teheran pledge of the Allies to work together in peace as in war: "The Society also believes that international cooperation will be the basis of a lasting peace, and that the physicians and scientists who meet on a neutral ground in their efforts to alleviate the sufferings of humanity have a moral obligation to be in the front line of such movements."[43]

In May 1943, the New York City organizing group set up its headquarters in the office of Leslie's company. Leslie accepted responsibility for the business and financial aspects of the new enterprise and is identified on the society's officer lists from the first to the last as business manager.

The New York City organizing group also hired Dorothy A. Halpern full time; she was fluent in Russian and experienced in editorial work. The group likewise dealt with the multitude of details associated with the society's first two major public events: a June 13 meeting at the Brooklyn Academy of Medicine formally sponsored by the Brooklyn chapter, whose chairman was Leo M. Davidoff, a distinguished neurosurgeon, and a June 18 testimonial dinner for the USSR's "medical ambassador" to the United States, Professor Vladimir V. Lebedenko, at the official launching of the society. This dinner, held at the Hotel Pennsylvania in Manhattan, was attended by over five hundred people and was noted in the *Journal of the American Medical Association* and elsewhere.[44]

Sigerist presided at the dinner honoring Lebedenko and Cannon and in the keynote address explained the purpose of the society. He said that the United States and the USSR "should become familiar with each other's purposes and achievements. The future welfare of the world may well depend largely upon the establishment of trust between them. . . . The people of the Soviet Union are said to look towards the United States for advances in methods of industrial production; we can well look to the Soviet Union for advances in methods of treating fairly the human factor in industry." And in addition, we have "a profound responsibility that they who have suffered supremely shall not have suffered in vain. As the promise of victory approaches realization, all nations which strive for justice and good will among men must put forth their most earnest efforts to build a better world—a world in which the miseries and horrors of war can be suppressed and every man can be assured the opportunity for 'life, liberty and the pursuit of happiness.' "[45]

Lebedenko, a leading Soviet neurosurgeon and professor at the First Moscow Medical Institute, had just been appointed representative of the Russian Red Cross to the United States.[46] He expressed unequivocal support for the society and its journal, making clear that this was official USSR policy: "[the journal will not only strengthen] the bonds of friendship and cultural understanding between our two great peoples, but will add to the enlightenment of the entire world and will prove an important step in the mutual sharing of scientific achievement among nations which will enrich the life of man after the plague of fascism has been cleansed from the earth."[47]

Disseminating Medical News from the USSR

The society's foremost activity was the *American Review of Soviet Medicine* (henceforth called the *Review*). Adhering to the format and style of Western medical journals, it presented current information on the full range of Soviet medical and public health practice, medical research, organization of health services, and training of health personnel.

The first issue appeared in October 1943; thereafter it continued bimonthly for four years and quarterly for its fifth and final year. The last issue appeared exactly five years after the first. Each issue (until the last three) had ninety-six pages plus annual index pages and unnumbered pages for photographs and advertisements; in other words, each of the first four volumes had about six hundred pages. Each volume (except the last) had fifty-one to fifty-eight translations of major Soviet articles, seventeen to twenty-six abstracts and clinical notes about Soviet medicine, five to ten survey articles, six to seventeen reviews of Soviet medical books, and twelve to twenty-four Soviet medical news items. There were also a few editorials—almost all by Sigerist—obituaries, society news items, and society library notes and acquisition lists.

Most of the scientific articles were reports of clinical research, and some, of laboratory and experimental research. Leading Soviet clinicians and researchers wrote about such subjects as military medicine and trauma surgery, including blood banking and blood substitutes; treatment and prevention of malaria, tuberculosis, and other infectious diseases; cancer etiology and surgery; neurophysiology, neurology, and neurosurgery; and the development of clinical and research resources, including medical education. A very few articles, mainly by Sigerist, reported on the organization of Soviet medical care. Some reports, like that about Alexander A. Bogomoletz's anti–old age (antireticular cytotoxic) serum, proved very questionable, while others, like that about the restoration of regular heart rhythm during fibrillation by a condenser discharge, led to highly valued and much used therapies in Western medicine.[48]

In solicited review articles, American medical experts summarized Soviet advances in various fields not previously reported in the Western medical literature. Charles R. Drew thus wrote on blood banking, Albert C. England Jr. on neurology, William P. Forrest on the Moscow emergency medical aid system, Michael B. Shimkin on medical education, Selman Waksman on microbiology, and Philip D. Wilson on orthopedic war injuries.[49]

The Soviet articles in the *Review* eschewed overt political statements.[50]

Occasionally, in their subject reviews, there is a nationalist (pro-Russian but not procommunist) coloration. Nonetheless, Sigerist was well aware of the political impact of even such relatively apolitical medical literature, asserting that "thousands of doctors [now] look to the USSR with great admiration, not only in this country but also abroad." [51]

The society's five-dollar annual membership fee included a journal subscription. In the second year (1944–45), individual membership peaked at about fifteen hundred, and institutional subscriptions also peaked, at about one thousand. The combined subscription list included persons in every state and seven countries. In addition, copies were distributed gratis to the USSR (three hundred), to advertisers, and, for promotion of memberships and subscriptions, to many other individuals and organizations. [52]

Publication of this ambitious, good-looking journal required the combined efforts of editorial board members and the business manager, the society's staff, and a host of volunteer Russian-speaking translators and editors—sixty-seven of whom were gratefully acknowledged in the last issue of the first volume, and about twice that many were similarly thanked for their help with the second volume. [53]

From the beginning, Sigerist and the other editors struggled to achieve a high scientific standard, accepting only a few of the articles they reviewed. [54] Many submissions presented long didactic subject reviews with few references, omitting the case histories, descriptions of procedures, and numerical data essential for understanding the clinical or scientific material being reported. Moreover, translation was a formidable task because of the shortage of translators and the unfamiliarity of nonphysician translators with Russian and English clinical and scientific terminology. For these reasons, many translations needed careful substantive editing. [55]

The editors had frequent, and at times in-depth, discussions of the quality of the journal. Some of their criticisms and those of readers concerned the translations, but the most fundamental problem was the quality of the original articles. [56] Succinctly stated by Vasili V. Parin, secretary-general of the USSR Academy of Medical Sciences, at an editorial board meeting of the *Review:* "Some of the articles selected, I notice, are not the best." [57] The essence of the problem was not selection judgment but the poor quality of much of the available literature. The editors frequently complained about having insufficient material to review and insufficient assistance from the Soviet medical leadership in finding the best contributions. This situation was reflected in repeated efforts by Sigerist and his fellow editors, Heiman and Mudd, to obtain more journals and books from the Soviet Union and to enlist the guidance of Soviet medical authorities in the selection process. The latter had been done in an informal and limited way by Lebedenko[58] and the visiting Soviet physicians, but Sigerist's hope was for a more institutionalized arrangement: "If the Academy of Medical Sciences could select articles for us, that would be of the most value."[59]

Nonetheless, as the American medical profession had practically no access to translated Soviet medical books and journals, the *Review* did fill the gap in English-language professional literature, and its contents were abstracted by the *Journal of the American Medical Association* and other U.S. medical journals.[60] Leslie, an outstanding typographer, gave unstinting attention to the journal's design and production so that it was visually attractive. Soviet medical leaders apparently regarded it highly.[61] During its brief existence, the *Review* achieved its two major explicit purposes—informing Americans about the modern character of Soviet medicine and facilitating friendship between medical professionals of the two countries.

After completing volume I in April 1944, Sigerist decided that in light of the large volume of work, a New York–based editor should be found.[62] This was not done immediately, but a complementary recommendation to set up an editorial board was implemented in July. Those initially chosen were Bernard D. Davis, Saul H. Fisher, Jacob Heiman, and Gregory Zilboorg, all New York City physicians who knew Russian well and had strong ties to Russia.[63]

The editorial board had its first meeting on October 11, 1944 in Heiman's office; Sigerist was not present.[64] In the October issue of that year, Heiman and Zilboorg are identified as the *Review*'s associate editors. Zilboorg, born in 1890 in Kiev, had both Russian and American medical degrees, was a board-certified psychiatrist and a psychoanalyst, and had a considerable public reputation as a lecturer, writer, and therapist for New York's cultural elite. Zilboorg had held a post in Russia's Kerensky government prior to coming to the United States; he was probably persona non grata in Moscow.[65] Heiman, born in 1892, was a general practitioner with an active practice and long-term involvement in cancer research. He and his wife, a dentist, were both members of the Communist Party.[66]

In late October, when Sigerist went to India for two and a half months, the associate editors assumed full editorial responsibility.[67] When Sigerist returned, he did not resume the kind of intensive editorial work he had earlier contributed, although he did give Heiman much advice and support. By May 1945, Sigerist was emphatic that Heiman should officially replace him as editor of the journal. He explained that the geographical distance between him and the headquarters of the society and its journal made continuous meticulous involvement difficult if not impossible, particularly as he had resolved to concentrate on his long postponed magnum opus, his projected eight-volume *History of Medicine*.[68] In September, Sigerist's resignation was accepted with regret by the society's national executive board and Heiman was appointed executive editor.[69] At the same time an energetic effort was made to expand the editorial board.[70]

Promoting Physician Exchanges and Medical Aid

In addition to the educational impact of the *Review,* the society's library and information service disseminated information about Soviet medicine in America and organized reports at public and professional meetings by Soviet physicians visiting the United States and by American physicians returning from visits to the USSR.

In February 1945, the society employed an experienced librarian, Russian-speaking Anne Cohen. By aggressive solicitation from both American and Soviet sources, the library grew rapidly; in December 1945 it had about eight hundred Soviet medical books and was receiving regularly thirty-five Soviet medical journals. In the librarian's first ten months, she answered about six hundred inquiries—from medical scientists and clinicians, newspaper reporters, patients who had read about new Soviet cures for their conditions, and even Vice President Henry A. Wallace.[71]

The society—its national leadership and members in various cities throughout the country—frequently hosted visiting Russian physicians, arranging for them to learn about American medicine firsthand and to tell American physicians about Soviet medicine. For society members this was an exciting and gratifying activity. Their warm, helpful, and practical assistance was recognized by both the visitors and the U.S. authorities who had official hosting responsibilities but usually couldn't provide Russian-speaking and USSR-friendly hosts.[72]

USSR reciprocity—provided mainly to the society's leadership—was touchingly hospitable despite the harsh accommodations for tourists and general food shortages. Heiman was the society's representative to the 220th Anniversary Celebration of the USSR Academy of Sciences in June 1945, an event remarkable in being held hardly a month following the cessation of European hostilities. After returning, at meetings with professional colleagues in a number of cities, Heiman gave moving accounts of the destruction of Soviet hospitals and universities and the resulting urgent need for medical supplies of all kinds.[73]

41. Some of the members attending the first annual meeting of the American-Soviet Medical Society, New York City, November 11, 1944. Standing, *left to right:* Gregory Zilboorg, N. N. Blokhin, Maria Guseva, Elizabeth F. Samsonova, N. N. Priorov, Alan Gregg, and Abraham Stone. Seated: Walter B. Cannon and Anna E. Chernasheva.

In the summer of 1946, the society's president, Stuart Mudd (who had succeeded Cannon after the latter's death), his wife Emily H. Mudd, a pioneer in marriage counseling, and Robert Leslie were invited by VOKS (All-Union Society for Cultural Relations with Foreign Countries) for a month's professional tour specially designed for them. Their reports were marked by their open admiration of the scientific, clinical, and administrative accomplishments they saw, as well as by gratitude for the friendliness shown to them everywhere.[74]

One other priority undertaking was the replenishment of the medical libraries of the USSR destroyed in the war. The society solicited and received American medical literature from publishers, medical libraries, research institutions, and individual medical scientists. Sigerist reported in February 1945 that 350 medical journals were being sent regularly to the Soviet Union and that an estimated total of ten thousand medical books and journals and three hundred 16 mm films had already been sent there.[75]

The society also tried to expand its membership of several thousand physicians, mainly clinicians, who supported its activities across the country. Included were a number of prominent academicians, a few of whom agreed to serve as regional vice-presidents—a major public relations asset.[76] Outside New York City, chapters were formally established in Los Angeles, Minneapolis, Philadelphia, San Francisco, and Washing-

42. Members attending the third annual meeting of the American-Soviet Medical Society, New York City, December 21–22, 1946. Sigerist is at the center of the dais.

ton, D.C. Their principal activity was to hold meetings at which Soviet medicine was presented by Russian physicians visiting the United States and by American physicians who had recently visited the USSR and to show Soviet medical films, notably "Experiments in the Revival of Organisms," with commentary by J. B. S. Haldane and "Soviet Medicine at the Front," with commentary by Lillian Hellman, playwright, and Frederick March, actor. The Philadelphians also staged the society's second annual meeting.[77] Stuart Mudd, a microbiologist at the University of Pennsylvania, was a very active member who served as society president for two years.[78]

The large and productive New York City chapter held five well-

attended public meetings, the last in April 1947. The New Yorkers also carried most of the responsibility for all but one of the society's major events: the first and third annual meetings, the Lebedenko testimonial dinner, the Cannon testimonial dinner, the Cannon memorial meeting, and the Sigerist farewell dinner. The New York City theater parties were a major source of revenue for the society.[79]

Although Sigerist considered the *Review* his primary responsibility, he also gave continuing attention to a variety of other organizational matters.[80] One of the most difficult was working with Soviet officialdom. Sigerist tried to solve this problem by a detailed June 1944 memorandum to Soviet officials about the society that included sections entitled "How we can help the Soviet medical workers" and "How the Soviet authorities can help us in our work"; one recommendation in this latter section was that a liaison committee representing the several concerned USSR agencies be established in Moscow.[81] Apparently this was never done.

The society's financial status was sound through its third fiscal year ending May 31, 1946. In that year its income was about $37,100 and its expenses about $39,500. Almost half of the income was from advertising, about 30 percent from membership dues and subscriptions, and the rest from contributions, theater parties, sales, etc. About a third of the expenses were for salaries, about half for printing and other journal expenses, and the rest for telephone, office supplies, etc.[82] Sigerist made an unusual contribution—he gave the second edition of his book on Soviet medicine to the society, asking in return only for a two hundred dollar subsidy to cover the expenses of the two-week stay in New York City he needed to update the first edition.[83]

The society ended its fourth fiscal year (through May 1947) with a deficit of eight thousand dollars resulting from a 5 percent increase in expenses and a 40 percent drop in advertising income.[84] The reason for the latter was all too clear.

The Postwar World's New Politics

America's domestic and international politics began to change in 1945 at about the time of the German surrender. The new politics erupted publicly a year later, on March 5, 1946, when Winston Churchill delivered his famous "iron curtain" speech in Fulton, Missouri, heralding the cold war.[85] President Harry Truman's personal and public enthusiasm for this call to arms against the "red menace" presaged a virulent decade-long renewal of American hostility to the Soviet Union and to U.S. citizens friendly to the USSR or even advocating a pragmatic relationship between the United States and the USSR.[86] The abrupt and sharp change in Truman's official position is underscored by comparing his anticommunist actions in the spring of 1946 with his December 14, 1945 message to the society's second annual meeting: "I wish to extend my greetings to the annual meeting of the American-Soviet Medical Society and my good wishes for a successful session. May the good offices of the medical profession help to bring about the betterment of humanity and assist in the building of a broader understanding as a foundation for a lasting peace."[87]

The cold war has been documented and analyzed by dozens of historians, political scientists, journalists, and participants.[88] Its origins have been variously attributed to ideological, economic, security/military, and partisan political considerations. Regardless of motivation, the cold war was aggressively and successfully sold by most of the nation's opinion makers, especially the mass media and the national political leadership. From March 1945 onward, American goodwill toward Russia declined sharply, and by the spring of 1946, the public's "generally positive attitudes [toward Russia were transformed] into generally negative ones." [89] Operationally this "meant that the country had to become organized for perpetual confrontation and for war." [90]

Like most liberals and leftists, health activists could see and feel the onset of the right-wing political inquisition: the 1946 election on rabid anticommunist platforms of Joseph R. McCarthy as a Wisconsin senator and Richard M. Nixon as a California congressman, the bitterly anti–New Deal and anti-Truman Congress, the administration's implementation of its crackdown on communists and radicals, the growing public hysteria as expressed in the media, the concern of private industry with subversive employees, and the denial of public meeting places to radical organizations.[91]

The political environment in the health field at this time was dominated by well-financed red baiting aimed at advocates of national health insurance by the AMA, its fronts, and political allies.[92] But particularly relevant to the society and its members was the attack by the House Committee on Un-American Activities (HUAC) on Communist Party "fronts" in 1946. Two of its priority targets were the National Council of American-Soviet Friendship and the Joint Anti-Fascist Refugee Committee (JAFRC). Both were subjected to well-publicized hearings, and the refusal of the leaders of both to cooperate with the committee resulted in their being cited for contempt of Congress.[93] As already mentioned, Sigerist and other society leaders were active in the national and local Councils of American-Soviet Friendship.

Losing the Battle for United States–USSR Medical Friendship

By 1947, many Americans had returned to a self-absorbed, politically conservative lifestyle, enjoying a higher living standard than ever before.[94] The Republicans controlled Congress for the first time since 1930, in a Congress best known for the Taft-Hartley Labor Relations Act restricting the rights and practices of labor unions and for the "Hollywood ten," a tragedy written and produced by HUAC.[95] President Truman's executive order established a federal employees loyalty program and legitimated the infamous attorney general's list;[96] Truman's doctrine of containment of the USSR began with economic and military aid to the anticommunist government in Greece, and Henry Wallace decided to run for president on a third-party ticket, a valiant but feeble attempt to recommit the nation to peaceful coexistence with the USSR and the rest of the world.

The *American Review of Soviet Medicine* was particularly vulnerable to the cold war. Sigerist's hope for a better supply of material for the journal was dashed by the renewed tension between the United States and the USSR. In fact, according to a long well-crafted appeal from Mudd to Andrei Gromyko, then USSR ambassador to the UN, on February 13, 1948, the contrary occurred: "During 1947 the receipt of manuscripts from the USSR fell off and finally ceased altogether, and the receipt of current journals and books in the biological and medical sciences has become infrequent and small in amount."[97] A requested meeting did not take place, and there is no reply from Gromyko in the American-Soviet Medical Society archive. Recent scholarship in Communist Party archives in Russia reveals that forces in the Soviet Union in 1947 had successfully campaigned to "radically curtail . . . the international activities of the Soviet scientific community."[98] Probably unaware of the ideological maneuvering in the USSR, Sigerist placed the full responsibility on the West and concluded that the situation had become hopeless: "The Russians seem to have written off the entire Western world, friend and foe, and you cannot blame them."[99]

The domestic expression of the cold war was equally devastating for the journal. Memberships and subscriptions dropped precipitously.[100] As early as February 1946, Leslie told Sigerist that three advertisers had canceled because of Sigerist's political views as reported in a major newspaper.[101] The *New York Journal American* of August 12, 1945, ran an article with the headline "Red 'Front' in Drive to Socialize U.S. Medicine" with an opening paragraph that began: "With the alleged advances of medicine under a Communist system utilized as a propaganda medium, the American-Soviet Medical Society is now building a nation-wide organization as part of the drive towards a socialized health program in the United States." The article detailed the leftist credentials of Cannon and Sigerist—in all likelihood based on information supplied by HUAC. The January 1946 issue of *Medical Economics*, the widely read commercial magazine for physicians, had an article with the headline "Sigerist Sees Kaiser Plan, Soviet System Parts of Same Pattern; Socialized-Medicine Proponent Lauds 'Efficiency' of Russian Program." The caption under a photo of Sigerist at a microphone begins: "U.S. Mouthpiece of Soviet Medicine." [102]

Although the society was not a formal public target of the witch hunters and was not placed on the attorney general's list, its president, Stuart Mudd, was attacked for communist and/or subversive political views and for his organizational activities.[103] At the University of Pennsylvania he was called "Dr. Muddski" by some colleagues and subjected to a formal hearing.[104] At the same time, Leslie was being investigated by the FBI.[105]

By the end of the fourth fiscal year, May 1947, Leslie reported that even with fewer issues a year, the expenses of the journal would be twice the five thousand dollars he anticipated as income from advertising.[106] "Thus, the picture at the present time looks pretty bleak." [107]

The final meetings of the national executive board naturally focused on the rapid deterioration of the enterprise. To reduce expenses, the staff was cut, the journal was made a quarterly, the library was given to the New York Academy of Medicine, and the office was also moved there. The planned fourth annual meeting never took place.[108] Just prior to his final departure for Switzerland in June 1947, Sigerist approved the retrenchment decisions.[109] From Switzerland he wrote the farewell editorial for the final issue of the *Review* in October 1948. This was quoted extensively in a *New York Times* story that served as a public obituary for the enterprise.[110]

The society's last gasp was a November 23, 1948, letter from the officers (Mudd, Schick, Stone, Shapiro, and Heiman) to the members, which informed them that publication of the *Review* had been suspended "because of high costs" and requested them to contribute ten dollars or more to pay off the debt.[111] In response, 162 contributions totaling eighteen hundred dollars were received though April 1949. The largest was one hundred dollars from Heiman, loyal to the bitter end, who in addition secured a thousand-dollar contribution from one of his patients.[112] At the end of June 1949, the society's office in the New York Academy of Medicine was closed, and the records of the society and its journal were left in storage in the basement of Leslie's home in Brooklyn.

Conclusion

The history of the American-Soviet Medical Society tells us much about Sigerist and the politics of his time. Sigerist's central role in the society's conception and implementation is clear. He had envisioned an organization for United States–USSR medical exchange and friendship, with a nationally distributed scientific journal as its major means for achieving these objectives. He then worked very effectively with friends and colleagues to bring the society and *Review* into being.

Sigerist's role was by no means confined to that of journal founder and editor. Whether it was writing the constitution, recruiting national leaders, dunning his wealthy friends, building on his close Soviet contacts, nurturing the society's membership, or personally promoting the society and its journal, he was systematic, industrious, and proficient. This was the work of a consummate organizer.

Sigerist invested his talents and time in the society and its journal when he was already heavily burdened by more traditionally defined medical history projects and administrative responsibilities at Johns Hopkins. This was a clear political decision, growing out of the commitment he had made in 1933 to inform the West about the virtues of socialized medicine in the Soviet Union. For some, these activities might seem an unfortunate digression from his scholarly work, but for Sigerist, the "true" historian *had* to combine theory and practice. He played out this conviction for the last time in the American-Soviet Medical Society.

In its public presentation, the society asserted that its focus on Soviet medicine was strictly scientific and professional, and it avoided visible identification with the Left.[113] Nonetheless, the society's basic purpose was surely political—promoting the acceptance, even admiration by Americans, of the world's first communist nation, its governmental health service, and its medical science. This is clear from Sigerist's own views and from the "comradely" ambience of the society's activities, generally devoid of criticism of anything Soviet.

Although this enterprise required the cooperation of Soviet officials and was managed by a group that included Communist Party members, it would be unfair to characterize the society simply as a CP "front" organization. The leadership was eclectic and took no orders from outside. Sigerist himself had longstanding candid commitments to state socialism and to state systems of medical care, but these commitments were based on his experiences, studies, and personal values—they were not imposed on him by any party in the United States or the USSR. His intellectual stature and political independence were the attributes that made others, communists and liberals alike, willing to work together to promote peace and international cooperation by means of communication between the medical professions of the great powers.

The birth of the American-Soviet Medical Society was facilitated by the military alliance of the United States and the USSR, and its death assured by the cold war offensive against the USSR and everything tainted or alleged to be tainted by communism. The parallel shift of attitudes in the Soviet Union is evidenced in Lebedenko's initial warm greetings and Gromyko's final deadly silence. The society and its journal, in short, were the products of United States–USSR relations both as hot war allies and as cold war enemies.

Notes

ASMS minutes, memoranda, letters, and other nonprint items whose location is not otherwise specified in the citations were, at the time this was written, in the American-Soviet Medical Society Archive, U.S. Health Left History Collection at the Institute of Social Medicine and Community Health, 206 N. 35th St., Philadelphia, PA 19104. In accord with the wishes of the executors of the Robert L. Leslie estate, the originals of the society's records have been transferred to the History of Medicine Division of the National Library of Medicine; the division has prepared a full finding guide. Photocopies and duplicates of ASMS items cited may be found in the Institute's ASMS Archive.

1. Walter J. Lear, "The History of the American-Soviet Medical Society," in progress.

2. *Life,* March 29, 1943.

3. See David Culbert, *Mission to Moscow* (Madison: University of Wisconsin Press, 1980) for a detailed account of how the U.S. wartime administration managed the making of this film.

4. Ralph B. Levering, *American Opinion and the Russian Alliance, 1939–1945* (Chapel Hill: University of North Carolina Press, 1976), 113–14.

5. George Sirgiovanni, *An Undercurrent of Suspicion: Anti-Communism in America during World War II* (New Brunswick: Transaction Publishers, 1990), 1–6.

6. Wilder Penfield, "The Recent Surgical Mission to the U.S.S.R.," *American Review of Soviet Medicine* (henceforth *ARSM*) (December 1943): 169–70. For a full report by the leader of the group see R. Watson-Jones, "Russian Surgeons and Russian Surgery," *British Medical Journal* (August 28, 1943): 276–77.

7. In 1942, exchange of medical information was already happening under the leadership of N. A. Semashko, head of the medical section of VOKS (All-Union Society for Cultural Relations with Foreign Countries) and Sir Alfred Webb-Johnson, president of the Royal Society of Surgeons and of the Anglo–Soviet Medical Council.

8. Henry E. Sigerist, *Socialized Medicine in the Soviet Union* (New York: W. W. Norton, 1937), 308.

9. Henry E. Sigerist, Diary, May 5, 1939. Yale University Library, Henry E. Sigerist Papers, Addition (June 1987), Biographical Data and Memorabilia, group 788, box 2. I am grateful to Theodore M. Brown for providing this item. When

the first issue of the *Review* was published, Sigerist noted that it had been conceived in 1938. *Autobiographical Writings,* ed. Nora Sigerist Beeson (Montreal: McGill University Press, 1966), Diary, October 15, 1943, 185.

10. Anon. (undoubtedly Jessica Smith), "Memorandum concerning preliminary meeting of a group to initiate an organization for medical aid to the Soviet Union, called by Dr. John A. Kingsbury and Dr. Henry Sigerist at the Commodore Hotel, Monday, July 2, 1941." Folder: Sigerist, Henry E., container B-19, John A. Kingsbury Papers, Manuscript Division, Library of Congress (henceforth referred to as Kingsbury Papers).

11. Maurice Isserman, *Which Side Were You On? The American Communist Party During the Second World War* (Middletown, Conn.: Wesleyan University Press, 1982), 129.

12. Levering, *American Opinion and the Russian Alliance,* 126–27.

13. Sigerist, "Americans Look at Soviet Medicine," February 1945, 2.

14. Louis Nemzer, "The Soviet Friendship Societies," *Public Opinion Quarterly* 3 (summer 1949): 276.

15. Levering, *American Opinion and the Russian Alliance,* 125–26.

16. Eleanor Bontecou, *The Federal Loyalty-Security Program* (Ithaca, New York: Cornell University Press, 1953), 190.

17. House Committee on Un-American Activities, *Hearings on H.R. 1884 and H.R. 2122,* 80th Cong., 1st sess., 66. See also Bontecou, *The Federal Loyalty-Security Program,* 356.

18. Sigerist, "Americans Look at Soviet Medicine," 3–4.

19. The three others were Leo M. Davidoff, Stuart Mudd, and Gregory Zilboorg. Many of the other persons involved in the council's Science Committee were veterans of the left activism of the late 1930s described in Peter J. Kuznick, *Beyond the Laboratory: Scientists as Political Activists in 1930s America* (Chicago: University of Chicago Press, 1987).

20. The other two were Ernest O. Lawrence, professor of physics, and Gilbert N. Lewis, professor of chemistry, both at the University of California. Anon., "Academy of Sciences of USSR Elects Americans, British to Honorary Membership," *Information Bulletin, Embassy of the USSR,* May 2, 1942, 1.

21. The papers presented at this November 7 panel were published in *Science in Soviet Russia* (Lancaster, Pa.: Jacques Cattell Press, 1944). See also "Soviet Scientists Lauded; Work Put on Par with Army's at Friendship Congress Here," *New York Times,* November 8, 1943, 21:1.

22. One who was both a leader of the ASMS and the CP's medical section (though closeted at the time) was Gerald I. Shapiro; I interviewed him December 27, 1981 and December 1, 1990. For an excellent overview of American Communism in the 1930s and 1940s, see Robbie Lieberman, *"My Song Is My Weapon": People's Songs, American Communism, and the Politics of Culture, 1930–1950* (Urbana: University of Illinois Press, 1989), 3–13.

23. *Autobiographical Writings,* Diary, November 14, 1942, 176.

24. Hannah Peters to Henry E. Sigerist, December 3, 1942; Henry E. Sigerist to Hannah Peters, December 17, 1942.

25. Alan F. Guttmacher, "In Memoriam [of Abraham Stone]," *Fertility and Sterility* 10 (1959): 421–23. Stone was a close professional colleague of Emily Mudd,

wife of Stuart Mudd who was initially a regional vice-president of the ASMS and, when Cannon died, became its president.

26. The Physicians Committee, Greenwich Village–Gramercy Park Committee, Russian War Relief, *Soviet War Medicine News*, A. Stone, M. Naftalin, eds. (mimeograph), January 1943.

27. Leslie also claimed to have done medical work for about ten years after graduating from Johns Hopkins Medical School in 1912, but there is no evidence that he ever practiced medicine. He achieved considerable distinction in typography. Interview of Robert L. Leslie by Lear, May 14, 1981; Jacob L. Chernofsky, "Humanitarian of the Graphic Arts World: Doc Leslie at 100," *AB, Bookman's Weekly*, December 16, 1986.

28. Interview of Shapiro by Lear, December 27, 1981 and December 1, 1990.

29. Interview of Shapiro by Lear.

30. Ibid. Although Shapiro did not recall further details of the origins of the society, he was clear that the CP did not try to direct or even monitor the ASMS; he stated he would have been involved in such direction or monitoring if it took place. Also, he noted, most of the society members who were members of the Party, except Heiman and himself, were not actively involved in the society. Policy and programmatic decisions were made largely by non-Party persons, who carried most of the organization's workload.

31. Abraham Stone to Henry E. Sigerist, January 22 and February 8, 1943.

32. *Autobiographical Writings*, Diary, February 5, 1943, 179–80.

33. Henry E. Sigerist to Abraham Stone, February 10 and 26, 1943.

34. For an evaluation of Cannon's politics see Saul Benison, "Walter B. Cannon and the Politics of Medical Science, 1920–1940," *Bulletin of the History of Medicine* 65 (1991): 234–51. For Eloesser's politics see Harris B. Shumacker, *Leo Eloesser, M.D.: Eulogy for a Free Spirit* (New York: Philosophical Library, 1982), esp. 303.

35. "Announcing: The American-Soviet Medical Society For the Exchange of Medical Information." Neither the draft nor the printed version is dated, but Sigerist received the printed version at the end of May 1943.

36. *Autobiographical Writings*, Diary, February 5, 1943, 180. See also Henry E. Sigerist to Abraham Stone, April 23, 1943.

37. Henry E. Sigerist to Hannah Peters, December 17, 1942.

38. Abraham Stone to Henry E. Sigerist, February 24, 1943.

39. Henry E. Sigerist to Dorothy Halpern, May 27, 1943. Before the prospectus was printed, Sigerist had prepared a list of over forty persons, mainly physicians, from fourteen different cities to whom it should be sent.

40. Henry E. Sigerist to Samuel Rubin, president of Fabergé, May 11, 1943.

41. Henry E. Sigerist to Dorothy Halpern, May 27, 1943.

42. Henry E. Sigerist to Abraham Stone, February 17, April 23, June 4, 1943; Henry E. Sigerist to Dorothy Halpern, June 7, August 8, December 21, 1943.

43. "Announcing the ASMS" (printed), 2.

44. Anon., "Society notes," *ARSM* 1 (1943): 89–92. Anon., "American-Soviet Medical Society Formed," *Journal of the American Medical Association* 22 (1943): 457; Anon., "Form Society for American-Soviet Medical Cooperation," *Journal of the Medical Society of the County of New York* 2 (1943): 9.

45. "Society News and Notes," *ARSM* 1 (October 1943): 91–92.

46. Lebedenko was the subject of a brief, but prominently placed story in the *New York Times,* June 18, 1942, 6: 3. See also Michael B. Shimkin, "Roads to Oz. I.: A Personal Account of Some U.S.–USSR Medical Exchanges and Contacts, 1942–1962," *Perspectives in Biology and Medicine* 22 (1979): 569.

47. Vladimir V. Lebedenko, "Greetings from the USSR," *ARSM* 1 (October 1943): 8.

48. For a contemporary medical view of the Bogomoletz serum see Shimkin, "Roads to Oz," 575, and A. Baird Hastings and Michael B. Shimkin, "Medical Research Mission to the Soviet Union," *Science* 103 (May 17, 1946): 605–8. Bernard Lown, an eminent Boston cardiologist, read the article by N. L. Gurvich and G. S. Yuniev, "Restoration of Regular Rhythm in the Mammalian Fibrillating Heart," when it appeared in *ARSM* 3 (February 1946): 236–39 and promptly developed this experimental work into a successful, still-indicated procedure for use in human beings. File folder for Bernard Lown, U.S. Health Left History Collection.

49. Charles R. Drew, "The Role of Soviet Investigators in the Development of the Blood Bank," *ARSM* 1 (April 1944): 360–69; Albert C. England Jr., "Recent Advances in Soviet Neurology," *ARSM* 4 (April 1947): 354–61; William P. Forrest, "Skoraya Pomoshch: The Moscow Emergency Medical Aid System," *ARSM* 5 (December 1947–January 1948): 9–14; Michael B. Shimkin, "The New Soviet Curriculum in Medicine," *ARSM* 4 (February 1947): 271–74; Selman A. Waksman, "Microbiology in the Soviet Union," *ARSM* 4 (April 1947): 314–21; Philip D. Wilson, "The Treatment of War Injuries of the Skeletal System," *ARSM* 2 (June 1945): 395–406.

50. Shimkin comments: "The [*Review*] avoided propaganda as assiduously as possible, and all contributions went through peer review." "Roads to Oz," 567–68. See also Walter Gellhorn, *Security, Loyalty, and Science* (Ithaca, N.Y.: Cornell University Press, 1950), 161.

51. Henry E. Sigerist to Robert Leslie, April 23, 1944.

52. [Leslie,] "Report on Memberships and Subscriptions, 9/4/45"; Robert Leslie to Stuart Mudd, March 31, 1947.

53. "Editors' Acknowledgments," *ARSM* 1 (August 1944): 576; 2 (August 1945): 576.

54. Henry E. Sigerist to Dorothy Halpern, April 20, 1944.

55. "Memo from Dorothy A. Halpern [to the Executive Committee] April 10, 1944"; Henry E. Sigerist to Jacob Heiman, February 26, 1945; minutes of meetings of the editorial board, January 7, March 18, May 19, July 29, 1945 and November 9, 1946; and minutes of the *Review*'s "Seminar Meeting" of July 11, 1946.

56. For example, Memo: "Thoughts at Random," Dorothy Halpern to Henry E. Sigerist, [August? 1943]: "The Vishnevski piece has been a bone in our throat. Dr. Saul Fisher read it very carefully and could not make head or tail of it. Said it sounded pompous and bombastic without facts and case histories to back it up. Have obtained the formulas from Lebedenko. When confronted with the possibility of cutting it out entirely, decided that, since Burdenko and others refer to the Vishnevski method, our best policy would be to condense the paper in such a

way to emphasize its highlights and omit its pompousness. Also to incorporate the formulas." Sigerist later writes: "More serious is the criticism of people who are sympathetic to our aims, admire Russian medicine but find some of the articles inaccurate and too brief so that they cannot be used. I had a long talk with two of our best Hopkins surgeons who were thrilled with Yurasov's paper on esophago-plasty. They had come to the same conclusion and used the same technique but their findings were based on a few cases only, while Yudin had infinitely more material available. They were thrilled because Yudin's much greater experience confirmed their own views but they were critical of the paper, found it inaccurate in many details." Henry E. Sigerist, "To the Members of the Executive Committee of the American-Soviet Medical Society," April 5, 1944, 2. See also Dorothy Halpern to Henry E. Sigerist, April 21, 1944.

57. Minutes of meeting of the editorial board, November 9, 1946.

58. Dorothy Halpern to Henry E. Sigerist, December 17, 1943.

59. Minutes of meeting of the editorial board, November 9, 1946.

60. Sigerist, "Americans Look at Soviet Medicine," 1.

61. Russian medical leaders reacted enthusiastically to the first issue of the *Review*, according to Halpern's report of Lebedenko's comments. Dorothy Halpern to Henry E. Sigerist, December 17, 1943.

62. Sigerist, "To the Members of the Executive Committee," April 5, 1944, 1; Henry E. Sigerist to Dorothy Halpern, July 24, 1944.

63. Henry E. Sigerist to Dorothy Halpern, July 24, 1944.

64. Minutes of meeting of the editorial board, October 11, 1944. See also Jacob Heiman to Henry E. Sigerist, October 16, 1944.

65. Anon., "Zilboorg, Gregory," *Directory of Medical Specialists 1942*, 1580; Anon., "[Obituary of] Gregory Zilboorg," *New York State Journal of Medicine*, 59 (1959): 4036. His Russian medical degree was from the Psychoneurological Institute in Leningrad, 1917, and his American degree was from Columbia University College of Physicians and Surgeons, 1926. Zilboorg and Sigerist had been good friends since the late 1920s.

66. Anon., "Heiman, Jacob," *AMA Directory 1950*, 1422; interview of Shapiro by Lear; Henry E. Sigerist to Robert Leslie, April 23, 1944.

67. Henry E. Sigerist to Jacob Heiman, October 18, 1944; Robert Leslie to Henry E. Sigerist, January 3, 1945.

68. Henry E. Sigerist to Robert Leslie, May 22, 1945. See also Henry E. Sigerist to Robert Leslie, September 12, 1945 and telegram from Sigerist to Leslie, September 13, 1945.

69. Minutes of meeting of the national executive board, September 14, 1945.

70. The October 1945 issue lists twenty-one editorial board members including the society's secretary, Stone, and two society regional vice-presidents, Stuart Mudd, professor of bacteriology at the University of Pennsylvania Medical School, and Bela Schick, professor of pediatrics at Mt. Sinai Hospital, New York City, and a number of other well-known academicians including Leo M. Davidoff, J. Bronfenbrenner, John F. Fulton, and Selman A. Waksman, as well as Leslie C. Dunn, chair of the Science Committee of the National Council of American-Soviet Friendship.

71. Anon., "Proceedings of the Second Annual Meeting, American-Soviet Medical Society, Philadelphia, Pa., December 15, 1945," 7-10. Vice President Wallace wanted to know more about an unidentified substance, reported in an AP story from Moscow, which was used to increase energy and reduce fatigue in soldiers. Searching the Soviet medical literature, Halpern found that the substance was actually Benzedrine. Henry E. Sigerist to Dorothy Halpern, June 6, 1944; Dorothy Halpern to Henry E. Sigerist, June 22 and 29, 1944.

72. File folders for chapters. See also Shimkin, "Roads to Oz," 584, and Thomas Parran to Robert Leslie, December 27, 1946.

73. Minutes of meeting of the national executive board, September 14, 1945; file folders for chapters.

74. Stuart Mudd, "Programs for Medicine and National Health in the USSR," *Science* 105 (1947): 269-73, 306-9; "Recent Observations on Programs for Medicine and Public Health in the USSR," *ARSM* 4 (June 1947): 464-71; 5 (December 1947-January 1948): 71-81. He also gave many oral reports, including a particularly noteworthy one at the December 2, 1946, Madison Square Garden rally sponsored by the National Council of American-Soviet Friendship. *New York Times,* December 3, 1946, 3: 13.

75. Sigerist, "Americans Look at Soviet Medicine," 2.

76. The original regional vice-presidents were Hugh Cabot of Boston, Charles R. Drew of Washington, Stuart Mudd of Philadelphia, Chauncey D. Leake of Galveston, Frances M. Pottenger of Los Angeles, Bela Schick of New York City, and Owen H. Wangensteen of Minneapolis.

77. Each of these chapters held two such meetings. Among the Soviet physician speakers were dermatologists, neurosurgeons, and orthopedists. Among the American physician speakers were Leslie Falk and W. Horsley Gantt as well as the society's officers. File folders for chapters.

78. Anon., "Our New President," *ARSM* 3 (February 1946): 196-97. See also "Stuart Mudd" [obituary], *Evening Bulletin,* May 8, 1975, and file for Stuart Mudd, U.S. Health Left History Collection.

79. File folder for New York City chapter.

80. Henry E. Sigerist to Dorothy Halpern, August 8, August 21, and December 21, 1943; Henry E. Sigerist to Robert Leslie, May 6, 1944. See also Sigerist, "To the Members of the Executive Committee," April 5, 1944, 1.

81. Sigerist, "Memorandum [to Soviet health authorities] concerning the American-Soviet Medical Society and the American Review of Soviet Medicine," [June 1, 1944]; Henry E. Sigerist to Dorothy Halpern, June 3, 1944.

82. File folder: Financial.

83. Henry E. Sigerist to Robert Leslie, September 21 and November 8, 1945. As a result, the society undertook major efforts to market the second edition (New York: Citadel Press, 1947). To promote sales, Sigerist autographed many hundreds of copies.

84. [Robert L. Leslie,] "Comparative statement of income and expense for the fiscal years ended May 31 [1945, 1946, 1947]."

85. Melvyn P. Leffler, *A Preponderance of Power: National Security, the Truman Administration and the Cold War* (Stanford, Calif.: Stanford University Press,

1992), 109; and John Lewis Gaddis, *The United States and the Origins of the Cold War* (New York: Columbia University Press, 1972), 307–9. The first major public use of the term "cold war" was in an April 16, 1947 speech by Bernard Baruch, a key advisor to the president; Eric Goldman, *The Crucial Decade—and After: America, 1945–1960* (New York: Alfred A. Knopf, 1966), 60.

86. Leffler, *A Preponderance of Power*, 100. See also Gaddis, *The United States and the Origins of the Cold War*, 313.

87. File folder for first annual meeting.

88. Of the huge number of books about the cold war, the most useful, in addition to those already cited, are Athan Theoharis, *Seeds of Repression: Harry S. Truman and the Origins of McCarthyism* (Chicago: Quadrangle Books, 1971); Alan Wolfe, *The Rise and Fall of the Soviet Threat: Domestic Sources of the Cold War Consensus* (Washington, D.C.: Institute of Policy Studies, 1984); Daniel Yergin, *Shattered Peace: The Origins of the Cold War and the National Security State* (Boston: Houghton Mifflin, 1977); I. F. Stone, *The Truman Era, 1945–1952* (Boston: Little, Brown and Co., 1988).

89. Levering, *American Opinion and the Russian Alliance*, 202, 204–5; Theoharis, *Seeds of Repression*, 101–2.

90. Yergin, *Shattered Peace*, 5–6.

91. For a good overview of the political situation in this period see David Caute, *The Great Fear: The Anti-Communist Purge under Truman and Eisenhower* (New York: Simon and Schuster, 1978), 25–35.

92. For a general overview of the AMA's red-baiting in the 1930s and 1940s, see Paul Starr, *The Social Transformation of American Medicine* (New York: Basic Books, 1982), 265–66, 280–89. For details about the sensationalist, right-wing AMA front, the National Physicians' Committee (1939–49), see Anon., "The Political Action Committee of Organized Medicine," *Physicians Forum Bulletin* (November 1944): 2–11; and Michael M. Davis, *Medical Care for Tomorrow* (New York: Harper & Brothers, 1955), 284–85.

93. Walter Goodman, *The Committee: The Extraordinary Career of the House Committee on Un-American Activities* (New York: Farrar, Straus and Giroux, 1968), 176–81; see also Caute, *The Great Fear*, 176–78 and Ellen W. Schrecker, *No Ivory Tower: McCarthyism and the Universities* (New York: Oxford University Press, 1986), 128–29.

94. Goldman, *The Crucial Decade*, 47–48.

95. HUAC's first hearings on the movie industry were held in October 1947, and Congress voted to cite the "Hollywood ten" for contempt November 24, 1947. Victor S. Navasky, *Naming Names* (New York: Viking Press, 1980), 78–85. For HUAC and other congressional political investigations, governmental loyalty and anticommunist activities, and the political inquisition in general see Caute, *The Great Fear;* Frank Donner, *The Age of Surveillance: The Aims and Methods of America's Political Intelligence System* (New York: Knopf, 1980); Gellhorn, *Security, Loyalty, and Science;* Goodman, *The Committee;* Bud Schultz and Ruth Schultz, *It Did Happen Here: Recollections of Political Repression in America* (Berkeley: University of California Press, 1989); Schrecker, *No Ivory Tower*, 3–11, 343–51.

96. "Executive Order 9835, Prescribing Procedures for the Administration of an Employees' Loyalty Program in the Executive Branch of Government" was promulgated on March 21, 1947. For a thorough treatment, see Bontecou, *The Federal Loyalty-Security Program.*

97. Stuart Mudd to Andrei Gromyko, February 13, 1948. See also R. Peiss, "Problems in the Acquisition of Foreign Scientific Publications," *Department of State Bulletin* 5 (1950), as cited in Gellhorn, *Security, Loyalty, and Science,* 264.

98. Nikolai Krementsov, "The 'KR' Affair: Soviet Science on the Threshold of the Cold War," unpublished manuscript. See also his *Stalinist Science* (forthcoming).

99. Henry E. Sigerist to John A. Kingsbury, April 23, 1948. Kingsbury Papers.

100. In the fall of 1946 Leslie reported to Sigerist: "The Anti-Soviet propaganda has affected our Society to the extent where we have lost a considerable membership—people are not renewing their subs. Also, advertisers are becoming very touchy and a number of accounts have cancelled their contracts. . . . I am getting to the point where I am despairing about the whole financial structure of our organization." Robert Leslie to Henry E. Sigerist, October 24, 1946. See also Gellhorn, *Security, Loyalty, and Science,* 162.

101. Robert Leslie to Henry E. Sigerist, February 18, 1946.

102. *Medical Economics* (January 1946): 93–99. For Sigerist's investigation for "loyalty" by the federal government see Elizabeth Fee's essay in this volume.

103. Bontecou, *The Federal Loyalty-Security Program,* 354. Mudd's name appears on lists of "subversives" in HUAC publications because he had published articles in *Soviet Russia Today* (about his trip to the Soviet Union) and was a sponsor of the National Committee to Defeat the Mundt-Nixon (Communist Control) Bill.

104. Interview of Shapiro by Lear: "His colleagues were calling him Muddski. . . . They were red-baiting him. In the beginning he could take it but it was getting so severe as time went on." Cf. interviews of Emily H. Mudd by Lear, December 29, 1980, and April 1, 1987, and file for Stuart Mudd in U.S. Health Left History Collection.

105. Robert Leslie to Henry E. Sigerist, December 26, 1947.

106. Minutes of ASMS staff meeting, "Discussion on Budget," June 18, 1947.

107. Robert Leslie to Stuart Mudd, March 31, 1947.

108. Minutes of meetings of the national executive board, September 17 and November 10, 1947.

109. Henry E. Sigerist to Robert Leslie, June 13, 1947.

110. Henry E. Sigerist, "Editorial," *ARSM* 5 (1948): 162; "Medical Exchange with Russia Ends," *New York Times,* November 19, 1948, 19: 3.

111. Mudd, Schick, Stone, Shapiro, and Heiman to members, November 23, 1948.

112. File folder: Financial.

113. "The Society never had any political ties of any kind. It was organized as a medical society, to satisfy a need strongly felt in the country, and to fill a gap in our periodical literature of medicine, with the sole end to make Russian medical experience available to us and our medical experience available to them. . . . Since we who have built up the Society and the *Review* are not guided by emo-

tions but by a sincere interest in medical science and by the desire to make results of research available to suffering humanity irrespective of border lines, we are determined to carry on as long as we possibly can . . . in spite of all momentary difficulties." Henry E. Sigerist, "Editorial: On American-Soviet Medical Relations," *ARSM* 5 (December 1947–January 1948): 6–8.

CHAPTER 13

Friendship and Philanthropy:
Henry Sigerist, Alan Gregg,
and the Rockefeller Foundation

Theodore M. Brown

Henry Sigerist's relationship with the Rockefeller Foundation seems full of puzzles and paradoxes. Why did the foundation provide such consistent and enthusiastic support for one of the country's most visible socialist intellectuals? Sigerist was, after all, a self-proclaimed Marxist, a prominent supporter of the Soviet Union, and a militant advocate of socialized medicine. In 1931, his identification as a socialist in Germany had already caused some hesitation about his appointment to the directorship of the Johns Hopkins Institute of the History of Medicine; by 1936, Sigerist was advocating the importance of a class analysis for explaining health status and the distribution of medical care; and by the late 1930s, he had become publicly prominent, signing his name to dozens of left-wing petitions and proclamations, and gracing the panels of United Front political meetings. In 1944, he was chosen by the newly elected socialist provincial government of Saskatchewan, Canada, as its adviser on the radical reorganization of medical care; in 1951, his first volume of the *History of Medicine* was immediately recognized as beginning a Marxian reinterpretation of medical history.

Despite Sigerist's growing fame as a socialist intellectual, Rockefeller philanthropy provided the consistent support that was essential for his American career and his continuing life of scholarship after retirement. In 1935, the Rockefeller Foundation awarded a three-year grant to the Institute of the History of Medicine; in 1938, it extended the grant for a ten-year period at an increased annual budget;[1] in 1942, during a particularly difficult political period, the foundation reaffirmed its support for Sigerist; and a few years later, it tried to help free him from administrative entanglements by offering additional funds for the Welch Medical Library. In the early 1950s, the foundation was well aware of the politically safer version of the social history of medicine being elaborated by Richard H. Shryock, who had succeeded Sigerist as director of the Hopkins Institute, yet it continued to support Sigerist even while facing difficult questions raised by the congressional investigation of its alleged backing of known subversives.[2]

One possible explanation for the foundation's behavior is that whatever his political views, Sigerist effectively promoted two of the most important items on the Rockefeller agenda: the rationalization of the financing and delivery of medical care and the refocusing of medical education to prepare young physicians for more comprehensive responsibilities in a reorganized system of practice. In this context, it may have been a relatively minor issue that Sigerist was also enthusiastic about Marxism and the Soviet Union. In the thirties, many respectable individuals shared these same political interests and values—leading scientists, intellectuals, artists, journalists, and entertainers were quite visibly pink and even red.[3] As long as Sigerist helped the foundation move toward its objectives, it may have seemed of little relevance that he traveled in these circles. Moreover, whatever Sigerist felt in private, he could be circumspect in public when the occasion demanded.[4] In the late 1940s, when the political climate had become dramatically different, one could more cynically assume that although the foundation did not instigate Sigerist's departure from America, its support for his relocation might have been a convenient way of removing from the scene someone who was becoming a political liability. Foundation representatives certainly made clear on several occasions that they were aware of Sigerist's growing notoriety and the difficulties it could cause.[5] They were also aware that one way to rechannel his considerable political energies was to "turn him loose" on his book.[6] In the 1950s it cost the foundation very little to keep Sigerist on European soil safely engaged in studying ancient medicine.

While this explanation for Rockefeller motivation has a certain plausibility, closer scrutiny suggests a more nuanced reading of events. Two other elements need to be added: the foundation was not a monolith, a mere extension of corporate capitalism, or a simple instrument of the trustees' interests, but a complex organization in which the professional staff—the "philanthropoids"[7]—had considerable authority and influence, often shaping foundation policy according to their own priorities while educating, persuading, and at times even manipulating the trustees. The other element is the personal friendship between Rockefeller Medical Sciences Director Alan Gregg and Henry Sigerist that grew amid institutional self-interest and administrative opportunism. According to several accounts, Gregg was a man of great depth, warmth, integrity, and loyalty; he early developed a tremendous admiration, respect, and affection for Sigerist and then never wavered—becoming in fact, as Sigerist himself acknowledged, his "guardian angel."[8]

This chapter is about that personal bond, how it grew, and what it meant to Sigerist's career. It traces a friendship that matured as Sigerist came to appreciate the ways in which Gregg's unusually sensitive understanding of medical politics and contemporary events closely matched his own. Gregg was certainly more sympathetic politically than might have been expected of a foundation official; although he usually assumed the conventional stances of a New Deal Democrat, his son remembered that he regularly voted socialist.[9] Moreover, Gregg empathized with Sigerist's frustrations at administrative clutter and university bureaucracy and his oscillations between political and intellectual work. Both emotionally and pragmatically, he supported Sigerist's deepest and at times most daunting scholarly ambitions. It became increasingly apparent to Sigerist that Gregg was a unique man in a very powerful position—one of the most influential figures in American interwar medicine—and one he could safely trust and even admire. The friendship that developed between these two men would prove to be Sigerist's most important professional relationship during the last two decades of his life.

Early Contacts

When Gregg and Sigerist first met in Leipzig in December 1929, the thirty-eight-year-old Sigerist had already been director of the Leipzig Institute of the History of Medicine for four years and in that brief period had transformed it into one of the most exciting intellectual centers in European medicine.[10] Serving in Paris as associate director of the Rockefeller Foundation's Division of Medical Education, Gregg, thirty-nine, was a rising star in the Rockefeller philanthropic world who in 1930 would take over as director of the reorganized and renamed Division of Medical Sciences.[11] Rockefeller interest in the history of medicine had already been well established. In November 1926, William Henry Welch, the beloved former dean of the Johns Hopkins Medical School and former director of its School of Hygiene and Public Health, had officially assumed new duties as professor of the history of medicine, occupying a chair endowed by the Rockefeller General Education Board for $200,000.[12] One major purpose of the chair was to encourage broad humanism rather than narrow scientism by using medical history as an instrument to widen Hopkins medical education from the restrictive training of "technical machine[s] competent to practice medicine" to the expansive rearing of physicians appreciative of the "intellectual cultural background" of the profession.[13] Two months before Gregg's visit to Leipzig, Sigerist's mentor and predecessor, Karl Sudhoff, had traveled to Baltimore to join in the official dedication of Welch's new Institute of the History of Medicine, now further endowed with another $250,000 from the General Education Board.[14]

When he arrived in Leipzig in December 1929, Gregg was undoubtedly aware of recent developments in Baltimore. He had been busy with an important set of related projects in the Division of Medical Education. Among other things, he was interested in promoting the greater centrality of psychiatry in medicine and of psychoanalytic and other psychological approaches within psychiatry.[15] He was also eager to find ways of sensitizing medical students and physicians to the social contexts and responsibilities of medical practice. In visits to Zagreb in January 1928 and to London in June 1929, for example, he had enthusiastically explored the "hygienic" and "sociological" aspects of medicine.[16] Gregg's interests thus intersected Sigerist's at several points. In Sigerist he found an accomplished young scholar, already recognized as a brilliant leader of the new "cultural" approach to medical history, who was also deeply concerned about the materialistic drift and subspecialty fragmentation of modern medicine.[17]

Gregg recorded his first impressions of Sigerist in his Rockefeller office diary. One entry, for the evening of December 15, summarized some light moments at a dinner party. "Very amusing evening at Thomas' house with Thomas, Sigerist, Sudhoff, Gildemeister and Schröder," Gregg noted. "Talked for 11 minutes on dreams without mentioning Psychoanalysis."[18] The next day Gregg recorded a more serious and private conversation with Sigerist:

Lunch with S. at his house. S. wants his institute to be the place where students get an idea of medicine as a whole, and takes special interest in them personally. . . . His orientation is obviously much more towards social medicine and the improvement of the average practitioner than was Sudhoff. . . . S. would like to . . . have the institute a center of student life. Is sure such a place would help very considerably to correct the most serious faults in German medical education which he considers to be unsynthesized specialization and the devil-take-the hindmost attitude of the teachers who do little more than lecture.[19]

Gregg seemed captivated by the meeting in Leipzig.

According to available sources, their next meeting did not take place until 1934, when both Gregg and Sigerist had been in the United States for some time, the former as director of medical sciences, based in the Rockefeller Foundation's New York City office, and the latter as director of the Johns Hopkins Institute of the History of Medicine. The Institute was funded by the General Education Board, a Rockefeller philanthropy administratively distinct from the Division of Medical Sciences, and Sigerist at first successfully pursued a few small supplementary grants from other foundations.[20] But Gregg remained interested in Sigerist and tracked him from a distance. He had originally been at work behind the scenes—and in correspondence with Sigerist—about arrangements for his fall 1931 lecture tour.[21] Gregg's interest had already been apprehended by Lewis H. Weed, the dean of the Johns Hopkins Medical School. The very day that Sigerist cabled his acceptance of the Hopkins offer, Weed called Gregg to report the news. Gregg recorded the call in his office diary. "Sigerist has accepted post in history of medicine at Hopkins," he noted. "This is very satisfactory news for the future of this subject in the U.S. since S. is competent not only as an historian but has real interest in social phases of medicine." [22]

The issue that brought Sigerist and Gregg together again face to face was finding support for Ludwig Edelstein, the Jewish classical philologist displaced from his post in Berlin by Nazi decrees. Sigerist approached Gregg, who was involved in refugee scholar relocation efforts. After a brief meeting in New York City, Gregg wrote to Sigerist in April 1934 to report that funds had been secured.[23] Their direct acquaintanceship thus renewed, Sigerist and Gregg met again in November, this time for a long discussion on Sigerist's central administrative preoccupation: obtaining funds to support the stable functioning of the Institute and his new projects in medical sociology.[24]

They met in Baltimore in Sigerist's office at the Institute. "Alan Gregg of the Rockefeller Foundation came to see me about the finances of the Institute," Sigerist noted in his diary. "I talked to him for many hours, giving him a detailed picture of the situation. He is a fine fellow, he understands immediately what you mean. I know that he will do for us whatever he can. If he fails it won't be his fault."[25] For his part, Gregg energetically pressed the issue. He met with Dean Weed and obtained an assurance that support for Sigerist was a high Hopkins priority.[26] He then prepared a memo for internal circulation at the foundation, which read:

> nowhere in the world are the records of development of social medicine in Italy, Russia, and Germany reviewed and distributed as is being done at the Hist. of Med. Inst. of Baltimore. . . . [This work] is much needed since historical perspective is extremely valuable in understanding social conditions that influence practice of medicine.[27]

Gregg was building a case for Rockefeller Foundation support of Sigerist's Institute, for which he obtained formal board approval in April 1935.[28]

The actual form of board action was a vote authorizing the Institute's transfer to the administrative and fiscal jurisdiction of the Medical Sciences Division. Endowment funds from the General Education Board would continue as before, but operating funds would be allocated as an "exceptional item" in the Rockefeller Foundation budget. For the three-year period from July 1, 1935, to June 30, 1938, that amount would be $12,500 per year, slightly less than Sigerist's formal request.[29] The expectations attached to the grant by the Rockefeller Foundation were that the Institute's teaching would continue to strive to "counteract the tendency of medical schools to place too great an emphasis on the purely scientific training of students" and that the Institute's research would increasingly shift in the "sociological" direction. Sigerist found these conditions perfectly congenial, as they were exactly in accord with his own wishes. After worrying for months that he might have to close the Institute, he was newly confident that instead, he was "safe for three more years."[30]

The Relationship Established

Now that Sigerist and Gregg were in official administrative contact, their personal relationship also had an opportunity to grow. Gregg took the initiative, inviting Sigerist in November 1935 to address his dinner club in New York City the following January.[31] Sigerist accepted, probably feeling that he could not possibly refuse. The evening turned out to be rather enjoyable—somewhat to Sigerist's surprise—as he found the club "an intelligent group . . . mostly of editors and journalists."[32] Gregg wrote to Sigerist a few days afterward to thank him for a "first rate [talk] . . . much appreciated by all."[33] To cultivate their friendship, he sent an old fee bill of the Georgia Medical Society, which Sigerist immediately offered to publish in the *Bulletin of the History of Medicine*.[34] Thus, while Sigerist in private could rail against the foundations and the "begging" they required, he was consistently cordial to Gregg, who, for his part, was positively effusive toward Sigerist.[35]

The two men also discovered a common interest in the Soviet Union. Sigerist was by now deeply committed to his next major project, his study, advertisement, and advocacy of the great social, medical, and public health experiments underway in Russia.[36] But Gregg—although he distributed money easily traceable to the "robber barons" and worked for the "philanthropic bosses"—was also quite an enthusiast in his own more subdued way. He had visited the Soviet Union in 1927 and had been impressed by what he had found.[37] He returned for a second visit some ten years later. Realizing that Sigerist had been on his own second trip during the summer of 1936 and was busily at work on his new book in early 1937, Gregg sent a postcard from the Soviet Union on January 30, 1937, with an eye-catching message:

> Dear Sigerist: Just finished a week in Russia. Striking contrast to conditions in 1927 when I was last there. . . . As someone said to me in Paris, "Give the Russians three more years like the last three and the Americans will get interested in what they *have* not what they *are!*"[38]

Later in 1937, after Sigerist had published *Socialized Medicine in the Soviet Union* with some trepidation, he and Gregg engaged in another revealing exchange about Russian medicine and public health.[39] Within weeks of the book's appearance, Gregg sent Sigerist material on the curricular programs of Soviet schools of hygiene, just received by the Rockefeller Foundation. Sigerist reported that he was "perfectly delighted" to receive the material, and added: "If I had known that you had this material in hand, I would have consulted it long ago and would have been able to add the curriculum to the appendices of my book."[40] While other friends communicated their anxieties about the book's dangerous political fallout, Gregg remained strongly supportive of Sigerist's Soviet enterprise in a quiet, steady, and upbeat way.[41]

Gregg's general support for Sigerist was expressed most profoundly in his careful work to renew and upgrade the foundation's grant to the Institute. In March 1937 he prepared a "Confidential Bulletin to the Trustees," fully a year before trustee action of any kind was required. The bulletin described the work of the Institute and its director in glowing terms, noting that at some of Sigerist's Hopkins lectures "he has an audience larger than the total enrollment of the School."[42] By May, Gregg was able to assure Sigerist that the chances of his grant being renewed were looking quite good.[43] When they met again, on January 10, 1938, they enjoyed a three-hour conversation on a wide range of topics. In his description of their meeting, Sigerist noted that Gregg "is a devoted friend of our Institute and I have no doubt that he will do for us whatever he can." He added: "He wants to get $15,000 for us for ten years. This would remove a disturbing element of uncertainty."[44]

Gregg was true to his word. On March 18, 1938, the Rockefeller trustees voted a ten-year grant, at $15,000 per year, beginning July 1, 1938.[45] The only conditions attached by the trustees were that the Institute focus on "study of the inter-relation of society and medicine," that its teaching emphasize "the social and ethical responsibilities implied in the practice of medicine," and that Sigerist continue as director. If he stepped down, since his work is "without known parallel," funding would continue for only one year, followed by a joint Hopkins-Rockefeller reassessment. Sigerist's major financial worries were over. Distracting budgetary concerns, which had reemerged in 1937, could now be put to rest. He felt newly confident, fully supported by a foundation officer who understood the quality and uniqueness of his contributions. Gregg had in fact pressed the Rockefeller Foundation to come through in splendid fashion, and Sigerist appreciated the significance of what he had managed to engineer.

In this warm new climate, a fuller friendship began to blossom. Sigerist told Gregg that he planned to "lead a public health seminar through the Soviet Union next June and July [1938]," and Gregg quickly responded with the names of leading physicians he thought might be invited to participate.[46] A month later, when Gregg was in Baltimore to work out details of a possible Hopkins chair in preventive medicine, he dropped by to "discuss matters" with Sigerist, thus keeping him informed and soliciting his advice on this potentially interesting development.[47] In April he sent Sigerist the year book of the Faculty of Medicine of Bangkok and, playing on Sigerist's well-known linguistic prowess, quipped: "It occurs to me that this is one of the few books I could send you that you can't read."[48]

The most interesting exchange occurred, however, in November 1938, after Sigerist's third visit to the Soviet Union. Sigerist had picked up a copy of Granville Hicks's biography of John Reed, the wealthy and socially prominent American turned revolutionary and Bolshevik propagandist, author of *Ten Days That Shook the World*, the sympathetic and widely read account of the Russian Revolution.[49] Sigerist discovered in

Reed's biography much that paralleled his own. He was moved to reflect that, like Reed, he once "cared just as little for the labor movement . . . and felt very superior as a member of the intelligentsia. Then came the [First World] war . . . and the great awakening." [50] But Sigerist also discovered that Reed had been a close friend of Alan Gregg, and that Gregg had, in fact, supplied noted left-wing author Hicks with much personal Reed material to help with the biography. [51] Now seeing his philanthropic ally in a surprising new light, Sigerist dropped Gregg a note on November 22: "I am just reading Granville Hicks' biography of John Reed, and I see that you knew him intimately. Some day you must tell me about him." [52] Sigerist's words suggested that he was now willing to distinguish Gregg as person from Gregg as foundation representative and hinted at his openness to a more reciprocal and more personal friendship. [53]

Friendship in the Forties

Quite a few months were to elapse before that more intimate bond actually began to form. Sigerist was furiously busy in the early part of 1939, then traveled to Europe for the summer, and spent the latter part of the year in South Africa. In early January 1940, soon after his return to the United States, he dropped Gregg a note acknowledging mail that had arrived during his absence and reminding Gregg of his recent travels. [54] Sigerist then entered a dark and depressing period as he reacted to ferocious political assaults at home and the intensification of the war in Europe. [55] In September he apologized to Gregg for his lapses as a correspondent and expressed his desire to see him "some time during the winter." [56] Two weeks later he sent Gregg a manuscript outlining a radically new approach to medical education and the training of the "social physician." [57] Gregg responded immediately with friendly comments followed three days later by a note occasioned by Sigerist's temporary hospitalization: "I learned through your secretary that you are having something done to your nose and throat. . . . I hope the temporary effects will soon pass away and the permanent result will make it all worth while. With best of luck—take good care of yourself." [58]

During February and March 1941, Sigerist and Gregg allowed themselves a series of direct, forthright, and vulnerable exchanges. Gregg sent Sigerist a draft of the first of his upcoming Terry lectures at Yale and solicited Sigerist's honest reactions. [59] Sigerist responded in less than a week with handwritten notes scribbled on the manuscript. Several letters later, on March 20, 1941, he teased Gregg: "You need not be afraid. This letter is not going to be as long as the one I sent you with the second lecture."[60] In the same letter, when describing the virtues of visiting lectureships, Sigerist freely "confessed" that when he first landed in Cape Town "where I did not know a soul, I was scared to death. I had to pull myself together but then it was a great satisfaction to see that we had to move three times into larger lecture halls." He closed the letter with his frankest confession of all: "Literary Eclampsia is a disease well known to me, and I can add to your description that you can have repeated attacks of it without developing any immunity."

Later in 1941 and in 1942, Gregg expressed friendship for Sigerist by continuing his unwavering support for the Institute and its director. By summer and fall 1941, Sigerist was feeling quite ill and depressed, troubled by a variety of physical ailments and distressed by Nazi aggression, particularly as it was directed against Switzerland and the Soviet Union.[61] He was disturbed by a flurry of political assaults, especially after Eugene Lyons cited him several times in *The Red Decade: The Stalinist Penetration of America* as a communist apologist and part of "Stalin's Fifth Column in America."[62] He probably realized that he was also under investigation by the FBI.[63] Wary of further political backlash, in July 1942 Sigerist requested that the *New Masses not* do an article about him at that moment.[64] Gregg, however, remained steadfast. He arranged for the work of the Institute and its innovative program in medical sociology to receive special praise in the December 1941 "Confidential Bulletin" to the Rockefeller trustees, and in October 1942 he sent Sigerist a strong letter of general affirmation: "I would be very happy if you would tell [your colleagues at the Institute] . . . of the consistent satisfaction I take in the continuing activities of the Institute," he wrote. "It is a hard time to survive in some ways, but surely it is a time when the knowledge and the points of view so active in the Institute are of special importance in the future of medicine in this country."[65] Deeply moved, Sigerist informed Gregg that his "very kind letter . . . went from office to office and was a great encouragement to all of us."[66]

The friendship between Sigerist and Gregg built on this solid base throughout 1943. In February, Gregg gently turned down, as outside foundation policy, Sigerist's request for a Rockefeller subsidy to the recently created *American Review of Soviet Medicine,* which Sigerist now edited, but helpfully suggested that the parent society apply for foundation funds to support a visiting Soviet lecturer.[67] Gregg also joined the American-Soviet Medical Society and attended several of its public functions.[68] In April he sent Sigerist a draft memo on the fundamentals of social medicine, drawn up for the edification of the Rockefeller trustees.[69] In response to Gregg's request for comments, Sigerist replied that he thought the draft "admirable."[70] In June Sigerist had a "long talk" with Gregg at foundation headquarters in New York City and afterward registered his overall impressions: "I like him very much. He is honest, sincere, eager and relatively unspoiled by his foundation work. He really means to be helpful."[71] In October he conveyed an even more enthusiastic assessment to Leslie Falk, former student and young medical associate who had recently met Gregg for the first time.[72] "[Your assessment] entirely confirms the opinion I have of Gregg," Sigerist wrote. "I have a tremendous admiration for him and without him, I should never have been able to carry on my work here. . . . He really is one of the most progressive forces in medicine in this country, and I still expect a great deal from him."[73]

Sigerist may not have been quite sure when he wrote these words exactly what he expected further from Gregg, but by the following March his ideas had clarified considerably. Sigerist had been increasingly miserable for some time; he was sick, tired, overworked, politically embattled, administratively burdened, and—most important—deeply depressed about his inability to start writing his projected masterwork, the multivolume *History of Medicine*.[74] By early 1944 he had persuaded himself that he must disentangle from the directorship of the Institute and break away from Johns Hopkins.[75] Sigerist understood clearly that Gregg's support was central to his plans, and on March 30 wrote to him requesting an "opportunity to talk to you briefly on a matter that I have very much at heart."[76] At a meeting in Gregg's office at the Rockefeller Foundation on April 12, Sigerist revealed his "secret."[77] He was pleased with the tenor of the conversation: "I have full confidence in him [Gregg], so that I could talk freely. I explained why I intended to leave Hopkins and he understood it very well. Now I feel free to act."[78] On April 20, Gregg assured Sigerist in unmistakable terms that the Rockefeller Foundation grant did "not imply any moral obligation . . . to continue in direction of the Institute."[79]

Gregg thus freed Sigerist to explore alternatives to Johns Hopkins. Sigerist first thought of a research post at Yale, an option he pursued with his friend, the physiologist and avid part-time medical historian John Fulton. He explained his situation to Fulton five days after meeting with Gregg, assuring him that he had already obtained Gregg's support and Rockefeller clearance to look into other options.[80] To Fulton's enthusiastic suggestion of a Yale post, Sigerist responded that it was "an immense satisfaction to know that men like you and Alan Gregg appreciate the situation in which I find myself" and that a research position in New

Haven would be "a pleasure and a privilege."[81] Fulton pursued the matter with the provost and selected members of the Yale Corporation, but budgetary problems and internal wrangling between the medical school and Yale alumni championing arts and science deflated the trial balloon. On February 3, 1945, Sigerist received a letter from Fulton announcing that the Yale appointment was off: "I cannot blame them," Sigerist noted in his diary, "but I am sorry because it would have been an ideal solution of my problem."[82]

With no positive news forthcoming from Yale, Sigerist tried to take matters into his own hands at Hopkins. He drew up a plan that would free him from his most onerous administrative burdens—the directorship of the Institute and the acting directorship of the Welch Library (added in October 1942)—and make him a research associate at half his regular salary.[83] Hopkins officials politely turned down his proposal, but Sigerist sent his memo on to Gregg, who thought it "makes a lot of sense."[84] Gregg also wrote secretly to Walter Stewart, Rockefeller trustee and a professor of economics at the Princeton Institute for Advanced Study, asking whether Stewart thought there might be a post for Sigerist at Princeton.[85] When nothing came of this effort, Gregg wrote a memorandum to Rockefeller Foundation President Raymond B. Fosdick, expressing his general "discouragement" about Sigerist's circumstances. "At a time when his life work ought to be bearing its major fruit," Gregg wrote, "[Sigerist] is expected by Hopkins to be a routine library administrator . . . The situation there gives me more or less the impression that I get from seeing a Steinway Grand used as a kitchen table."[86]

Sigerist's situation changed dramatically in May 1945. On May 3 Gregg wrote to share a new idea: "We [the Rockefeller Foundation] might be prepared to contribute the salary of a medical librarian so as to relieve you from that work entirely and at the same time give assurance that the present assistance plus the librarian would be continued to 1956."[87] Within four days, however, Gregg received a phone call with the news that Sigerist had been "laid up with [a] heart attack."[88] Sigerist's personal physician, Hopkins Chief of Medicine Warfield T. Longcope, had already told Sigerist in April that for reasons of health, he ought to resign the library job. Longcope assured Sigerist that he would communicate his considered medical judgment to Hopkins President Bowman and Medical School Dean Chesney.[89] In the wake of Sigerist's hospitalization, Bowman and Chesney agreed to Longcope's recommendation, effective the middle of May.[90] After first calling with the news, Sigerist wrote Gregg in early June to express his gratitude for "all you have done for me."[91]

Gregg did not wish to let matters rest there. He still felt that Bowman had failed to address Sigerist's situation with sufficient sensitivity and seriousness. They met at Rockefeller Foundation headquarters on July 18, 1945, and both were well prepared. Bowman began by attempting to "astound" Gregg by telling him in confidence the "whole story" of Sigerist's political involvements.[92] Gregg made a show of surprise and took a few notes on Bowman's "revelations." But he then brushed these remarks aside and told Bowman that he could most effectively "mitigate S's political activities" by "turning Sigerist loose on the book."[93] Gregg then returned strategically to his idea of a Rockefeller-supported program in medical librarianship, obviously dangling it as a fiscal carrot to win Sigerist's release from library administration. His goal was clear: to use Rockefeller funds to buy Sigerist out of his most burdensome, intrusive, and depressing Hopkins encumbrance, thus freeing him to get on with his book. Earlier that very week, Sigerist started writing his *History of Medicine*.[94]

Sigerist worked hard at his book during the summer, fall, and early winter of 1945. In January and February 1946, he was still productively engaged and reported to Gregg that his health was much better and that he hoped "to finish Volume I this year and be able to produce one volume every year."[95] That summer Sigerist and his family returned to Switzerland for the first time in seven years. The experience confirmed his developing sense that he not only had to leave library administration, but also the directorship of the Institute, Johns Hopkins, and the United States. By November, he had decided that he wanted to give up his chair, return to Europe, and settle in a little village in the Ticino region of Switzerland. "I am determined now to leave the University at the end of this academic year," he wrote in his diary. "Of course we will be very poor, but I hope to get a fellowship from the Rockefeller Foundation."[96] By late November, he had drafted a letter of resignation, but before sending it to Bowman, he wanted to check with Gregg.[97] On December 27 he wrote a five-page double-spaced letter to Gregg, obviously meant for further circulation within the foundation. He explained his intentions and asked for $5,000 per year for three years: $3,000 per year for a fellowship, $1,500 for a secretary, and $500 for books, photographs, and general office supplies.[98] He had reached his Rubicon. "*Alea iacta est!*" Sigerist wrote in his diary.[99]

Gregg of course wanted to help, but he and the foundation had a delicate political problem on their hands. If Rockefeller simply provided the support Sigerist requested and continued funding the Hopkins Institute for only one year after his departure as previously stipulated, it would face a very disgruntled Hopkins administration. That administration would feel further aggrieved when it found out that Yale—with Gregg's knowledge—had acted competitively and surreptitiously.[100] Rockefeller President Fosdick, impatient with such political niceties, wrote Gregg a note strongly urging a grant to Sigerist, "one of the outstanding scholars of our time." If the foundation did not make the grant, Fosdick suggested, it would be as if "after a lifetime of research, Darwin had come to us and had wanted a breathing space in which to write his *Origin of Species;* I hope we would have had the good judgment to grant his request."[101] Others in the foundation were more circumspect, and Gregg tried judiciously to steer a middle course. He told Sigerist on the telephone that "it would not be correct for us to make any comment upon his plan to retire to Switzerland and suggested that he would have to come to a decision without comment one way or the other from here."[102] Meanwhile, behind the scenes, he deftly helped with other options.

The best option came from Harvey Cushing's widow, her daughters, and their husbands. Prodded by Sigerist's friends who also knew the Cushings and their kin, a plan was hatched to establish a "Cushing Professorship" at Yale, which Sigerist could occupy in absentia.[103] Mrs. Cushing remembered the warmth and admiration her deceased husband had felt for Sigerist, and her son-in-law John Hay ["Jock"] Whitney, husband of Cushing's daughter Betsey, now took the lead. He arranged for a three-year grant to Sigerist as incumbent of the Cushing Chair while Sigerist was, in fact, to reside in Switzerland. Whitney and others in the family would provide funds that Yale would collect and disburse to Sigerist, approximately $7,000 for the first year and $5,000 per year for the following two.[104] Official contributors included Mr. and Mrs. John Hay Whitney, the Helen Hay Whitney Trust, the William S. Paley Foundation (Paley was another Cushing son-in-law), Mrs. Harvey Cushing, and Mr. S. S. Spivack. Spivack was Jock Whitney's associate assigned the task of organizing the gift and negotiating with both Yale University and with Sigerist. At key points in the complex process he turned for guidance to Alan Gregg.

Gregg and Spivack had their first contact on January 2, 1947. Spivack called to express interest in Sigerist and to inquire about the Rockefeller Foundation's possible role in supporting his return to Switzerland.[105] Once Gregg explained the situation, Spivack understood the constraints upon the foundation but enlisted Gregg's personal aid in working out details of the alternative arrangements that were rapidly taking shape. He dropped by Gregg's office to discuss matters at length. Gregg noted their conversation in his office diary.

S. [Spivack] much impressed by Sigerist and asks whether three years grant at $5,000 per year might not be better [than] five years at $7,000. I said I thought the latter would be much better. . . . Said I saw no reason why the matter could not be handled through Yale University as the Whitney people apparently would like to do it, i.e., a Cushing Professor to be held by Sigerist *in absentia*.[106]

Sigerist felt sufficiently confident in the as yet uncompleted negotiations to send his letter of resignation to Bowman. Two and a half months later he learned that his mother had found a suitable house in the village of Pura, in the Ticino region of Switzerland.[107] A telegram informed him that the house was called "Casa Serena," which he took as an excellent omen.[108] As Sigerist looked forward to his translocation back to Europe and to what he projected as a period of peace and tranquility in which he would complete his *History of Medicine*, it is no wonder that he thought of Gregg — who had watched over him so often — as his "guardian angel."

The Last Decade

Although Henry Sigerist and Alan Gregg never saw one another again, their friendship continued after Sigerist's return to Europe. Correspondence over the next decade was sparse, but it was rich with feeling, especially on Gregg's side. The first contact in what was to be the last decade of both their lives was a letter from Sigerist to Gregg in April 1948. Sigerist endorsed the appointment of Richard H. Shryock to the directorship of the Johns Hopkins Institute politely, positively, and a bit formally, adding that since Gregg had "always shown so much sympathetic interest in the Institute . . . I felt you might wish to know what my attitude towards Shryock was."[109] He also touched on more personal topics. He was expecting to see Andrija Štampar, the Yugoslavian social medicine and public health leader, who was much admired by Gregg. He missed his American students — from whom he received "really touching" letters "almost every day" — and other old American friends. He hoped, in particular, that Gregg might come and visit "here some day."

When Gregg responded, it was with a friendly, handwritten note of many pages. He told Sigerist he had heard that his [Gregg's] "health was drunk in Pura, and whenever that is done in an unauthorized and spontaneous fashion I feel an equally undemanding response welling up in pleasure."[110] He chatted about Truman's election and what he hoped it meant for the future of socialized medicine in America. He commented on recent changes at the Rockefeller Foundation and his growing frustration with the "routine pound of the office," then told Sigerist that he was looking forward to retirement and the freedom to write. He thus confessed that he "sympathized with your decision perhaps more fully than you could have guessed."

Sigerist wrote to Gregg several times in 1950 as his anxieties peaked about the continuation of his research appointment. His three-year research appointment had been formally renewed by Yale after a little delay and confusion, but the more important issue, funding, was still unresolved as the year drew to a close. The major problem was that Jock Whitney or those speaking for him had become skeptical about Sigerist's productivity and the likelihood of his completion of the history project.[111] When Whitney reluctantly sent final payment on the initial grant after eight month's delay, he accompanied the check with a note clearly stating that his payment was "the third and final installment required under the terms of my letter dated May 7, 1947."[112] Then, in a seemingly sudden reversal, Whitney's associate Samuel C. Park asked John Fulton whether Yale "would be willing, or be able, to furnish in some way half of the required [sum to continue support for Sigerist's project]."[113] Fulton immediately began exploring external sources for the "Yale" half, estimated at $3,000 per year for five years.

Within weeks Gregg became officially and enthusiastically involved. Since the foundation now supported the Hopkins Institute under the direction of Shryock, there were no institutional impediments to direct Rockefeller aid to Sigerist. Gregg wrote Fulton in late January 1951 that he would "pick up the preliminary moves in connection with a contribution from here to help keep Sigerist at his work."[114] After a discussion in Gregg's office, Fulton wrote to Sigerist on February 27, 1951, that "Alan Gregg . . . is prepared to recommend allocation of $3,000 a year for five years beginning April 1st."[115] Sigerist responded with the observation that "the latest news is very encouraging. Gregg has always been a very loyal friend."[116] As anticipated, on Gregg's urging the Rockefeller trustees approved the grant on April 4, commenting in the official resolution that "the proposed grant would give assistance over five years to the work of the world's leading medical historian at the most productive and important period of his career."[117] But almost as soon as the Rockefeller board concluded its vote, arrangements began to unravel as Jock Whitney backed out of what had seemed his clear commitment to a matching grant. Fulton became very agitated, worrying about reactions at Yale and the Rockefeller Foundation and fearing that Sigerist out of desperation would accept an offer from the University of Berne that he really did not want to take.[118] Fulton also speculated that Whitney was probably "infected" by the climate of witch-hunting hysteria, which added current political concerns to his longstanding doubts about Sigerist's productivity.[119] Mostly, however, Fulton felt stymied and unable to salvage the suddenly disastrous situation.

Once again, Alan Gregg stepped in as Henry Sigerist's "guardian angel." He urged Fulton to do whatever he possibly could to prevent Sigerist from "spill[ing] the milk" and opting precipitously for Berne.[120] Next Gregg considered various indirect ways of getting to Whitney. He spoke with Dr. Duckett Jones, an officer of the Helen Hay Whitney Foundation and Jock Whitney's special adviser on medical affairs.[121] Gregg then called Fulton and told him to contact Jones directly.[122] Jones talked to Gregg again, checked some facts with Fulton, and within a few days persuaded Jock Whitney to reconsider his recent decision "in light of action taken by the Rockefeller Foundation."[123] A week later, on June 14, 1951, Fulton was officially advised that "through a combined contribution of Mrs. Vincent Astor (Cushing's daughter Mary Benedict Cushing) and the John Hay Whitney Foundation an annual grant aggregating $3,000 for the next five years will be made to Dr. Sigerist to match the grant made by the Rockefeller Foundation."[124] Mastermind behind the scenes, Gregg had done it again.

The unsettling events of the spring and early summer of 1951 took their toll on Sigerist. In one diary entry he confessed that he had made "practically no progress with volume II of the History. . . . somehow I felt paralyzed, frozen."[125] Overwhelmed by feelings of depression and guilt, Sigerist seems to have communicated at least the latter to Gregg, who responded with a handwritten note.

> Your letter devoted more space than it should have to the complications that might have accompanied your leaving Johns Hopkins; that is, complications which you refer to as "a vague feeling of guilt toward the Foundation." If the Pope can act for God I can act for the Foundation! And I assure you that my feelings of disappointment centered around the J. H. University in not creating the sort of circumstances that were conducive and appropriate for the work you can do. So please enjoy all the comforts of plenary absolution given gladly and without hesitation.[126]

This was one of the last letters of substance Gregg wrote to Sigerist. He maintained an active interest during the next few years, of course, and in August 1955 was among the small group of "Henry Sigerist's close friends" to receive a private memo from John Fulton reporting on Sigerist's recovery from a rather severe stroke.[127] It is fitting that the last piece of direct correspondence seems to have been written by Sigerist to

43. Alan Gregg in a reflective mood at his retirement home, Big Sur, California.

Gregg, on February 24, 1955. Sigerist had just learned that Gregg had retired to a house in Big Sur, California. "I was delighted to hear that you
have found your 'Casa Serena' too," Sigerist wrote.[128] Sigerist knew that
after a lifetime of battles his guardian angel had earned his own well-
deserved period of serenity.

Friendship that had developed amid the opportunistic negotiations between an ambitious scholar and a major foundation thus turned ultimately
to true philanthropy—a bilateral generosity of spirit between two men
who in the end genuinely cared about one another. Gregg granted Sigerist
freedom from remorse and guilt, whatever his actual productivity, and
Sigerist wished Gregg true peace after years of successful but debilitating
realpolitik. It was this deep personal connection that most immediately
explains the last five years of the Rockefeller Foundation's support for
Henry E. Sigerist, Marxist historian of medicine, during the declining
years of his career. But even when Sigerist was at the height of his powers,
personal friendship emerged as an important element in his dealings with
the Rockefeller Foundation. While no part of either Gregg's or Sigerist's
initial motivation, friendship grew within an instrumental relationship

whereby the foundation bought Sigerist's talents and Sigerist gained some measure of financial security. Ironically, this friendship assured a steady flow of funds from a major corporate philanthropy to a leading critic of the capitalist order.

Notes

1. In January 1938, assured that the Rockefeller Foundation was about to award to the Institute this ten-year, $150,000 grant, Sigerist became rather self-righteous as he reflected on the irony of the grant. "It is pretty liberal, after all, that the Foundation supports me in spite of my radical attitude," he wrote. "I do not hesitate to accept the money. It is nothing but social justice that this money should serve the ends for which I am fighting." Henry E. Sigerist, Diary, January 10, 1938. Yale University Library, Henry E. Sigerist Papers, Addition (June 1987), Biographical Data and Memorabilia, group 788, box 2 (hereafter cited as Diary); partially excerpted in Nora Sigerist Beeson, ed., *Henry E. Sigerist: Autobiographical Writings* (Montreal: McGill University Press, 1966), 130. In the following references, where specific manuscript diary entries are included in the selection published by Nora Sigerist Beeson, both the manuscript and published references are given; where diary entries were not included in that volume, only the manuscript diary entry is cited.

2. For the Foundation's assessment of Marxian and non-Marxian social history, see the interoffice memo written by Robert S. Morison, "JHU-Institute of the History of Medicine, 1950–1952," October 20, 1952. Rockefeller Foundation Archives, Rockefeller Archive Center, North Tarrytown, N.Y. (hereafter cited as RFA), record group 1.1, series 200, box 93. For Congress' investigation of the Rockefeller and other foundations during the McCarthy era, see Ben Whitaker, *The Foundations: An Anatomy of Philanthropy and Society* (London: Eyre Methuen, 1974), 106–9.

3. See, for example, Harvey Klehr, *The Heyday of American Communism: The Depression Decade* (New York: Basic Books, 1984). Cf. Peter J. Kuznick, *Beyond the Laboratory: Scientists as Political Activists in 1930s America* (Chicago: University of Chicago Press, 1987).

4. Privately, in his diary, Sigerist commented caustically on the political spinelessness of the large foundations. "Like other foundations the Rosenwald Fund is afraid of approaching problems of medical service and has organized a special committee for that purpose that it can repudiate at any time," he noted. "It proves once more that problems of public welfare cannot be solved by bodies that have their own financial interests to protect." Henry E. Sigerist, Diary, April 13, 1937. Sigerist never expressed these sentiments in public.

5. Robert A. Lambert to M. C. Balfour, October 18, 1944. RFA. Record group 1.1, series 200, box 93. Alan Gregg, Office Diary, January 2, 1947, RFA.

6. Alan Gregg, Office Diary, July 18, 1945. RFA.

7. The term "philanthropoid" was Gregg's original, self-derisive coinage. He used it, for example, in his letter to Sigerist dated February 29, 1952. Yale Uni-

versity Library, Henry E. Sigerist Papers (hereafter cited as Sigerist Papers/Yale), General Correspondence, 1947–57, group 788, series 1, box 13.

8. Henry E. Sigerist, "Response," *Bulletin of the History of Medicine* 22 (1948): 41–42.

9. As cited by Wilder Penfield, *The Difficult Art of Giving: The Epic of Alan Gregg* (Boston: Little, Brown and Co., 1967), 309.

10. For Sigerist's Leipzig years, see the essay by Ingrid Kästner in this volume.

11. For an overview of Gregg's career at this time, see Theodore M. Brown, "Alan Gregg and the Rockefeller Foundation's Support of Franz Alexander's Psychosomatic Research," *Bulletin of the History of Medicine* 61 (1987): 159–64.

12. Simon Flexner and James Thomas Flexner, *William Henry Welch and the Heroic Age of American Medicine* (New York: Viking, 1941), 419.

13. This language is from the "Proposal for a Medical Library at the Johns Hopkins University," October 8, 1925. The Ferdinand Hamburger Jr. Archives of the Johns Hopkins University, Records of the Office of the President, 1903–63, file 28.9 (Institute of the History of Medicine). (Hereafter cited as Hamburger Archives/Hopkins.)

14. Flexner and Flexner, *William Henry Welch*, 438–39.

15. Theodore M. Brown, "Alan Gregg and the Rockefeller Foundation," 161–67.

16. Entries dated January 26, 1928, and June 23, 1929, in Alan Gregg's Office Diary. RFA.

17. See the essays by Elizabeth Fee and Theodore M. Brown and by Ingrid Kästner in this volume.

18. Alan Gregg, Office Diary, December 15, 1929. RFA.

19. Ibid., December 16, 1929.

20. For the administrative complexities and tensions in the Rockefeller philanthropies, see Robert E. Kohler, *Partners in Science. Foundations and Natural Scientists, 1900–1945* (Chicago: University of Chicago Press, 1991), 233–62. For Sigerist's early efforts with other foundations, see, for example, Henry E. Sigerist to Ludwig Kast, July 28, 1932. Sigerist Papers/Yale, General Correspondence, 1931–46, group 788, series 1, box 5.

21. Mary L. Waite to Henry E. Sigerist, September 23, 1931. Sigerist Papers/Yale, Professional Activities, group 788, series 2, box 3.

22. Alan Gregg, Office Diary, April 30, 1932. RFA.

23. Alan Gregg to Henry E. Sigerist, April 2, 1934. RFA. Record group 1.1, series 200, box 93.

24. For Sigerist's concern with this issue, see, for example, his Diary entries for December 4, 1933; December 19, 1933; May 24, 1934; October 23, 1934; November 26, 1934; December 12, 1934.

25. Henry E. Sigerist, Diary, November 19, 1934.

26. Alan Gregg, Office Diary, November 19, 1934. RFA.

27. Alan Gregg, "RF Interoffice Memo: Interview of AG with Prof. Henry Sigerist, at Baltimore, Nov. 19, 1934." RFA. Record group 1.1, series 200, box 93.

28. "RF Staff Conference—March 21, 1935" and "Resolution RF35056 (4/17/35)." RFA. Record group 1.1, series 200, box 93.

29. "Resolution RF35056 (4/17/35)." Sigerist had requested $15,000 per year, using somewhat inflated estimates for projected Institute expenditures on travel, office furniture, book purchases, etc. Henry E. Sigerist, "Memorandum for a Plan of Studies of the Social Aspects of Medicine." Hamburger Archives/Hopkins.

30. Henry E. Sigerist, Diary, February 8, 1935, and April 17, 1935.

31. Henry E. Sigerist to Alan Gregg, November 20, 1935. The Johns Hopkins Medical Institutions, Alan Mason Chesney Archives, Henry E. Sigerist Papers (hereafter cited as Chesney Archives/Hopkins), box 46.

32. Henry E. Sigerist, Diary, January 22, 1936.

33. Alan Gregg to Henry E. Sigerist, January 27, 1936. Chesney Archives/Hopkins, box 46.

34. Henry E. Sigerist to Alan Gregg, January 29, 1936. Chesney Archives/Hopkins, box 46.

35. Henry E. Sigerist, Diary, October 13, 1935.

36. For Sigerist's Soviet interests at this time, see the essays by John Hutchinson and Walter Lear in this volume.

37. For the "robber barons" phrase, see Henry E. Sigerist, Diary, February 1, 1936. He attributes the "philanthropic bosses" phrase to Yale's John Peters. Henry E. Sigerist, Diary, April 17, 1937; *Autobiographical Writings,* 123. For Gregg's 1927 visit to the Soviet Union, see Wilder Penfield, *The Difficult Art of Giving,* 190-95. Cf. Gregg's Office Diary, December 5-19, 1927. RFA. On the Rockefeller interest in the Soviet Union during the 1920s, see David C. Engerman, "The Rockefellers and American Aid to Soviet Russia," *Research Reports from the Rockefeller Archive Center,* spring 1994, 8-10.

38. Alan Gregg to Henry E. Sigerist, January 30, 1937. Chesney Archives/Hopkins, box 46.

39. For Sigerist's trepidation, see his Diary entries for March 22, 1937, and October 28, 1937; *Autobiographical Writings,* 122, 128.

40. Henry E. Sigerist to Alan Gregg, November 26, 1937. Chesney Archives/ Hopkins, box 46.

41. For expressed anxieties, see Sigerist's Diary entry for November 21, 1937; *Autobiographical Writings,* 128-29.

42. Excerpt, "Confidential Bulletin to Trustees," March 1937. RFA. Record group 1.1, series 200, box 93.

43. Henry E. Sigerist to Alan Gregg, May 11, 1937. Chesney Archives/Hopkins, box 46.

44. Henry E. Sigerist, Diary, January 10, 1938; *Autobiographical Writings,* 130.

45. "Resolution RF38022 (3/18/38)." RFA. Record group 1.1, series 200, box 93.

46. Henry E. Sigerist to Alan Gregg, January 26, 1938; Alan Gregg to Henry E. Sigerist, February 17, 1938. Chesney Archives/Hopkins, box 46.

47. Henry E. Sigerist, Diary, March 23, 1938.

48. Alan Gregg to Henry E. Sigerist, April 27, 1938. Chesney Archives/Hopkins, box 46.

49. "John Reed," *Dictionary of American Biography,* vol. 8 (New York: Scribner's, 1935), 451-52; Granville Hicks, *John Reed: The Making of a Revolutionary* (New York: Macmillan, 1937).

50. Henry E. Sigerist, Diary, November 27, 1938; *Autobiographical Writings*, 140.

51. On Hicks's role in the left-wing culture of the thirties, see Warren L. Susman, *Culture as History* (New York: Pantheon, 1973), 174. For Gregg's friendship with Reed and help with the book, see Hicks, *John Reed,* 34, 45, 59–60, 404, 408–9.

52. Henry E. Sigerist to Alan Gregg, November 22, 1938. RFA. Record group 1.1, series 200, box 93.

53. It is telling that on the very day he wrote the note to Gregg, Sigerist wrote an entry in his diary that underscored the same distinction between the person and the institutional position of another foundation official, Keppel of the Carnegie Foundation: "There is nothing I detest more than Cocktail Parties . . . And when such parties are given to worship a foundation fool they are particularly unpleasant; although, I must say, Weed's party today was not quite so bad because the hero, Mr. Keppel, was quite human." Henry E. Sigerist, Diary, November 22, 1938.

54. Henry E. Sigerist to Alan Gregg, January 10, 1940. RFA. Record group 1.1, series 200, box 93.

55. See chapter by Elizabeth Fee in this volume.

56. Henry E. Sigerist to Alan Gregg, September 6, 1940. RFA. Record group 1.1, series 200, box 93.

57. Henry E. Sigerist to Alan Gregg, September 23, 1940. Chesney Archives/ Hopkins, box 46. For Sigerist's original work on this curricular plan, see Henry E. Sigerist, Diary, February 21, 1940, and February 24, 1940; *Autobiographical Writings,* 164.

58. Alan Gregg to Henry E. Sigerist, September 30, 1940; Alan Gregg to Henry E. Sigerist, October 3, 1940. Chesney Archives/Hopkins, box 46.

59. Alan Gregg to Henry E. Sigerist, February 18, 1941. Chesney Archives/ Hopkins, box 46.

60. Henry E. Sigerist to Alan Gregg, March 20, 1941. Chesney Archives/Hopkins, box 46.

61. See, for example, Henry E. Sigerist, Diary entries for July 5, July 9, August 1, August 23, September 2, September 4, 1941; *Autobiographical Writings,* 172–75.

62. Indianapolis: Bobbs-Merrill, 1941, 10, 249, 254, 259, and especially 247. For one reaction to the book of direct significance to Sigerist, see Marshall Winchester to Isaiah Bowman, April 7, 1942. Hamburger Archives/Hopkins.

63. For FBI investigation, see File on Henry Ernest Sigerist, U.S. Department of Justice, Federal Bureau of Investigation, Documents referred from the Immigration and Naturalization Service. This partially declassified FBI file was obtained via a Freedom of Information Act request by Corinne Sutter-Brown.

64. Handwritten note dated July 10, 1942, by Sigerist's secretary, on copy of telegram from *New Masses* to Henry E. Sigerist, July 8, 1942. Chesney Archives/ Hopkins, box 88.

65. Alan Gregg to Henry E. Sigerist, October 19, 1942. RFA. Record group 1.1, series 200, box 93. See also "Confidential Bulletin to Trustees," December 1941. RFA. Record group 1.1, series 200, box 93.

66. Henry E. Sigerist to Alan Gregg, October 21, 1942. Chesney Archives/Hopkins, box 46.

67. Alan Gregg to Henry E. Sigerist, February 25, 1943. Chesney Archives/Hopkins, box 46.

68. See fig. 41.

69. Alan Gregg to Henry E. Sigerist, April 1, 1943. Chesney Archives/Hopkins, box 46.

70. Henry E. Sigerist to Alan Gregg, April 8, 1943. Chesney Archives/Hopkins, box 46.

71. Henry E. Sigerist, Diary, June 18, 1943; *Autobiographical Writings,* 182–83.

72. Leslie Falk to Henry E. Sigerist, October 6, 1943. Chesney Archives/Hopkins, box 38.

73. Henry E. Sigerist to Leslie Falk, October 11, 1943. Chesney Archives/Hopkins, box 38.

74. For Sigerist's mental and physical state at this time, see the essay by Elizabeth Fee and Theodore M. Brown in this volume. See also Henry E. Sigerist, Diary, June 12, 1943; September 11, 1943; November 4, 1943; November 26, 1943; *Autobiographical Writings,* 182, 184–85.

75. Henry E. Sigerist, Diary, March 15, 1944; *Autobiographical Writings,* 186. This entry may be compared with his entry for July 10, 1943, where he expressed less resolve and more a frustrated "wish" to be free.

76. Henry E. Sigerist to Alan Gregg, March 30, 1944. Chesney Archives/Hopkins, box 46.

77. Alan Gregg, Office Diary, April 12, 1944. RFA.

78. Henry E. Sigerist, Diary, April 12, 1944.

79. Alan Gregg to Henry E. Sigerist, April 20, 1944. RFA. Record group 1.1, series 200, box 93.

80. Henry E. Sigerist to John Fulton, April 17, 1944. Sigerist Papers/Yale, Addition (1981), Correspondence, group 788, series 1, box 1.

81. John Fulton to Henry E. Sigerist, April 20, 1944 and Henry E. Sigerist to John Fulton, April 22, 1944. Sigerist Papers/Yale, Addition (1981), Correspondence, group 788, series 1, box 1.

82. Henry E. Sigerist, Diary, February 3, 1945.

83. Ibid., February 23, 1945; *Autobiographical Writings,* 193–94.

84. Henry E. Sigerist, Diary, March 6, 1945; *Autobiographical Writings,* 194. Alan Gregg to Henry E. Sigerist, March 26, 1945. RFA. Record group 1.1, series 200, box 93.

85. Alan Gregg to Walter Stewart, March 26, 1945. RFA. Record group 1.1, series 200, box 93.

86. Alan Gregg to Raymond B. Fosdick, April 27, 1945. RFA. Record group 1.1, series 200, box 93.

87. Alan Gregg to Henry E. Sigerist, May 3, 1945. RFA. Record group 1.I, series 200, box 93.

88. Alan Gregg, Office Diary, May 7, 1945. RFA. Sigerist's daughter Nora Sigerist Beeson remembers that her father was admitted to the hospital for "rest because of overwork." Personal communication, 1994.

89. Henry E. Sigerist, Diary, April 10, 1945; *Autobiographical Writings,* 194.

90. "Library Committee Minutes Meeting of May 9, 1945." Hamburger Ar-

chives/Hopkins. Henry E. Sigerist to Leslie Falk, May 15, 1945, Chesney Archives/ Hopkins, box 38.

91. Henry E. Sigerist to Alan Gregg, June 9, 1945. RFA. Record group 1.1, series 200, box 93.

92. "Memorandum of a Talk with Dr. Alan Gregg (July 18, 1945)." Hamburger Archives/Hopkins.

93. Alan Gregg, Office Diary, July 18, 1945. RFA.

94. Henry E. Sigerist, Diary, July 15, 1945; *Autobiographical Writings,* 195.

95. Henry E. Sigerist to Alan Gregg, February 12, 1946. RFA. Record group 1.1, series 200, box 93.

96. Henry E. Sigerist, Diary, November 12, 1946; *Autobiographical Writings,* 201–2.

97. Henry E. Sigerist, Diary, November 29, 1946.

98. Henry E. Sigerist to Alan Gregg, December 27, 1946. RFA. Record group 1.1, series 200, box 93.

99. Henry E. Sigerist, Diary, December 27, 1946; *Autobiographical Writings,* 203.

100. For some indication of these feelings, see Alan M. Chesney to Isaiah Bowman, October 17, 1947 and Isaiah Bowman to Alan M. Chesney, October 20, 1947. Hamburger Archives/Hopkins. See also "RSM [Robert S. Morison] Interview," May 20, 1947. RFA. Record group 1.1, series 200, box 93.

101. Raymond Fosdick to Alan Gregg, January 2, 1947. RFA. Record group 1.1, series 200, box 93.

102. Alan Gregg, Office Diary, January 6, 1947. RFA.

103. The official account can be found in the *Seventh Annual Report of the Historical Library,* Yale University School of Medicine, June 30, 1947, 7–8. For another view of events that emphasizes his own role, see Gregory Zilboorg to Henry E. Sigerist, January 8, 1947. Sigerist Papers/Yale, Addition (1981), Correspondence, group 788, series 1, box 1.

104. John Hay Whitney to John Fulton, May 7, 1947. Sigerist Papers/Yale, Addition (1981), Correspondence, group 788, series 1, box 1. Cf. "Records of the Yale Corporation," June 16, 1947. Sigerist Papers/Yale, Addition (1981), Correspondence, group 788, series 1, box 1.

105. Alan Gregg, Office Diary, January 2, 1947. RFA.

106. Ibid., January 15, 1947.

107. Ibid., March 29, 1947; *Autobiographical Writings,* 207–8.

108. Henry E. Sigerist, Diary, April 6, 1947; *Autobiographical Writings,* 208.

109. Henry E. Sigerist to Alan Gregg, April 24, 1948. RFA. Record group 1.1, series 200, box 93.

110. Alan Gregg to Henry E. Sigerist, November 5, 1948. Sigerist Papers/Yale, General Correspondence, 1947–57, group 788, series 1, box 13.

111. John Fulton to Henry E. Sigerist, September 9, 1950; John Fulton to Henry E. Sigerist, September 28, 1950. Sigerist Papers/Yale, Addition (1981), Correspondence, group 788, series 1, box 1.

112. John Hay Whitney to John Fulton, February 6, 1950. Sigerist Papers/Yale, Addition (1981), Correspondence, group 788, series 1, box 1.

113. Samuel C. Park to John Fulton, November 2, 1950. Sigerist Papers/Yale, Addition (1981), Correspondence, group 788, series 1, box 3.

114. Alan Gregg to John Fulton, January 22, 1951. Sigerist Papers/Yale, Addition (1981), Correspondence, group 788, series 1, box 3.

115. John Fulton to Henry E. Sigerist, February 27, 1951. Sigerist Papers/Yale, Addition (1981), Correspondence, group 788, series 1, box 1.

116. Henry E. Sigerist to John Fulton, March 5[?], 1951. Sigerist Papers/Yale, Addition (1981), Correspondence, group 788, series 1, box 1.

117. "Resolution RF51218 (4/4/51)." RFA. Record group 1.2, series 200A, box 164.

118. John Fulton to S. S. Spivack, April 22, 1951. Sigerist Papers/Yale, Addition (1981), Correspondence, group 788, series 1, box 3.

119. John Fulton to Henry E. Sigerist, April 27, 1951. Sigerist Papers/Yale, Addition (1981), Correspondence, group 788, series 1, box 1. It is interesting to note that FBI agents were, in fact, actively investigating Sigerist in the spring of 1951 and filed another official report on May 5, 1951, after several months of fieldwork. See FBI File on Henry Ernest Sigerist.

120. Madeline Stanton to Alan Gregg, May 10, 1951. Sigerist Papers/Yale, Addition (1981), Correspondence, group 788, series 1, box 3.

121. Alan Gregg to Robert S. Morison, handwritten note on letter from John Fulton to Alan Gregg, May 25, 1951. RFA. Record group 1.2, series 200A, box 164.

122. John Fulton to Duckett Jones, May 28, 1951. Sigerist Papers/Yale, Addition (1981), Correspondence, group 788, series 1, box 3.

123. Duckett Jones to John Fulton, June 5, 1951. Sigerist Papers/Yale, Addition (1981), Correspondence, group 788, series 1, box 3. John Fulton to Henry E. Sigerist, June 7, 1951. Sigerist Papers/Yale, Addition (1981), Correspondence, group 788, series 1, box 1.

124. Samuel Park to John Fulton, June 14, 1951. Sigerist Papers/Yale, Addition (1981), Correspondence, group 788, series 1, box 3.

125. Henry E. Sigerist, Diary, December 31, 1951; *Autobiographical Writings*, 237.

126. Alan Gregg to Henry E. Sigerist, February 29, 1952. Sigerist Papers/Yale, General Correspondence, 1947–57, group 788, series 1, box 13.

127. John Fulton, "A Day in Pura," August 26, 1955. Sigerist Papers/Yale, Addition (1981), Correspondence, group 788, series 1, box 1. This group of friends seems to have been identical to the "Henry E. Sigerist Research Fund Committee," which raised private funds to support Sigerist's historical work in the last years of his life. The members of the Committee were Erwin Ackerknecht, Esther Lucille Brown, Leslie Falk, John F. Fulton, Iago Galdston, Alan Gregg, Robert Leslie, Genevieve Miller, Milton I. Roemer, George Rosen, George Silver, Ilza Veith, and Gregory Zilboorg. See John F. Fulton, "Preface" to Henry E. Sigerist, *A History of Medicine*, vol. II (New York: Oxford University Press, 1961), vi.

128. Henry E. Sigerist to Alan Gregg, February 24, 1955. Sigerist Papers/Yale, General Correspondence, 1947–57, group 788, series 1, box 13.

PART 4

Sigerist's Legacy

CHAPTER 14

Sociological Vision and Pedagogic Mission: Henry Sigerist's Medical Sociology

Milton I. Roemer, Leslie A. Falk,
and Theodore M. Brown

Henry Sigerist's impact on the practice of medical history in the United States would be influenced by professional traditions and national politics; by contrast, his contribution to medical sociology was undermined by the vast transformation of that field itself. When Sigerist, in the thirties, first conceived his ambitious project in the "Sociology of Medicine," the sociological enterprise was still believed to stand at the intersection of social analysis and social reform. Not yet entirely differentiated from economics, political science, anthropology, and social work, "sociology" referred to a generally socioeconomic and politicocultural, as opposed to a genetic or geographic, style of analysis. It was broadly understood by intellectuals and policy makers, even by many sociologists, as a countervailing point of view and a moral disposition rather than as a specialized academic discipline.[1] But within a decade and a half, sociology became so narrowly focused and rigidly technical that Sigerist's kind of sociology—inspirational and influential in its time—was judged irrelevant to the professional field.

Those who shared Sigerist's vision made no mark on sociological prac-

tice in the late forties and fifties, even though many he inspired participated actively in medical care reform and health policy debate. Sigerist's
sociology, crucial to his sense of overall mission, was a product of its
time. It was an expression of the thirties, not so much as an emerging academic discipline but as a compelling, comparative, and implicitly political
approach to the evolving contemporary relations between medicine and
society. As George Rosen put it, for Sigerist sociology was "a tool . . .
[and] a means of contributing to the urgent present problems of medicine
and of helping to prepare the future."[2]

To understand the attributes of what Sigerist called "sociology" and to
appreciate its significance in his overall career, this essay considers medical sociology in three parts. First, it reviews basic trends in the social
analysis of medicine in the period from the 1910s to the mid-1930s, when
Sigerist became active in the field. Then, against this background, it highlights Sigerist's own emphases and the contributions he made in his writing and teaching. Third, it suggests why Sigerist's sociological ideas and
actions influenced a generation of American health policy activists but
not the later academic field of medical sociology.

Social Aspects of Medicine, 1910–1936

Serious exploration of the social aspects of modern medicine began in the
1910s and 1920s. Those involved in these early efforts were only occasionally academically trained "sociologists" in the current professional sense
of the term. Bernhard J. Stern, for example, published his Columbia University Ph.D. dissertation, *Social Factors in Medical Progress,* in 1927.[3] But
Stern was a rare exception among sociologists, who, for the most part,
ignored medical topics.[4] More often, early twentieth-century students of
the social aspects of medicine were either economists or reform-minded
physicians.[5]

Among the economists were Irving Fisher, Harry H. Moore, Michael
Davis, Edgar Sydenstricker, C. Rufus Rorem, and I. S. Falk.[6] Fisher was
a pioneering mathematical economist who became involved in many
health-related causes. A Yale professor, he was a founder of the Committee of One Hundred on National Health, which, beginning in 1906,
advocated the creation of a federal department of health. From 1915 to
1917, he was president of the American Association for Labor Legislation
at the peak of its campaign for compulsory national health insurance.[7]
Harry H. Moore, an economist with the U.S. Public Health Service, produced in 1927 the first broad overview of the American health system by

a single author, *American Medicine and the People's Health*.[8] Moore was also the first director of the twenty-eight-volume report of the Committee on the Costs of Medical Care (CCMC). These volumes appeared between 1929 and 1932 and established a framework for the analysis of the U.S. health system. Despite its name, the CCMC examined not just economics but also epidemiology, manpower, facilities, patterns of delivery, and current health needs—social and organizational issues well beyond the singular issue of costs.[9]

Michael Davis was also deeply involved with the CCMC and, indeed, had initially helped organize the committee.[10] Holder of a Ph.D. from Columbia University, where he had studied sociology, psychology, and education, Davis was director of the Boston Dispensary from 1910 to 1920 and secretary of New York City's Committee on Dispensary Development from 1920 to 1927. In both positions, Davis investigated ways to organize, finance, and deliver comprehensive and socially responsive curative and preventive services.[11] In 1928 he became director of medical services at the Julius Rosenwald Fund, an influential post he held until 1937, when he became chairman of the Committee on Research in Medical Economics (financed by the Rockefeller Foundation). He had written a number of important books, including *Clinics, Hospitals and Health Centers* (1927), *The Crisis in Hospital Finance* (1932), and *Public Medical Services* (1937).

Edgar Sydenstricker was likewise active in the work of the CCMC.[12] Trained in economics, Sydenstricker was chief of the Office of Statistical Investigation of the U.S. Public Health Service from 1920 to 1928 and director of research at the Milbank Memorial Fund from 1928 to 1935. In 1935 he was appointed administrative head of the Milbank Fund and also directed the study of President Franklin Roosevelt's Committee on Economic Security entitled "Risks to Economic Security Arising Out of Ill-Health." Earlier in his distinguished career, he had studied (with Joseph Goldberger) the incidence of pellagra in southern mill villages and demonstrated the close association between the occurrence of pellagra and low socioeconomic status.[13]

Two other economists closely associated with the CCMC deserve mention—C. Rufus Rorem and I. S. Falk. Rorem was formally trained in economics, while Falk was initially schooled in bacteriology and immunology.[14] By 1929, however, both Rorem and Falk had become deeply interested in health economics and other social aspects of medical care. Rorem was appointed a staff economist to the CCMC, Falk became associate director, and each worked on an important series of CCMC studies. Rorem produced, among others, *The Public's Investment in Hospi-*

tals (1930), *Private Group Clinics* (1931), and *The "Municipal Doctor" System in Rural Saskatchewan* (1931); Falk contributed *A Community Medical Service Organized under Industrial Auspices in Roanoke Rapids, North Carolina* (1932) and *Organized Medical Services at Fort Benning, Georgia* (1932), among several other titles.

In his *American Medicine* (1934) Henry Sigerist warmly applauded the efforts of the CCMC and specifically cited the studies of Rorem, Falk, Davis, Moore, and others closely associated with the work of the committee.[15] Sigerist, in fact, based his crucial chapter six—on evolving American relations between physicians and patients—primarily on data extracted from CCMC publications and related studies. Claiming that these publications were "equally absorbing to medical men and to sociologists," Sigerist noted that they led to the recognition that "medical care is not a technical problem, which can be considered separately . . . [but] is much more a sociological problem." [16] He thus acknowledged that early twentieth-century economists, especially those connected with the CCMC, had helped educate him about the American substance and perhaps even the general significance of "medical sociology."

A small international group of socially minded physicians active during the same years also contributed to Sigerist's understanding of the comparative sociology of medicine. These physicians all combined scholarly analysis with hard-headed pragmatism in their efforts to bring about significant change in the provision of health care and related social services. They were Isaac Rubinow, Arthur Newsholme, Andrija Štampar, and René Sand.

Rubinow was a Russian-born, American-trained physician and Ph.D. economist who played a major role in the American campaign for compulsory health insurance in the 1910s.[17] He also wrote substantial scholarly works on social insurance from a comparative international perspective. Rubinow spent the years from 1919 to 1922 in Palestine organizing the American Zionist Medical Unit. With a group of physicians and a total staff of five hundred working on fixed salaries, he set up hospitals, infant welfare stations, and a rural health care program. From his return to the United States in 1923 until his death in 1936, Rubinow was active in the broadly based campaign for social security legislation. He served briefly as a consultant to President Roosevelt's Committee on Economic Security and in 1934 published a book, *The Quest for Security,* which was similar in spirit to several of Sigerist's. It was a work on social insurance based on historical and comparative analysis but written for the general public in accessible fashion, conveying "theory, prophesy and program." [18]

Arthur Newsholme was a distinguished figure in public health and social medicine whose career spanned the half century from the 1880s to the 1930s.[19] After British medical training and a brief stint in general practice, he became a local medical officer of health. During that same period he carried out influential studies on the relations between poverty and health, tuberculosis control, the social aspects of infant and maternal health, and many other topics. From 1908 to 1919 he served as principal medical officer to England's Local Government Board, thus acting as, in effect, the director of England's public health service. During those eleven years he witnessed and supported Britain's adoption of a health insurance scheme and strongly advocated the organization of more comprehensive, publicly funded diagnostic and therapeutic services. He retired from government service in 1919 and accepted an invitation to become professor of public health administration at the just founded Johns Hopkins School of Hygiene and Public Health. Here and elsewhere in the United States he strongly supported state-organized medical services.

In 1919, Newsholme gave a lecture at the New York Academy of Medicine entitled "The Increasing Socialisation of Medicine."[20] In the 1920s he wrote several books, most notably, *Public Health and Insurance* (1920) and *Health Problems in Organized Society: Studies in the Social Aspects of Health* (1927). In 1931 he published in three volumes the results of a comprehensive study commissioned by the Milbank Memorial Fund, *International Studies on the Relation between the Private and Official Practice of Medicine*. In 1933, with John A. Kingsbury, secretary of the Milbank Fund, he wrote what was, in effect, the fourth volume, *Red Medicine: Socialized Health in Soviet Russia*. Sigerist had long been aware of Newsholme's work and cited his studies with respect and enthusiasm.

Andrija Štampar was another socially oriented physician of the early twentieth century who strongly influenced Sigerist's conception of comparative medical sociology. Štampar was a Croatian-born, Viennese-trained public health leader of great energy and political courage who published widely but was best known for his tangible and practical successes.[21] In 1925 he edited and wrote much of a wide-ranging two-volume work on social medicine.[22] Štampar had already been appointed director of public health in the newly created country of Yugoslavia in 1919, at the unusually early age of thirty-one. In that office he established more than 250 social medicine units, including rural health stations, epidemiological research centers, antivenereal and antituberculosis dispensaries, and maternal and child health centers. He believed that health care ought to be a free public service that the state had the responsibility to provide. In

1931 his progressive views caused him political trouble in Yugoslavia, and he left to work with the Health Organization of the League of Nations, then spent three years in China. In 1938 he was in the United States and visited Henry Sigerist at Johns Hopkins. This, in part, is how Sigerist described the visit:

> We crowded around him and asked him to tell us about his work in Yugoslavia. . . . He knew that public health is determined by social and economic conditions, and that it is silly to distribute drugs where food is needed. He therefore approached his task in the broadest possible way, helping the people not only to improve their health but their living and working conditions as well.[23]

One final influence should be noted: Belgian physician René Sand, a major figure in the field of social and international medicine.[24] Sand founded the Belgian Social Medicine Association in 1912 and moved to Paris in 1921 as secretary-general of the League of Red Cross Societies. Under his leadership, the work of the league increasingly focused on broadly conceived projects in child welfare and health education. Sand was also prominent in a variety of international organizations concerned with hospitals, social work, and public health. In 1937 he returned to Brussels to become secretary-general of the Belgian ministry of health. Perhaps most significant, however, was his publication in 1934 of the influential book, *L'Économie Humaine par la Médecine Sociale,* available in an English translation in 1936 under the title *Health and Human Progress: An Essay in Sociological Medicine.*[25] Sand's book presented rich and varied data on the influence of social, economic, occupational, and educational factors on morbidity and mortality and summed up major findings in a chapter entitled "Inequality of the Social Classes in Respect to Sickness and Death." It is also notable that the first chapter, called "The Advent of Sociological Medicine," included the following prescription: "the whole of medicine, both preventive and curative, must be enlightened by social science, associated with social service."[26] Sand's book drew attention to the importance of "sociological" approaches within medicine just as Henry Sigerist was developing his own interest in medical sociology.

The Sociological Contributions of Henry Sigerist

Henry Sigerist's enthusiasm for medical sociology thus developed against a background of considerable and growing interest in the social aspects of medicine. American economists and an international group of socially minded physicians in the early twentieth century had generated widespread interest in the subject. Sigerist followed their work eagerly. In 1934 he explicitly labeled these broad interests "sociological" and, in *American Medicine* and other writings, enunciated his own strong and increasingly clearly articulated views on medical sociology.

Sigerist had, in fact, first begun to publish on sociological themes in the 1920s when he was director of the Institute of the History of Medicine in Leipzig. Especially in his later Leipzig years, he wrote essays on social issues in medicine that began to rival his synthetic historical essays on scientific, philosophical, and conceptual themes. Most notable were his essays "The Special Position of the Sick"[27] and "The Physician and the Environment."[28] In the latter essay he argued that the relationship between patient and physician had changed from relative isolation to deeper social integration, so that in modern society individuals felt a social obligation toward health and physicians functioned in ways increasingly dependent on the state. Then, in 1931, Sigerist published *Man and Medicine: An Introduction to Medical Knowledge.*[29] He addressed this book to medical students, but it is not a simplified textbook of medicine. Throughout his text, Sigerist examines relevant social problems, highlights the history of public health and health insurance, and analyzes the social and economic conditions that shaped health services in the past.

Henry Sigerist's fifteen years in the United States were his most fruitful with regard to medical sociology. In 1937, he published his first book on the Soviet health system, *Socialized Medicine in the Soviet Union.*[30] Two books with broad historical, comparative, and social sweep soon followed, both derived from lecture series, *Medicine and Human Welfare* (1941)[31] at Yale, and *Civilization and Disease* (1943)[32] at Cornell. In these books, Sigerist makes abundantly clear that much of his interest in medical history had shifted to exploring the social context of health status and health services. Historical analysis could reveal the social determinants of health and disease in the past, just as comparative contemporary study could reveal those determinants in the present.

Some of Sigerist's best sociological work in the thirties was published in the form of short essays. For example, in 1933 he presented "The Physician's Profession through the Ages," which underscored modern tendencies toward specialization, mutual social obligation, and compulsory health insurance.[33] In 1934, his "Trends towards Socialized Medicine" elaborated these themes.[34] In 1936, Sigerist analyzed stages in the institutional development of the hospital, first evident in Europe and then rapidly recapitulated in the United States.[35] In "Historical Background of Industrial and Occupational Diseases," he keyed major works in the history of occupational medicine to the social, economic, and industrial circumstances in which they had been written.[36] He also generated considerable interest with his 1939 article "The Realities of Socialized Medicine," in which he argued that some form of socialization of medical services was imminent, as the inevitable long-term consequence of industrialization.[37] Any physician who opposed this inexorable course of worldwide development, in which medicine continuously moved from private relationship to social institution, might be competent in medical science but "knows very little about economics and sociology." [38]

At the same time, Sigerist actively developed what was to become widely influential teaching in medical sociology. After some early pedagogic experimentation at Johns Hopkins, in 1934 he announced his plan to expose Hopkins medical students to medical history first and then lead them "gradually . . . into the field of sociology." [39] By the 1935–36 academic year, now with help from the Rockefeller Foundation, the Institute's teaching included two "sociological" courses (so designated), "Social Aspects of Medicine" and a sociological seminar whose primary goal was to assist students in the preparation of original papers.[40] Sigerist also helped promote a student-initiated "Social Problems Forum" that included "The Protection of Health in the Soviet Union" (Sigerist), "The Development of Public Health Work in the Eastern Health District of Baltimore" (H. S. Mustard), and "Economic Security Against Sickness" (I. S. Falk).[41] By 1938, the Institute's teaching included a formal course, "Current Events," led by Sigerist, which included such lecures as "Cooperative Health Associations," "The Washington Group Health Association," and "The National Health Inventory of the United States Public Health Service." [42] In 1938 Sigerist also met once a week with a group of students from the School of Hygiene and Public Health for a study of "Medical Economics in the United States." [43] In 1939 he devoted his sociological seminar to "socialized medicine" and assigned twenty-eight students from the Medical School and the School of Hygiene and Public Health to report in detail on the demographic, social, economic, and health service features of Baltimore and twenty-three Maryland counties.[44] The year 1940–41 represented perhaps the peak of Sigerist's sociological teaching, with separate courses on the social aspects of medicine in historical perspective, medical economics, and current events.[45] In any event, he continued his sociological teaching throughout his tenure as director of the Institute and developed the subject most fully in his seminars.[46]

Inspired by these teaching engagements and the enthusiasm of his students, Sigerist formulated plans for an ambitious and synthetic sociological treatise. In 1938 he first publicly announced his intention to publish a "two volume Sociology of Medicine."[47] He later indicated that he would incorporate material on the economics of medicine and expand the work to four volumes.[48] In 1943 he wrote, "The plan of the *Sociology* . . . [has developed] rapidly. While it was rather hazy in the beginning, its outlines became clearer with every year. . . . The one-volume book soon developed into a four-volume plan."[49] A fragment found among Sigerist's papers hints broadly at how he planned to arrange the four volumes:

Sociology of Medicine: General Plan
1. Medicine as a Social Science
2. Health Insurance
3. State Medicine
4. Problems of Various Countries.[50]

In 1946 Sigerist published a detailed outline of a "systematic course" on the sociology and economics of medicine that provides clearer insight into how the four-volume treatise might actually have been organized.

  I. *Foundations*
     1. Structure of an industrial society
     2. The new technology of medicine
  II. *The incidence of illness*
     1. Recent changes in the incidence of illness
     2. Social distribution of illness
  III. *Supply and distribution of medical personnel and equipment*
     1. Physicians (general practitioners and specialists), dentists, nurses, technicians, etc.
     2. Hospitals, sanatoria, laboratories, etc.
     3. Public health services
     4. Industrial health services
  IV. *The costs of illness*
     1. Costs of medical care
       a. Costs of personnel (incomes of physicians, dentists, etc.)
       b. Hospital economics
       c. Costs of drugs and appliances
       d. Miscellaneous expenditures
     2. Loss of wages
     3. Capital losses through premature deaths
  V. *Methods to meet the cost of illness*
     1. Voluntary insurance
       a. Mutual benefit societies
       b. Commercial insurance

c. Private group clinics with prepayment plans

d. Cooperative health associations

e. Group hospitalization (Blue Cross)

f. Medical service plans of medical societies

g. Rural health plans under the Federal Government

2. Compulsory insurance

a. History, principles, scope

b. Groups covered

c. Benefits

d. Cost, premiums, remuneration of physicians

e. Administration

3. Public Services

a. Expansion of public health services

b. From Zemstvo to Soviet medicine

VI. *Recent trends in medical organization*

1. Group practice

2. Health centers

3. Health districts

4. Special problems of rural health services

5. Democratic control of health service

VII. *Critical summary and outlook.*[51]

While Sigerist never completed his projected sociological treatise, it seems clear what empirical material he intended it to contain. It is also clear from his publications—both essays and books—what its principal theoretical conceptions would likely have been. A few central framing notions recur frequently in Sigerist's published sociological writings:

Disease has social as well as physical, chemical, and biological causes. How income is earned is the best determinant of class position which in turn determines the occurrence of certain diseases.

The tasks assigned the physician are determined primarily by the social and economic structure of society and by the technical and scientific means available to medicine at the time.

There is an increasing tendency in modern society to liberate the physician from economic bonds, from the necessity to sell his services on the open market, a necessity that prevents him from settling where he is needed most, in poor districts, and forces him to practice where the per capita income of the population is large enough to assure him an adequate income.

The organization of medical services is a world-wide development. In some countries the process is finished and services completely organized, others are halfway in the development, and in others it is just beginning, but no country can escape the trend.[52]

One final idea completed the conceptual foundation of Sigerist's sociology. Indeed, in many ways this idea was the single most important component and the energy source for the whole system: the notion that one must not only understand how health systems have come to be and currently operate but must also work actively to usher in the future. Sigerist missed no occasion to draw lessons from history and from the comparative study of health systems that could serve as guides to contemporary action. Thus he wrote and taught in a way designed to motivate and inspire. As James Mackintosh has written, Sigerist deliberately translated social theory into social action because he was "so constituted that he could not stand aside and watch."[53] Many of his sociological books, papers, lectures, and seminars concluded with an exhortation. The reader or audience was called on to work for the attainment of better health and improved health services for the people.

Sigerist's Impact

Sigerist was a powerful force in American medicine from the early thirties to the mid-forties. Since he did not believe that his advocacy reduced the objectivity of his scholarship, he unleashed the combined power of his erudition, his insights, and his passionate call for social change on health professionals, especially a generation of students eager for inspiration and leadership, and on the public. Not all of his students at Johns Hopkins understood everything that he presented, but many of those who comprehended his central message became deeply devoted to him. He left an indelible imprint on those who saw him lecture, heard him address student meetings, or had the privilege of participating in his seminars. With his charisma, charm, energy, and good humor, he turned on sympathetic students like so many light switches. They speeded up in his presence and came to share the thrill of his ideas and his vision.

Several of Sigerist's most devoted students went on to become key figures in the fields of public health, community and preventive medicine, and health care organization. In their subsequent careers, they translated into action, on the local, national, and international level, the sorts of things that Sigerist had been most keen to develop in the sphere of medical sociology.[54] One of the authors of this essay (M. R.), for example, served as chief of the Section on Social and Occupational Health of the World Health Organization and as director of Medical and Hospital Services in the Province of Saskatchewan, Canada, before settling into an academic career at UCLA. Another author (L.A.F.) worked in the U.S. Public Health Service and was then medical administrator of the United Mine Workers of America Welfare Fund for the Pittsburgh Area, before becoming professor and chair of the Department of Community and Occupational Health at Meharry Medical College. George Silver was director of the Eastern Health District of the Baltimore City Health Department, chief of the Division of Social Medicine at Montefiore Hospital in the Bronx, New York, and deputy to the assistant secretary for health in the Department of Health, Education, and Welfare in Washington, D.C., before becoming professor of Public Health at Yale. Milton Terris punctuated an academic career in public health and preventive medicine at SUNY Buffalo and New York Medical College with a term as head of the Chronic Disease Unit, Division of Epidemiology, of the Public Health Research Institute in New York City, followed by a term as president of the American Public Health Association in 1966–67. Many hundreds, perhaps even thousands, of others took Sigerist as their most important "life's model" and, in their careers as clinicians, researchers, administrators, and teachers, worked hard to convert his general sociological principles into concrete programs and reforms.

While thus never forgotten by his faithful disciples, in the later forties and fifties Sigerist's influence was greatly diminished. This was partly due, of course, to the impact of the cold war and the McCarthy era, which had devastating effects on the promotion of progressive ideas and principles in general. Moreover, Sigerist's legacy was abandoned in the course of the specialized professional evolution of the field of medical sociology. As it developed after World War II, formal medical sociology departed more and more sharply from the area of study and advocacy Sigerist had so effectively promoted in the thirties and early forties. A chasm of incomprehension began to separate those physicians and others who vividly remembered and were still inspired by Sigerist's "medical sociology" and those Ph.D.-trained academicians who developed professional careers in the emerging subdiscipline of the same name but who had never heard of Sigerist.

The fate of Bernhard Stern was likewise indicative of changes under way in the postwar years. As we have noted, Stern was a pioneer academically trained medical sociologist. He was also an avowed Marxist who had helped found and edit the left-leaning journal *Science and Society,* to which Sigerist had contributed an essay on "Science and Democracy" in 1938.[55] Stern published prolifically in the forties, his books including *Society and Medical Progress* (1941), *American Medical Practice in the Per-*

spectives of a Century (1945), and *Medical Services by Government* (1946).[56] In the first of these he expressed his "especial appreciation" to Henry Sigerist and included a chapter "Income and Health" very consistent with Sigerist's viewpoint.[57] Stern continued to conceptualize and write in broad, economically sensitive, and politically outspoken terms, and this made his intellectual style seem increasingly anachronistic in American social science by the beginning of the fifties. Stern's separation from the mainstream, combined with his unpopular politics, extinguished his reputation as a leading medical sociologist. He did not obtain an academic post commensurate with his intellectual accomplishments and, soon after his death in 1956, was largely forgotten by the more narrowly focused practitioners of the field he had helped to found.[58]

The mainstream of 1950s medical sociology flowed in a few restricted channels.[59] One directed energy and effort to exploring the medical utilization patterns and health care practices of various segments of the population. A second focused on the professional behavior of physicians and the professionalization process of medical education. A third was concerned with the doctor-patient relationship and the organization of health care personnel and institutions. A fourth concentrated attention on the social epidemiology of mental illness and the internal working of psychiatric hospitals. What all these investigations in the mainstream had in common was their attempt to achieve "objectivity" by following the models of behavioral and/or natural science. In practice, this meant that medical sociology became increasingly "scientific" by narrowing its focus, purifying its methodology, and restricting its interpretive goals.

In the decades since the fifties, medical sociology became even more narrowly focused and increasingly decontextualized. Much of the work developed in strongly psychological and highly quantitative directions. Every effort was made to obtain subtle measurements and complicated statistical correlations, and in many cases, the collection and analysis of "neutral" quantifiable data seem to have driven the research rather than having been part of the process of answering broadly formulated questions. In short, "medical sociology" as Sigerist had conceived it was increasingly replaced by a more refined yet more limited enterprise that grew in precision but often missed the "big picture." It also became so hypervigilant about scientific validity and objectivity that it left out not only the politics but also the passion that once animated the discipline.[60] Sigerist never gave up on the direct utility of his "sociological" scholarship; mainstream medical sociology gave up on what he had stood and hoped for.

In the nineties, there are hopeful signs that Sigerist's work and his passionate commitment are being recovered. Those committed to preserving the legacy and renewing the spirit of Henry E. Sigerist should remember these lines written shortly after his death:

> almost regardless of criticism of some of his professional colleagues, he had the courage always to identify himself with what he regarded as the interests of the common people. His work in every country enriched not only historical scholarship but was directed to hastening the social application of medicine for the common good. To no master of social medicine are more people, great and humble, indebted. Henry Sigerist wrote, acted, and lived as a citizen of the world.[61]

Notes

1. Albert J. Reiss, "Sociology: The Field," in *International Encyclopedia of the Social Sciences,* vol. 15, ed. David L. Sills (New York: Macmillan Company and The Free Press, 1968), 1-23, esp. 4-6, 9-13. For other helpful works on the history of sociology, see Wolf Lepenies, *Between Literature and Science: The Rise of Sociology* (Cambridge: Cambridge University Press, 1988); Dorothy Ross, *The Origins of American Social Science* (Cambridge: Cambridge University Press, 1991); Thomas L. Haskell, *The Emergence of Professional Social Science* (Urbana: University of Illinois Press, 1977); Mary O. Furner, *Advocacy and Objectivity* (Lexington: University of Kentucky Press, 1975); Robert C. Bannister, *Sociology and Scientism* (Chapel Hill: University of North Carolina Press, 1987); Cecil E. Greek, *The Religious Origins of American Sociology* (New York: Garland Publishing, 1992).

2. George Rosen, "H. E. Sigerist, Social Historian of Medicine," *Science* 126 (1957): 551-52.

3. New York: Columbia University Press, 1927. Stern's basic theme was the lag between biomedical advance and social application as exemplified in societal resistance to medical innovation from Leonardo da Vinci's dissections in the early sixteenth century to Pasteur's bacteriological discoveries in the late nineteenth. On Stern and his unusual career, see Samuel W. Bloom and Ruth E. Zambrana, "Trends and Developments in the Sociology of Medicine," in *Advances in Medical Social Science,* vol. 1, ed. Jullio L. Ruffini (New York: Gordon and Breach, 1983), 75-76.

4. The *American Journal of Sociology* published only one article in this area in the period from 1895 to 1935. That article, "Sociology Applied to the Field of Health," appearing in vol. 28 (1922-23): 319-25, was written by Florence Meredith, M.D., professor of preventive medicine and hygiene, Woman's Medical College of Pennsylvania and lecturer in medicine, Smith College of Social Work. Dr. Meredith was primarily concerned with promoting the medical social worker as the "connecting link between individual patients and doctors . . . [and] between medical science and other forces working for human betterment." Thus her article, although published in a professional journal, used "sociology" in its broad, non-specialized sense, in which social reform advocacy and what would today be considered social work practice figured significantly. Two books published by physi-

cians earlier in the twentieth century also used "medical sociology" in Meredith's sense. One was *Essays in Medical Sociology* (1902) by pioneering woman physician Elizabeth Blackwell; the other was *Medical Sociology: A Series of Observations upon the Sociology of Health and the Relations of Medicine to Society* (1909) by the former editor of the *New York State Journal of Medicine*, James Peter Warbasse.

5. Given the institutional locus of sociological study in early twentieth-century American universities, the predominance of economists should not be surprising. As Robert Church writes, "academic sociology developed, by and large, within economics departments." Robert Church, "The Economists Study Society: Sociologists at Harvard, 1891–1902," in *Social Sciences at Harvard 1860–1920*, ed. Paul S. Buck (Cambridge: Harvard University Press, 1965), 21. Even the famous German sociologist Max Weber held an appointment in economics. See Albert Reiss, "Sociology: The Field," 12.

6. On the role of these economists and others in early twentieth-century health care discussions, see Daniel M. Fox, "From Reform to Relativism: A History of Economists and Health Care," *Milbank Memorial Fund Quarterly* 57 (1979): 297–336, esp. 302–13.

7. John Perry Miller, "Irving Fisher," *Dictionary of American Biography*, suppl. 4 (New York: Charles Scribner's Sons, 1974), 272–76. See also Irving Norton Fisher, *My Father: Irving Fisher* (New York: Comet Press, 1956).

8. New York: Appleton, 1927. On Moore, see *Who Was Who in America*, vol. 2 (Chicago: A. N. Marquis, 1950), 380.

9. The CCMC reports included titles such as the following: *The Extent of Illness and of Physical and Mental Defects Prevailing in the United States* (1929); *Hospital Service for Patients of Moderate Means* (1930); *Private Group Clinics* (1931); *Community Medical Services Organized under Industrial Auspices in Roanoke Rapids, North Carolina* (1932); *Medical Care for the American People: The Final Report of the Committee on the Costs of Medical Care* (1932).

10. S. Galishoff, "Michael Marks Davis," in *Dictionary of American Medical Biography*, eds. Martin Kaufman et al. (Westport, Conn.: Greenwood Press, 1984), vol. I, 186–87. See also *Who Was Who in America*, vol. 5 (Chicago: A. N. Marquis, 1973), 173.

11. See George Rosen, "Michael M. Davis: Pioneer in Medical Care," *American Journal of Public Health* 62 (1972): 321–23 and Ralph E. Pumphrey, "Michael Davis and the Transformation of the Boston Dispensary," *Bulletin of the History of Medicine* 49 (1975): 451–65.

12. Dorothy G. Wiehl, "Edgar Sydenstricker: A Memoir," in *The Challenge of Facts: Selected Public Health Papers of Edgar Sydenstricker*, ed. Richard V. Kasius (New York: Prodist, 1974), 3–17. See also Dorothy G. Wiehl, "Edgar Sydenstricker," *Dictionary of American Biography*, suppl. 2 (New York: Charles Scribner's Sons, 1958), 645–47, and M. Kaufman, "Edgar Sydenstricker," in *Dictionary of American Medical Biography*, eds. Martin Kaufman et al. (Westport, Conn.: Greenwood Press, 1984), vol. II, 730.

13. Milton Terris, ed., *Goldberger on Pellagra* (Baton Rouge: Louisiana State University Press, 1964) and Stephen J. Kunitz, "Hookworm and Pellagra: Exemplary Diseases in the New South," *Journal of Health and Social Behavior* 29 (1988): 144–45.

14. On Rorem, see *Who Was Who in America*, vol. 9 (Chicago: A. N. Marquis,

1989), 307; on Falk, see *Who Was Who in America,* vol. 8 (Chicago: A. N. Marquis, 1985), 132.

15. *American Medicine* was first published in German in 1933, then in an English translation by Hildegard Nagel in New York by W. W. Norton in 1934. In the Norton edition Sigerist's principal text references to the CCMC occur on pp. 187–90, and his bibliographical citations are on pp. 296–300.

16. Sigerist, *American Medicine,* 188–89.

17. Neva R. Deardorff, "Isaac Max Rubinow," *Dictionary of American Biography,* suppl. 2 (New York: Charles Scribner's Sons, 1958), 585–87. See also J. Lee Kreader, "Isaac Max Rubinow: Pioneering Specialist in Social Insurance," *Social Service Review* 50 (1976): 402–25. For Rubinow's role during the compulsory health campaign of the 1910s, see Ronald L. Numbers, *Almost Persuaded: American Physicians and Compulsory Health Insurance, 1912–1920* (Baltimore: Johns Hopkins Press, 1978), passim.

18. President Roosevelt acknowledged reading the book with "great interest"; see Kreader, "Isaac Max Rubinow," 419.

19. On Newsholme, see Arthur S. MacNalty, "Sir Arthur Newsholme," *The Dictionary of National Biography,* suppl. 6 (London: Oxford University Press, 1959), 625–26, and obituaries in *Lancet* 1 (1943): 696 and *British Medical Journal* 1 (1943): 680–81. See also John M. Eyler, "The Sick Poor and the State: Arthur Newsholme on Poverty, Disease, and Responsibility," in *Framing Disease,* eds. Charles E. Rosenberg and Janet Golden (New Brunswick: Rutgers University Press, 1992), 276–96.

20. Arthur Newsholme, *The Last Thirty Years in Public Health* (London: George Allen and Unwin, 1936), 255.

21. On Štampar, see Slobodan Lang, "A Corner of History: Andrija Štampar, 1888–1958," *Preventive Medicine* 4 (1975): 591–95; Henry van Zile Hyde, "A Tribute to Andrija Štampar," *American Journal of Public Health* 48 (1958): 1578–82; and "A Pioneer in the Balkans," *Lancet* 2 (1966): 100–101.

22. Štampar's work was published in Zagreb under the title *Socijalna Medicina.*

23. Henry Sigerist, "Yugoslavia and the Eleventh International Congress of the History of Medicine," originally published in *Bulletin of the History of Medicine* 7 (1939): 99–147. Reprinted in *Henry Sigerist on the Sociology of Medicine,* ed. Milton I. Roemer (New York: MD Publications, 1960), 89–117; these remarks are on 111–13.

24. *Lancet* 2 (1953): 576, and *American Journal of Public Health* 43 (1953): 1476–77.

25. New York: Macmillan, 1936.

26. Sand, *Health and Human Progress,* 13.

27. Originally published as "Die Sonderstellung des Kranken," *Kyklos* 2 (1929): 11–20. Reprinted in English translation in *Henry E. Sigerist on the Sociology of Medicine,* 9–22.

28. Originally published as "Der Arzt und die Umwelt," *Deutsche Medizinische Wochenschrift* 2 (1931): 1049–51. Reprinted in English translation in *Henry Sigerist on the Sociology of Medicine,* 3–8.

29. Originally published in German as *Einführung in die Medizin* (Leipzig: Georg Thieme Verlag, 1931); the English translation was published as *Man and Medicine. An Introduction to Medical Knowledge* (New York: W. W. Norton, 1932).

30. New York: W. W. Norton, 1937.

31. New Haven: Yale University Press, 1941.

32. Ithaca: Cornell University Press, 1943.

33. Originally published in *Bulletin of the New York Academy of Medicine,* 2nd series, 9 (1933): 661–76. Republished in *Henry E. Sigerist on the History of Medicine,* ed. Felix Marti-Ibañez (New York: MD Publications, 1960), 3–15.

34. Originally published in *Problems of Health Conservation* (New York: Milbank Memorial Fund, 1934), 78–83. Reprinted in *Henry E. Sigerist on the Sociology of Medicine,* 23–27.

35. Henry E. Sigerist, "An Outline of the Development of the Hospital," *Bulletin of the History of Medicine* 4 (1936): 573–81. Reprinted in *Henry E. Sigerist on Sociology of Medicine,* 319–26.

36. Originally published in *Bulletin of the New York Academy of Medicine,* 2nd series, 12 (1936): 597–609. Reprinted in *Henry E. Sigerist on the History of Medicine,* 46–56.

37. Originally published in *Atlantic Monthly* 163 (1939): 794–804. Reprinted in *Henry E. Sigerist on the Sociology of Medicine,* 180–96.

38. *Henry E. Sigerist on the Sociology of Medicine,* 193.

39. *Bulletin of the History of Medicine* 2 (1934): 408.

40. Ibid., 3 (1935): 698. For the Rockefeller Foundation's interest in and support of Sigerist's sociological teaching, see Theodore M. Brown's essay in this volume.

41. *Bulletin of the History of Medicine* 4 (1936): 606–7.

42. Ibid., 6 (1938): 863.

43. Ibid., 6 (1938): 864.

44. Ibid., 7 (1939): 854.

45. Ibid., 8 (1940): 1131 and 10 (1941): 381–86.

46. Ibid., 12 (1942): 451; 14 (1943): 263–64; 16 (1944): 205; 18 (1945): 234; 20 (1946): 382.

47. Ibid., 6 (1938): 860.

48. Ibid., 10 (1941): 373; 12 (1942): 446.

49. Ibid., 14 (1943): 253.

50. *Henry E. Sigerist on the Sociology of Medicine,* xii.

51. Sigerist, *The University at the Crossroads* (New York: Henry Schumann, 1946), 138–39.

52. These excerpts are from a longer list published by Leslie A. Falk, "Medical Sociology: The Contributions of Dr. Henry E. Sigerist," *Journal of the History of Medicine and Allied Sciences* 13 (1958): 214–28, esp. 218–21.

53. James M. Mackintosh, "Foreword. Henry Sigerist: Medical Sociologist," in *Henry E. Sigerist on the Sociology of Medicine,* viii.

54. Career synopses that follow in this paragraph are derived from entries in *Directory of Medical Specialists,* 25th ed., vol. 2 (Wilmette, Ill.: Macmillan, 1991).

55. *Science and Society* 2 (1938): 291–99.

56. Stern, *Society and Medical Progress* (Princeton: Princeton University Press, 1941); id., *American Medical Practice in the Perspectives of a Century* (New York: Commonwealth Fund, 1945); id., *Medical Services by Government: Local, State and Federal* (New York: Commonwealth Fund, 1946).

57. Stern, *Society and Medical Progress,* vii, 126–41.

58. Bloom and Zambrana, "Trends and Developments in the Sociology of Medicine," 76.

59. The generalization about the state of medical sociology contained in the remainder of this paragraph and the following one are derived primarily from Bloom and Zambrana, "Trends and Developments in the Sociology of Medicine," and Robert Straus, "The Nature and Status of Medical Sociology," *American Sociological Review* 22 (1957): 200–204.

60. For parallel observations about the closely related field of medical economics, see Daniel M. Fox, "From Reform to Relativism."

61. Milton I. Roemer, "Henry Ernest Sigerist: Internationalist of Social Medicine," *Journal of the History of Medicine and Allied Sciences* 13 (1958): 243.

CHAPTER 15

"Anything but *Amabilis*": Henry Sigerist's Impact on the History of Medicine in America

Theodore M. Brown and Elizabeth Fee

> They [Cushing, Welch, Klebs, Fulton, et al.] all belong to the Osler school of *historia amabilis*. They "had a good time" studying history. Their subjects were limited and never offensive. . . . My history is anything but *amabilis*, but is meant to be stirring, to drive people to action.[1]
>
> *August 20, 1943*

By the summer of 1943, Henry Sigerist had been devoting himself to the intellectual and organizational needs of the history of medicine in the United States for more than ten years. He had built the core program of the Johns Hopkins Institute and had cultivated efforts to raise the professional standing of the field above its largely amateur style and status. In his frequent lecture trips around the country he had encouraged numerous medical history clubs and other local activities. Sigerist continued to edit the *Bulletin of the History of Medicine,* which he had founded a decade earlier, now using it to provide a forum for the uneven efforts of the members of the American Association for the History of Medicine and its constituent societies and to set higher standards through diplomatic example. He worked closely with the association to mold it into a more inclusive yet more professional organization, simultaneously formalizing a representative structure and creating prizes and distinguished lecture-ships to reward and showcase the best work. He arranged "Graduate Weeks" at Hopkins to provide training for established and aspiring his-torians of medicine. By 1943, although he had reached a peak of success, he was also feeling trapped because the burdens of his responsibilities seemed unrelenting while the pleasure he derived from his organizational triumphs was diminishing.

Sigerist was now moving in novel directions. He was enthusiastically cultivating the new field he called medical sociology and writing about re-cent trends in the reorganization of medical care. Within medical history, his primary interest had shifted in a more sociohistorical and political di-rection. This change was perhaps most clearly seen that year in his essay "From Bismarck to Beveridge," which he intended to be the first chap-ter of a new book on social welfare legislation. He was also editing the *American Review of Soviet Medicine* and lecturing widely on Soviet medi-cine and medical care reform. Yet while engaged in these new activities, Sigerist was still bound by the requirements of his discipline-building role; as the leading historian of medicine in the country, he knew he was expected to write books and articles on more conventional topics, deliver congratulatory guest lectures, sustain the activities of the association and the flow of contributions to the *Bulletin,* review countless manuscripts, entertain constant visitors, and daily answer a mountain of mail.

Sigerist's expression of exasperation with the *amabilis* historians must be understood in the context of these divided loyalties. On one level, his statement quoted above—written in his diary and repeated in a letter to Genevieve Miller—displays his impatience with the self-congratulatory assurance of many of the genteel physician-historians. He was offended by the constriction of their vision to the heroic and the anecdotal and irri-tated with their comfortable presumption that history could be written part-time, as a hobby, to entertain or inspire. But perhaps Sigerist was aware that he had much in common with the *amabilis* historians. Like them, he saw the history of medicine as part of medicine. From his per-spective, and from theirs, the field of medical history was directed to the concerns of physicians. While calling for a more politically progressive history, Sigerist made it clear that his primary intended audience would still be medical—students, young physicians, and others in the profession. His goals for the history of medicine were essentially instrumental: to in-fluence contemporary medicine, health policy, and physicians' behavior and values. However sophisticated it became, the history of medicine was not some isolated academic discourse concerned with abstract principles of historiography; it was a guide to action.

Sigerist's dual loyalties—to professionalization and to medical relevance—are critical to understanding his impact on the history of medicine as a scholarly endeavor in the United States. They do much to explain his initial recruitment to the directorship of the Institute, provide the key to his actual successes and failures, and yield insights about his relationship to the development of the field during his sojourn in America.

Before Sigerist: The History of Medicine in the United States

When Sigerist arrived in the United States, interest in the history of medicine was already longstanding, widespread, and lively. The subject had been studied and taught for at least a century, going back to Robley Dunglison's lectures at the University of Virginia in the late 1820s.[2] Since the late eighteenth century and continuing into the early nineteenth century, a number of physicians had published local and general accounts of the history of medicine—mainly as a way of establishing their particular orientation to contemporary medical issues.[3] In the same period, physician-historians had also published biographical dictionaries, histories of epidemic disease, and surveys of ancient texts.[4] In 1854, the catalogue of Penn Medical University explained that it offered medical history as a means of elevating the social standing of physicians and for "the scientific dignity and self-possession it gives to the physician in his intercourse with the erudite portion of the community who naturally look down upon any physician as being an ignoramus, who does not know the history of his own profession."[5] As Genevieve Miller notes, "many professional leaders in all parts of the country became bibliophiles, as book collecting came to be equated with gentility."[6] In the latter part of the nineteenth century, medical men published translations of European works on medical history, general histories based on European sources, and even some critical reviews of American medical developments.[7] In the 1890s, a number of medical schools introduced courses of lectures in the history of medicine.[8]

John Shaw Billings, the organizer of the Surgeon General's Library and the compiler of the *Index Medicus* and the *Index-Catalogue of the Surgeon General's Library*, was the person most directly responsible for bringing the high standards of European scholarship in the history of medicine to the United States. In 1876, he had been appointed Lecturer in the history and literature of medicine at Johns Hopkins University; he was sufficiently familiar with the primary sources and scholarly literature to feel comfortable criticizing contemporary European scholars on the basis of his own careful reading of the original texts.[9] Lecturing in his first year of teaching to about fifty students, he presented a sophisticated approach to the historiography of medicine, insisting that medicine could not be understood in isolation from general culture. In 1887 he explained: "To attempt to isolate the history of medicine, and to comprehend its curious ebbs and flows of doctrine, from medical writings only, is like cutting a narrow strip from the centre of a piece of tapestry and speculating upon the origin and purpose of the cut threads and fragments of patterns that may be found in it." [10]

The most vividly remembered and influential teacher of the history of medicine in the early years at Johns Hopkins was not Billings, however, but the charismatic professor of medicine, William Osler, known to many simply as "the Chief." Osler, an enthusiast for the history of medicine, rejected arguments that the field needed to be taught as a separate subject; instead, it should be integrated into clinical teaching. On the wards and in the outpatient departments, Osler would frequently touch on the historical aspects of the medical topic under review; he invited his fourth-year students, two at a time, to his home for dinner, showed them first editions, read a paragraph or two, and talked about cultural themes.[11] His clinical teaching was suffused with a historical sensibility. With William Henry Welch, Howard Kelly, and some thirty other Hopkins doctors, Osler founded the Johns Hopkins Hospital Historical Club in 1890. The club quickly became an important element in the life of the medical institutions, a place where students could listen to historical lectures by eminent medical men.[12] According to Eugene Fauntleroy Cordell, a contemporary at the University of Maryland, the club "exercised a profound influence not only locally, but throughout the entire country. . . . there are few who have any claims to distinction in this field in the United States who have not been its guests." [13]

The principal appeal of medical history to Osler and his Hopkins colleagues and to many other physician enthusiasts was its integrative and inspirational potential. Osler's history was infused with a deep sense of the timeless virtue and high calling of the medical profession. As Philip Teigen argues, "the profession" served as his central integrative concept, and he frequently emphasized "its noble ancestry, its remarkable solidarity, its progressive character, and its singular benevolence." [14] Looking in the mirror of the history of medicine, physicians could be inspired by the exertions and triumphs of their heroic forbears.

Many less famous physician-historians also subscribed to the Oslerian faith. As Cordell explained, medical history could provide the "high ideals and the inspiration that come from a contemplation of the examples, the lives, the achievements, of the great men of the past." He regretted the contemporary materialist emphasis on money and asserted that exposure to medical history would help physicians resist the downward slide to "mere mechanical work that looks at nothing beyond gain." [15] In a similar vein, Lewis S. Pilcher, a noted surgeon, would later describe medical history as "an antitoxin for medical commercialism." [16]

When Osler left the United States in 1905 to become Regius Professor of Medicine at Oxford, interest in the history of medicine continued to grow and his influence remained dominant. New medical history clubs were created in Philadelphia, Chicago, New York, and Boston, the latter two drawing 75 and 125 members to their inaugural meetings. [17] Charles N. B. Camac, one of Osler's house officers, published the first American medical history source book in 1909. [18] The most influential medicohistorical publication, however, was Fielding H. Garrison's *Introduction to the History of Medicine,* first published in 1913. [19] Garrison, a junior colleague and successor to John Shaw Billings, spent most of his career at the Library of the Surgeon-General's Office, now the National Library of Medicine. Here he exhibited "prodigious industry," gradually collecting the materials for a single-volume survey of the history of medicine from "primitive" medicine to the present.

For Garrison, medical biography was the essence of medical history; as Henry Viets admiringly described his *Introduction:* "The bare outlines of events are interspersed with exquisite, thumbnail biographies of physicians. . . . A few words, a brief characterization, a penetrating analysis, and the man stands before us as clear as his portrait." [20] F. N. L. Poynter described Garrison's book as "a well-ordered survey of a vast quantity of documentary material, each item of which he had himself examined, catalogued and studied." [21]

Garrison's text became an essential reference point for the history of medicine. It provided an accumulation of useful information and served as a handy outline accessible to the average physician, student, librarian, or bookseller. It quickly became the standard work in the field: used in medical schools as a textbook, kept on the shelves of all medical libraries, and referred to in the historical preambles of innumerable medical case reports. [22] The availability of Garrison's text made it easier to offer lecture courses in the history of medicine, and courses were introduced at Harvard and the Universities of Pittsburgh, Oregon, San Francisco, Chicago, and Washington. [23]

Several new journals were now established to publish papers in the history of medicine. Most were ephemeral, like *The Medical Pickwick: A Monthly Magazine of Wit and Wisdom* and *The Aesculapian.* One of the more successful and relatively long-lived was *Medical Life,* published by Victor Robinson. Robinson (born Victor Rabinowitz) built his career as a medical editor, publisher, and historian but was initially better known as the author of such works as *Comrade Kropotkin, An Essay on Hasheesh,* and *Pioneers of Birth Control*—radical interests that made their way into the pages of *Medical Life* alongside more conventional topics such as the serialized *Life of Jacob Henle.*[24] The journal promoted itself as the official organ of "The American Society of Medical History," an apparently informal group of like-minded friends who met on occasion in New York City and were presumably open to a wider variety of opinion than the more conservative physicians of the Oslerian school. The group identified with *Medical Life* was clearly interested in European scholarship on the history of medicine, and Robinson counted among the members of his international editorial board such luminaries as Arturo Castiglioni, Max Neuburger, Karl Sudhoff, and Henry Sigerist. For a memorial volume to mark the occasion of Robinson's sixtieth birthday, Castiglioni and Sigerist both noted that *Medical Life,* by translating their work, had provided their first opportunities to address an American audience.[25] Robinson's Froben Press published volumes of collected essays by Max Neuburger and Karl Sudhoff, in addition to many of Robinson's own works.[26] Sigerist wrote that he had been surprised, on his arrival in America, to find that Robinson was not given the credit he deserved within medical history circles: "Medical history in those days was a somewhat aristocratic and restricted subject and you had written a book on such a wicked man as Kropotkin, an anarchist like Sacco and Vanzetti. You were a fighter and reformer, interested in a number of subjects that were not looked upon as orthodox."[27]

Under Robinson's leadership, *Medical Life* was a lively and eccentric publication, combining outspoken political views, progressive attitudes toward sexuality, translations of leading European historical scholars, discussions of balneology and the philosophy of history, biographies of Jewish physicians, and a liberal helping of advertisements for spas, nutritional supplements, mineral waters, medical products, and appliances.

By contrast, *Annals of Medical History,* founded in 1917, and edited by Francis R. Packard, declared that it would be maintained "on the highest plane."[28] As the editor later explained: "no advertisements swelled its bulk or marred its beauty, and there were no vulgar facetiae to derogate from its dignity."[29] The journal was legitimated by the presence of Fielding Garrison and Charles Singer, the leading American and English historians of medicine, among the associate editors; otherwise, the journal was Oslerian in style and content and aimed to represent the high cultural aspirations of the medical profession. Osler himself—now Sir William Osler at Oxford—was an associate editor; all eleven of the other original associate editors were Osler's well-placed American friends, students, or colleagues. Among them were such leading clinicians as George Dock, Charles Dana, Abraham Jacobi, Howard Kelly, and Harvey Cushing. The publisher, Paul B. Hoeber, had earlier reprinted the English medical classic *The Gold-Headed Cane,* which was reviewed in the *Annals* as conveying "the best traditions of Anglo-Saxon medicine."[30] Hoeber's medical bookstore and collection of rare medical books was known as a rendezvous for "the local collecting fraternity," many of whom were recruited as associate editors.

In keeping with their high-toned intentions, the *Annals* editors were proud of its large pages, beautiful illustrations, and typographical elegance, and recommended that physicians might place copies in their waiting rooms as "attractive reading for the cultured layman as well as for the doctor."[31] Although the journal was devoted to "the cultural aspects of medicine" and aimed at a display of learning, excessive erudition was not expected. As one of the associate editors commented in his review of Henry Sigerist's edition of the letters of Albrecht von Haller to Johannes Gesner: "it is to be regretted that the erudite editor has not translated the letters, as there are few physicians, and the reviewer is not one of them, who remember their Latin well enough to read the book with pleasure or satisfaction."[32]

As the valedictory number of the *Annals* in 1942 summarized its contributions:

> From its opening article . . . this periodical has maintained a high and constantly uniformly dignified level of usefulness, much authoritative material of scientific value appearing in its columns, together with much that was of cultural or entertaining value to other elements of its clientele, and a few perhaps trivial, but never cheap or undignified contributions.[33]

The author of this tribute, Edward Krumbhaar, was an associate editor of the *Annals* and a founding member of the American Association for the History of Medicine. Several members of the Oslerian circle, gathered at the College of Physicians of Philadelphia, had started the association in 1924. The next year, this group called a meeting attended by about thirty of the prominent medical men assembled in Washington, D.C., for the Congress of American Physicians and Surgeons. At subsequent meetings, a few historical papers were presented, followed by a dinner at which "non-members including ladies" were welcome.[34] For the most part, attendance at these history of medicine sessions was restricted to those already assembled in Atlantic City for the annual meetings of the elite Association of American Physicians. Contributors in these early days included Harvey Cushing, William Henry Welch, Charles N. B. Camac, and Lewellys F. Barker—Osler's successor as professor of medicine at Hopkins. Scholarly publication was not a requirement, although Krumbhaar notes that "any essayists who wanted to publish their efforts could always be accommodated, generally by our fellow member, Francis R. Packard."[35]

In these years, however, the most interesting developments in the history of medicine were taking place in Baltimore. William Henry Welch, like many other medical leaders in the 1920s, was concerned that the increasing scientific and technological sophistication of medicine was leading to the fragmentation of a once unified profession. Physicians, he warned, could become mere technicians, specialists in a narrow field but "devoid of the intellectual, cultural background so necessary for broadening the physician's influence."[36] To counter these centrifugal tendencies, he urged the creation of a central library within the Johns Hopkins Medical Institutions, where investigators and clinicians could come together in a unified intellectual atmosphere.[37] As a capstone to the library, Welch suggested the creation of a chair in the history of medicine. Teaching in the history of medicine would provide the "human note" needed to "make the physician a gentleman of culture."[38]

The Welch Medical Library at Johns Hopkins was funded by the General Education Board of the Rockefeller philanthropies. Welch, rejecting the board's offer of a chair, proposed Fielding H. Garrison as the first professor of the history of medicine. "For me to take such a chair at my age," Welch explained, "would merely emphasize the spirit of dilettantism in which the subject is regarded and pursued generally in this country."[39] The General Education Board, however, countered that its grant was conditional upon Welch's acceptance of the position. Welch was now in a difficult situation. He had always insisted that the men selected for Hopkins professorships have the most demanding professional training, and he clearly recognized that he was himself only an amateur historian. Although eventually "yielding on the matter of scholarly competence," as Donald Fleming notes, Welch "always kept before him the two objects of laying a proper foundation for rigorous work and quickly finding a successor more fit than himself to build upon it."[40]

When looking for professional talent and high scholarly standards, Welch usually turned to Europe. On an extended European trip, he bought books for the library, familiarized himself with professional scholarship in the history of medicine, and visited its most prominent representatives.[41] He went to the University of Leipzig, where two decades before, Karl Sudhoff had established the world's first institute of the history of medicine. Although still actively at work, Sudhoff was formally retired, his place as director now filled by his young protégé, Henry Sigerist. Welch was deeply impressed by the scale and scholarly productivity of the Institute and returned to Baltimore with an expanded vision: instead of a single chair, he would build a fully staffed institute like Sudhoff's.

Welch was still somewhat ambivalent about the primary mission of the professor to be appointed in the history of medicine: was this individual to teach and inspire medical students and imbue them with a cultural antidote to narrow specialization or should he be viewed as the chief researcher leading a team of specialized scholars? When the library and Institute were dedicated in 1929, Welch expressed this ambivalence by inviting two major speakers.[42] To open the Institute, he chose Karl Sudhoff, as the embodiment of the disinterested German scholarly ideal; a man of broad learning, with decades of experience in archival and philological research. To open the library, he selected Harvey Cushing, a distinguished surgeon, an inspirational medical teacher, Osler's Pulitzer Prize–winning biographer, and the leading representative of the Oslerian historical tradition in America. Each man spoke in characteristic terms: Sudhoff emphasized the importance of painstaking scholarly work, while Cushing warned against creating yet another group of specialists and hoped that a leader of the right personality could bring the "scattered and subdivided" profession out of "the wilderness and again bind it together."[43]

Torn between these two views in choosing his successor, Welch first argued that scholarship was the most essential requirement for the position. He thus offered the post to Charles Singer, a physician-scholar. When Singer declined, Welch reversed himself and now declared that what was needed was not a scholar but "a leader and inspiring lecturer; a man who would interest the medical students and younger members of the faculty."[44] He thus proposed Harvey Cushing for the professorship. When Cushing vacillated and ultimately declined, saying "I am not a historian and never will be,"[45] Welch again reversed himself, declared that the position required a recognized scholar and, with Cushing's blessing, offered the position to Sudhoff's Leipzig successor, Henry Sigerist.

Sigerist Takes Over

Although Sigerist combined the virtues of Cushing and Sudhoff in being both an inspirational teacher and a superb scholar, his primary mission at the Hopkins Institute was clearly to establish a beachhead of German scholarship in America.[46] He was already well aware of the amateur status of the history of medicine as practiced in America and was committed to transforming it in the image of the more professional European model. In a survey of medical history teaching, undertaken in 1927 and published in English in 1929, Sigerist had noted that most European countries had established chairs in medical history, and Germany had eleven specialized academic appointments: "there is, perhaps, in no other land such an interest in medico-historical studies as in Germany. From all sides young physicians crowd the few institutes to receive their medical historical education."[47] By contrast, in the United States, "medico-historical education is still a matter of chance."[48] Other than at Johns Hopkins, medical history was taught "chiefly unofficially" by medical school professors at the University of Maryland, the University of California at Berkeley, Harvard University, Northwestern University, the University of Wisconsin, Cornell University, the University of Pennsylvania, and Washington University.[49] In other words, medical history was not considered a true academic specialty but the avocation of some self-selected professors from the medical or clinical sciences. Undaunted, Sigerist recognized the opportunity presented in America. He wrote—in private—of the Johns Hopkins Institute in early 1932: "The Institute is a superb instrument which has only to be tuned and played. Then the Old Ladies Home will amount to something."[50]

Sigerist's first task was to build a professional Institute staff. He had inherited several staff members recruited by Welch: Fielding Garrison served as head of the library as well as lecturer in the history of medicine, and John Rathbone Oliver, a popular teacher of the history of medicine at the University of Maryland, offered a course of lectures at Hopkins. Sigerist wanted to add several accomplished European scholars and had obtained a guarantee that he could bring his *Privatdozent,* Owsei Temkin, from Leipzig to Baltimore. Temkin, who had a full command of Greek, Latin, Arabic, and Hebrew, in addition to several modern languages, was an exemplar of the kind of scholar Sigerist hoped to nurture and reproduce. He was delighted in early 1934 when he was able to bring another German scholar, Ludwig Edelstein, to the Institute, saying that his ar-

44. Sigerist, standing beneath a portrait of Karl Sudhoff, in his office at the Johns Hopkins Institute of the History of Medicine.

rival meant that "the Institute will rest on the solid basis of German philology."[51]

To set a high standard of scholarly research and showcase the work of the Institute staff members, Sigerist began in 1933 to publish the *Bulletin of the Institute of the History of Medicine* as a special supplement of the *Bulletin of the Johns Hopkins Hospital*. The first issue carried Temkin's article "The Doctrine of Epilepsy in the Hippocratic Writings" and Garrison's hundred-page bibliography of the history of medicine.[52] This issue established a high scholarly standard, typified by the daunting methodological dictum with which Temkin began his article: "The purpose of the following study is to analyze all the [relevant] passages in the writing of the Hippocratic collection . . . making use of philological methods where these are necessary for the understanding of the original meaning."[53]

Subsequent issues of the *Bulletin* identified it even more clearly with the German scholarly tradition. The next volume included five papers in celebration of Karl Sudhoff's eightieth birthday. Each member of the Institute staff contributed a paper on some aspect of Sudhoff's work—as historian, bibliographer, philologist, medievalist, and rediscoverer of Paracelsus.[54]

Sigerist implied that he had been personally chosen to inherit Sudhoff's mantle of medieval scholarship: his account of his own research agenda and summer's research in Italy began with a long and dramatic retelling of his first meetings with Sudhoff.[55] He reinforced this identification by publishing a photograph of himself with Leica camera and bound volumes of manuscripts: a working medievalist in Sudhoff's image (see fig. 34).

In his diary for June 1934, Sigerist reflected with satisfaction on his accomplishment in establishing the *Bulletin:* "It has a definite function in the country—to publish the results of original research, to propagate medical history not as a hobby but as a science, a historical discipline."[56] To his readers, he explained, more tactfully: "All papers that bring new facts, the results of new investigations or new interpretations of known facts are welcome. . . . I want the Bulletin to be scholarly but not dry."[57]

In 1934, Sigerist's friend, mentor, and protector, William Henry Welch, died. Sigerist immediately realized that Welch's death removed a living guarantor of his American legitimacy. He now wrapped himself in the mantle of Welch, just as he had earlier surrounded himself with the aura of Sudhoff. He began the first issue of the *Bulletin* for 1935 by publishing an address that Welch had previously given on the history of pathology.[58] At the same time, he announced he would start reprinting an "Old Hopkins Picture" in each number of the *Bulletin.* The first one he chose was a photograph of the Hopkins graduating class of 1897, surrounding a be-whiskered Welch and accompanied by their dog, "Popsy." The second "Old Hopkins Picture" showed Sir William Osler in his office at the Hopkins Hospital in 1890. Subsequent pictures displayed Welch's place of work, the old pathology building; a group of Hopkins interns proudly framing "The Chief"; Welch astride a mule in China in 1915; and, as the crowning glory, an artist's sketch of a winged William Osler, radiating light and hovering on a cloud atop the Johns Hopkins dome, the image entitled: "The Saint—Johns Hopkins Hospital." In the English-language edition of *The Great Doctors,* Sigerist added an admiring new biography of Osler and emphasized the significance of Johns Hopkins as the pinnacle of American medicine.[59] By the end of 1935, he had clearly surrounded himself and his *Bulletin* with the iconography of the Hopkins medical greats.

Sigerist now began to follow a new strategy of inclusion, reaching out beyond the halls of Hopkins to court the allegiance of medical historians throughout the country. Although his first reports in the *Bulletin* of "Medical-Historical Activities in the United States" recounted only the doings of the Hopkins faculty, in later 1935 issues, he extended his cov-

45. "Saint Osler," printed in the *Bulletin* for 1935 as "Old Hopkins Picture No. 10."

erage to include accounts of the meetings of the Charleston Medical History Club of South Carolina, the Medical History Club of Honolulu, and the Innominate Society of Louisville, Kentucky.[60] In 1936, he presented medicohistorical news from Washington, D.C.; New Orleans; Chapel Hill, North Carolina; Nashville, Tennessee; New Haven, Connecticut; Cleveland; Philadelphia; Iowa City; and New York City. He also published the wildly eclectic program of the twelfth annual meeting of the American Association for the History of Medicine in Atlantic City. Half of the ten papers were presented by members of the Hopkins faculty, and the others belonged to what Sigerist termed the *"amabilis"* school of medical history. Thus, while Ludwig Edelstein delivered a paper "Greek Medicine in Relation to Religion," Louis H. Clerf presented "Historical Notes on Foreign Bodies in the Food and Air Passages," Owsei Temkin presented "Haller's Scientific Controversies," and Howard Dittrick entertained the group with a lantern-slide presentation, "Some Old Hospitals in Spain." [61]

In public, Sigerist was gracious, welcoming the amateur historians, contributing to their programs, and publishing accounts of their meetings. He first cultivated their friendship and later tried to raise their standards of scholarship through gentle encouragement. In 1937, Sigerist was elected president of the Association of the History of Medicine, clear indication of his acceptance by the majority of historically minded physicians. In private, however, he was less complimentary about his colleagues. In 1937, he noted in his diary, "Meeting of the American Association for the History of Medicine over which I had to preside. Many papers, some good, some poor. The society must be reorganized from the bottom. The way it is now it cannot live and cannot die." [62]

Part of Sigerist's strategy was to focus on the teaching of medical history as a way of bridging the interests of amateur medical historians and professional scholars. Thus, his presidential address to the American Association for the History of Medicine in 1937 presented a broad proposal for the future teaching of the history of medicine in America.[63] Laying aside any contentious current questions about the quality of historical research and publication, Sigerist appealed to the authority of medical leaders—Billings, Halsted, Kelly, Osler, and Welch—to argue for the utility of medical history in turning "mere technicians" into "highly cultured personalities." [64] Medical students, he claimed, were themselves demanding instruction in the history of medicine. He had surveyed the deans of seventy-seven medical schools and discovered that some fifty-four (70 percent) provided lectures or courses in the history of medicine although, for the most part, medical history teaching was still a voluntary activity undertaken by professors of anatomy, surgery, or internal medicine.

Sigerist was careful to praise the Oslerian approach of integrating references to medical history, personalities, and original sources into clinical teaching. At the same time, he suggested, such instruction did not obviate the need for systematic courses in medical history, to give the student "a continuous picture of the development of medicine, and to make him realize where we came from, at what point we are standing today, and what our coming tasks will be."[65] In addition to basic lecture courses giving students a clear orientation to the history of their profession, more advanced training in medical history should be available to students desiring specialized instruction and should be provided by persons familiar with the appropriate research methods.

Sigerist then laid out an ambitious plan for the extension and upgrading of medical history instruction, with himself and the Johns Hopkins Institute at the hub of a national network. The Institute would provide postgraduate courses and serve as a "center of information" for the whole country. Other regional universities could develop medical history departments to serve as centers for instruction within their geographic area. Gradually, as those responsible for teaching medical history had ready access to expert sources of information, the standards of teaching across the country would improve.[66]

With a similar sense of purpose, Sigerist began to transform the American Association for the History of Medicine into a professional organization. As secretary in 1938–39, he was instrumental in the adoption of a dramatically new constitution and bylaws, to go into effect in January 1939.[67] The new constitution strengthened the association and enlarged its membership by including constituent societies in a new category of corporate membership. Any organization—a society, institute, or library—having a purpose similar to that of the association was eligible to be voted a constituent society. In one move, Sigerist brought all local medical history clubs and societies under the umbrella of the association and implicitly encouraged new ones to form. No longer a small and self-selected club, the governing council now included the association's officers, past presidents, and delegates from each of the constituent societies. Sigerist assured local societies that they would benefit by publishing their annual reports in the *Bulletin* and by being kept informed about events around the country.[68] Constituent societies were asked to encourage their members to join the association as individuals, and a newly effective system of collecting dues increased the organization's treasury.

Sigerist used the *Bulletin of the History of Medicine* to consolidate the new federated organization of the association. Effective in January 1939, he made the *Bulletin of the History of Medicine* the official organ of both the American Association for the History of Medicine and the Johns Hopkins Institute, changing its name to reflect the new status.[69] The association agreed to pay the Institute four dollars of the five-dollar individual membership dues and six dollars of the ten-dollar constituent society dues for publishing the *Bulletin*.[70] With one step, Sigerist thus solved the financial problems of the *Bulletin* and obtained a stable readership; the association gained a journal, and the *Bulletin* published every paper presented at the annual association meetings.

Sigerist was simultaneously director of the Institute, editor of the *Bulletin,* and secretary of the association and was extremely effective in all three positions. The association grew rapidly: in 1926, it had 62 members, and in 1939, 328 members. Sigerist proposed "an effort to increase our membership planfully" to 500 members in 1940, increasing by at least 50 new members each year until reaching 800 members, which he considered "not too ambitious a figure considering the large number of physicians in this country."[71] In fact, membership climbed to 450 in 1943, dipped just after the war, and then climbed again to around 500 by the end of the decade.

When the association as a gentleman's club had been drifting, Sigerist had taken control. He now instituted ways of recognizing promising young scholars, upgrading standards, and rewarding long-term contributions. He established the annual Fielding H. Garrison lecture and the William Osler medal, the latter presented for the best essay written by a medical student. Arturo Castiglioni, George Sarton, and Francis Packard were the first three Garrison lecturers selected; two were recognized scholars and the third, a well-known representative of the Oslerian circle.

To exemplify the highest standards of scholarship, Sigerist encouraged his Hopkins staff to give papers at the annual meetings of the association. With regard to the other papers, the fact that publication implied the possibility of critical scrutiny doubtless served as a goad to greater rigor. Following the prescription of his 1937 presidential address, Sigerist then instituted a form of continuing education for recognized and aspiring historians of medicine. At the "Graduate Weeks" organized at Johns Hopkins in 1938 and 1939, participants joined in an intensive week-long program of lectures, seminars, exhibitions, and entertainments provided by the Institute staff.[72] These carefully prepared programs helped establish the Hopkins Institute as the central reference point for the history of medicine.

By taking control of the American Association for the History of Medicine (AAHM) and installing the *Bulletin* as its official publication, Sigerist effectively coopted all competition and hastened the decline and demise of rival journals. *Medical Life* ceased publication in 1939; its editor, Victor Robinson, became an enthusiastic participant in the 1938 Graduate Week, the New York Society for Medical History's representative on the council of the association, a contributor to the AAHM program, and a *Bulletin* author. The *Annals of Medical History* folded in 1942, in part because of the deaths of several leaders of the *amabilis* school—Harvey Cushing, Charles Camac, and David Riesman—but also because it had lost a major part of its mission. The papers once placed in the *Annals* were now automatically being published in the *Bulletin*. In the same year that the *Annals* suspended publication, its editor, Francis Packard, delivered the Garrison lecture, which was duly printed in the *Bulletin*.[73]

Triumph and Transition

Sigerist had succeeded in gaining almost singular control of the history of medicine in America, but he found there were unintended consequences of success. He had accepted responsibility for publishing all papers presented at the AAHM, all reports of constituent societies, and all details of their business transactions, the total amounting annually to hundreds of pages. The *Bulletin* thus swelled to impossibly bloated dimensions. The 1940 issue, for example, amounted to 1,415 pages of text. In 1941, Sigerist said he was "terrified" to realize that the *Bulletin* had tripled in size within eight years and concluded that "Much to my regret I am obliged not only to stop the growth of the *Bulletin* but to reduce its size to about 1200 pages a year."[74] Unwilling to offend the rank and file of the AAHM by judging the quality of their submissions, Sigerist suggested that authors not submit seriatim chapters of forthcoming books or lengthy annotated bibliographies. The latter comments were clearly directed at the gentlemen-amateurs: "With many people bibliography has become a game, a very fascinating and an expensive one. There is no objection to games as long as the players bear the costs of their entertainment . . . in the future, I must refuse to publish fanciful bibliographies."[75]

Sigerist was beginning to lose enthusiasm for his self-appointed task of organizing and upgrading the field. While feeling constrained to limit the growth of the *Bulletin,* he also expressed declining interest in organizing the Institute's major postgraduate program. In 1941, aware that he had just passed his fiftieth birthday and his twentieth year in the United States, Sigerist confessed that he had "no inspiration" for conducting more Graduate Weeks. He apologized that despite the demand for more postgraduate courses, he had canceled plans for that year: "There is nothing that I am more afraid of than setting a pattern or establishing a routine and then having it followed by the mere force of inertia." [76]

Sigerist was deeply troubled about the outbreak of war and its potential implications for scholarship. Insisting that historical work must continue and that cultural contributions were even more urgently needed at times of national and international crisis, he noted that students—despite an accelerated curriculum—were eager for history of medicine courses because they felt themselves in the midst of a "gigantic historical process" they wanted to understand. [77] Sigerist reported that in spite of the war mobilization, the membership of the AAHM was climbing and that "the majority of our members in active service continued to pay dues and asked to have our journal sent to their army camps." [78]

The war also presented an opportunity to solve some of his administrative problems. Paper was now a scarce wartime commodity; Sigerist was forced, as a patriotic duty, to limit both the number of pages and number of issues of the *Bulletin.* At the same time, he was relieved of the obligation for publishing the wearying transactions of the association because, from 1943 to 1946, the AAHM suspended its annual meetings and conducted its minimum essential business in radically abbreviated executive sessions. Sigerist had considerably more draft material than room to print it, and he was free to select the papers he wanted to publish. Thanks to the war, he had achieved editorial control. The quality of the *Bulletin* improved dramatically.

Sigerist now published more papers by his staff and other scholars whose careers he wished to promote. Although Owsei Temkin was burdened with war-related responsibilities, he was able to finish his definitive study of epilepsy, *The Falling Sickness,* and to produce several other papers. [79] Ludwig Edelstein wrote a major monograph on the Hippocratic oath, published as the first supplement to the *Bulletin* in 1943. While Edelstein and his wife Emma were correcting the proofs of their path-breaking scholarly work on the Asclepian cult, he also prepared several papers for the *Bulletin.* [80] Genevieve Miller, who had started as a graduate student, now became Sigerist's research secretary and a full member of the staff, editing a series of bibliographies on the history of American medicine and, in 1944, being appointed the *Bulletin*'s associate editor. Emerging as the Institute's specialist in American medicine, Miller published editions of William Beaumont's early notebooks, Benjamin McCready's history of occupational diseases, and several papers on American medical history.[81]

Sigerist was able to add new scholars to the Institute staff. In 1941, a fellowship from the Carnegie Corporation allowed him to provide a two-year stipend for Israel Drabkin, a historian of ancient science. Drabkin came to the Institute with his wife, Miriam, who was also a scholar of note. While Israel started work on his translation of Caelius Aurelianus's book on acute and chronic diseases, Miriam published several papers in the *Bulletin* on ancient and medieval medicine.[82] Sigerist was delighted to add Erwin Ackerknecht to the Institute staff in January 1942. Ackerknecht, who as Sigerist's student in Leipzig had written a brilliant thesis on the German medical reform movement of 1848, was a leading European scholar with an interesting political past.[83] In addition to working on medicine and history in Germany, he had studied social anthropology at the University of Paris before emigrating to the United States. As an Institute fellow, he immediately became one of its most productive and prolific members.[84] His papers and monographs on the social and psychological aspects of "primitive" medicine were remarkable for their range and sophisticated use of history, ethnology, and psychiatry. His study of malaria in the Upper Mississippi Valley presented surprising epidemiologically based findings that medical therapies had little impact on the history of the disease.[85] When Ackerknecht left the Institute in 1945 for a position at the Museum of Natural History in New York City, Sigerist described as "irreparable" the loss of this "mature and original scholar at the height of his productivity."[86]

In 1944, Sigerist admitted his first and only successful Ph.D. student, Ilza Veith. Veith, another European scholar, had studied medicine in Switzerland and Austria and was developing as a specialist in the history of Chinese medicine.[87] Her thesis was a translation of the ancient text known as *The Yellow Emperor's Classic of Internal Medicine,* published in 1949.[88] Veith's interest in oriental medicine added new breadth to the Institute. Sigerist had consistently promoted this field, starting with the appointment of Edward H. Hume, formerly dean of the Hunan-Yale College of Medicine, as lecturer in 1938. Sigerist noted with considerable pride that, together, the Institute staff could handle texts in at least sixteen languages.[89]

Sigerist also cultivated promising young scholars such as Milton Roemer, Milton Terris, and George Rosen, adding them to his stable of regular contributors to the *Bulletin*. He first met Roemer at a New York gathering of progressive young doctors and encouraged his interests in medical history and social medicine. Roemer published several articles in the *Bulletin* and was to become a lifelong friend and admirer, shaping much of his future career on Sigerist's ideals.[90] Terris was a student at the Hopkins School of Hygiene and Public Health when he met Sigerist, who was quick to publish his fine seminar paper in the *Bulletin,* thus beginning a long friendship.[91] George Rosen first contacted Sigerist when, as an American medical student studying in Germany, he was looking for a medicohistorical thesis topic. On his return to the United States, Rosen became a constant correspondent, frequent visitor, and prolific author, publishing a steady stream of articles in the *Bulletin* and elsewhere, as well as an impressive number of books and monographs.[92] Taking Sigerist as the central reference point for his life and career, he continued to publish significant work in the history of medicine and public health while holding a series of prominent positions in public health and health education; he would later become professor of the history of medicine and public health at Yale.[93]

In 1943, when Sigerist started publishing book reviews in the *Bulletin,* he carefully chose the books to be reviewed and the reviewers; only a select few were allowed this privilege. These penetrating and critical reviews, published in the main by Ackerknecht, Temkin, Edelstein, Rosen, Drabkin, Miller, and Veith, embodied the new scholarly standards he now had an opportunity to enforce.[94] Sigerist also held out the rewards of inclusion and recognition to a coterie of especially favored scholars whose articles he regularly published: the eminent Europeans Max Neuburger and Walter Pagel, the distinguished Americans Loren MacKinney and Lynn Thorndike, and promising newcomers such as Saul Jarcho and Whitfield Bell. These, together with the Institute circle, all belonged to the cadre of — in effect — "professional" historians of medicine. For these few years, Sigerist was able to stimulate and then shape their work into impressive displays of scholarship. He reflected on the *Bulletin* for 1943 with satisfaction: "we published several numbers which I think were rather attractive. Thus the February number . . . was entirely devoted to English medicine and medicine in English literature. The April number . . . dealing with the history of public health and social medicine, and in May we had an American number. . . . we plan an issue that will commemorate Vesalius and his *Fabrica*. . . . All in all, I think the *Bulletin* has improved."[95]

Whatever gratification Sigerist justifiably derived from the *Bulletin* for 1943, and for 1944 and 1945 as well, in 1946 he again faced the prospect of losing his hard-won editorial control. In May of that year, the American Association for the History of Medicine resumed its annual meetings, and its members presented a series of papers which Sigerist was obliged to publish. He was therefore delighted to welcome a new journal, the *Journal of the History of Medicine and Allied Sciences*, edited by George Rosen. Sigerist hailed the new publication with enthusiasm and relief: "When a child is born the world rejoices. And when a child is born after years of death and destruction, the creation of a new life appears like a miracle, like a great promise, and the joy we feel over it is the deeper."[96]

Sigerist described Rosen as a man of "progressive attitude," "tremendous working capacity," and "undoubtedly ... one of the most able medical historians of the younger generation." He declared that together, the *Bulletin* and the *Journal* would promote research and interest in the history of medicine; they would not compete but would "supplement one another in the happiest way."[97] Rosen echoed these sentiments in his editorial for the first number of the *Journal* and added: "We do not want to cultivate medical history as a mere search for antiquities, a kind of hunt for curios, but rather as a vital, integral part of medicine."[98] He distinguished the *Journal* from the *Bulletin* by stating that the *Journal* would not publish bibliographies or "papers of a philological nature"; the *Bulletin* was the proper channel for these kinds of studies. In fact, Rosen's editorial board and his roster of frequently published authors would be almost indistinguishable from the group of historians already identified as *Bulletin* regulars. With another American scholarly journal representing the history of medicine, Sigerist felt relieved of the pressure to expand the *Bulletin*. As long as his was the only journal in the field, he had felt "forced to expand" to provide researchers with an outlet for their work; now that there was another excellent journal, the *Bulletin* could afford to limit its number of pages "without causing any harm to the field of medical history."[99]

Sigerist was now intent on a more general objective. He was organizing his various professional activities and responsibilities so that others could take them over without disrupting the continuing development of medical history in the United States. He had for some time been thinking about leaving Hopkins and, in January 1947, formally resigned his Institute chair, effective July 1, 1947. Sigerist relinquished his editorial responsibilities for the *Bulletin* and Genevieve Miller, who had been associate editor since 1944, took over as acting editor.

Sigerist could resign with a clear conscience and a sense of accomplishment. The next generation of medical historians—his friends, students, and younger colleagues whose careers he had facilitated and cultivated—

were now becoming established in secure positions around the country. Erwin Ackerknecht had accepted a professorship in the history of medicine at the University of Wisconsin—the first new chair in this field in America and only the second full-time position after Sigerist's at Hopkins. Ludwig Edelstein had accepted a chair in classical languages and literature at the University of Washington in Seattle; soon after, he was appointed professor of Greek at the University of California at Berkeley. Ilza Veith was finishing her Ph.D. and would soon move to an assistant professorship in medical history at the University of Chicago. George Rosen was making his reputation as a leader in public health and was on his way to becoming professor and head of the department of health education at the School of Public Health at Columbia University.

At the Johns Hopkins Institute, Owsei Temkin was securely established as associate professor of the history of medicine; his teaching and research ranged widely, covering medical history from antiquity through the nineteenth century. In 1949, he took over as editor of the *Bulletin of the History of Medicine* and maintained this responsibility for many years. After staying at the Institute for an additional year, Genevieve Miller decided to continue her doctoral studies at Cornell University; she later accepted an assistant professorship at Case Western Reserve.

Owsei Temkin's tenure at the Institute guaranteed the continuation of the high standards of European scholarship that Sigerist had worked to establish. Miller's leaving, however, created a gap in the history of American medicine, a field Sigerist had enthusiastically encouraged. The appointment of Richard Harrison Shryock as the new director of the Institute ensured the further development of that field at the highest levels of scholarship.

Shryock was, for many, a surprising and controversial choice. Those closest to Sigerist—Temkin, Ackerknecht, and Rosen—were all physician-historians, but Shryock, a distinguished professional historian who had completed his doctorate in American history at the University of Pennsylvania, had no medical training and had never previously taught medical students. A professor of history first at Duke University and then at Pennsylvania, he had however been president of the History of Science Society in 1941–42 and was elected president of the American Association for the History of Medicine for a two-year term in 1946. As a pioneer among general historians in his explorations of American medical and public health history, Shryock brought to the subject a decidedly sociological perspective.[100] In 1936, he had published a major work, *The Development of Modern Medicine*, which traced the emergence of medical science as an integral part of larger social, economic, and general cultural developments.[101]

Shryock visited Sigerist at the Institute in May 1935, as he was getting the book ready for publication. Sigerist had clearly seen a copy of the manuscript, for he noted in his diary, "Then Prof. Shryock of Duke University. He has just written an excellent book on the Modernization of Medical Science, a sociological approach to the subject. I took him for lunch to the University Club." [102] Two years later, Shryock presented a paper, "The Historian Looks at Medicine," at the annual meeting of the American Association for the History of Medicine, and Sigerist promptly published it in the *Bulletin*.[103] This was Shryock's first and only publication in the *Bulletin* before his remarks at the farewell dinner for Henry Sigerist in 1947.[104]

In the intervening period, Shryock and Sigerist had the opportunity to get to know each other fairly well. Shryock had attended the Institute's Graduate Weeks in 1938 and 1939. Both men served on the Committee on Research in the History of American Medicine, appointed by the Association for the History of Medicine in 1939, with Shryock as a member and Sigerist as chair. In 1941, they exchanged positions, with Shryock serving as chair. The committee began preparing bibliographies of the history of medicine, publishing the first in 1940 and others annually thereafter.[105] In 1943, Shryock was elected vice president of the association, effective 1944, while Sigerist continued his critical role as *Bulletin* editor; although the association suspended its annual meetings during the war years, Shryock and Sigerist continued to meet as members of the governing council.

When Shryock was appointed William Henry Welch Professor of the History of Medicine and Institute director at Johns Hopkins, he was not Sigerist's first choice for the position. But Sigerist acquiesced to the decision, noting that "Shryock would have limitations in so far as he is not a physician—but he could compensate for this easily through his staff. He is a good administrator and teacher, is able to make friends and would undoubtedly bring money to the Institute." [106] In print, Sigerist would wax more enthusiastic, describing Shryock as "a social historian of vision . . . [who] looked at medicine and saw a great deal that the professional historians of medicine never noticed." [107] Privately, Sigerist could reassure himself that Shryock would allow Temkin's abilities and interests to counterbalance his own so that between them, the Institute would be in good hands. Where Temkin represented the European philological and philosophical traditions, Shryock was an imaginative and well-connected American academic, with interests in new disciplinary developments and in the more recent past. Sigerist could confidently leave the Institute in their care.

After Sigerist

The balance between Shryock and Temkin in temperament and research interests was reflected at the Institute in several ways. One was the division of teaching responsibilities. Temkin taught the first half of the introductory course on the history of medicine and followed this with a series of specialized seminars on ancient and medieval medicine and the history of anatomy and pathology. Shryock taught the second half of the introductory course, covering the nineteenth and twentieth centuries, a general course on the history of public health, and a specialized course on the history of modern science. Temkin later recalled that "in our division of labor, the teaching of medical students and house staffs fell to me" whereas Shryock's teaching of the history of medicine "was done chiefly in the School of Arts and Sciences, where he held an appointment in the department of history."[108]

Shryock, with the more sociological orientation, directed much of his attention away from the medical students and toward graduate students specializing in history and the history of science. Temkin gave special attention to the medical students but was relatively uninterested in sociological issues or in addressing the contemporary problems of medical care. Neither man taught medical history or medical sociology from Sigerist's essentially political perspective. Even in Shryock's ostensibly "sociological" teaching, there was none of Sigerist's urgent advocacy. Instead, Shryock's medical sociology was clipped, "shorn of its political overtones."[109]

Shryock's muted liberal approach was derived from his own temperament, background, and experiences and reinforced by the political climate of the times.[110] It would not have been safe or acceptable during the cold war fifties to articulate the kinds of views that had drawn such attention to Sigerist in the thirties and early forties. Also shaping Shryock's perspective was his interest in the history of science, a scholarly field that was developing very rapidly in what has been termed the "internalist" mode, following Koyré's close analyses of classic scientific texts.[111] Koyré read these texts with exquisite attention to their structure and inner coherence but paid minimal attention to their social context.

Shryock intended, as one of the Institute's goals, to cultivate the history of science and in 1951, arranged for Henry Guerlac, Cornell's rising young star, to spend a semester at Johns Hopkins as a visiting lecturer in the history of science. In 1952, Shryock negotiated a similar position for Alexander Koyré himself. In integrating the history of science into the Institute's academic program, Shryock emphasized the scientific content of medicine, thus moving in the direction of identifying medicine with science, and health progress with the applications of medical science. He was also actively writing about the history of American medical research. In 1947, he published *American Medical Research: Past and Present* and the next year, his paper on American indifference to basic science during the nineteenth century.[112]

Shryock's view of the ideally close relationship between science, medicine, and their histories contrasts with Sigerist's conception of the necessary distinctiveness and independence of the history of medicine. Most sharply articulating this difference in his debate with the preeminent historian of science, George Sarton, in the mid-1930s, Sigerist had argued: "Medicine is not a *branch of science* and never will be. If medicine is a science, then it is a social science."[113] He insisted that the history of medical science was only a small part of the history of medicine: "The history of medicine in a very large sense is the history of the relationships between physician and patient, between the medical profession . . . and society. . . . The morbidity of a given period, in other words the task with which the physician is confronted, is the result of endless social and economic factors. If you want to understand the development of medicine in the 19th century, you will have to study the industrial revolution first."[114] Furthermore, because access to medical care depended on social class and most people derived little direct benefit from medical research, a comprehensive history of medicine had more in common with social and economic history than the history of thought. These insights—so central to Sigerist's conception of the meaning and purpose of medical history—faded as the Institute under Shryock moved toward identifying its interests with the history of science.

By the early 1950s, most historians of medicine beyond the confines of the Institute—even those who had been closest to Sigerist—likewise drifted away from the political version of sociological history. Younger men who had shown early enthusiasm for the combination of political activism and the social history of medicine—most notably Milton Roemer and Milton Terris—were engaged in struggles around social medicine, public health, and the organization of medical care and were defending themselves against the political backlash in the McCarthy era.[115] Preoccupied with these demanding matters and finding the field moving in directions less relevant to their contemporary concerns, they did not sustain their former level of activity in historical research.

Better-established medical historians with a social orientation kept up their efforts in the early fifties, but even their succession of books, papers, and reviews showed evidence of caution. George Rosen, for example, who sharply distinguished between Shryock's book *The Development of Modern Medicine,* as an "introductory" and "pioneer" effort to create a social history of medicine, and Sigerist's first volume of *A History of Medicine,* which he described as a masterful, commanding synthesis "on a grand scale," scattered his own efforts in several directions and produced no major scholarly work in the early fifties to match his previous books on miners' diseases and medical specialization.[116] Even Erwin Ackerknecht, who published an impressive series of papers on nineteenth-century French public health and social hygiene and, in 1953, his biography of Rudolf Virchow, was producing politically cautious work.[117] As Owsei Temkin has implied, the bland emphasis of Ackerknecht's biography on chronology and coverage contrasts with the obviously Marxist analysis of his Leipzig thesis on Virchow and the reform movement of 1848.[118]

Other changes were under way in the fifties. The successor generation that Sigerist had so carefully cultivated still dominated the field intellectually, as was evident in their scholarship, their series of major awards and recognitions, and their general productivity.[119] But historians of medicine of amateur status had by no means disappeared and continued to enjoy a prominent role in the fifties. Notable signs were the appearance of *amabilis*-style Osleriana and other indications of the genre; the appointment of John Fulton—scientist, Cushing biographer, and bibliophile—as Sterling Professor of the History of Medicine at Yale in 1951; and Fulton's displacement, in the same year, of George Rosen as editor of the *Journal of the History of Medicine.*[120] When Erwin Ackerknecht departed for Switzerland in 1957, leaving an obvious gap in the ranks of professional medical historians, he was replaced by a series of visiting German scholars who had a limited impact on the American scene and returned to Europe after varying, usually brief, stays in Wisconsin.[121]

In his Garrison lecture of 1956, F. N. L. Poynter captured the mood of the day when he eloquently defended the contributions of amateur historians.[122] Although he acknowledged the accomplishments of professional scholars in the history of medicine, he criticized "that academic *hubris* with which specialists often regard the work of those who are not of their specialty" and suggested that medical historians needed to be "refreshed and stimulated" by contact with contemporary medical thought and practice. Without such contacts, their scholarship could easily become "mere pedantry and antiquarianism."[123]

Perhaps more clearly indicative of the unresolved tensions of the field was the quick rise but dramatic exit of Lloyd G. Stevenson as a major new presence. A young physician who, during his medical training, had written a lengthy biography of Frederick Banting, Stevenson indicated his desire to become a professional historian by enrolling as a graduate student in the Hopkins Institute in 1947 to study for his Ph.D. under Temkin.[124] Completing his historical thesis in two years, he was quickly recruited to editorial boards and committee chairmanships in a field eager to engage the talents of a man qualified in both medicine and history. Despite this red-carpet treatment, Stevenson did not sustain his earlier work in a consistent way. In the early 1950s, he published a few promising papers and a volume of biographical snapshots and expository selections of Nobel laureates, but in 1956, he was recruited from his position as historian of medicine at McGill University to become dean of the medical faculty. Thus achieving great success in his primary field of medicine, he did not return full-time to history until completing a seven-year term as dean and moving to Yale in the early sixties.

Stevenson's move from historical scholarship to medical school administration and back again was indicative of fundamental difficulties in the field in the fifties and sixties. While medical historians slowly recruited major new talent to their ranks, adding, for example, the physician-historians Lester King and Donald Bates, and the Ph.D.-historians John Duffy and Charles Rosenberg, many remained ambivalent about their journey toward professionalization. This ambivalence was reflected in the continuing intense concern over the role of medical history in medical education, still usually taken on by part-time and amateur historians.[125] After the infusion of new training grants by federal and philanthropic agencies in the late fifties and early sixties, attention turned to the institutional circumstances of the field. One major discussion occurred at a 1966 conference sponsored by the Josiah Macy Jr. Foundation and the National Library of Medicine, at which medical school administrators and historians of medicine and science gathered to discuss the best strategies for developing academic programs and teaching in the history of medicine. As John Z. Bowers indicated in his introductory remarks, medical schools were interested in the history of medicine but uncertain as to its scope or the best training for academic teachers. At this conference, only Ph.D. historians, notably those most closely identified with the history of science, unqualifiedly endorsed professionalization in the sense of creating an autonomous academic discipline. Other participants, George Rosen and Owsei Temkin in particular, sided with the medical school administrators and amateur historians in insisting on the medical relevance of the field to students and clinical practitioners. Professors of medical history should be part of the medical school and sensitive to its concerns. Temkin expressed this point of view most forcefully:

> I see a great danger. If the place of the medical historian is on the campus, then the intellectual problems of the environment will subtly influence him, and he will drift more and more away from the problems of the medical school. These problems may be uncomfortable for him, but they are there, and I think he has an obligation to them. And this obligation he will increasingly shirk if he is on the university campus. . . . I think that our responsibilities—and this factor I think overrides convenience and congeniality—primarily lie with the medical school.[126]

These issues are still not resolved today, and since the sixties, the history of science and the history of medicine have followed divergent paths of development. The history of science has largely been institutionalized in history departments or in small units within faculties of arts and sciences. The annual meetings and publications of the national organization, the History of Science Society, are characterized by sophisticated professional discourse conducted—almost exclusively—by full-time practitioners of the discipline, either Ph.D.s or Ph.D.s-in-training. Scientists are rarely in evidence, and their direct concerns are seldom addressed by history of science professionals, who are more interested in issues internal to their own academic discipline.

In the history of medicine, by contrast, although a significant number of appointments have been added to history and history of science departments, teachers of the discipline are frequently to be found on medical school faculties.[127] Often, a penumbra of amateur medical history clubs and societies adds to the culture of the medical school environment.[128] The meetings of the American Association for the History of Medicine are still relatively small, attended by a significant number of full-time medical practitioners with avocational interests in history and, despite the increased presence and influence of Ph.D.s and doctoral students, are suffused with an unmistakable medical presence and tone. This medical orientation is reflected in the concerted efforts of the organization's leadership over the last twenty-five years to achieve an M.D./Ph.D. balance in program committee membership and papers presented at the annual meetings and to alternate the association's presidency, whenever possible, between M.D.s and Ph.D.s.

Henry Sigerist presumably would have endorsed these efforts to retain the medical focus of the American Association for the History of Medicine. His abiding conviction was that the history of medicine must be relevant to the concerns of physicians:

> Why should a physician undertake the labour of consulting the past, of recreating it in history if it were not that he felt driven to such a task by medical considerations. History is an instrument of life and medical history is an instrument of medical life. It is a vital part of the theory of medicine and contributes ultimately towards the common goal, the improvement of the people's health.[129]

Sigerist had worked to raise scholarly work in America beyond an amateur to a professional level, leaving a lasting legacy in the Hopkins Institute and other full-time departments, the *Bulletin,* and the association. Yet he would certainly have agreed with his successor in the William H. Welch Chair, Owsei Temkin, that the pathway taken by the history of science was inappropriate for the history of medicine. Sigerist cherished a belief and more, an optimism, that the history of medicine professionally cultivated and enthusiastically disseminated could make a significant impact on the world of medicine by influencing policy and the organization of practice. History of medicine was "anything but *amabilis*"; it was also far too important and too rich in possibilities to be restricted to the insulated preoccupations of an autonomous scholarly profession.

Notes

1. Henry E. Sigerist, Diary, August 20, 1943. Yale University Library, Henry E. Sigerist Papers, Addition (June 1987), Biographical Data and Memoirs, group 788, box 1 (hereafter, Henry E. Sigerist, Diary); Nora Sigerist Beeson, ed., *Henry E. Sigerist: Autobiographical Writings* (Montreal: McGill University Press, 1966), 184.

2. Robley Dunglison, *History of Medicine from the Earliest Ages to the Commencement of the Nineteenth Century,* ed. Richard J. Dunglison (Philadelphia: Lindsay and Blakiston, 1872).

3. See, for example, Peter Middleton, *A Medical Discourse, or An Historical Inquiry into the Ancient and Present State of Medicine* (New York: Hugh Gaine, 1768); Benjamin Waterhouse, *The Rise, Progress, and Present State of Medicine* (Boston: Thomas and John Fleet, 1792). For a brief discussion of these and similar titles, see "An Exhibit of the History of Medical Historiography," *Bulletin of the History of Medicine* 26 (1952): 277–87. See also Ludwig Edelstein, "Medical Historiography One Hundred Years Ago," *Bulletin of the History of Medicine* 21

(1947): 495–511; W. B. McDaniel, "A View of 19th Century Medical Historiography in the United States of America," *Bulletin of the History of Medicine* 33 (1959): 415–35; Genevieve Miller, "In Praise of Amateurs: Medical History in America before Garrison," *Bulletin of the History of Medicine* 47 (1973): 586–615.

4. James Thacher, *American Medical Biography* (Boston: Richardson and Lord, 1828); [Wilson Jewell], "A History of Quarantine. Report of the Committee on Quarantine," in *Proceedings and Debates of the Third National Quarantine and Sanitary Convention* (New York: E. Jones, 1859), 247–97; John Redmond Coxe, *The Writings of Hippocrates and Galen* (Philadelphia: Lindsay and Blakiston, 1846).

5. As quoted by Genevieve Miller, "Medical History," in *The Education of American Physicians,* ed. Ronald L. Numbers (Berkeley: University of California Press, 1980), 292.

6. Ibid., 293.

7. Johann Herman Baas, *Outlines of the History of Medicine and the Medical Profession,* trans. Henry E. Handerson (New York: Vail, 1889); Roswell Park, *An Epitome of the History of Medicine* (Philadelphia: F. A. Davis, 1897); Edward H. Clarke et al., *A Century of American Medicine, 1776–1876* (Philadelphia: H. C. Lea, 1876).

8. Miller, "Medical History," 296–97.

9. See Sanford V. Larkey, "John Shaw Billings and the History of Medicine," *Bulletin of the History of Medicine* 6 (1938): 360–76.

10. John Shaw Billings, "The History of Medicine," *Boston Medical and Surgical Journal* 118 (1888): 29.

11. For a vivid first-hand account of Osler's clinical teaching, see Joseph H. Pratt, *A Year with Osler: Notes Taken at his Clinics in The Johns Hopkins Hospital* (Baltimore: Johns Hopkins Press, 1949). For Osler's famous Saturday evening dinners, see Harvey Cushing, *The Life of Sir William Osler* (Oxford: Clarendon Press, 1925), vol. 1, 428–29, 440, 445, 548.

12. Many of Osler's most influential historical papers were first presented at the club and later published in the *Johns Hopkins Hospital Bulletin.* His famous "An Alabama Student," for example, was read at the club in January 1895 and published in the *Bulletin* in January 1896. It is reprinted in William Osler, *An Alabama Student and Other Biographical Essays* (Toronto: Oxford University Press, 1908).

13. Eugene F. Cordell, "The Importance of the Study of the History of Medicine," *Medical Library and Historical Journal* 2 (1904): 272.

14. Philip M. Teigen, "William Osler's Historiography: A Rhetorical Analysis," *Canadian Bulletin for the History of Medicine* 3 (1986): 33.

15. Cordell, "The Importance of the Study of the History of Medicine," 273.

16. Lewis S. Pilcher, "An Antitoxin for Medical Commercialism: Being Some Considerations as to the Value and Place in Medical Undergraduate Instruction of the History and Memorials of Medicine," *Physician and Surgeon* 34 (1912): 145–58.

17. E. B. Krumbhaar, "Notes on the Early Days of the American Association for the History of Medicine," *Bulletin of the History of Medicine* 23 (1949): 577–82; Miller, "Medical History," 299.

18. C. N. B. Camac, *Epoch-Making Contributions to Medicine, Surgery and the Allied Sciences, Being Reprints of Those Communications Which First Con-*

veyed Epoch-Making Observations to the Scientific World together with Biographical Sketches of the Observers (Philadelphia: W. B. Saunders, 1909).

19. Fielding H. Garrison, *Introduction to the History of Medicine* (Philadelphia: W. B. Saunders, 1913).

20. Henry R. Viets, "Fielding H. Garrison and His Influence on American Medicine," *Bulletin of the History of Medicine* 5 (1937): 349.

21. F. N. L. Poynter, "Medicine and the Historian," *Bulletin of the History of Medicine* 30 (1956): 420.

22. Claudius Frank Mayer, "The Literary Activity of Fielding H. Garrison, M.D.," *Bulletin of the History of Medicine* 5 (1937): 378-87.

23. Miller, "Medical History," 301.

24. Victor Robinson, *Comrade Kropotkin* (New York: Froben Press, 1908), *An Essay on Hasheesh* (New York: Froben Press, 1912), *Pioneers of Birth Control* (New York: Froben Press, 1919), and *The Life of Jacob Henle* (New York: Froben Press, 1921). See Solomon R. Kagan, ed., *Victor Robinson Memorial Volume: Essays on the History of Medicine* (New York: Froben Press, 1948).

25. Henry E. Sigerist, "A Tribute to Victor Robinson," and "A Tribute from Dr. Arturo Castiglioni," in *Victor Robinson Memorial Volume*, xi–xii, xiii–xv.

26. Karl Sudhoff, *Essays in the History of Medicine*, ed. Fielding H. Garrison (New York: Froben Press, 1926); Max Neuberger, *Essays in the History of Medicine*, ed. Fielding H. Garrison (New York: Froben Press, 1930).

27. Henry E. Sigerist, "A Tribute to Victor Robinson," xii.

28. Francis R. Packard, "Editorial," *Annals of Medical History* 1 (1917): 102.

29. Francis R. Packard, "Editorial," *Annals of Medical History* 10 (1928): 504.

30. Francis R. Packard, "Review of *The Gold-Headed Cane*," *Annals of Medical History* 5 (1923): 411.

31. Francis R. Packard, "Editorial," *Annals of Medical History* 10 (1928): 504.

32. David Riesman, "Review of *Albrecht von Hallers Briefe an Johannes Gesner (1728-1777)*," *Annals of Medical History* 7 (1925): 102.

33. Edward B. Krumbhaar, "A Note of Appreciation," *Annals of Medical History*, 3rd series, 4 (1942): 533.

34. Edward B. Krumbhaar, "Notes on the Early Days of the American Association of the History of Medicine," *Bulletin of the History of Medicine* 23 (1949): 578.

35. Ibid., 579-80.

36. "Proposal for the Establishment of an Institute of the History of Medicine at the Johns Hopkins University," n.d., 1. The Ferdinand Hamburger Jr. Archives of the Johns Hopkins University, Records of the Office of the President, 1903-63, file 28.9 (Institute of the History of Medicine). All further references to the Hamburger Archives are to materials in this file.

37. "Proposal for a Medical Library at the Johns Hopkins University," October 8, 1925. Hamburger Archives.

38. "Proposal for the Establishment of an Institute of the History of Medicine at the Johns Hopkins University," n.d., 3. Hamburger Archives.

39. Simon Flexner and James T. Flexner, *William Henry Welch and the Heroic Age of American Medicine* (New York: Viking Press, 1941), 418.

40. Donald Fleming, *William H. Welch and the Rise of Modern Medicine* (Boston: Little, Brown and Co., 1954), 198.

41. For the history of medical historiography in Europe, see especially Owsei Temkin, "An Essay on the Usefulness of Medical History for Medicine," *Bulletin of the History of Medicine* 19 (1946): 9–47; F. N. L. Poynter, "Medicine and the Historian," *Bulletin of the History of Medicine* 30 (1956): 420, also offers useful insights and observations.

42. Editorial, "Inauguration of the Department of the History of Medicine of the Johns Hopkins University, and the Opening of the William H. Welch Medical Library," *Annals of the History of Medicine* n.s. 2 (1930): 122–23.

43. Harvey Cushing, "The Binding Influence of a Library on a Subdivided Profession," *Bulletin of the Johns Hopkins Hospital* 46 (1930): 30.

44. Joseph S. Ames, "Recollection of Dr. Welch, as sent to Simon Flexner," May 31, 1934, 3. Hamburger Archives.

45. Harvey Cushing to Joseph S. Ames, November 9, 1931. Hamburger Archives.

46. See Genevieve Miller's chapter in this volume.

47. Henry E. Sigerist, "History of Medicine in Academic Teaching: Results of a Questionnaire of the Institute," *Medical Life* 36 (1929): 55.

48. Ibid., 44.

49. At the time, John R. Oliver, a psychiatrist, taught medical history at the University of Maryland; Herbert M. Evans, professor of anatomy, taught the subject at Berkeley; Edward C. Streeter gave lectures at Harvard; Morris Fishbein, then clinical professor of medicine, at Northwestern University; William S. Miller, professor of anatomy, at Wisconsin; and Charles L. Dana, professor of nervous diseases, at Cornell. No professors were named at the University of Pennsylvania or Washington University, although both schools claimed to offer some instruction in medical history. Sigerist, "History of Medicine in Academic Teaching," 41–55.

50. Henry E. Sigerist, Diary, January 26, 1932; *Autobiographical Writings,* 76.

51. Henry E. Sigerist, Diary, March 5, 1934.

52. Owsei Temkin, "The Doctrine of Epilepsy in the Hippocratic Writings," *Bulletin of the History of Medicine* 1 (1933): 277–322; Fielding H. Garrison, "Revised Students' Checklist of Texts Illustrating the History of Medicine with References for Collateral Reading," *Bulletin of the History of Medicine* 1 (1933): 333–434.

53. Temkin, "The Doctrine of Epilepsy in the Hippocratic Writings," 277.

54. *Bulletin of the History of Medicine* 2 (1934). Henry E. Sigerist, "Karl Sudhoff, the Man and the Historian," 3–6; Fielding H. Garrison, "Karl Sudhoff as Editor and Bibliographer," 7–9; John Rathbone Oliver, "Karl Sudhoff as a Classical Philologian," 10–15; Owsei Temkin, "Karl Sudhoff, a Rediscoverer of Paracelsus," 16–21; Henry E. Sigerist, "Karl Sudhoff the Medievalist," 22–25.

55. Henry E. Sigerist, "The Medical Literature of the Early Middle Ages. A Program—and a Report of a Summer of Research in Italy," *Bulletin of the History of Medicine* 2 (1934): 26–52.

56. Henry E. Sigerist, Diary, June 2, 1934; *Autobiographical Writings,* 96.

57. Henry E. Sigerist, "Epilogue to Volume II," *Bulletin of the Institute of the History of Medicine* 2 (1934): 612.

58. "Address by Dr. William Henry Welch on the History of Pathology," *Bulletin of the Institute of the History of Medicine* 3 (1935): 1–18.

59. Henry E. Sigerist, *The Great Doctors* (New York: W. W. Norton, 1933).

60. "Medical-Historical Activities in the United States," *Bulletin of the Institute of the History of Medicine* 3 (1935): 610–11, 756–58.

61. "Medical-Historical Activities in the United States," *Bulletin of the Institute of the History of Medicine* 4 (1936): 514.

62. Henry E. Sigerist, Diary, May 3, 1937; *Autobiographical Writings*, 124.

63. Henry E. Sigerist, "Medical History in the Medical Schools of the United States," *Bulletin of the History of Medicine* 7 (1939): 627–62.

64. Ibid., 629.

65. Ibid., 652.

66. Ibid., 657–58.

67. "American Association of the History of Medicine: Constitution and By-Laws," *Bulletin of the History of Medicine* 6 (1938): 670–76.

68. Ibid., 834.

69. Previously, it had been the *Bulletin of the Institute of the History of Medicine;* henceforth it would be known simply as the *Bulletin of the History of Medicine.* The *Bulletin* remained the property of the Institute and as editor, the director of the Institute retained full control of editorial policy, although he agreed to "consult" with the council about publishing association materials.

70. "Association of the History of Medicine: Report of the Annual Meeting," *Bulletin of the History of Medicine* 7 (1939): 836.

71. Henry E. Sigerist, "Meeting of the Council," *Bulletin of the History of Medicine* 7 (1939): 833.

72. Henry E. Sigerist, "Report of the Activities of the Institute of the History of Medicine of the Johns Hopkins University During the Academic Year 1937–1938," *Bulletin of the History of Medicine* 6 (1938): 864–71; Henry E. Sigerist, "Report of the Activities of the Institute of the History of Medicine of the Johns Hopkins University during the Academic Year 1938–1939," *Bulletin of the History of Medicine* 7 (1939): 856–65.

73. Francis R. Packard, "Medical Case Histories in a Colonial Hospital," *Bulletin of the History of Medicine* 12 (1942): 145–68.

74. Henry E. Sigerist, "Waste and Economy in the Publication of Research," *Bulletin of the History of Medicine* 9 (1941): 1–2.

75. Ibid., 5.

76. Henry E. Sigerist, "The Johns Hopkins Institute of the History of Medicine during the Academic Year 1940–1941," *Bulletin of the History of Medicine* 10 (1941): 388.

77. Henry E. Sigerist, "Editorial: On the Threshold of Another Year of War," *Bulletin of the History of Medicine* 13 (1943): 2.

78. Ibid., 4.

79. Owsei Temkin, *The Falling Sickness: A History of Epilepsy from the Greeks to the Beginnings of Modern Neurology* (Baltimore: Johns Hopkins Press, 1945); Owsei Temkin and Sanford V. Larkey, "John Bannister and the Pulmonary Circulation," in *Essays in Biology, in Honor of Herbert M. Evans* (Berkeley: University of California Press, 1943), 285–92; Owsei Temkin and William L. Straus Jr., "Vesalius and the Problem of Variability," *Bulletin of the History of Medicine* 14 (1943): 609–33.

80. Ludwig Edelstein, *The Hippocratic Oath: Text, Translation and Interpretation*, suppl. 1, *Bulletin of the History of Medicine* (Baltimore: Johns Hopkins Press, 1943); Emma J. Edelstein and Ludwig Edelstein, *Asclepius. A Collection and Interpretation of the Testimonies*, 2 vols. (Baltimore: Johns Hopkins Press, 1945); Ludwig Edelstein, "Vesalius, the Humanist," *Bulletin of the History of Medicine* 14 (1943): 547-61; "On Sydenham and Cervantes," in *Bulletin of the History of Medicine*, suppl. 3, *Essays in the History of Medicine Presented to Professor Arturo Castiglioni on the Occasion of His 70th Birthday* (Baltimore: Johns Hopkins Press, 1944), 55-61.

81. Genevieve Miller, ed., *William Beaumont's Formative Years: Two Early Notebooks, 1811-1821. With Annotations and an Introductory Essay* (New York: Henry Schuman, 1946); Benjamin W. McCready, *On the Influence of Trades, Professions, and Occupations in the United States, in the Production of Disease*, new edition with introductory essay by Genevieve Miller (Baltimore: Johns Hopkins Press, 1943); Genevieve Miller, "A Nineteenth Century Medical School: Washington University of Baltimore," *Bulletin of the History of Medicine* 14 (1943): 14-29; Genevieve Miller, "The Study of American Medical History," *Bulletin of the History of Medicine* 17 (1945): 1-8.

82. Miriam Drabkin, "A Select Bibliography of Greek and Roman Medicine," *Bulletin of the History of Medicine* 11 (1942): 399-408; Miriam Drabkin, "Select Pages from Medieval Medical Manuscripts," *Bulletin of the History of Medicine* 11 (1942): 409-36. In 1946, Miriam Drabkin was employed by Henry Schuman as assistant editor of the *Journal of the History of Medicine and Allied Sciences*.

83. See Paul Cranefield, "Erwin H. Ackerknecht, 1906-1988," *Journal of the History of Medicine and Allied Sciences* 45 (1990): 145-49; Owsei Temkin, "In Memoriam: Erwin H. Ackerknecht," *Bulletin of the History of Medicine* 63 (1989): 273-75.

84. Ackerknecht's publications in this period are extensive and include Erwin H. Ackerknecht, "Primitive Medicine and Culture Pattern," *Bulletin of the History of Medicine* 12 (1942): 545-74; "Psychopathology, Primitive Medicine and Primitive Culture," *Bulletin of the History of Medicine* 14 (1943): 30-67; "White Indians," *Bulletin of the History of Medicine* 15 (1944): 15-35.

85. Erwin H. Ackerknecht, *Malaria in the Upper Mississippi Valley 1760-1900*, suppl. 4, *Bulletin of the History of Medicine* (Baltimore: Johns Hopkins Press, 1945).

86. Henry E. Sigerist, "The Johns Hopkins Institute of the History of Medicine during the Academic Year 1944-1945," *Bulletin of the History of Medicine* 18 (1945): 229.

87. Ilza Veith, "Government Control and Medicine in Eleventh Century China," *Bulletin of the History of Medicine* 14 (1943): 159-72.

88. Ilza Veith, *Huang Ti Nei Ching Su Wĕn. The Yellow Emperor's Classic of Internal Medicine* (Baltimore: Williams and Wilkins, 1949).

89. Henry E. Sigerist, "Medical History in the United States: Past—Present—Future," *Bulletin of the History of Medicine* 22 (1948): 57.

90. One of Roemer's earlier articles published in the *Bulletin*, for example, was Milton I. Roemer, "Government's Role in American Medicine—A Brief Historical Survey," *Bulletin of the History of Medicine* 18 (1945): 146-68.

91. Milton Terris, "An Early System of Compulsory Health Insurance in the

United States, 1798–1884," *Bulletin of the History of Medicine* 15 (1944): 433–44.

92. George Rosen, "The Medical Aspects of the Controversy over Factory Conditions in New England, 1840–1850," *Bulletin of the History of Medicine* 15 (1944): 483–97; George Rosen, "An Eighteenth Century Plan for a National Health Service," *Bulletin of the History of Medicine* 16 (1944): 429–36; George Rosen, *The History of Miners' Diseases: A Medical and Social Interpretation* (New York: Schuman's, 1943); George Rosen, *The Specialization of Medicine* (New York: Froben Press, 1944); George Rosen, *Fees and Fee Bills: Some Economic Aspects of Medical Practice in 19th-Century America,* suppl. 6, *Bulletin of the History of Medicine* (Baltimore: Johns Hopkins Press, 1946). For a more complete listing, see the bibliography in *Healing and History: Essays for George Rosen,* ed. Charles E. Rosenberg (New York: Science History Publications, 1979), 252–62.

93. On Rosen, see Edward T. Morman, "George Rosen, Public Health, and History," in George Rosen, *A History of Public Health,* expanded edition (Baltimore: Johns Hopkins University Press, 1993), lxix–lxxxviii; Elizabeth Fee and Edward T. Morman, "Doing History, Making Revolution: The Aspirations of Henry E. Sigerist and George Rosen," in *Doctors, Politics and Society: Historical Essays,* eds. Dorothy Porter and Roy Porter (Amsterdam: Rodopi, 1993), 275–311; Saul Benison, "George Rosen: An Appreciation," *Journal of the History of Medicine and Allied Sciences* 33 (1978): 245–53; and Charles E. Rosenberg, "George Rosen and the Social History of Medicine," in *Healing and History,* ed. Charles E. Rosenberg (New York: Science History Publications, 1979): 1–5.

94. Sigerist bore "the wrath of authors who cannot stand criticism" and defended his policy of critical book reviews in Henry E. Sigerist, "Preface to Volume XXI," *Bulletin of the History of Medicine* 21 (1947): 3.

95. Henry E. Sigerist, "The Johns Hopkins Institute of the History of Medicine during the Academic Year 1942–1943," *Bulletin of the History of Medicine* 14 (1943): 260.

96. Henry E. Sigerist, "A Welcome to the *Journal of the History of Medicine and Allied Sciences,*" *Bulletin of the History of Medicine* 19 (1946): 115.

97. Ibid., 117.

98. George Rosen, "What Is Past, Is Prologue," *Journal of the History of Medicine and Allied Sciences* 1 (1946): 4.

99. Henry E. Sigerist, "Preface to Volume XXI," *Bulletin of the History of Medicine* 21 (1947): 2–3.

100. See, for example, Richard H. Shryock, "The Origins and Significance of the Public Health Movement in the United States," *Annals of Medical History* n.s. 1 (1929): 645–65; Richard H. Shryock, "Medical Sources and the Social Historian," *American Historical Review* 41 (1936): 458–73.

101. Richard H. Shryock, *The Development of Modern Medicine: An Interpretation of the Social and Scientific Factors Involved* (Philadelphia: University of Pennsylvania Press, 1936).

102. Henry E. Sigerist, Diary, May 13, 1935.

103. Richard H. Shryock, "The Historian Looks at Medicine," *Bulletin of the History of Medicine* 5 (1937): 887–94.

104. Richard H. Shryock, "Henry E. Sigerist: His Influence upon Medical History in the United States," *Bulletin of the History of Medicine* 22 (1948): 19–24.

105. For the first bibliography, see "Bibliography of the History of Medicine

in the United States and Canada—1939," *Bulletin of the History of Medicine* 8 (1940): 619–35.

106. Henry E. Sigerist to John F. Fulton, January 12, 1949. Sigerist Papers/Yale, General Correspondence, 1947–57, group 788, series 1, box 12.

107. Henry E. Sigerist, "Review of Richard Harrison Shryock, *The Development of Modern Medicine* and *American Medical Research, Past and Present*," *Bulletin of the History of Medicine* 25 (1951): 193.

108. Owsei Temkin, *The Double Face of Janus and Other Essays in the History of Medicine* (Baltimore: Johns Hopkins University Press, 1977), 29, 32.

109. Owsei Temkin, *Double Face of Janus,* 29.

110. Only two years younger than Sigerist, he grew up in Philadelphia. When Richard was five, his father died, and he was raised by his mother, a member of an old Connecticut family. His ambition to study medicine was thwarted because of the family's financial difficulties. See Whitfield J. Bell Jr., "Richard H. Shryock: Life and Work of a Historian," *Journal of the History of Medicine and Allied Sciences* 29 (1974): 15–31.

111. Arnold Thackray, "Science: Has Its Present Past a Future?" *Minnesota Studies in the Philosophy of Science* 5 (1970): 112–33; Arnold Thackray and Robert K. Merton, "On Discipline Building: The Paradoxes of George Sarton," *Isis* 63 (1972): 473–95.

112. Richard H. Shryock, *American Medical Research: Past and Present* (New York: Commonwealth Fund, 1947); Richard H. Shryock, "American Indifference to Basic Science during the Nineteenth Century," *Archives Internationales d'Histoire des Sciences* 5 (1948): 50–65.

113. Henry E. Sigerist, "The History of Medicine *and* the History of Science," *Bulletin of the Institute of the History of Medicine* 4 (1936): 4–5.

114. Ibid., 5.

115. For examples of their earlier historical contributions, in addition to papers previously cited, see Milton I. Roemer, "Medicine and Social Criticism: A Comment on George Rosen's Article," *Bulletin of the History of Medicine* 11 (1942): 228–34, and Milton Terris, "Hermann Biggs' Contribution to the Modern Concept of the Health Center," *Bulletin of the History of Medicine* 20 (1946): 387–412. For the activities of these men and several of their like-minded colleagues in the late forties and early fifties, see especially the correspondence between Milton I. Roemer and Henry E. Sigerist, Sigerist Papers/Yale, General Correspondence, 1947–57, group 788, series 1, box 20.

116. George Rosen, *The History of Miners' Diseases: A Medical and Social Interpretation* (New York: Schuman's, 1942); George Rosen, *The Specialization of Medicine* (New York: Froben Books, 1944). For his comments on Shryock's and Sigerist's work, see George Rosen, "Levels of Integration in Medical Historiography," *Journal of the History of Medicine and Allied Sciences* 4 (1949): 460–67; George Rosen, "The New History of Medicine: A Review," *Journal of the History of Medicine and Allied Sciences* 6 (1951): 516–22.

117. Erwin H. Ackerknecht, "Hygiene in France," *Bulletin of the History of Medicine* 22 (1948): 117–55; Erwin H. Ackerknecht, *Rudolf Virchow: Doctor, Statesman, Anthropologist* (Madison: University of Wisconsin Press, 1953).

118. Owsei Temkin, "In Memoriam: Erwin H. Ackerknecht," *Bulletin of the History of Medicine* 63 (1989): 273–74.

119. The first Welch medal for work of outstanding scholarly merit was awarded to Sigerist in 1950; Owsei Temkin received the award in 1952, and Erwin H. Ackerknecht in 1953. Ackerknecht held the Garrison lectureship in 1948, and Israel E. Drabkin in 1951.

120. In 1949, both the *Bulletin of the History of Medicine* and the *Journal of the History of Medicine and Allied Sciences* devoted special issues to celebrating the centennial of Osler's birth. For other samples of Osleriana, see Henry R. Viets, "A Roving Commission: The Doctor Calls on Some of His Friends," *Bulletin of the History of Medicine* 22 (1948): 363–72, and Robert J. Hunter, "The Curse of Ernulphus: An Anecdote about Sir William Osler and Dr. Ellery Hughes," *Bulletin of the History of Medicine* 25 (1951): 554–58. For Rosen's distress at his displacement by John Fulton, see George Rosen to Henry E. Sigerist, December 8, 1951. Sigerist Papers/Yale, General Correspondence, 1947–57, group 788, series 1, box 21.

121. "Medico-Historical News and Activities," *Bulletin of the History of Medicine* 31 (1957): 580; 32 (1958): 476; 33 (1959): 383–84; 35 (1961): 179. The scholar of longest tenure was a Swiss, Nikolaus Mani, who worked on the history of liver research. *Bulletin of the History of Medicine* 39 (1965): 184.

122. F. N. L. Poynter, "Medicine and the Historian," *Bulletin of the History of Medicine* 30 (1956): 420–35.

123. Ibid., 431–33.

124. Lloyd G. Stevenson, *Sir Frederick Banting* (Toronto: Ryerson Press, 1946). See Leonard G. Wilson, "Lloyd Grenfell Stevenson (1918–1988): Medical Historian and Man of Letters," *Journal of the History of Medicine and Allied Sciences* 43 (1988): 377–85; Gert H. Brieger, "In Memoriam: Lloyd Grenfell Stevenson (1918– 1988)," *Bulletin of the History of Medicine* 62 (1988): 628–30; Edward C. Atwater, "Lloyd Grenfell Stevenson: A Personal Recollection," *Bulletin of the History of Medicine* 62 (1988): 630–31.

125. George Rosen, "The Place of History in Medical Education," and "Partial Abstract of Discussion," *Bulletin of the History of Medicine* 22 (1948): 594– 629; Richard H. Shryock, Iago Galdston, and Owsei Temkin, "Committee on the Teaching of Medical History," *Bulletin of the History of Medicine* 25 (1951): 571– 77; D. A. Tucker Jr. et al., "Committee to Survey the Teaching of the History of Medicine in American and Canadian Medical Schools," *Bulletin of the History of Medicine* 26 (1952): 562–78; 28 (1954): 354–58; 29 (1955): 535–44; 30 (1956): 365–69; Richard H. Shryock, "Conference on the Teaching of Medical History," *Bulletin of the History of Medicine* 28 (1954): 560–65.

126. Owsei Temkin, "Discussion of 'The History of Medicine as a Part of the University Complex,'" in *Education in the History of Medicine*, ed. John B. Blake (New York: Hafner, 1968), 101.

127. The last extensive survey of medical history teaching was Genevieve Miller, "The Teaching of Medical History in the United States and Canada: Report of a Field Survey," *Bulletin of the History of Medicine* 43 (1969): 259–69; Genevieve Miller, "The Teaching of Medical History in the United States and Canada: Report on Individual Schools," *Bulletin of the History of Medicine* 43 (1969): 344–75; 444–72; 553–86. For a more recent discussion by a number of leading teachers of medical history, see Jerome J. Bylebyl, ed., *Teaching the History of Medicine at a Medical Center* (Baltimore: Johns Hopkins University Press, 1982).

128. In 1966, Donald G. Bates commented astutely on the complex ecology of the medical school environment; see Bates, "The History of Medicine as a Part of the University Complex," in *Education in the History of Medicine,* 86–88.

129. Henry E. Sigerist, "The History of Medicine *and* the History of Science," 7.

Nora Sigerist Beeson holds a Ph.D. in Slavic languages and literature. She has worked as a researcher, translator, writer, and editor for *Current Digest of the Soviet Press, American Slavic and East European Review, Encyclopedia of World Art, Encyclopedia Britannica, New Columbia Encyclopedia,* the Metropolitan Museum of Art, Harry N. Abrams, Inc., and the Architectural History Foundation.

Marcel H. Bickel received his training in pharmacology in Switzerland and the United States. From 1947 until 1957, he was in frequent contact with Sigerist. Until 1993, he was professor of pharmacology at University of Bern School of Medicine. He has published actively in the history of medicine and has served as president of the Schweizische Gesellschaft für Geschichte der Medizin und der Naturwissenschaften, the Swiss society for the history of medicine and the sciences.

Theodore M. Brown holds a Ph.D. in history of science from Princeton University and was a postdoctoral fellow at the Johns Hopkins Institute of the History of Medicine. He teaches in the Departments of History and of Community and Preventive Medicine at the University of Rochester. His research focuses on the intellectual and social history of medicine and psychiatry, on European and American health policy and educational practice, and on the American health left.

Leslie A. Falk, M.D., was a protegé of Henry Sigerist who participated in his sociological seminars at Johns Hopkins in 1941–42. He was a member of the Oxford University team that made penicillin safe for human use. He spoke on behalf of the students at Sigerist's farewell dinner in 1947. Since that time, Dr. Falk has been a leader in social medicine, serving as a medical administrator for the United Mine Workers of America Welfare Fund and as chair of the Department of Community and Occupational Health at Meharry Medical College.

Elizabeth Fee is chief of the History of Medicine Division of the National Library of Medicine and adjunct professor of history and health policy at the Johns Hopkins School of Hygiene and Public Health. She is author of *Disease and Discovery* (1987) and coeditor of *AIDS: The Burdens of History* (1988), *A History of Education in Public Health* (1991), *AIDS: The Making of a Chronic Disease* (1992), and *Women's Health, Politics, and Power* (1994). She serves as contributing editor for history of the *American Journal of Public Health* and as an editor of *Social History of Medicine*.

John F. Hutchinson is professor of history at Simon Fraser University in Burnaby, British Columbia. His *Politics and Public Health in Revolutionary Russia, 1890–1918* appeared in 1990 as did a collection of essays entitled *Health and Society in Revolutionary Russia*, which he edited jointly with Susan Gross Solomon. His history of the international Red Cross, entitled *Champions of Charity: States, War and the Rise of the Red Cross*, was published by Westview/Harper Collins in 1996.

Ingrid Kästner is lecturer in the history of medicine at Leipzig University, Karl-Sudhoff-Institut. She was previously lecturer in pharmacology and toxicology, and her research on epilepsy was awarded the Leibniz Prize in 1986. Dr. Kästner is currently working on the history of psychiatry, medicine in Germany from 1933 to 1945, and women in medicine. She is coeditor and coauthor of *Sigmund Freud: Hirnforscher, Neurologe, Psychotherapeut* (1989) and *575 Jahre Medizinische Fakultät der Universität Leipzig* (1990).

Walter J. Lear, M.D., is a former public health official and medical care administrator and a longtime activist in the health left, peace, civil rights, and gay movements. He is founder and president of the Institute of Social Medicine and Community Health. Dr. Lear currently works as a historian of health activism in the United States. His publications include a history of the early years of the Physicians Forum, biographical essays on politically active physicians, and the entry "Health Left" in the *Encyclopedia of the American Left*.

Michael McVaugh is professor of history at the University of North Carolina (Chapel Hill). He is a coeditor of the continuing series *Arnaldi de Villanova Opera Medica Omnia;* his recently published *Medicine before the Plague: Practitioners and Their Patients in the Crown of Aragon, 1285–1345* (Cambridge, 1993), was awarded the William H. Welch Medal of the American Association for the History of Medicine. He is currently preparing a transcription (with commentary) of the *Chirurgia Magna* of Guy de Chauliac, the last great Latin surgical textbook of the Middle Ages.

Genevieve Miller, Ph.D., is associate professor emeritus of history of science, Case Western Reserve University School of Medicine, and retired director of the Howard Dittrick Museum of Historical Medicine, Cleveland, Ohio. From 1935 to 1948, she was student, research secretary to Henry Sigerist, assistant in the history of medicine, and instructor at the Johns Hopkins Institute of the History of Medicine. She is the author of numerous publications on the history of American medicine and editor of *A Bibliography of the Writings of Henry E. Sigerist* (1966).

Milton I. Roemer, M.D., M.P.H., also holds a masters degree in sociology. Since 1962, he has been a professor in the School of Public Health at the University of California, Los Angeles. Dr. Roemer has served at all levels of health administration—county, state, national, and international. Working with the World Health Organization and as an international consultant, he has studied health care organization in seventy-two countries and has published extensively on this subject. In 1983, the American Public Health Association awarded him the Sedgwick Memorial Medal for Distinguished Service in Public Health.

Owsei Temkin was born in Minsk, Belarus, in 1902, and received his education in Leipzig, Germany, where he obtained his medical doctorate and later taught medical history at the university. In 1932 he moved to the Institute of the History of Medicine at the Johns Hopkins University with his mentor, Henry Sigerist. At the time, Dr. Temkin was "Associate" (assistant professor); he retired in 1968 with the title of William H. Welch Professor Emeritus of the History of Medicine. A preeminent scholar, his publications cover the entire field of the history of medicine, with a special emphasis on ancient medicine.

Ilza Veith was born in Germany and studied at the medical schools of Geneva and Vienna. Emigrating to the United States, she obtained her Ph.D. from the Johns Hopkins Institute of the History of Medicine in 1947, specializing in Oriental medicine. She later taught at the University of Chicago and the University of California, San Francisco. She is the author of *The Yellow Emperor's Classic of Internal Medicine* (1949) and

Hysteria: The History of a Disease (1965), among other works in the history of medicine.

Heinrich von Staden is professor of classics and comparative literature at Yale University and a member of the core faculty in history of science and medicine. He is the author of *Herophilus: The Art of Medicine in Early Alexandria* (Cambridge, 1989), which won the William H. Welch Medal and the Goodwin Award of Merit, and of numerous articles on Greek and Roman medicine and on ancient Greek culture and its modern reception.

Page numbers in italic denote illustrations.

179, 180, 186, 300; health problems, 2, 77, 91, 101, 106, 189, 296, 297, 298, 299, 304; hobbies, 108-10, *110*, *111*; political notoriety, 3, 56, 58, 114; and religion, 87–88, 93–94; retirement, 2, 58, 78; in Swiss army, 25, *26*, *27*, 230; travels (*see specific countries*)

Sigerist, Marguerite (sister), 16, 19, 20, 21, 22

Sigerist, Miranda (granddaughter), 116

Sigerist, Nora (daughter). *See* Beeson, Nora Sigerist (daughter)

Silver, George, 4, 326

Silverman, Charlotte, 218

Singer, Charles, 67, 122, 338, 341

Singer, Dorothea Waley, 67

Sixties, changes in the history of medicine in the, 359, 360

Smith, Jessica, 261

Social Factors in Medical Progress (Stern), 316

Social hygiene: legislation, 181; in the Soviet Union, 243

Social insurance: old age, 205; temporary disability, 208; unemployment, 205. *See also* Socialized medicine

Social medicine, 54, 187, 217, 292, 293, 297, 302, 319, 328, 352, 357

Social Security Act of 1935, 202-3, 205, 211, 215

Social Security Charter Committee, 216

Socialism, 56, 113, 184, 186, 199, 202, 229, 230, 233, 234, 242, 249, 252

Socialized medicine, 139, 197, 199, 202, 209, 210, 211, 213, 214, 230, 233, 278, 288, 297, 302, 319, 322, 357. *See also* Health insurance

Socialized Medicine in the Soviet Union (Sigerist), 2, 3, 141, 183, 184, 199, 209, 229, 230, 236-40, 244, 246-51, 261, 294, 321

Society and Medical Progress (Stern), 326

Society for the History of Pharmacy, 52

Society of German Naturalists and Physicians, 44

Sociologists, 54, 204, 315, 316, 318, 326, 327

Sociology, and medicine, 75, 187, 188, 189, 204, 315-28, 334

Sociology (Sigerist), 185, 186, 187, 323-24

Solomon, Susan Gross, 243

Solov'ev, Z. P., 238, 240

South Africa, Sigerist's travels in, 2, 112, 113, 185, 213

Soviet Russia Today, 250, 251, 261

Soviet Union, 71, 105, 112, 168, 182, 183, 190, 199, 202, 210, 229; purges, 242, 246, 252; Sigerist's visits to, 207, 230, 232, 234, 238-39, 244, 246, 250, 294, 295. *See also* Medicine, Soviet

Spalteholz, Werner, 43

Spanish Civil War, 210, 265

Spengler, Oswald, 126

Spinoza, Baruch, 232

Spivack, S. S., 301

Sprengel, Kurt, 132

Stakhanov, Aleksei, 250

Stalin, Josef, 242, 243, 246, 251-52

Štampar, Andrija, 65, 217, 302, 318, 319

Stanford University Medical School, 265

State University of New York–Buffalo, 326

Stern, Bernhard J., 316, 326-27

Stevenson, Lloyd G., 5, 359

Stewart, Walter, 299

Sticker, Georg, 43

Stimson, Dorothy, 63

Stochasticism, 139

Stock market crash of 1929, 200

Stone, Abraham, 263, 264, 265, 271, 277

Stone, Hannah, 263

Strachey, John, 237

Strashun, Ilya Davidovich, 53, 56, 230

Studien und Texte zur frühmittelalterlichen Rezeptliteratur (Sigerist), 30, 124, 165

Studien zur Geschichte der Medizin (Sudhoff), 163

Sudhoff, Karl, 1, 25, 42, 43, 44, 46, 48, 49, 54–55, 58, 66, 67, *100*, 122-23, 124, 125, 132, 133, 163, 164, 165, 166, 189, 291, 292, 338, 341, 343; influence on Sigerist's career, 27, 28, 29, 32, 33-34, 35, 36, 37, 174, 180, 181

Surgeon General's Library, 335. *See also* National Library of Medicine

Surgery, 32, 35, 37, *171*, 347

Susruta, 155

Swiss Society of the History of Medicine and Sciences, 32

Switzerland, 2, 18, 21, 37, 58, 101, 112, 114, 168, 179, 184, 185, 187, 217, 246, 277, 300, 351, 358; involvement in World War I, 25, 27; in World War II, 113, 297

Sydenstricker, Edgar, 203, 316, 317

Sze Ma-chien, 154